Daily Keys to Success

Essentials for a Thriving Career and Life

Randy Kay

Upword Media

DAILY KEYS TO SUCCESS: Essentials for a Thriving Career and Life by Randy Kay

www.dailykeystosuccess.com
www.randywkay.com

Edited by Peggy Matthews Rose
Cover designed by Alexander von Ness
Interior designed by Ellie Searl, Publishista® www.publishista.com

Published in the United States of America

ISBN: 978-0-9854589-2-8
LCCN: 2013948900

UPWORD MEDIA

1042 N. El Camino Real
Encinitas, CA 92024-1322
www.upwordmedia.com

To Renee, the woman with the key to my heart,
and to my parents, Robert and Norma Kay, who persevered
through World War II and the Great Depression, and then handed
the keys to success to me.

INTRODUCTION

GETTING TO KNOW SUCCESS

FOR YEARS I RESENTED THE word *success*. To me it represented the superficial aspiration of making lots of money or achieving the status of some superstar on the world's stage. Trying to become like so-and-so just made me feel like more of a failure because my ideal concept of success only convinced me that I could not be like someone else. Then it dawned on me—I only needed to live out my own definition of success!

I know that may sound silly or too simplistic, but when you think of yourself as one of a kind and your success as unique to you, then you stop comparing yourself to others. You stop striving after someone else's goals and start living out the journey especially prepared for you. That paradigm shift is completely freeing. You don't have to fit some preconceived idea of success; you need only be true to your own purpose in life. You need only live *your* dream—not someone else's. And once you realize this, you are free to grow into the person you were created to be.

Sure, there are common skills and abilities we all must practice in order to live in this world. I wrote this book to give everyone a common foundation for success that allows you to relate effectively with others while finding your own success. You can't just live on an island and be successful—success is directly related to others. However, it's the contributions we make, not the possessions we accumulate, that ultimately define success. You can enjoy that new car, or live in the place of your dreams—enjoy life! But at the end of your journey these will mean nothing. It's what you created that gives you satisfaction. It's whom you benefitted that brings you peace. So go ahead and live life to the fullest. But make sure to build the treasures that matter most to you. Make sure to grow yourself into your own ideal—the very best of you. Define *your* success.

HOW DO YOU DEFINE SUCCESS?

HOW IS SUCCESS DEFINED? ONLY you can really answer that. Often the measures of success are achievement-oriented, as in realizing a meaningful career and contributing to the betterment of others. Or success can pertain to personal fulfillment, as in your satisfaction with life. As a general rule, success begins from the inside out, by first finding your purpose and passion and then developing your skills and abilities to achieve something of significance. As a practice, success is both a journey of discovery and a destination of accomplishment.

Each step along the way represents a process entirely unique for you. Consider that the journey and destination for an oil company executive would probably be very different from those of a Catholic monk, as would be the case with a college student and a senior retiree. Your success is specific to you, and no one can take the same journey or reach the same destination.

What is common is that each of us desires that feeling of completion when the task is finished, or we seek that satisfaction from attaining some aspiration. Success helps to complete us, whether it's being successful as a parent or as a professional. We all need to feel purposeful and accomplished in life in order to realize a sense of fulfillment. Without it we feel frustrated and unfinished.

For the healthy individual, the journey to success is never finished—and therefore, ever inspiring. We can never rest on our laurels because there always exists another need, another goal to achieve, or a hurdle to overcome. For those disciplined enough to stay focused on the process, the destination becomes inevitable. That's because successful people make a habit of improving their skills and abilities so that even if the intended destination must be rerouted to something else, their new path will invariably lead to an outcome that's even better. It's their commitment to continuous improvement that leads to success.

SUCCESS AS GIVING

I'M OFTEN ASKED FOR MY single definition of success, and after much thought I've devised a universal definition to the best of my ability: if you intend something, and you achieve it, that's success. Success for me is when I see my contributions reflected in the success of someone else. I cannot imagine living wholly unto myself, for my selfish interests. Some of the most successful people I've known are the greatest givers. Their joy comes from seeing the twinkle of success in the eyes of those they've influenced. There is a principle of reciprocity that makes giving a win-win. It is explained in one of my favorite pasages from Luke 6:38: "Give, and it will be given to you. A good measure, pressed down, shaken together and running over, will be poured into your lap. For with the measure you use, it will be measured to you."

That's why I wrote *Daily Keys to Success*. It's my legacy for my children, my friends, my associates—anyone (such as you) who wishes to do more, be more, and see more success in others. I hope in reading this book you will see success is intrinsically tied in with giving, and that by applying all of the keys you will experience joy and satisfaction. I believe each of us is born with a purpose to leave this world with the imprints of our goodness, uniqueness, and loving-kindness. Sure, some of us will get rich in the process, but it's the wealth that cannot be defined in possessions or currency that leaves a lasting imprint.

My own personal journey has brought me before hundreds of these amazing achievers. When I designed and facilitated training programs for corporations such as Johnson & Johnson and worked as a consultant for several Fortune 500 companies, I followed the personal development of thousands of rising stars within their organizations. As an executive in marketing, operations, and sales for some of the largest health-care companies in the world, I experienced the joy of helping people achieve their goals in the face of daunting challenges. When I served as a chief executive officer for a biotech company, a media company, and my current strategic development firm *TenorCorp*, I developed my own abilities to initiate and lead innovative expansions on a macro scale. Over a thirty-plus-year career, I've studied from some of the best success masters, I've taught more classes and conducted more seminars to more professionals than I care to remember, and I've learned countless lessons on how to be successful from people and experience. Even more important than my professional accomplishments has been my joy in living a successful marriage, seeing both my son and daughter reach their potential, and helping others succeed. I may not know you, but if I've touched you in some positive way, this gives me joy!

What Do the Experts Say?

When I sat down to plan *Daily Keys to Success*, the huge volume of information from my own personal experience, along with the advice from and examples of success experts, distinguished enterprisers, laudable leaders, best-seller authors, top psychologists, philanthropists, and common people who live admirable lives proved overwhelming. Soliciting more than five hundred people for their keys to success produced a myriad of answers. I synthesized a treasure trove of information into common thematic elements, and then further defined the causes for success into ten groupings: *behavioral skills*, *self-awareness*, *health* (physical, psychological, and spiritual), *general well-being* (satisfaction with life), *social adaptation*, *generosity*, *relationship building* (of family, friends, associates), *discipline* (planning, good habits), *financial management*, and *leadership*. Within these groupings were hundreds of success keys. I then made sure to include the most commonly recommended keys to success as expressed by all my sources and confirmed by my own experiences. Since all the keys were important, I decided to form daily tips for learning, reinforcement, and encouragement, with varying relevance, depending on the life course of the reader. I wanted this book to serve as a lasting resource—something you can turn to anytime you need encouragement or a reminder. Achieving success is first and foremost a day-by-day journey.

THE METHOD FOR ACHIEVING SUCCESS

WHILE DEVELOPING THIS BOOK, I discovered that the factors for success are numerous and applicable for each person, both on a personal and a professional level. The impetus for a healthy career is generated from discovering one's calling, then one's talents, then next developing one's abilities for targeted purposes. Toward this end the study of success in life and work must come from a broad course of learning, but the focus of one's energies must be narrow in finding one's purpose. To claim that only a few habits, steps, or laws will get you to your destination discounts the massive amount of knowledge and insights that are required for people in general to succeed.

There are not seven steps to success, or twenty, or even one hundred—there are at least 366 keys to success that I have documented and written about in *Daily Keys to Success*. Imagine unlocking your potential day by day through developing the skills, knowledge, and understanding of proven principles that have helped bring about the personal success of people for generations. That's the power of a study that requires only minutes of your time each day, so that in one year you will have learned the lessons of success for your own life.

THE WAY WE LEARN

I HAVE FOUND THAT PEOPLE tend to learn better when they are not inundated with information. Also, thematic insights like those expressed in several best sellers serve to reinforce only a few ideas, and I wanted to represent hundreds of key success factors from a broad spectrum of choices. I have read inspiring books written by some great writers who presented fresh ideas, which made me want to rush out and practice my newfound understanding. Then months or years later, I forgot the essence of those books, and perhaps at best only one or two key takeaways remained. That is why I decided to create snippets of insights that could serve as quick reference guides for years to come. You can go back months after reading a topic and in only a few minutes refresh your key takeaway.

You may choose to read about these keys beginning with January, or you may choose to skip to those that appear most relevant to you—how you do it really doesn't matter. It only matters that you do it. Some keys may be new to you, while others will serve as reminders. As a success trainer of thousands, I've learned that our minds work in such a way that we tend to screen information based on what's most relevant to us. Those "aha" moments occur when something new or timely clarifies a piece of the puzzle in our brains. My hope is that *Daily Keys to Success* will help you glean some fresh awareness with which to further your journey on the road to success.

Personal Commitment

I HAVE ENTITLED EACH KEY to success with a commitment because success always follows a personal promise to act. That's why you will see each key headlined with the statement: "I will _________ [do something]." If you commit to each of these keys, your success *will* happen. The key to learning begins with staying on purpose. This success devotional is intended to teach you how to think and not to do your thinking for you. Consequently, if you pick up this book and simply read a page, you are wasting your time. As soon as any thought stimulates your mind or your heart, you can put the book down and just meditate on it. I call this form of learning *resonance training*, which is a personalized form of changing habits by routinely taking only one or two understandings that evoke in you a desire to change your behavior, and then applying this change to your normal way of doing things over a period of at least twenty days. So after reading your daily devotional, carry on through your day with a commitment to incorporate your key learning into your daily activities, and then consciously continue this for about a month so it becomes intuitive. This is *resonance learning*—finding what's most relevant for your life. If a key is important to you, it will stick.

I encourage you not to read more than one success key each day. Don't attempt to assimilate the varying concepts in this success devotional all at once. Our brains are not wired to take in a data dump of information and concepts. Try recalling what you learned from a seminar you attended long ago, or a book you read a few years or even a few months back. Chances are you might recall one to three key takeaways—if that—but none of us can absorb the superabundance of information imparted by them. That's why I opted to write a daily devotional instead of a book detailing emerging concepts or a step-by-step process for changing how you go about achieving success. You need to allow what resonates with you (the "aha" or an important reminder) to settle. Commit something new or fresh to your daily life based on what you've read that day, preferably in the morning. It's amazing what one change a day can do to bring you to a point of greater success. Just imagine what 365 committed days of success training can do for the rest of your life!

BEGIN THE JOURNEY

NOW LET'S BEGIN YOUR DAILY journey to success. Don't concern yourself with getting to your destination; simply be content with improving a little each day. Enjoy the experience of getting better. Remain confident in your abilities. Stay on purpose. Follow your dreams. Build on your talents and develop your skills. Be content with your station in life and your future possibilities. Your best awaits you. Remember, your best is singular to you. Your success cannot be defined by anyone but you. You will know it when it happens—no one else can know it for you. No one else can understand when you've arrived. Only you can live your life, and only you can experience your success. The most wonderful part of your journey and destination is that others will reap the benefits of your success—and it's because you made it happen! You took the time and made the effort to make your success. Congratulations—you are opening the door to your success through unlocking the keys to your potential. I hope you enjoy your daily keys to success. May they unlock for you a lifetime of *your* success!

~ Randy W. Kay

JANUARY

GET READY FOR NEW

JANUARY 1

I will live in the present

Each New Year brings with it resolutions to achieve something in the future. Some of these decisions include rectifying failures from the past. The truth is, neither the past nor the future exists. We only have the present, and increasing demands coupled with the stresses of life often obscure it. Staying focused on "now" forces attention onto the situations and people who truly matter. Not only does living in the present have a dramatic effect on our emotional well-being, but the detrimental effects of stress on our body are lessened as well. It also makes us more effective.

Slowing down and realizing we can only influence what's happening right now allows us to focus on life one opportunity at a time. It eliminates distractions that can impede our ability to be effective and get things done.

Getting sidetracked usually means we are looking too far ahead or too far behind. As our attention narrows, our awareness merges with the action we are performing, and we gain a sense of personal power over it, so that anything we do in the moment will seem almost effortless.

Center yourself in the moment right now: take a deep, slow breath. Count to five and then exhale slowly. Accept any emotions, situations, and thoughts without any need to reconcile them. Stop confusing situations with useless conjecture and self-defeating worry. Overthinking and self-evaluation are two of our greatest impediments. Keep life simple by focusing thoughts and actions only on what's significant.

Approach familiar surroundings with what some call a "beginner's mind"—find a new sight, sound, or smell with no need to judge any of it. Slow down to savor the moment. Appreciate life as it is instead of looking to tomorrow or dwelling on the past, and peace as well as increased efficiency will follow.

Life centers all around *now*, and now has always been about our life. If we're not living in the present, we're relinquishing our life. Now is our most precious possession—don't waste it on anything else.

"Life is a sequence of moments all called now." ~ weheartit.com

JANUARY 2

I will control my awareness and thoughts

Have you ever misperceived a situation because you were too stressed, angry with someone, or felt some bias from others? Such factors can cloud our thinking and rob us of our happiness. We can train ourselves to think rationally, clearly, and positively, no matter the situation.

When feeling overwhelmed, our self-confidence suffers. We become less positive. We constantly communicate with ourselves through self-talk, and when we doubt our abilities, we set ourselves up for failure, and this invariably hurts our performance.

One approach to counteract this self-doubt is to consciously note our thoughts—either physically write them down or make mental records of how we talk to ourselves. Then look for habits of thought, repetitive stories, or words that feed into a negative narrative.

Assess the validity of the narrative. Is it rational or imagined? Ask for feedback from others to confirm or refute questions about performance. If our negative thoughts tell us we are not up to the job or an undertaking, we should benchmark against others who are in similar positions, or who have succeeded in ways similar to what we expect of ourselves, and compare our qualifications to the actual standards required of the job or task.

Sometimes our personal bias may inflate our impression of others, so clarify the (measureable) requirements of whatever needs to be accomplished. If they are not met, adjust the performance. If they are being met or are tracking toward completion, that's success!

If we've established clear requirements, and we are doing our best to meet them, then anyone with a fair perspective should view our work positively. If not, they are being unfair and we need to accept that as their bias, not as our reality. We need to keep telling ourselves the truth to turn our negative thoughts into positive ones.

For irrational feelings of failure, we can tell ourselves things like, "I am competent at this. I have worked diligently to meet the requirements. I will succeed." If someone or something outside of our control feeds into the negative narrative, we can tell ourselves things like, "Fair people will recognize my success. I am not going to believe irrational criticism."

Positive assertions turn our self-speak into a positive narrative, enabling us to succeed because of ourselves.

"You become what you think about most of the time." ~ Brian Tracy

JANUARY 3

I will be self-confident

We are more likely to be persuaded by someone who appears self-confident, stands straight, holds his chin up, speaks crisply, who answers questions without any hint of doubt, and who is forthright in admitting he doesn't have an answer. If you don't fit that description, the good news is you can learn to be self-confident.

Self-confidence is exhibited in body posture, how you speak, the words you use, and your overall behavior. It's standing up to what you believe is right, taking risks, owning-up to your failures, being gracious in accepting praise as well as criticism, remaining positive and optimistic, and admitting your mistakes with a forward-thinking attitude.

You start developing confidence when you believe in your ability to achieve goals that are important to you, with the conviction that if you work diligently toward those goals, you will succeed. Invariably, challenges will arise. However, your confidence building happens when you understand that you can overcome these difficulties, that you can handle anything that comes your way, and that you have a right to a fulfilling and successful life.

Approval from others may not be within your control, but self-confidence comes from a belief that your best is enough, that you are capable of doing what needs to be done, and that you can master any task if you dedicate yourself to it. One of the best ways to accomplish this attitude is to take notice of your past achievements as evidence of your future potential. Notice what strengths you and others have observed about you that led to your successes.

Set yourself up for success by establishing goals that are optimally suited to your strengths—start small and work-up from there—and celebrate your successes along the way. Be cognizant of what actions, thoughts, and influences went into your achievement of these goals, and fix those pictures into a positive mental image of what you can achieve.

Don't be overconfident or under-confident. Be honest and simply fill in your knowledge and skill gaps, and build upon your strengths. The more you *gradually* stretch yourself, the more self-confidence you will build. Self-confidence is a process of setting realistic and increasingly challenging goals that leave a trail of achievements along the way.

"Nothing builds self-esteem and self-confidence like accomplishment." ~ Thomas Carlyle

JANUARY 4

I will attend to my well-being

Independence from our brokenness requires that we be made whole. And, wholeness can only occur when we've achieved a high level of satisfaction with each of our six primary areas in life: **Career**, **Social, Spiritual, Community, Financial,** and **Physical.** List these six and rate your level of satisfaction with each from one to ten, with one being the lowest level of satisfaction, and ten being the highest level of satisfaction. Now average your level of satisfaction by adding your scores for each and dividing by six. How did you score? If your average score was seven or above, then you are thriving. If you average between five and six, you are striving in life. If you scored four or below you are struggling, and you need to seriously consider making some changes and seek help.

Which areas give you the least satisfaction and why? What people, factors, qualities, or missing pieces must change in order to get you back to a healthy level of well-being? Eliminate those toxins that are slowly poisoning you. Don't just believe that old adage that "everything in moderation" is good—poison in moderation is *not* good. If you need to add some piece in order to make life whole, then do it—whether it be attending a club or church to find new relationships, finding a new job or position, changing your diet, putting together a budget, or moving. You need to start now. If your physical well-being is suffering, exercise just a little longer and you will be more satisfied with life, as confirmed by a study at the National Institutes of Health. If you scored high in one area, don't just be content with maintaining the status quo. We should always build on our strengths and improve our weak areas.

Someone who scores tens in all five areas but only a one in one area will still need to improve the one, but the higher areas will tend to compensate for the lower ones. Still, our goal should be to increase our satisfaction to a seven or above in all areas of life.

"A sad soul can kill you quicker than a germ." ~ John Steinbeck

JANUARY 5

I will be resilient

Results are usually not perfect the first time you try something. In a world with shifting goals and expectations, people are often forced to get the job done with less than adequate preparation. If you're the type of person who feels uncomfortable when you can't be your best at something or when things don't go according to plan, you'll always be subject to feeling disappointed when situations fall out of your control.

According to experts, one of the best ways to deal with life's disappointments and the anxiety they cause is to be resilient. Resilience is defined by the ability to adapt to challenging circumstances. When you are resilient, your confidence is not dependent on your performance. You can play a lousy game of golf, shooting well over one hundred—someone who is not resilient might feel she's not a great player.

But if you're resilient, you can still get enthused by how much you learned from those mistakes and how you are improving your abilities. You can also appreciate how much value the game brings to you regardless of your score. That's a very freeing attitude to adopt.

Unfortunately we've been taught to strive for greatness while missing the benefits of just enjoying and learning the "game." The irony is that a resilient attitude actually leads to greatness—as a byproduct, not a motivation. The key is to acknowledge that one—or even two or a hundred—screwups do not define you. Resilient people are consumed with the journey as much if not more than the destination, and that journey is about learning and growing. They are curious about life and eager to embrace new challenges because their expectations are not self-limiting, not solely dependent on others, and they are not bound by the game's scorecard.

When things don't go according to plan, allow yourself some flexibility to improvise. Reward yourself for just trying instead of criticizing yourself for not being the best, or even close. This attitude will allow you to try and try again—to face the next challenge with greater self-confidence and have a lot more fun in the process.

"Once you're caught in the mousetrap, why not eat the cheese?" ~ The Covert Comic

"If you learn something from a defeat it isn't a loss." ~ Autumn Worcester

January 6

I will develop my brand

Alex said to Mary, "I am the man of your dreams." Though a little presumptuous, Alex nevertheless believed in marketing himself directly. After dating Alex for several weeks, laughing together, and generally enjoying Alex's company, Mary said, "I believe that you are the man of my dreams." Alex had successfully branded his message with Mary.

The difference between sales/marketing and branding is essentially this: sales/marketing is telling the customer about your product or service, whereas branding is about what your customer believes your product or service can do for them.

Scott Bedbury, one of the most successful branding gurus of the twentieth century, was president of marketing during Starbucks's rise to preeminence within the coffee industry. As head of advertising for Nike he transformed the brand image into something spectacular, using the tag line "Just Do It." Suddenly Nike went from being an image about sneakers to a product about values and esprit. Bedbury wrote a book called *A Brand World: Eight Principles for Achieving Brand Leadership in the Twenty-First Century* (Penguin Books, 2003) in which he tells about transforming Starbuck's brand core identity from "engineering a great cup of coffee" to "providing a great coffee experience." "We wanted to reward our customers with consistently better service, not a sometimes cheaper cup of coffee," he said.

Declaring "relevance, simplicity, and humanity—not technology—will distinguish brands in the future," Bedbury proposed a humanistic approach to branding by championing two key aspects of a brand: love and trust, he says, are critical for success. No amount of advertising can help a company or product if it lacks a soul or heart, he explains, since both are required for marketing to resonate with consumers.

Mary felt that Alex loved her more than any of her other suitors because he was radically different from the others. In winning Mary, Alex had followed the advice of leading marketing and branding experts. See what your competitors are doing, and then do something completely and originally different—something that makes the customer feel special, wanted, and cherished.

"A brand for a company is like a reputation for a person." ~ Jeff Bezos

JANUARY 7

I will focus for ten minutes a day

Ten minutes—focus? Focus on what? On getting something done? On watching a potted plant grow? The answer is both. Ten minutes is the new conceptual time paradigm in our fast-paced world. Instead of thinking about huge chunks of time, consider ten minutes a day to both boost your focus and attention, and to get something accomplished.

In *The Emotional Life of Your Brain: How Its Unique Patterns Affect the Way You Think, Feel, and Live--and How You Can Change Them* (Hudson Street Press, 2012), authors Richard J. Davidson, PhD and Sharon Begley discuss their study of the neural base of emotions and how we can train our emotional styles to achieve greater success. One of the emotional styles they discuss is your attention style, which is your ability to screen out distractions and unimportant things as opposed to having a "monkey mind"—thoughts jumping from topic to topic, which involves both cognitive and emotional elements.

If you'd like to boost your focus and attention, Davidson recommends two disciplines for taking time every day for ten minutes in a quiet place.

The first discipline is intended to train your mind to just focus. With your eyes wide open, focus on an object (a picture, a plant). Keep your eyes trained on it for ten minutes, and if your thoughts wander, bring them back to the object.

If you're looking to change something in your life, like rearranging something, spending more time with the family, or learning a new skill, you'll want to practice the second discipline. The fact that you're setting aside time to bring something new into your life for a short period each day compounds itself into something more significant over a longer period, and therefore you gain a tremendously enriched sense of accomplishment.

Start by asking yourself: "What's one area in my life I could improve upon?" This is a very doable approach to clearing out the "getting around to it" mental depot that leads to consistent frustration and stress. Maybe it seems like a little change, like spending ten minutes a day with your child or partner, but it can be transforming.

Think about taking a flight from San Francisco to New York City. If the pilot changes course by just a few degrees, you could end up in a Southern tropical paradise. Small degrees of change, such as focusing attention on an object for ten minutes, or committing ten minutes to that important thing you've been hoping to do will positively transform your way of living.

"There are only ten minutes in the life of a pear when it is perfect to eat." ~ Ralph Waldo Emerson

JANUARY 8

I will embrace change

Unsettledness naturally follows change, and we begin asking or saying something like, "Did I make the right decision?" or "This isn't what I wanted." Emotions fluctuate between excitement and fear, between joy and unhappiness. All of these reactions only prove that we are human.

Managing change is what makes the difference between thriving and just acceptance. Resigning yourself to uncertainty must be the first step. Set reasonable expectations with the understanding that nothing lasts forever. By not marrying yourself to the result you can remain flexible as to the outcome.

Choosing to manage the controllable aspects of the change must also occur in tandem with reflecting on your own core values and purpose in order to remain centered. Successful change leaders persevere without surrendering to inevitable obstacles through an adaptable attitude that continually seeks innovative solutions. They maintain a positive can-do approach by dwelling on future possibilities rather than current challenges.

These leaders also see things as they can be by visualizing the big picture and adjusting their direction as needed. Adaptability doesn't always mean just going with the flow; it also involves helping to redirect the flow when necessary. There's something about making a commitment and putting yourself in the way of change that invites success. Consider R. H. Macy, the founder of the large department store chain. He started seven failed businesses before finally hitting it big with his store in New York City.

However, despite any positive turn of events from adapting to changing events, none of it matters unless people experiencing change remain committed to their physical and spiritual health. Many experts view faith as the most important stabilizing factor to help us go through change, followed by good eating habits and regular exercise. Remaining faithful to what is most important will balance an otherwise unstable environment. Look to your faith, loved ones, purpose, and values, which should always remain constant. They serve as your anchor when the waves of change become too rough.

"Sometimes good things fall apart so better things can fall together." ~ Marilyn Monroe

"I may not have gone where I intended to go, but I think I ended up where I intended to be." ~ Douglas Adams

JANUARY 9

I will get in the "zone"

We've all heard about sports players "getting in the zone" —that place where their mental and physical abilities are at peak performance. That sense of exhilaration comes from the thrill of competition, which stretches the athlete's trained abilities to reach their maximum potential.

We can also attain that same level of positive flow in work and in our home life. In fact, longtime "happiness researcher" Mihaly Csikszentmihalyi wrote a popular book about this dynamic called *Flow: The Psychology of Optimal Experience* (HarperCollins Publisher, 1990). He writes: "We have all experienced times, when, instead of being buffeted by anonymous forces, we do feel in control of our actions, masters of our own fate . . . moments like these are not passive, receptive, relaxing times . . . the best moments usually occur when a person's body or mind is stretched to its limits in a voluntary effort to accomplish something difficult and worthwhile." That adrenaline rush accompanied with a release of endorphins creates a pleasant sense of honed purpose within us.

It is important to continually stretch ourselves with more complex and challenging goals in order to make life more meaningful. In *Flow*, the author sets out four major components of an activity that will tend to make anything we do more enjoyable: 1) we confront tasks we have a chance of completing, 2) we must be able to concentrate on what we are doing, 3) there are clear goals, and 4) there is immediate feedback. When these four elements are enacted, whether in a team environment or singularly (via self-discipline), an almost effortless engagement occurs that lifts us from the monotony of life into the zone of peak work-through and enjoyment—the irony being that we are in absolute control, but we almost lose our "self" until the experience is over.

The key is to not just be challenged by something; it's more like immersing ourselves in an activity with stretch goals that keep our mental blinders on, preventing us from becoming distracted until we've reached the finish line. Practicing the mental discipline of placing blinders around our thinking helps us to remain focused on our actions. Nothing else seems to matter and the resulting feeling of flow gives us a natural high. Tap into that feeling.

"It's a very strange feeling. It's as if time slows down and you see everything so clearly."
~ Excerpt from Mind Games: Inspirational lessons from the world's finest sports stars, Grout and Perrin (Capstone, 2006)

JANUARY 10

I will not mistake perfection with progress

Perfectionism may work if you are a surgeon required to operate with pinpoint accuracy, but over time it can lead to stress, self-ridicule, and hyper-criticalness that causes an unalterable adherence to strict standards of performance. Perfectionism reduces creativity and risk taking, which runs counter to the growing need for adaptability in the global marketplace.

"There's a difference between excellence and perfection," explains Miriam Adderholdt, a psychology instructor at Davidson Community College in North Carolina and author of *Perfectionism: What's Bad about Being Too Good?* (Free Spirit Publshing, 1999). Excellence arises from enjoying what you're doing, appreciating what you've learned, and developing confidence. Perfectionism involves finding mistakes no matter how well you or the other person is doing.

Offering constructive criticism to yourself and others is always forward focused, as in, "How can I do better next time?" It is a way of showing empathy with others who have failed, as well as forgiving yourself when you've fallen short, and being specific about improvements that must be made while avoiding general accusations. Genuine praises should always outnumber criticisms. Give yourself some self-praise and learn to celebrate growth as much as accomplishment.

Contrary to popular opinion, perfectionists are often low-producers due to their extreme fear of failure. If you find yourself falling into that trap, reevaluate your goals by establishing some quick wins first before increasing their difficulty. Instead of aiming for 100 percent, go for a lower percent and focus more on the process than the end goal. Ask yourself questions like "What's the worst that can happen?" and "What can I learn from my mistakes?" Perfectionism often leads to disappointment, whereas excellence leads to progress.

"Don't mistake activity with achievement." ~ John Wooden

"The maxim 'Nothing prevails but perfection' may be spelled PARALYSIS."
~ Winston Churchill

"We all want progress, but if you're on the wrong road, progress means doing an about-turn and walking back to the right road; in that case, the man who turns back soonest is the most progressive." ~ C. S. Lewis

JANUARY 11

I will assess my key skills

Honestly answer each question AS you go along: Given a limited budget, will you cut back in other areas in order to develop yourself or your team? Do you use the same approach to motivate each person? Do you understand the difference between leadership and management? If you answered a resounding "yes" to all three, your leadership and management skills are strong.

Next answer these questions: When you need to make a decision, do you pick the first good solution you find? When you face a problem, do you immediately begin looking for potential solutions? When a setback occurs, do you maintain a clear focus on the situation with positivity and objectivity? If you answered all with "yes" without any hesitation, then your problem-solving and decision-making skills are strong.

Now answer these: Are you able to communicate your needs and ensure that your message is clearly understood? When conflict arises, do you remain calm by using your communication skills to find a resolution? When discussing a situation with someone, do you try to stay ahead of the conversation by actively thinking about what you are going to say next? If your answers are a bold "yes" to each, then your communication skills are strong.

Here are your next questions: Do you routinely set goals for yourself and track your progress until you've achieved them? When managing your workload, do you know your priorities? Do you rarely lose time during the day because of uncertainty as to what needs to get done? If your "yes" for each answer was without a doubt, then your planning skills are strong.

Here are your final questions: Do you approach life with confidence and with a high self-esteem? Does the work you do reflect your values in alignment with the goals you've set for yourself? When you face a setback, do you routinely focus on the situation positively and objectively? If your answer was without question "yes" to all three, then your mastery over yourself is strong.

Of course, these questions are a very simple and quick assessment of your basic success skills. Assuming you've been honest, focus your development on the areas in need of the most improvement going forward.

"Happiness will come when we test our skills towards some meaningful purpose." ~ John Stossel

JANUARY 12

I will create a mission statement

Imagine a marathon runner who has no clue as to where the finish line is. She might prepare for a ten-mile race when in fact the finish line extends twenty-six miles from the starting point. What if an artist randomly applies paint to canvas with no vision as to what the final picture should look like? Those who live with no direction and no idea as to their desired end rarely create their life's masterpiece, and they rarely finish the race well.

Conversely, those with a mission that clearly defines their desired outcome and the criteria for attaining it tend to live life to the fullest. Do you have a mission statement for your life? If not try writing one now. Instill within your mission statement value, credibility, inspiration, and specificity. Make it memorable and pithy. Then test it with others to gain their feedback and suggestions. Walt Disney had a wonderful mission statement that simply stated, "Make people happy." This mission inspired the greatness with which Disney pioneered a new frontier in premier entertainment.

A properly stated mission for life articulates the picture or dream one desires at the end of their ultimate contribution in life. Think of it in this way: How would you like your one-to-three sentence obituary to read? Or if writing your obit is a little too eerie, think of that one quintessential achievement you desire. Your aspiration in life is the inspiration for your mission. Make it simple yet profound, because your mission statement will act as your guidepost throughout life. Print and keep your brief mission statement in your purse or wallet and reference it regularly as a reminder of your final masterpiece. And since no one stays the same, check it and revise it once in a while to ensure it reflects your current direction in life.

"The most effective way I know to begin with the end in mind is to develop a personal mission statement or philosophy or creed. It focuses on what you want to be (character) and do (contributions and achievements) and on the values or principles upon which being and doing are based." ~ Stephen Covey

"Everyone has his own specific vocation or mission in life . . . therein he cannot be replaced, nor can his life be repeated. Thus, everyone's task is unique as is his specific opportunity to implement it." ~ Viktor Frankl

JANUARY 13

I will be a truth seeker

We are all students in life, regardless of how much we know. Things constantly unfold, and as soon as we find out the answers, someone has changed the questions. A truth seeker learns from experiences and from others, but never simply accepts a majority rule or even social norms as the way it must be. The entire community around you may be wrong regarding certain points, but if you want to be a truth seeker, you may need to stand alone in determining the objective truth based on a compilation of sources filtered through your own finite understanding.

You will make decisions that may never be fully validated, yet the probably of your being right compels you to think that maybe you know the answer, and so you choose to act with all you know at the time. Realizing that you may be wrong is the voice of wisdom telling you that there's always more to know. As a truth seeker, you deal with terms such as *probability*, *likelihood*, and *maybe*. That's not a bad thing—it just means you will never shut the door on new ideas or concepts that may enter into your world of reality.

A scientist seeking the truth arrives at a conclusion while recognizing the uncertainty in life, just as a professional must act based on the probability that he or she knows the answer. As long as we're aware that there may be more to know, we can be at peace simply knowing we did the best we could at the time. If we believe with absolute certainty, then our eyes may be closed to revelations that present themselves to us.

An open mind need not exist in an unsettled state for perpetuity; it simply needs to revisit its ordered way of thinking should some disclosure arise, or should the truth surprisingly show up from some unknown source. We can arrive at a conclusion without closing all questioning by critically analyzing our ideas based on new information. Creativity and innovation put new ideas to the test, and when combined with critical thinking, the truth may be revealed.

Take the time to reflect on whether your truth is based just on what you want to believe or some personal bias, or if you've honestly appraised the value of your truth against a standard higher than yourself. Changing your mind is not always a bad thing. It means you are willing to factor new evidence into your way of thinking.

"Even if you are a minority of one, the truth is the truth." ~ Mahatma Gandhi

JANUARY 14

I will think like a child

A semi loaded with boxes traveled along a highway going from San Jose to Los Angeles. As the driver entered the city, he was confronted with a low-arching overpass and he was worried about the clearance. The truck driver decided to go under the overpass, and his truck got stuck. He quickly tried to go in reverse after failing to move forward, but to no avail—his truck was completely wedged between the road and the overpass. He then lit some flares to deter any other vehicles from rear-ending the truck. When emergency vehicles arrived, the workers tried almost everything to dislodge the truck. They could not remove any of the tightly banded boxes from the truck to reduce its height.

Then a mother pulled to the side of the highway, allowing her seven–year-old son to run up to the workers along the side shouting, "I've got it! I've got it!" "Got what?" asked the chief emergency worker. The child answered, "Let the air out of the truck's tires, move it past the overpass, and then pump up the tires again!" The workers did just that—problem solved!

Leave it to a child. Some of the most brilliant scholars (like Einstein) have long advocated this philosophy: it is productive and sometimes essential for people to think like children to achieve success as adults. Old habits of thinking and commonly accepted patterns of behavior clog our ability to accept free-flowing ideas. Sometimes we need to view things from a fresh perspective, unfettered by age. "Children are designed by evolution to be extremely good learners—to be able to think about anything that's interesting and important in the world around them," says Alison Gopnik, a professor of psychology and an affiliate professor at the University of California, Berkley. "When you look at their brains, they're extremely flexible, so they can change what they think based on new evidence very quickly and easily."

She further explains that as adults we tend to focus only on the things that are most relevant to us, making us more close-minded and unable or unwilling to consider the broadest possible range of opportunities. Gopnik suggests adopting more of the inquisitive approach to things that adults tend to lack by becoming more hesitant to ask questions. Keeping an open mind and releasing preconceptions is key to not overthinking a problem with prejudiced answers.

"It took me four years to paint like Raphael,
but a lifetime to paint like a child." ~ *Pablo Picasso*

JANUARY 15

I will start Mapping in Reverse (MIR)

While achievements present some level of satisfaction, they pale if not congruent with our dreams. Envision the best that you wish to be and do: therein resides your dream. Once you've discovered that place you want to be, work backward from there.

This concept is called Mapping in Reverse (MIR). After you first create the end point in your imagination, you draw up a blueprint for getting there. The key is to flip that blueprint so that you are starting immediately with the end point. In other words, you would picture yourself doing what you dream about first, and then find a way to support your continuance and development of the end point/dream. In this way you won't become frustrated through the twists and turns of getting there, which causes many people to just give up on their dream.

MIR is about immediately connecting with your dream. For example, Erin dreamed of writing a book in order to leave a legacy for her family, so she started writing—without delay. Realizing your dreams does not always necessitate uprooting yourself from job or home. Many choose volunteering as a wonderful way in which to immerse themselves in their dream. Sometimes our dream is not a position but rather a change in attitude. Naomi wished to be more patient, so she carved out a sabbatical to relieve her stress and worked weekends at a soup kitchen as a way of stabilizing her emotions.

By jumping immediately into the dream, we connect the sequence of our steps in reverse, beginning with the desired end point as our reality. Steve Wozniak, cofounder of Apple, used MIR after dreaming that he would have a computer someday—so he made one. MIR allows a person who dreams of being a master chef to start cooking classes, or a banker who dreams of being a police officer to start as a police volunteer, or to fill out an application and complete police academy training.

As children we learned to dream big, and as adults we learned to accept reality. But reality need not be an exception to our dreams. In truth we can enter into our dream without delay by working backward from its end point in order to justify our reality. If we fail to follow our dream, someone during our lifetime may hire us to fulfill his or her dream. Try starting from the end to fulfill yours—*now*.

"Start with a goal and reverse engineer it." ~ Brian Fling, Mobile 2.0 guru

JANUARY 16

I will embrace being one of a kind

"On your mark, get set, go!" With that send-off, Ida and her fellow competitors began racing to the finish line. All the racers finished except Ida, who hardly moved an inch. The judge instantly declared Ida as the last-place finisher—the loser—and poor Ida lived most of her life thinking she was a failure. Then one day someone placed Ida in a pool to compete with a group of turtles. Ida won!—because Ida was actually a goldfish.

Ida, like all of us, was uniquely designed to function for a purpose, but only if fitted in the right place. Our singularity makes each of us experts—standouts—because of our one-of-a-kind ability and not because of anyone or anything else. As Walt Disney once said, "The more you are like yourself, the less you are like anyone else, which makes you unique."

Your strength lies in your inherent abilities. Learn to know your assets, what separates you from others. List them and cherish them. Use your uniqueness to brand yourself as "You, Inc.," and through practice you won't have to tell people why you are special—your characteristics will tell them for you.

Don't be ashamed because you are different or unusual. Underneath the pretenses that every person uses to cover their "flaws" and peculiarities is the unfiltered persona that represents the genuine self. A priceless work of art loses its value if copied, and what some view as flaws are considered masterpieces by others (consider that the famous *Venus de Milo* statue has no arms). Albert Einstein was a misfit in the traditional school system, where his primary-school teachers reported that "the child had a powerful and lingering distaste of authority," coupled with his late-developing speech. He did, however, excel at math and physics.

So instead of trying to emulate someone else, or striving to be proficient in a field you're not good at, embrace yourself even if oddly shaped or strangely wired, and think as the eccentric artist Salvador Dali did: "I am not strange, I am just not normal." Normal is vastly overrated. You are an original design. Don't try to be a copy.

"You are the only you God made . . . God made you and broke the mold."
~ Max Lucado

"Don't compare yourself with anyone in this world . . . if you do so, you are insulting yourself." ~ Bill Gates

JANUARY 17

I will escape the Boiling Frog Syndrome

If you drop a frog in a pot of boiling water, it will instantly try to climb out. However, if you gently place it in a pot of lukewarm water and turn the heat on low, it will float there calmly. As the water gradually heats up, the frog, unaware of its deadly changing environment, before long boils to death. Many people are like the boiling frog—too comfortable in their situation to realize that to remain there means gradual harm or death. Some who remain in an abusive relationship allow it to continue until the abuse becomes accepted and rationalized, and as the abuses intensify, the abused person becomes resigned to the hopelessness of their reality.

The same dynamic happens in an unsatisfying job. You can get slowly "cooked to death" while complacently or fearfully just getting by . . . until retirement—if you can make it that long. The "boiling frog syndrome" even impacts those who live a sedentary life because they resent the time or energy required to exercise, gradually sacrificing their health. Some who pass over an opportunity because it appears too threatening can eventually succumb to boredom or regret—attitudes guaranteed to lead to an unsatisfying life.

And then there's the boiling frog syndrome that affects fast-food eaters, whose poor diets can clog their arteries because they just don't want to hassle with shopping for healthful foods, or they just prefer the taste of fatty foods. Our body requires activity in order to thrive, just as a healthy lifestyle includes mixing things up once in a while, trying something new, like piano lessons once a month or cooking a new recipe. Even small modifications to the daily routine can eventually lead to a more healthful norm.

Finding an accountability partner can bolster your resolve, like an exercise partner or a mentor. Each barrier crossed in trying something new sets up greater confidence to take on even greater challenges. It's important to remember your victories along the way, and if you've failed a time or two or more, simply begin again—try a different path, or start something completely new.

A stagnant life can breed disease, just as a vibrant life often leads to vitality. Good habits are comforting in a positive way and should not be confused with becoming too comfortable with bad habits. The healthy life requires a mix of both new and old.

"One is never wounded by the love one gives, only by the love one expects."
~ Marty Rubin, author of Boiled Frog Syndrome

JANUARY 18

I will seek opportunity instead of just climbing the ladder

Climbing the proverbial corporate ladder does not automatically lead to success—sometimes it just leads to another rung. More important than just climbing higher in the hierarchy is getting closer to your personal best. The greatest leaders seek opportunity, not status. When asked for the best advice ever given to him, IBM CEO and chairman Sam Palmisano answered: "The best advice was from a former boss who told me, 'Don't view your career as a linear progression.' He advised me to take horizontal rather than vertical steps, to try out situations that are unstructured, to learn different ways of working, and to get outside of headquarters and experience different cultures."

Some of the most successful people never rose to the ranks of CEO or president; however, they did expand their limited abilities to break through boundaries in achieving something greater than themselves. They became satisfied through achievement, not status. A new paradigm for getting ahead focuses on incremental personal and collective growth versus attaining rank.

In his breakthrough reasoning for human motivation called Theory Z, Abraham Maslow attempted to combine the entrepreneurial spirit of the American worker with the dedication of the Japanese worker by theorizing that higher productivity and satisfaction could be achieved through less frequent promotions and a greater commitment to advancing the entire organization. In other words, working for *us* versus just for *me*. As personal status becomes more irrelevant, it frees the individual to seek areas of greater challenge minus the burden of just getting ahead.

The term *intrepreneur* was coined in the 1980s to mean someone who displays the same characteristics as an entrepreneur but remains with an organization as an employee. In today's workplace, organizations that encourage intrepreneurship (e.g., risk-takers, innovators) foster a culture that harvests potential by tapping into the positive energy of workers instead of tacitly condoning political maneuvering, which can damage morale and stifle productivity. When people within an organization start overriding their desires to simply get ahead with an earnest desire to learn, create, and contribute to the organization, both the employees and company thrive. Success is not a position—it's a contribution.

"As we look ahead into the next century, leaders will be those who empower others." ~ Bill Gates

JANUARY 19

I will clarify my values

Clarifying your work values in your life and career is essential. Your values are both intrinsic (relating to how you live your life) and extrinsic (relating to the by-product of what you do). An intrinsic value might be "helping people," while an example of an extrinsic value is "having prestige."

Try taking a *values inventory* by creating a list of your values and rating them in order of importance. This will help you to match your values with the choices you must make, and it also helps you with making decisions. One famous case study illustrates how rating an intrinsic value "of doing the right thing" ahead of an extrinsic value of "making lots of money" can dramatically affect the outcome of a company and its people.

In 1982 someone laced Tylenol capsules with cyanide, which resulted in several deaths. At that point Tylenol represented Johnson & Johnson's (J&J's) greatest profit-maker. Losing it would potentially ruin the company. Within weeks its market share dropped from 37 percent to 7 percent, and the company's stock plummeted. Governed by J&J's credo (value statement) without regard to the consequences, Chairman James Burke ordered a halt to production and pulled all twenty-two million Tylenol capsules from retailer shelves. By 1985, Tylenol's market share was fully restored with J&J's new tamper-resistant product. Burke stated: "Later we realized that no meeting had been called to make the first critical decision. Every one of us knew what we had to do. There was no need to meet. We had the credo to guide us."

Highlighting one of the greatest market recoveries in history, this story demonstrates the advantage of establishing concrete values that will endure through all situations, including crises. This truth applies to individuals the same as it applies to companies. Until we clarify our values and commit them to memory, our actions will tend toward convenience and survival, or others' influences. Absent solid values, our reactions will typically follow the path of least resistance. The rock of our character consists of immutable standards of behavior that safeguard our most important values. We build our foundation for growth upon each of these values, and in this case, J&J doing the right thing eventually led to them succeeding.

"As a man thinks in his heart, so is he." ~ David, the psalmist

JANUARY 20

I will make myself irreplaceable

The old adage is that nobody is indispensable. While it's true that organizations often downsize and sometimes eliminate positions irrespective of an individual's talent, those performers who continually develop their skills while going above and beyond expectations tend to be more irreplaceable.

With twenty-four hours allocated to each human being, how we use these hours each day will determine our level of success. Dedicating time to the most important tasks requires a prioritization of responsibilities based on stakeholder or management input and the potential return on investment. In other words, do *not* major in the minors. Making good decisions involves the ability to invest in those areas with the highest visible return—ones that will command notice—making yourself invaluable to others by meeting unmet needs—being remarkable.

Research completed by the authors Judy Free and Traci Maddox for *The Essential Employee: The Adventures of Carmen Senz* (Sage Peak Associates, Inc., 2008) revealed behaviors considered by executives, supervisors, and coworkers as the most valuable in the workplace. Employees who practice these behaviors distinguish themselves with a reputation deemed necessary within the organization.

Free and Maddox developed an acronym for these behaviors: REACH. It stands for: 1) Results—meet or exceed measurable goals, communicate routinely with your supervisor and others involved in the project, and let your successes be known; 2) Enthusiasm—a positive "can-do" approach will not only make others enjoy your company but it also signals to supervisors that you are committed to the success of the organization; 3) Attitude—when things go wrong (and they will), focus on the positives and the possibilities—helping and encouraging others elevates the mood within the workplace and also expresses your gratitude for your job; 4) Cooperation—volunteering to help others, being accountable, thanking those who help you, taking ownership for successes as well as failures, and giving credit to those who deserve it demonstrates the essential quality of good teamwork; and 5) Honor—allow your values to be your constant in an ever-changing environment so others can see that in the shifting nature of things your solid moral foundation stands strong, worthy of respect, and indispensable!

"In order to be irreplaceable one must always be different." ~ Coco Chanel

JANUARY 21

I will reinvent the future

Wouldn't it be great if you could predict the future? Well, you can—to some extent. Past performance usually predicts future performance. Problems in the past tend to repeat themselves unless the causes for them are eliminated and replaced with solutions. The old adage that history repeats itself proves correct more often than not. So being a student of history in your environment is critical. Ask: what has worked and what hasn't worked in the past? If you take your car into a repair shop more than once and they can't fix it, you should probably find another shop. Likewise, if you've experienced difficulty with something in the past, you likely need to find a different approach.

One of the best ways to predict the future is to reinvent it. That happens when we declare our intention and then critically evaluate how to turn future *probabilities* into future *possibilities.* A critical mind-set consistently evaluates how to do things more effectively—better than before.

Planning is crucial, including developing fallback plans in case of failure. One of the major causes of failure is falling behind, so staying on task is critical, along with establishing daily responsibilities so there remains time for assessing potential problems and opportunities. This also includes eliminating unnecessary tasks that can keep you mired in the minutia and cloud your perspective from a ten-thousand-foot level.

Reoccurring problems happen when you stay in the same place, using the same perspective, being fearful of the new. Spotting potentialities requires viewing *all* the variables within your sphere of impact. Looking at the big picture allows you to anticipate needs so that you can evaluate all the ramifications involved in improving processes.

Involve others and delegate effectively in order to engage more eyes on the issues, thereby expanding your awareness. Always ask yourself the question: how can we do things better?

"Before you act, listen. Before you read, think. Before you spend, earn. Before you criticize, wait. Before you pray, forgive. Before you quit, try." ~ Ernest Hemingway

"The windshield is bigger than the rearview mirror." ~ Tom Daschle

JANUARY 22

I will be a good salesperson

Selling is a *listen-acknowledge-respond* cycle, not a talk-present-convince process. Most ineffective salespeople try to convince someone of their product's benefit, frequently talking over the other person. Great salespeople listen to their customers' personal (not just professional) wants. They acknowledge the merit of their wants, and then through a series of engrossing (thought-provoking) questions guide the customer to a realization that their product's benefits will create a personal win for them as well as a professional win.

A personal win is subjective to the buyer. It is provided to the buyer by satisfying his self-interests, such as giving the buyer something that enhances his respect among his peers. Whereas a professional win would be giving the buyer something to help him perform his job better.

Consider this sales situation: Annie is trying to sell her neighbor some Girl Scout cookies. Beyond saying hello, one of her first questions is not to ask her neighbor if she wants to buy cookies—that would be Annie's want. Instead she asks a more thought-provoking question: "Ms. Neighbor, what first came to mind when you saw me in my uniform selling cookies at the door?" Ms. Neighbor scratches her head and says: "Well, honestly, I thought, here comes one of about twenty Girl Scouts I'm going to have to buy cookies from." So Ms. Neighbor's *personal win or wish* is to not be constantly hassled by girls selling cookies.

Annie remains unflappable, chuckles, and says, "Thank for your honesty. I can imagine how much of a nuisance that would cause anyone [Annie shows empathy]. Would it help if I could ask the scout leader to assign only one canvasser to your block [Annie offers a solution for achieving her customer's *personal win*]?"

You see where this is going? Annie listened to her neighbor's most pressing concern, she acknowledged it in order to demonstrate she was listening, and then she addressed the *customer's* want, not her own. She also sold Ms. Neighbor five boxes of cookies because she eliminated her competition! Zig Ziglar puts it this way: "Stop selling, start helping." The art of the sale involves actively and empathetically listening to others' needs, and then meeting those wants/needs first.

"You can close more business in two months by becoming interested in other people than you can in two years by trying to get people interested in you." ~ *Dale Carnegie*

JANUARY 23

I will practice the Social Interaction Rule

Most know the Golden Rule from Matthew 7:12 of the Bible: "Do unto others as you would have them do unto you." The *Social Interaction Rule (SIR)* states: "Treat people in the manner to which they are most receptive." People respond differently depending on their behavioral style, and this makes SIR an effective interaction tool.

Essentially two categories describe the vast majority of people: they are either *extroverts* or *introverts*, and they are either *sensing* (feeling) or *judging* (appraising). The combinations of each type generally determine a person's behavioral style. An extrovert/sensing person is called an *Expressive.* An extrovert/judging person is called a *Director.* An introvert/sensing person is called an *Amiable.* An introvert/judging person is called an *Analyzer. Expressives* enjoy being the life of the party and are motivated by social interaction, so the SIR is to engage them with spirited conversation. *Directors* want action and tend to believe their way is the only way, so the SIR is to be forthright with them with little or no banter (cut to the point). *Amiables* want everyone to get along, and they tend to be the caretakers, so the SIR is to avoid conflict with them and to ask them questions about family, friends, etc. *Analyzers* enjoy solving problems and tend to be numbers-oriented, so the SIR is to present them with statistics, information, proof—they thrive on reasoning and calculations.

You can determine a person's type by their mannerisms, social interactions, and accouterments. Amiables tend to include lots of family pictures in their office. Directors are proud to display their awards and achievements. Expressives appreciate luncheon meetings, and Analyzers eat pie charts for lunch. When interacting with each type, reflect those behaviors to which they respond most positively.

Don't assume your likes are their likes—one size does not fit all. When with an Expressive, be gregarious; with a Director be straightforward; be affable with an Amiable; and speak or act logically with an Analyzer. Each behavioral type desires a different way of interaction that mirrors what they want, so be adaptable to each type by reflecting those behaviors with which each style is most comfortable.

"If you contemplate the Golden Rule, it turns out to be an injunction to live by grace rather than by what you think other people deserve." ~ Deepak Chopra

JANUARY 24

I will practice the law of attraction

The commonly accepted law of attraction, which represents one of the most influential paths to success, says that people will naturally gravitate toward the perception they have of themselves. This means people can control their thoughts, feelings, and interpretations to attract the attention of people attracted to those attributes.

So how you perceive yourself (either consciously or unconsciously) may reveal that person to others and in turn create the expectations imposed by your thoughts. Think confidently about yourself and you will invite others' attention. Believe in your ability to succeed in something and you will invite that success into your life. Conversely, expect to fail and you will probably fail. How you perceive yourself reflects how others tend to perceive you.

Now, does this mean that at age eighty-five someone who believes himself to be an NFL linebacker will become one? Of course not—that would be delusional thinking; however, if that eighty-five-year-old thought and truly felt like a strong, athletic person, he would display those attributes to others, some of whom might in turn create for the eighty-five-year-old opportunities to accommodate that persona—such as someone inviting him to go for a power walk. Hence, because of the law of attraction, you help shape the environment around you.

So to create the world in which you wish to live, you must first know what you want, pray that God will give you the wherewithal, and then you must expect it. Don't just wish for it—*expect* it. This means that you are in a constant mode of anticipation—a hope that cannot be extinguished. This doesn't mean that you are entirely responsible for the bad that happens in your life. You didn't bring all these things on by thinking negatively—some circumstances are of course beyond our control (natural disasters, evildoers who randomly attack others). The law of attraction applies to intentional people who, even in the face of tragedy, can turn accidents into opportunities, such as someone who lost a loved one becoming a grief counselor to help others. The law does guarantee a compelling attraction of openings that nurture our expectations to their fullest actualization. It's a little like earnestly believing in your potential or future as if you are already there. If you do that, invariably, you will get there!

"He is greatest whose strength carries up the most hearts by the attraction of his own." ~ Henry Beecher

JANUARY 25

I will choose my circle of friends carefully

Staying the right course requires choosing wise counselors and accountability partners. George Washington surrounded himself with Hamilton and Jefferson to help him weigh decisions. Only after heeding his mother's advice did Washington at an early age decide not to follow his childhood dream of joining the British navy and instead went on to become commander in chief of the entire military forces of the United States of America. Throughout history, people who made a difference have done so not by themselves but through the counsel of others.

The people with whom we spend the most time often influence us the most. Who we surround ourselves with will determine whether we rise to the heights of the solution-makers or sink to the depths of the naysayers. That, coupled with constant learning, determines success, and who better to learn from than those whose present skills are superior to our own?

A team of three-to-five accountability partners who meet at least once a month will invariably strengthen each other's abilities, especially if at least one of them acts as a mentor/coach willing to interact more frequently with us. Ad hoc members of our advisory team should also include respected authors/speakers whose books or tapes we've gone through. Networking groups such as clubs, seminars, and Internet groups are great ways to stay plugged in with others to seek advice. Diversity, as with people outside our own company or profession, also adds different perspectives. For personal challenges, such as getting in shape or competing, accountability partners help push us to the finish line.

Surround ourselves with the people we want to be like, and we will become more like them. Having an honest and committed accountability group or partner can be the single greatest asset for life and career.

"The best advisor is one who can be your ally, advocate, and adversary when he or she needs to be." – Carol M. Roberts.

"If you hang out with chickens, you're going to cluck, and if you hang out with eagles you're going to fly." ~ Steve Maraboli

JANUARY 26

I will not allow my environment to dictate my success

Living as a child in one of the poorest areas in Detroit, laughed at and joked about each day in school, this self-proclaimed "stupidest kid in fifth grade" went on to become the chief of pediatric neurosurgery at John Hopkins University Hospital and received the Presidential Medal of Freedom in 2008. Benjamin Carson grew up in a gang-infested neighborhood that killed both his older cousins. The teasing and desperation of Carson's environment turned him into an angry and desperate youngster.

Eager to save her two sons, Carson's single mother and domestic worker, Sonya Carson, one day prayed to God for wisdom as to how to raise her children. The answer came to turn off the TV and require her children to read two books a week. Though she could not read, Sonya Carson insisted that each boy write a report of the books they read while she pretended to grade each paper written. In a year and a half, Ben Carson went from the bottom to the top of his class.

While still struggling with extreme anger issues, a revelation came to Carson one day that transformed his life. He realized that people with bad tempers surround themselves with people who are self-centered. "Once you learn to step outside the center of the equation, and are able to look in from the outside, it is very difficult for people to make you angry, and you have a much better perspective, and fortunately I was able to gain that before I ended in jail or reform school or the grave," he explains.

Carson's life serves as an example of how we can achieve victory over circumstances through reading, discipline, and an "others-focused" perspective, which makes our environment more irrelevant. As he says, "Successful people don't have fewer problems. They have determined that nothing will stop them from going forward."

"Happiness doesn't result from what we get, but from what we give." – Ben Carson

"Success is determined not by whether or not you face obstacles, but by your reaction to them. And if you look at these obstacles as a containing fence, they become your excuse for failure. If you look at them as a hurdle, each one strengthens you for the next." ~ Ben Carson

JANUARY 27

I will love what I do

Doing what you love to do is complicated. Not all passionate endeavors lead to a paycheck. Sometimes delayed gratification must be practiced first. Even Einstein had moments when he wanted to enjoy his love of sailing right away but told himself that he should finish what he was working on first.

Loving what you do is much easier; however, it requires a paradigm shift. It begins with changing your common view of doing work for someone else, or a company. That perspective feeds into a fatalist perspective that can be demotivating when others disappoint you. Think of your work as a journey to develop your skills and relationships. So the journey is not about finding your next job; it's about realizing how all your efforts create a mosaic of experiences that make you a richer human being. This way your title or occupation does not define you.

Consider instead how you want to spend your time. What skill do you want to develop, what kinds of people will teach you something, what work instills within you the desire to do more? Sometimes you can grow opportunities in your current position. There's a quote from the movie *The Peaceful Warrior* (DEJ Productions, 2006) that speaks to loving what you do: "A warrior does not give up what he loves. He finds the love in what he does." You may compromise your passion for a while waiting to find a new experience that will rekindle your dream with deeper understanding.

Discover the love of what you do in all aspects of your life while keeping in mind opportunities for the next adventure. Experiment with new ideas and insights, and push your physical and mental limits. Keep learning until your brain hurts. Surround yourself with people who've accomplished what you admire. This way your journey can evolve into something truly inspiring.

"The biggest mistake people make in life is not trying to make a living at doing what they most enjoy." – Malcolm Forbes

"I have looked in the mirror every morning and asked myself: 'If today were the last day of my life, would I want to do what I am about to do today?' And whenever the answer has been 'No' for too many days in a row, I know I need to change something." ~ Steve Jobs

JANUARY 28

I will use my imperfections to help others

We all have them—imperfections that make us undesirable or ill fitted to our community surroundings. But social pressures cause us to want to be perfect. Chin tucks and weight reduction represent two of the fastest growing categories of "self-improvement." Sometimes our imperfections happen suddenly, as with Joni Eareckson Tada, who at the age of seventeen suffered paralysis from the shoulders down after a dive into Chesapeake Bay. Along with her body, many of Joni's dreams were instantly fractured in that moment.

After much suffering she turned her life in new directions. She learned to paint with the brush in her mouth, and wrote about her Christian faith—her struggles and victories—in order to benefit others dealing with disabilities. Almost fifty top-selling books later, with several beautiful pieces of artwork to her credit and countless awards, Joni continued to encourage the mentally, emotionally, and physically challenged through weekly broadcasts, summer family camps for persons with disabilities, donating wheelchairs for the underprivileged throughout the world, and numerous speaking engagements that would exhaust even the most able-bodied person.

To Joni, her success is not represented by a series of personal victories but rather in the way she used her disability to help others and to show the love of God. Altruism is grossly underrated and appearance is sadly overrated in a society that values perfect people. As with Joni, we can use our imperfections to help others overcome theirs, and we can grow stronger because of them.

To help you get there, ask yourself: if someone you loved had your imperfection (whether emotional-mental, physical, or a character flaw), what would you say to her? When you've arrived at the answer to that question, turn it around and tell yourself that answer. Find your strength through your imperfection, and then help others through the affinity you develop from your own suffering. Try using your flaws as a healing force by sharing your story and showing empathy for the struggles of others.

"I have found the paradox that if you love until it hurts, there can be no more hurt, only more love." ~ Mother Teresa

"Sometimes God allows what he hates to accomplish what he loves." ~Joni Eareckson Tada

JANUARY 29

I will not worry about the future

If given the chance, would you wish to know the future? Keep in mind that all the inevitable accidents, the failures, the sickness, and the losses ahead of you would come with that revelation. Now suppose that, after knowing the future, you could change it. However, besides not repeating some mistakes or avoiding devastating accidents, you would also miss the benefits of the trials that lay ahead of you. Perhaps you wouldn't have taken that job if you had known it would end so abruptly, or you might have refused that relationship that caused so much heartache. In doing so you also might have failed to gain some wisdom about how to choose a better job, having not learned from the former one. You might not know the joys and the pitfalls that could have benefited you from the failed relationship you passed over, ensuring the next relationship would be more fulfilling.

The future is shielded from us for a reason. Given the chance, most of us would avoid everything painful in our lives. If so, we would remain in a stunted state of delusion, unable to overcome most of life's challenges. Trials serve to strengthen us and help us develop wisdom.

Our most genuine worries typically are not imagined or planned; they are the kind that blindside us, like a three a.m. call—and then worry makes it three a.m. over and over again. Since we cannot plan our lives to filter out all trials, we must allow life to happen to us. The key is to face the good and the bad with equal thankfulness, since both serve to complete us.

The path of least resistance is also the path of least growth. When confronted with the unplanned, dive into it, and don't always take the easiest way out. If crisis arrives, just get through the moment, and then the day, and then the next day after that, and so forth. Remember that the memory is kind. It often assuages the harshness of pain and loss over time as the past forms a mosaic that eventually blends into a future that includes a stronger you.

We cannot dwell on future possibilities without losing the hope of today. Your destiny begins with your willingness to accept the future enthusiastically. It's your journey—anticipate a life that will leave you stronger and wiser.

"Ask yourself this question: 'Will this matter a year from now?'" ~ Richard Carlson, Don't Sweat the Small Stuff (Hyperion, 1997)

JANUARY 30

I will contribute to the team

Never underestimate the value of teamwork. So many set out to be leaders but lose sight of the fact that a true leader is defined by the quality of his actions and the integrity of his decisions. Leaders do not seek after attention. They protect the interest of their team without worrying about who gets the credit for the success of the team. Effective leaders say "we" instead of "I," and inspire enthusiasm versus fear. They practice the TEAM concept.

TEAM is an acronym that stands for Together Everyone Achieves More. Teamwork begins with a commitment to the team's vision. Leaders must communicate clear expectations to the team, and in their absence, good team members must define the expectations. Individual contributors on the team should be reminded of why they are on the team, their roles and responsibilities, and of how important they are to the team.

If you or another member are not fully committed to meeting the objectives of the team, success will not happen. So as the teamwork leader you must determine the reason for the lack of commitment. Ask yourself: "Do the team members perceive their value, and have their expectations been heard and adequately addressed?"

Keep in mind that you don't have to be in an official position as a "leader" to practice effective leadership within a team—leadership is a choice, not a position. If you support the team by celebrating the team's success and by taking the initiative for seeing that tasks get done, others will notice you as a leader. The key is to know your strengths and to find a role within the team that offers you the opportunity to do what you do well.

The single most valuable asset to a team is reliability, so keep your commitments. Be an involved communicator with the group. Stay positive even when being constructively critical. Remaining flexible to the changing dynamics of the team demonstrates your own adaptability, which is hugely important in any team environment. Stay focused on the results, not on yourself. Remember that the greatest benefit of working together is that it gives you the opportunity to accomplish more than you can do by yourself.

"Teamwork is so important that it is virtually impossible for you to reach the heights of your capabilities or make the money that you want without becoming very good at it." ~ Brian Tracy

JANUARY 31

I will establish SMART goals

SMART is an acronym for achieving goals that stands for Specific Measurable Attainable Realistic (and Relevant) Timely, and it's smart because it keeps you from spinning your wheels! This acronym first appeared in a November 1981 issue of *Management Review* (vol. 70, issue 11), and to this day it represents the standard by which many organizations establish goals.

The process of being SMART begins with everyone being clear as to the outcome-based goals (i.e., the destination), so that everyone on the team or organization understands what is the desired outcome. An outcome-based goal should provide clear direction. Begin formulating these goals by thinking about the big picture, and then start at the end and work backward so that you can stay focused. Goals like "enjoy life more" or "get healthy" are too vague; hence, the first importance of a goal is to be specific, such as "read one book every month" or "lose ten pounds by March by exercising four times a week." These two goals are measureable with a quantity and a deadline.

In some cases you may want to keep a log in order to track progress against the goal. Your goal should inspire you to change by offering enough motivation to do so. Having an accountability partner or being a part of a group may help maintain your mojo during lower peak times. Don't establish goals that are not under your control, such as a goal for your boss "to be nicer"—goals for other people typically are not readily attainable.

Goals should require you to stretch your capacity without being impossible to attain. Realistic goals may need to be broken down into smaller goals, with a corresponding plan to graduate their degree of difficulty based on time and quantity.

Finally, ask yourself: "When will the goal be completed?" Choosing a time or date should be expeditious. Open-ended goals don't establish any sense of urgency to encourage progress. Saying, "I will lose thirty pounds by midyear" is fine, but stating, "I will lose an average of three pounds a week" is even better. This way you can routinely track your progress by planning regular updates to gauge your progress. Once you've done all that, revisit and revise your goals consistently to incorporate any changes that may have occurred along the way.

"If it isn't measureable, it cannot be managed." ~ Jack Welch

FEBRUARY

NEXT STEPS

FEBRUARY 1

I will think outside the box

At one public relations firm, employees at a roundtable session were given the task of making a chemical company look sexy. Sitting at a table strewn with little toys, putty, and squeeze balls, they were asked, "Tell me an idea excited by the word *chemicals*," and then the moderator showed a picture of children playing in a field with the caption: "What chemicals should they be playing around?" They were given a few minutes to jot down concepts.

This is the type of experience that can foster greater out-of-the-box thinking—by providing a potential negative and turning it into a positive. Providing prompts like that provocative question stimulated creative thinking by connecting concepts to seemingly disparate words or phrases, while avoiding the pitfall of scattered thinking. Too much freedom can actually stifle practical creative thinking, so some framework is necessary without creating too-rigid boundaries.

Spontaneous inspirations that challenge paradigms trigger the mind to go places seemingly unrelated to the challenge, and then force a way to funnel these ideas into a workable concept. Think of associations that seem totally unrelated, such as the word *stars* to *vacuums*, or *oranges* to *cars*. Most of the time when presented with outrageous links you will become energized with a type of playful exuberance to place the randomness together. Try starting with a negative association, like *toxic* and *chemicals*, and turn it into a positive, like *life* and *chemicals*.

Consciously eliminate the filters of your thinking to begin considering the ridiculous or what may seem incorrect. Afterward you can mold it into something more practical. The key is to circumvent your programmed way of thinking in order to conceptualize something new and fresh.

"The greatest danger for most of us is not that our aim is too high and we miss it, but that it is too low and we reach it." ~ Michelangelo

"The most pathetic person in the world is someone who has sight, but has no vision." ~ Helen Keller

"Vision is the art of seeing the invisible." ~ Jonathan Swift

FEBRUARY 2

I will not be afraid to make mistakes

Without mistakes, no progress would be made. Mistakes teach us in a way far superior to any other experience. Mistakes grow our perspective and understanding as long as they are followed up with a commitment to "not do that again," which is a type of negative reinforcement that precludes us from making similar mistakes. The key is to analyze the details of what caused the mistake in order to develop an alternative pathway that avoids the root cause of the mistake the next time.

Most problems include a series of steps that must be taken in order to reach a solution. Deductive reasoning causes the brain to eliminate those steps that do not lead to the next, and so forth, until the final answer is achieved. Mistakes usually occur by taking large leaps of faith that do not follow an ordered sequence of reasoning, or they can occur inevitably, as part of learning, such as trying to figure out pieces to a puzzle. Educated guesses almost always factor into any reasoning since we human beings are not all-knowing. After going through a defined process, sometimes we need to take a risk.

The important consideration in making an educated guess is to do it with gusto. Don't just dip your toes into the pool—you need to eventually start swimming. By diving in you can correct any mistakes from that process of discovery. Of course, some activities do not allow for such guessing, as with a surgeon repairing a heart valve, but even the surgeon must make some mistakes before becoming an expert (preferably on cadavers first). Programming the artificial intelligence of software uses this technique of checking for error and then taking alternative paths. Human intelligence operates similarly.

"Success makes a lousy teacher," said Bill Gates in response to the inevitability of making mistakes. Mistakes make us humble and give us insight, and those are good things even though they hurt in the short term. To try and then make a mistake is better than never having tried in the first place.

"People who make no mistakes lack boldness and the spirit of adventure. They are the brakes on the wheels of progress." ~ Norman Vincent Peale

FEBRUARY 3

I will define the reality around me

There is a woman (for the sake of privacy, we will call her Edith), who at the age of forty-eight had never stepped one foot outside New York City (NYC). To Edith, her entire reality was that city. While employed as a hotel manager, Edith eventually was asked by her company to visit some other hotels outside NYC to investigate ways in which the company could improve. This out-of-town assignment terrified Edith. Her right brain hemisphere, as it is for each of us, was mostly concerned about the present circumstances, unable to separate her limited awareness from the world around her. Edith thought the outside world was a dangerous place because her "right brain" told her so.

The left brain hemisphere, however, thinks methodically, by picking out events in the past and using them to predict the future. The longer Edith allowed her experience to be confined to NYC only, the more she enabled her right hemisphere and disabled her left hemisphere. If the right brain had its way, it would only consider the here and now, with no concept of the difference between people or places, and no perception of the past or future.

Defining reality uses both sides of the brain by factoring in personal experience, reality as defined by others, and the dictionary definition of reality, which is "the state of being actual or true." However, by consciously choosing our beliefs, our reality is what we make it. Edith eventually decided to travel to other cities, and in the process expanded her reality by subconsciously connecting the right hemisphere to the left hemisphere—she took a chance. She changed her reality by changing her thoughts, and we can do the same.

Connecting the two sides of our brain to expand our reality requires openness to change, which leads to the creation of a new external reality that assimilates the "tried and true" with the "potential and possible." We must define our reality as a starting point but not as an end point. Keep an open mind toward creating a more positive outlook, and live life with an attitude of expectancy. In Edith's case, she now loves traveling to different places.

"The first act of a leader is to define reality. The last is to say thank you. In between, the leader is a servant." ~ Max De Pree

"If the facts don't fit the theory, change the facts." ~ Albert Einstein

FEBRUARY 4

I will promote myself

Self-promotion has gotten a bad name because too many use it to the detriment of others. Used constructively, self-promotion allows others to see your value so that they can benefit from it, with some added benefits to you. And if you don't do it, who will?

The foundation of a strong promotion campaign is to find great ideas and content to share. Setting up a self-hosted web page is a good way to get started. You can also start a blog with articles showcasing your expertise through your own Wordpress site, and create an e-mail address from your own URL. Post accomplishments using a photo gallery or pages for individual projects. You can also create a Twitter account and invite people within your field. LinkedIn is a must for professionals, with over two hundred million subscribers and counting, because it helps you to actively manage your personal viability in the expanding economy. Chances are every savvy professional who has scheduled a meeting with you has looked at your profile before the meeting.

Spend time responding to messages, tweets, and e-mails, as these represent others who have expressed an interest in what you do, and try to give them information helpful to them. Don't make yourself a pest by consistently communicating with people who don't respond to you—this only shows desperation. Make sure not to over communicate by filling up mailboxes, voice mail, and such, using the qualifier that if it isn't a response or if it doesn't include some added benefit to the other person, don't send it.

Attend events, trade shows, and career groups that specialize in your primary area of interest. Networking is king in promoting yourself. Don't embellish your experiences but make sure to show a consistent theme of success (results) in your own area of expertise. Try understanding those you're reaching out to and remain sensitive to their needs when promoting your own. Make sure to build your promotions around your talents and strengths so that others will take you seriously. And don't forget to be confident.

"The day you stop promoting yourself is the day you stop advancing. Opportunities rarely go to the most qualified, but rather to those who can promote themselves the best and who are in the right place at the right time."

~ Jim Murray, from Becoming CEO (and Staying There)

FEBRUARY 5

I will find my niche

What is it that separates you from ninety-percent of the people out there? Ask yourself this question: "What do people consistently ask my advice about?" This will give you your first clue as to your personal niche. Next, honestly assess your strengths and weaknesses, and determine which of your strengths is most unique within the universe around you. Your personal niche reflects the sum of your personhood and includes behavioral style, personality, talents, skills, experience, and even appearance.

After you've discovered what makes you unique and sought after, make a list of those characteristics you most appreciate about yourself, and then describe your dream position. Compare your characteristics to those you feel are generally lacking within your dream position. In other words, what do you offer that others in your dream position generally do not provide? Are there any unmet needs? If so, use these to your advantage by promoting your personal niche—what makes you special, the quality that makes people seek you out.

People tend to make a greater impact if they're known as the "go-to person." This requires that you find your personal brand that will draw more people to you. But don't become overly concerned if you can't identify a defined personal brand. The most important part of being you is not to put up a façade. Be honest about yourself, or others may see you as a fake. Listen to your heart. When you close the gap between realizing your unique qualities and discovering where you want to go, then you're ready to leap into the place your inner voice is calling you to.

Then it's time to take the risk. Niche businesses are great ideas for entrepreneurs who can develop their talents and experiences into a niche expertise. Hobbies sometimes can turn into businesses, but avoid enterprises that are purely interests without identifying a neglected market space. Use your niche characteristics to make a difference. You need to know how big the market is and how you can broaden it. Also, consider partnering with other similar niche businesses and with those whose unique qualities complement yours to leverage your opportunities.

"Everyone has a niche in life. This is what I meant to do." ~ Audrey Rosenstein

FEBRUARY 6

I will know when to stop talking

In the movie *Jerry Maguire* (Gracie Films and Tri-Star Pictures, 1996), Dorothy, played by Renee Zellweger, and Jerry (Tom Cruise) fall in love, but it takes time and a fair amount of wooing by Jerry. When Dorothy is finally willing to kiss her beau, Jerry continues to talk over her, until she says, "Shut up, just shut . . . You had me at hello." Jerry suffered from the common communication problem of overselling. Talking over someone else is one of the most frequent errors made by salespeople, and one that affects any interaction in which someone is trying to convince another, such as interviewing.

Conversing in such a way that the other person doesn't lose interest requires an understanding of body language, like foot tapping, glazed eyes, and checking the watch—all signs of boredom. Run-on sentences can be fatal, so being concise is important: no more than ten sentences and no responses more than half a minute long. Avoid going off on a tangent. If you don't understand the question, ask for clarification.

Check as to whether the other person has heard enough before assuming you should say more. Don't be afraid of pauses, as they allow the other person to ponder your answers. If you catch yourself having over-talked, apologize and quickly move on. Don't try to overcompensate by responding with curt answers like a yes or no unless the other person requests it. Anything missed in a conversation can be covered in an email or a follow-up talk. Convincing someone is eighty-percent listening and twenty-percent talking. Learn when enough is enough.

"[Overselling] gives the buyer a reason to pause and ask themselves: maybe I'm paying too much, or maybe this is more than what I need." ~ Colleen Francis

"[People] have two ears and one mouth for a reason. The formula for sales success is 80 percent listening and 20 percent talking." ~ Lori Turner-Wilson

'Formula for success: under promise and over deliver." ~ Tom Peters

FEBRUARY 7

I will tell the good with the bad

Delivering bad news isn't fun, unless you're a sadist, which of course does *not* describe any readers of this book. The good news is that there are effective ways to share negative messages like "it's over." You just need to understand how others hear you.

Most of us use selective listening. We hear, or prefer to hear, the good news over the bad. According to a study at the University College London, in the general population eighty to ninety percent of us revise our negative self-image when told we are smarter or more attractive, but hearing that we are more stupid or uglier causes less revision of a positive self-image. To some extent this has been interpreted as a defense mechanism that allows us to handle bad news with less trauma.

But there is a downside to rose-colored perspectives. Shrugging off what we deem negative may prevent us from preparing for potential tragedies, even make us reckless. So should we accentuate the bad? Not really. According to Drs. James Shepperd and Marie Helweg-Larsen, the good news predominance in which we are inclined to only accept positive comments made about us tends to be less common in people with depression, making it likely that the optimist's view of life is healthy for our well-being, and helps to motivate us.

There is, however, a proper way to *tell* the bad news. Always tell bad news face-to-face, and document good news in writing if possible. Your sentiments should be sincere, not contrived. Generally the bad news should be expressed as soon as possible, since people don't want to feel like they've been deceived or betrayed if what's potentially damaging to them is hidden over an extended time. Give the receiver of bad news an advance warning, saying something like "things have changed" without going into details, but don't keep them worrying too long. Begin the conversation objectively with the facts, followed by genuine empathy, and concluded with some encouragement. Remember, people tend to hear the good news and discount the bad news, so you may need to repeat the bad news, but always do so with a dose of hope for the future.

"Bad news isn't wine. It doesn't improve with age." ~ Colin Powell

"You don't hear things that are bad about your company unless you ask. It is easy to hear good tidings, but you have to scratch to get the bad news." ~ Thomas J. Watson

FEBRUARY 8

I will make a positive first impression

In just under five seconds it's over—the first impression. Your appearance, your demeanor, your body language, and your first words create that quick assessment that takes place during that first meeting. So whether during your career or social life, these first encounters will probably influence your relationships for their entirety and are therefore critically important.

But don't allow the anxiety of a first meeting to make you overly controlled. In advance of the first meeting, try to learn something about the other person before you get together. For instance: Does he play golf or have any other interests? When you are meeting people for the first time, approach them with a genuine interest in getting to know who they are. Often this leads to a more engaging conversation since your interest in the other person will likely trigger their interest in you.

You must appear at ease in order to relax the other person. Take deep breaths and imagine you are meeting an old friend, even if greeting the potential new friend causes the jitters. Show up for the meeting at least ten minutes in advance, and certainly don't be late. You don't need to look like someone out of *Vogue*, but you do need to make your appearance appropriate to the place and situation. What you want to convey should be reflected in your dress: neatly pressed, well-tailored, color-coordinated, and shoes-shined business attire generally fit in the professional setting; use more casual dress for informal settings.

Try to mirror the dress and grooming of the person with whom you will be meeting by doing some investigating (look for pictures of them or ask others). Learn the social norms in their setting. Ensure that your attire fits the culture and country. In some professional settings formal attired is not warranted.

Get a good haircut or style in advance of the meeting. Guys: shave, trim eyebrows, nose hair, etc. You can express your individuality if it does not stand out too much. Greet the other person with a genuine smile—not a forced one. Exude confidence by making eye contact. Use a firm handshake, stand erect, and avoid nervous habits. Remain positive and courteous, turn off your phone, ask the person about their day, use their name, and just *be you.*

"One never gets a second chance to make a first impression. But remember that the first impression is not the last chance to make a good impression." ~ Author Unknown

FEBRUARY 9

I will dress for success

That model on the cover of *GQ* magazine may be your image of a successful appearance, but if you're working at a funky "shoes-off" kind of place, it may not get you far. On the other hand, a teeshirt may not flatter that tummy others want to rub for good luck. In an era of changing norms, dressing for success can be complicated. So when uncertain, dress traditionally. You can usually dress down, but rarely can you dress up in a hurry. Conservative dress is the best default if unsure. However, the best means for fitting the paradigm of success is to understand the corporate or social culture. Attending a formal event in cutoffs will make someone a sure pariah, while that same outfit at a company barbeque on Saturday can make a person appear more human.

At work, keep in mind that presentation matters even when people say it doesn't. Jeans may be tolerated on casual Fridays, but not that old pair with the tears or stains. Dress in the workplace as though your next client may walk through the door at any moment because those around you will feel even more respected (and respect you) if you take the time to make the right statement.

Before entering a new environment, you can always ask about the dress code. If no parameters exist, generally subtle class trumps flashy dress. Look at the models in the classier (or business attire) sections of department stores to gain ideas, if need be. Wear gray, blue, or black outfits, polished black shoes, tailored shirts, and matching slacks (for men). Socks or stockings should match the color of the outfit. Select white or blue shirts for men, skirts that rest just above the knee for women, or pants/pantsuits. Office-appropriate pantyhose, moderate heels, or polished flats fit well in professional settings. Sweaters are fine. Adorn yourself with modest jewelry and go light on the makeup. Always dress for the environment, the task, the season, and the region, and you'll look great!

"Dress for success. Image is very important. People judge you by the way you look on the outside." ~ Brian Tracy

"You cannot climb the ladder of success dressed in the costume of failure." ~ Zig Ziglar

FEBRUARY 10

I will use proper etiquette

Etiquette varies based on social functions like ceremonies and dining, but it's not as difficult as you might imagine. Generally, you should treat people in the same manner that they desire from you, in a polite fashion that you would expect of people who care about people.

Etiquette is the art of respecting others and their needs. General etiquette applies to all situations: when meeting someone, offer to shake their hand and say "nice to meet you"; say "thank you" and "please"; do not wear a hat indoors; cover your mouth when sneezing or coughing; say "hello" instead of "hi" or "what's up"; and acknowledge the other person with a nod and a smile in passing.

When dining, never leave your dirty napkin on the table—place it on the chair; never eat with your hands, unless you're consuming bread or some other finger food; never speak with your mouth full; never blow your nose at the table; keep you elbows off the table and hands on the lap when not in use; use duplicate silverware from left to right; turn cell phones off; use the drink to your right and the bread dish to your left; wait until all of your dinner guests are seated and served before eating; never bite down on your fork or utensil.

In social settings never appear impatient; don't make noises during shows; eliminate vulgar language. When entertaining others, don't ask people to remove their shoes, but if you must, offer them slippers; initially offer each guest a refreshment; introduce guests; manage conversations to make sure no one is left out and inappropriate conversations are stopped; dissuade controversial subjects.

With regard to communications, always return calls within twenty-four hours. Don't use email to reprimand others or to deal with controversial subjects. Never shout. Don't keep someone waiting or on hold for more than thirty seconds, even if it requires coming back to the caller before making him or her wait again. Don't text, email, or answer calls, except in emergencies, while others are talking to you. Be considerate of others at all times.

"Etiquette means behaving yourself a little better than is absolutely essential."
~ Will Cuppy

"Nothing is less important than which fork you use. Etiquette is the science of living. It embraces everything. It is ethics. It is honor." ~ Emily Post

FEBRUARY 11

I will persevere

Debra sat before her manager in tears. After almost two weeks of sales training, she could no longer bear the pressures. Debra passed her tests, she even excelled at some presentations, but she didn't participate much with the class, and worst of all, after she stood outside an Operating Room to witness a procedure, she nearly fainted. Her apparent frailties portended poorly for her potential success as a surgical sales representative in one of the most challenging territories in the U.S.—New York City.

"Maybe this is not the right fit for you," her manager said.

"I can do this," Debra responded. So with reservations Debra's company allowed her to continue on a probationary status.

Fast-forward twelve years. Debra won every major sales award offered by the company and became one of the most successful sales persons in its history. Ask Debra the key to her success and she will say, "I never give up, and when someone tells me to give it up, I try even harder." That is the mantra of a successful person, and it's spelled p-e-r-s-e-v-e-r-a-n-c-e.

Winston Churchill's famous "Never give up, never give in…" speech at the Harrow School in 1941 preceeded Germany's failed attempt to bomb England—a turning point in World War II—by three years. Faith in oneself, as Churchill demonstrated, leads to a moral conviction that can override seeming defeat in pursuit of a fixed goal. Psychologists suggest that people trying to develop perseverance must think positively. Failure is not an option. That requires self-control when doubts arise in order to maintain a view of the horizon through the din of others declaring defeat. Perseverance is a mindset that must be trained through sheer resolve.

"Most of the important things in the world have been accomplished by people who have kept on trying when there seemed to be no hope at all." ~ Dale Carnegie

"You've got to say, 'I think that if I keep working at this and want it badly enough I can have it.' It's called perseverance." ~ Lee Iacocca

"Perseverance is failing nineteen times and succeeding the twentieth." ~ Julie Andrews

FEBRUARY 12

I will be an innovator

Business and leadership professors at Brigham Young University, INSEAD (France), and Harvard interviewed nearly 100 innovative entrepreneurs and leaders to see what makes them think. The results were published in *The Innovator's DNA*, in which the authors detail four behavioral skills: questioning, observing, networking, and experimenting. Only one was a cognitive skill: the skill of associating, defined as making connections across apparently unrelated fields, problems or ideas. This means, they explain, that essentially everyone has some capacity for creativity and innovative thinking. It simply requires a change in behavior. They claim that the skill for producing innovative ideas is associating, and note that some people generate more association than others, partly because of the way their brains are wired.

Associative thinking is what we commonly term "free association"—the mental process of making associations between a subject and all pertinent present factors without drawing on past experience. These researchers assert that associative thinking can be triggered by questioning, observing, networking and experimenting—behaviors that innovators use.

So why do some people use these behaviors more often than others? The researchers concluded that it has to do with courage. The more people put these skills into practice, the more confident they become.

Choose which of these characteristics—questioning, observing, networking, or experimenting—you need to practice more often. Maybe it's one, more than one, or all four. Start challenging yourself in these areas, at work and at home, by establishing at least one area for improvement, and using those skills to turn a problem into a solution.

"Innovation distinguishes between a leader and a follower." ~ Steve Jobs

"Learning and innovation go hand in hand. The arrogance of success is to think that what you did yesterday will be sufficient for tomorrow." ~ William Pollard

"Replace either or thinking with plus thinking." ~ Craig Hickman

FEBRUARY 13

I will simplify

When you reach the freedom to say *no* to the things you don't want in life and replace them with what matters most, your life becomes simpler. Your better, simpler life may resemble a placid field of flowing grass, or it may be more akin to the hustle and bustle of the city. Each person has unique special interests and wants.

So the first step in priotizing is to separate the important things from the most irrelevant things by listing ten of each, top to bottom. Think about what you would want to retain after retiring to some idyllic place. Therein lie your essentials.

Next, scrutinize your routine to weed out unnecessary habits that have encroached on vital life sources like health, loved ones, career, and rest. Establish a regimen that will help you complete household tasks by doing chores on specific days or times of the month.

Communication piles rob us of valuable time, and the more gadgets we use (computer, phone, answering machine) the more diligent we must be in reducing clutter. For electronic messages, read once and act upon it and/or discard it. Place filters on junk mail if possible. Any files or saved messages over six months and definitely over one year should be trashed unless they relate to deeds, warranties, and other important documents. Go paperless as much as possible. Store all need-to-have items in one place using containers or electronic files. Designate at least one cleanup day a quarter to getting rid of old DVDs, CDs, books, and other dated goods. And de-clutter you workspaces by making them appear clean and simple. You can easily donate things to charities or trash them if damaged.

Pledge today to stop buying as many nice-to-have items as possible. Consider renting instead of purchasing, or use the library for those "must reads." Things you buy should be used within 30 days, or longer for emergency items, and a good qualifier is to ask yourself if you have anything like it that could satisfy your need.

And remember, you don't have to do it all. Ask for help. Delegate tasks if possible. Life is better when it's simple.

"The ability to simplify means to eliminate the unnecessary so that the necessary can speak." ~ H. Hofmann

"Everything should be made as simple as possible, but not simpler." ~ Albert Einstein

FEBRUARY 14

I will pay it forward

A wealthy old man sat alone in the atrium of a senior home all alone, with no family or friends that would speak to him. He had lived a life of material gains without giving much value to others. This is a sad but all-too-common story.

Gains measured by the lives we give to make us richer in spirit and relationships. According to a report produced by the mentoring group Catalyst, they also produce financial rewards. Catalyst's study found that high potential talent who'd been themselves mentored and helped along the way are more likely to "pay it forward." Paying it forward, by helping others succeed, pays back by benefitting not only the protégé, but also through career advancement and compensation for those providing the assistance—as much as $25,075 in additional compensation between 2008 and 2010, according to the report. This personal bonus may be because helping develop others creates more visibility and respect for the help provider, leading to greater reward and recognition for going the extra mile.

Paying it forward is an essential element of success, because it benefits everyone involved. "It's a virtuous circle that leads to more of the same," said Ilene H. Lang, President and CEO of Catalyst. We often think of paying it forward as performing charitable work, based on the book-turned-movie in which a teacher gives a voluntary, extra-credit assignment: "Think of an idea for world change, and put it into action." One young boy decides to do something good for three people. When they ask how they can pay it back, the boy tells them they have to, "Pay it forward." So nine people get helped, and so forth. The same principle that applies in charity applies in the workplace and anywhere we come and go. It's all about helping others, not expecting anything in return, and requiring of the receiver that they pay the favor forward to others in their life.

This type of "pay it forward" giving has an exponential effect in creating a better environment of success for everyone involved. Try it, by offering to mentor a new hire, or by simply buying an extra coffee for a fellow worker. Make sure to tell the other person that you want nothing in return. You simply want them to consider doing something good for someone else. In time, that kindness will come full circle to you.

"It is not how much we give but how much love we put into giving." ~ Mother Teresa

FEBRUARY 15

I will live a life of significance

Most children aspire to greatness. They may dream of being a professional sports star, a celebrity, or maybe even President of the United States. As the years progress, the adult that child becomes will look back, likely not at the great star she'd hoped to be, but at having lived a life of significance because she turned many opportunities into realities.

Our culture often equates significance with position or major achievement. That kind of perspective robs us of the opportunity to make each moment significant. Significance finds itself in taking advantage of the present circumstances, over and over again. Its signifier is not just the sense of doing something great, but of how we have grown, and what we have gained through learning. Finding meaning and purpose leads to significance through living life to the fullest *as we see it*, not as others expect it.

Positive first experiences, whether a specific occasion, or a career, or in relationship create lasting impressions. However, too often we forget what made those things special. That "first time" thrill gives way to a life of monotony. Reignite those passions by remembering what made them special in the first place, and then infusing those qualities back into your life. Perhaps it was the first time you met someone, or the first time you did something together with the people you met in your career or in your personal time.

The moments we dedicate to building relationships are the building blocks of significance. At the end of life, few, if any, wish they had spent one more day at the office. Possessions mean little in comparison to relationships. You are significant not because of what you have, but because of what you did with and for others in the moments that defined your life.

Create a vision for the future that appreciates the process of making it happen along the way. Refresh life through the lense of your first-time experiences.

"Enthusiasm releases the drive to carry you over obstacles and adds significance to all you do." ~ Norman Vincent Peale

"Our greatest fear as individuals should not be of failure but of succeeding at things in life that don't really matter." ~ Tim Kizziar

FEBRUARY 16

I will place my loved ones first

How often do we say the most important thing in our life is a loved one, and yet spend our energy in places that neglect them? The demands of work and everyday pressures sometimes crowd out time for family and friends, so it's important to recommit to placing others first.

Find out what makes your loved ones happy. Trite as it may sound, too often we fail to ask them. Or their hearts may have changed over the years, and what gave them joy in the past no longer hits the mark. Ask your spouse or significant other what aspect of your relationship she or he most enjoys, as well as those they find less fulfilling. Routines such as Friday night movies, date nights, or meals together can be reminders of how you value your relationship.

Consider, too, what makes *you* happy. Do you appreciate your alone time? Believe it or not, even regular time apart can help to offset the disorder that normal life brings. Kids' unrestricted minds can devise some very creative solutions, so include them in the conversation when appropriate.

Be careful not to assume too much. Instead share your needs and wants with one another regularly—then reprioritize your commitments as necessary. If more time away from work is necessary (or more time at work is needed), see what you can work out with your employer. Piled-up chores can be accomplished by declaring a "family day," dedicated to cleaning and celebrated with a fun activity when the work is done.

Let's all prioritize the time we have with loved ones to enjoy a stroll, a bike ride, a picnic lunch or whatever activity seems to accommodate special friends and family. These little things are not so small after all. They are the ways we express our caring.

Putting first people first is the mark of a healthy life. Cherish the ones you love.
"When you look at your life, the greatest happinesses are family happinesses." ~ *Dr. Joyce Brothers*

"Love does not die easily. It is a living thing. It thrives in the face of all of life's hazards, save one—neglect." ~ *Andrew Carnegie*

FEBRUARY 17

I will move on

Isabelle left a voice mail on her friend's answering machine. "I need to talk! I am in trouble!" After retrieving the message, her friend ran down the backstairs of their apartment complex and pounded on Isabelle's door. Isabelle pulled the door open and smiled, a drift of cinnamon wafting from the mouth of the coffee cup in her hand.

"What's the crisis?" her breathless friend asked.

"I saw a picture of Martin and it triggered every hurtful emotion," Isabelle answered.

"That was twelve years ago!" her friend said, not a little perturbed.

What do you think is Isabelle's problem? It's not the loss of Martin. It is the fact that she can't move on. Moving past a failed relationship or a lost job requires that we let go of the hating, the "what ifs," the wondering about what they are doing or whom they are with. Determine to move to the other side of the relationship or job. Be ready to take on new challenges and new relationships. Get away to a quiet place to actively engage in forgiving those who have hurt you—including yourself.

Brain scientists suggest nearly twenty percent of us suffer from "complicated grief," or an inaccurate romantic view of a lost relationship. Tell yourself the truth: *it wasn't that good. In fact, it probably was pretty bad.* Any loss must be healed through the grieving process, but issues that linger longer than a year indicate you are harboring resentment. You're cheating your future by holding onto those hurts.

Find yourself a counselor if needed and force yourself to dwell on possibilities that may never have occurred if you were still at that place, or with that person. Rekindle lost relationships. Appreciate your current position, or network to find a new one. Realize that nothing lasts forever. Immerse yourself in the present, cherry pick the past, and be thankful.

"Cry. Forgive. Learn. Move on. Let your tears water the seeds of your future happiness." ~ Steve Maraboli

"The amount of happiness that you have depends on the amount of freedom you have in your heart." ~ Thich Nhat Hanh

FEBRUARY 18

I will sleep on it

Hurried by someone, or after some unsettling situation the immediate choices we make are vulnerable, and therefore potentially dangerous. Misconceived decisions can lead to debt and discouragement. We are the "gotta have it now" generation with our fast food, real time streaming, online shopping, and multiple communication modes as examples. The typical modus operandi in the business world is change, merge, divest.

Taking it slowly is almost considered a sin, but it can be our saving grace. The resulting impulsivity from an overcharged environment can result in worsening outcomes due to careless decisions. Rushed behavior can be counterproductive if we don't thoroughly consider the potential ramifications. It's important to always think through possible results, allowing choices to bake for a while.

Reactions often result in opposing reactions, such as the negative affect on company morale (aka, productivity) through a hasty choice to acquire new technology that doesn't work. Impulse buying or decision-making can affect one's ability to cover future emergency needs.

Identifying the long-term negative consequences of an impulsive decision increases our awareness through the simple exercise of listing out the short-term and long-term pros and cons. Because impulsivity does sometimes provide temporary relief for anxiety or fear, one way of reducing the likelihood of an impulsive behavior is to use a time-out. Walk away for a while. Consciously make the choice to delay your decision in consideration of the big picture. Sleep on it. Your decision tomorrow will be less emotional and better reasoned.

"It is a common experience that a problem difficult at night is resolved in the morning after the committee of sleep has worked on It." ~ John Steinbeck

"Think twice before you speak, because your words and influence will plant the seed of either success or failure in the mind of another." ~ Napoleon Hill

FEBRUARY 19

I will be humble

People who have achieved success and fortune tend to lose their humility and become at least a little arrogant. They falsely assume they did it all themselves, saying in essence, "It's all about me." When we allow success to go to our head, stress levels elevate and satisfaction with life gradually fades. Arrogance causes people to stop liking you, and eventually you stop liking yourself.

In our "only the strongest survive" culture of today, humility is often viewed as a weakness. Actually it's a tremendous gesture of strength, a demonstration of your confidence, since you've *chosen* to be humble. Humiliation, a negative event, usually happens at the decision of someone else. Being humble is a decision *you* made. Humility is a compelling virtue that attracts people to you and makes you more persuasive. A humble person sees others as inherently valuable, and doesn't derive his or her identity from his/her accomplishments.

Conversely, we often distort how others view us, sometimes thinking ourselves funnier or more adept than we really are. The fact is, our jokes are at times not really as funny as we think they are. Our intellect is never as superb as it seems to our limited purview. Our achievements and our status are never as great or lofty as the highest level possible.

Here's the crème de le crème: we will all be dead in 200 years and nothing of our social rank will matter to anyone living at that time. So why not be humble about it?

That old Chinese proverb holds true: *Never let success go to your head, and never let failure go to your heart.* Each person, from the beggar on the street to the President of the United States, deserves the foundational level of respect that comes with being God's creation. Take time to know people's stories. Ask them questions, remember their names, and listen to their concerns. Applaud others' successes while being quietly thankful for your own. This is true humility.

"The minute you're satisfied with where you are, you aren't there anymore." ~ Hall of Famer Tony Gwynn

FEBRUARY 20

I will be a strategic thinker

Strategic thinking is a critical skill for achieving success in both your personal and professional life. It involves setting short-term as well as long-term goals, making effective plans, anticipating the unexpected, analyzing all facets of your surroundings, and tapping resources that help to meet goals.

While most focus on what's ahead, strategic thinkers look in all directions to look for blockbuster solutions. They question the status quo by challenging accepted beliefs, uncovering unproductive habits within organizations, and rethinking problems to identify hidden root causes. They are great at connecting the dots by engaging thought leaders and identifying interrelated key links between solution providers. Trusting their guts as well as their minds, strategic thinkers assimilate information, cut through hidden agendas, and make decisions that factor in the divergent views of their wide network of sources without overanalyzing. They are constant learners, looking for cutting-edge information while challenging others to rethink approaches.

Are you a strategic thinker? If not, battle the tendency to think tactically. Aim to look at things more critically from a higher level, at systems instead of parts. Strategic thinking focuses on relationships, the environment, possible outcomes, totality, the larger processes, and looping feedback. Start at a 10,000-foot view and drill down from there. Don't focus on the problem but on the larger system, to identify why problems happen. Don't jump to conclusions without a comprehensive solutions approach that insists on a new paradigm.

"The best way to predict the future is to invent It."
~ Alan Kay, father of the personal computer

"There is nothing so useless as doing efficiently that which should not be done at all." ~ Peter Drucker

"Strategy without tactics is the slowest route to victory. Tactics without strategy is the noise before defeat." ~ Sun Tzu

FEBRUARY 21

I will retain my self-respect

What do former president Bill Clinton, actress Drew Barrymore, Elizabeth I (Queen of England), and evangelist Joyce Meyer have in common? They are all survivors of abuse. The list could have gone on to include hundreds of accomplished persons who overcame horrible tragedies by maintaining their self-respect. Perhaps you've experienced some form of abuse, or someone has belittled you at work or socially. If so, just remember that to develop self-respect means to arm yourself with the self-confidence to handle rejection.

Self-respect means being secure in who you are, regardless of what others say. If others criticize you, try to detach yourself from the personal attack by deflecting it as mere opinion or unfair bias. If possible, use it as a learning experience. Too often we compare our limitations to others' strengths, when in fact none of us is without imperfections. We need to stop benchmarking our value against others. Value is not based on the rise and fall of your attempts to succeed or on your social status, but rather on your inherent value as a human being. Self-respect happens when we value our own qualities as well as those of others.

The confidence that comes from self-respect lies not on the foundation of feeling superior, but in appreciating the uniqueness of each individual's intrinsic worth. Self-hatred, the opposite of self-respect, comes from the inability to accept our flaws and mistakes, or a lack of forgiveness. Moving on, letting go of the past, is essential to attaining self-respect.

Contrary to popular belief, self-respect is not self-absorption. It is a selfless endeavor that considers human value as a quality not to be earned or displayed, but appreciated in everyone.

"Keep away from people who try to belittle your ambitions. Small people always do that. But the really great make you feel that you, too, can become great." ~ Mark Twain

"That you may retain your self-respect, it is better to displease the people by doing what you know is right, than to temporarily please them by doing what you know is wrong." ~ William J.H. Boetcker

FEBRUARY 22

I will be diligent

We often talk about hard work—giving 100% of your efforts—but it's not really hard work that defines the key to success: it's diligence. Diligence is defined as a careful and persistent work or effort.

There's a saying that reads: "Wherefore, now let every man learn his duty, and to act in the office in which he is appointed, in all diligence." Diligence imbues a sense of tenacity and commitment to finishing a job well done. It means learning what someone—your boss, your spouse, your co-worker, or God—expects of you, devising a plan to achieve it, being persistent in your work, and blessing others through your work and personal life. Diligence is not just an approach to work, it's an approach to life in general.

A practical application of diligence is doing something with gusto. We should be diligent in all aspects of life. We should diligently seek after wisdom. We should diligently pursue our goals. We should diligently build our relationships. We should diligently serve others in need. We should diligently meet all of our job requirements. We should diligently dedicate time to rest and relax. Diligence leads to a satisfying life. How do you feel at the end of a hard-worked day? Satisfied? Relieved? That's the nature of human beings. We cannot be fully satisfied until we've been diligent with the things given to us.

Whatever we do, in work or in play, we should do it with all of our heart. Half-hearted approaches lead to a half-hearted fulfillment. By giving it our all, the return comes back to us in feelings of contentment. The result of just working hard doesn't always translate into success. However, the result of working *diligently* maximizes each effort to its fullest capacity—and that almost always means success.

"If people knew how hard I worked to get my mastery, it wouldn't seem so wonderful at all." ~ Michelangelo

"Things may come to those who wait, but only the things left by those who hustle." ~ Abraham Lincoln

FEBRUARY 23

I will let my work speak for itself

Successful people don't need to boast about their work. They just do it. Our actions speak for themselves. They also serve as evidence of our character. Even when someone demeans you, the best safeguard against their words having any lasting effect is to do a good job.

One of the most irritating ways people talk is by bragging. It's one thing to promote yourself as a professional, but outside of a job interview, boasting should be confined to speaking alone in front of a mirror, if at all. If you're trying to impress someone in order to fit into a group or class of people, the likelihood of boasting working to your benefit is small. Groucho Marx said, "I wouldn't join any club that would have me as a member." He has a point! Any club requiring boastfulness or arrogance probably isn't a place we would want to belong.

We need to allow people to accept us as we are, even letting our faults show once in awhile, or we risk needing to continually pretend we are the braggarts we appeared to be from the start. People who continually look on our outward appearance are shallow and not worth a lasting relationship.

Generally people honor actions over just words. Setting yourself up for success means promising only what you know is realistic, and then working to over-deliver whenever possible. If you must promote your work to attract new clients, then network with others and showcase examples of your product or service. The art of gracefully promoting your abilities involves getting your work noticed, not you. Our work offers a portrait of our character—one that hopefully speaks of integrity, commitment, quality, and honesty.

"When your work speaks for itself, don't interrupt." ~ Henry J. Kaiser

"A superior man is modest in his speech, but exceeds in his actions." ~ Confucius

"Bragging actually dilutes the positive feelings you receive from an accomplishment or something you are proud of. To make matters worse, the more you try to prove yourself, the more others will avoid you, talk behind your back about your insecure need to brag, and perhaps even resent you." ~ Richard Carlson

FEBRUARY 24

I will inspire others

Think of the person who's most inspired you. Perhaps a former teacher inspired you to pursue a career. Perhaps a parent or a boss encouraged you in some special way. What was it about that person that inspired you? Chances are that person saw in you abilities and talents you didn't know you had. Their encouragement then motivated you toward some goal. You respected them, and no doubt they cared about you and served as a good role model.

Now ask yourself—who have you inspired? You might be surprised at how many you've already influenced. Most of us never confess our admiration to the one who inspired us. To inspire others, you need to be inspired *through* others. You need to surround yourself with the people, knowledge, and environment that bring out the best in you. People who inspire others are byproducts of a life abundant with positive experiences. No one can inspire others if their spiritual tank is only half full. Let your rich and varied experiences impart valuable wisdom to someone who's never been where you've been, or done what you've done.

Inspiration also happens when we are transparent, declaring our failures as well as our successes. We don't relate to perfect idols, but to those who share our emotions. Word pictures, stories, or common identification with another often resonate inspiration.

We communicate best with others when we create a common identity with them, such as with an associative expression like, "I can relate to your fear of a new job because I've felt the same way. Let me tell you about it…" To be inspiring, you must identify with the other person and challenge him or her to reach new heights of success. Create a vision of what that person can attain, and then give him or her the confidence to go after it.

"If your actions inspire others to dream more, learn more, do more and become more you are a leader." ~ John Quincy Adams

"You can buy a person's hands but you can't buy his heart. His heart is where his enthusiasm, his loyalty is." ~ Stephen Covey

FEBRUARY 25

I will take risks

Each day, Jimmy's mother would take him to swimming lessons—and Jimmy would refuse to jump in the pool. No matter what his mother or instructor told him, the red-headed little boy would just sit in the poolside chair, his head resting on his clenched knuckles. Jimmy, like most of us, feared failure. One day his dad went to lessons with Jimmy. The dad said, "I have a fear of water too, Jimmy, but if you jump, I'll jump with you." The five-year-old looked up to the top of his dad's six-foot-three-inch frame and said, "OK." Jimmy and his dad jumped into the pool hand-in-hand.

We all have a choice to let fear grip us, or take a leap of faith into the unknown. Sometimes we need a mentor to hold our hand, like Jimmy, but that leap into darkness always requires faith—faith in you, faith in God (if you believe), faith that failure never lasts and victories always triumph. People who achieve their dreams dare to step out of their comfort zone. If you believe in God, there is no uncertainty, because he has control over all things and he will always accomplish his good purpose. If you don't believe in God, simply understanding your emotions and that anxiety is irrelevant to your decision helps guards against the anxiety risk-taking produces. Said another way, if you decide to leap, you will have already (subconsciously or otherwise) thought through your most fearful emotions. The rest is simply downhill.

People who expect to fail don't take risks. People who expect to learn or succeed when taking a risk always succeed in achieving one of those goals. It's a conviction that the experience is worth the potential downside because something will be learned, and learning leads to progress. So just do it!

"I am always doing that which I cannot do, in order that I may learn how to do it." ~ Pablo Picasso

"You'll always miss 100% of the shots you don't take." ~ Wayne Gretzky

"It's not because things are difficult that we dare not venture. It's because we dare not venture that they are difficult." ~ Seneca

FEBRUARY 26

I will create a thriving environment

People thrive in environments where they feel safe, supported, and respected. Putting people at ease helps them mentally motivated. We've all heard the saying, "I've got your back," meaning, "I'll protect you from any negative fallout." It indicates a trust level that removes any threat of consequences than can hinder their productivity. It also creates a learning environment that focuses on making progress, versus one that makes them feel they "have to cover their own derriere." Creating a pleasant work or social environment fosters more creativity and increases collaboration between people.

If you want to create a thriving environment, get to know the people in your circle of influence. Ask them about their experiences, their likes, and their dislikes. Spend one-on-one time with each person to create personal connections. Provide frequent positive feedback and praise their achievements, large and small. Encourage freedom of expression by promoting each person's talents. Give them special projects or allow them to plan special occasions like birthday parties or team celebrations. In a work environment, allow employees to express their opinions anonymously through a suggestion box, and then announce improvements based on those suggestions. Meet at least weekly with individuals and with the larger team at least monthly to share successes, progress against goals, and to recognize individual achievements. Allow others to meet with you to discuss their most important issues. Make it clear that everyone is to be treated with respect and that destructive behavior will not be tolerated. Finally, create a fun environment replete with cheerful decorations and even toys to bring out the child in each of us.

A fun, trusting, open, nurturing, and challenging environment that encourages productivity motivates people to flourish.

"A business has to be involving, it has to be fun, and it has to exercise your creative instincts." ~ Richard Branson, Founder, Virgin Enterprises

"Hell, there are no rules here—we're trying to accomplish something." ~ Thomas Edison

FEBRUARY 27

I will remember people's names

"Hey, great to see you again, ____." It's embarrassing when we forget someone's name. A person's name is the most pleasant sound in the room to them, and when we forget that name, it can translate into the biggest insult.

When you first meet someone, a good exercise is to spell their name to yourself, or ask them to spell it if it is unique. Then repeat their name at least three times during conversation, without overdoing it, in order to commit the name to memory. Allow the person's name to form an impression with you by observing the person's physical characteristics, and using your senses to concentrate on that person while associating the name with him or her. By using the name immediately after meeting, and repeating it silently to yourself, you deposit it into your memory bank. You might even comment on the name, without overly focusing on its ethnicity. Before leaving, say the name again. Log it into your smart phone or jot it down afterwards.

Another name-remembering technique is to associate the person's physical appearance with an image implied by the name. If you exaggerate the image and place it into a story,you can create an indelible image—like carving it on the person's forehead. Any physical feature or associative property (voice, position, locale, oddity) you can relate to the name helps create a more lasting memory. You might also associate the name to a sound, story, feeling, rhyme or any other word association, such as: *David* (the *Goliath – he's tall*) Archer (picture him *shooting a bow and arrow*); *Mary* (quite *contrary*); *Rich Toproff* seems like a *rich guy to top it off.*

If all else fails, ask someone in the room to remind you of the person's name, and if in doubt—don't guess. It's best to just admit you forgot, rather than using the wrong name.

"If you want to win friends, make it a point to remember them. If you remember my name, you pay me a subtle compliment; you indicate that I have made an impression on you. Remember my name and you add to my feeling of importance." ~ *Dale Carnegie*

"Forgive your enemies, but never forget their names." ~ *John F. Kennedy*

FEBRUARY 28

I will practice good politics

Politicking has gotten a bad reputation. Some think of it as manipulation, but first and foremost it represents a form of communication, and it is one of your most critical skills toward success. Just working hard will not necessarily promote your status in a company. Good politics begins with creating a hierarchal organizational chart for your environment, so that everyone understands who makes the final decisions. Realize that politics occur within any organization, whether in a social group or in the workplace. It's critical to understand how to effectively deal with it.

To begin with, there are three types of people in any environment: 1) your *Supporters,* who care about you and will support just about anything you do; 2) your *Saboteurs,* who will do anything to undermine or sabotage your efforts; and, 3) your *Sideliners,* who are neutral because they haven't yet made up their mind about you. They stand on the sidelines and are neither for or against you. It's the *Sideliners* you must win over, because if you gain their support you will have a majority on your side. Spend time understanding the needs and motivations of the *Sideliners.* Help their causes by lending them a hand and by encouraging their efforts. If politics is not your style, consider a more entrepreneurial or smaller environment.

In any event, don't be a pest by smothering others with attention. Be genuine in applauding the *Sideliners'* achievements without overdoing it. Don't try to please everyone. Volunteer for philanthropic events within your organization. When *Saboteurs* deliberately undermine your efforts and/or talk behind your back, confront them directly. Be careful to be tactfully assertive, especially if the *Saboteur* is in a position of influence. Organizations usually reward good team players, so try reconciliation if possible before burning those bridges with the *Saboteurs.* Reinforce your *Supporter* relationships. Let them help you build bridges to the *Sideliners* through their networks and through their mentoring, advice, and advocacy. Good politics is about increasing your positive perceptions within the organization by leveraging your influence among the different groups so that most become your Supporters.

"In our seeking for economic and political progress, we all go up—or else we all go down." ~ F.D. Roosevelt

FEBRUARY 29

I will understand consumer marketing

A basic understanding of marketing can help us promote our ideas as well as our products or services. Marketing at its core is getting people to want what you have to offer. Marketing or branding traditionally focuses on people's top-of-mind desires, such as a new car or a, new tube of toothpaste. Impulse buyers go for the latest trend and are typically early adopters of new things. Traditional buyers want only that which is comfortable, tried and tested.

The fundamental task of marketing is to inculcate a "want" based on peoples' emotional and reasoning logic, that will ideally shape their self-identity and product/service identity into a compelling story. Effective branding evokes a future want and is basically tagging how you want to market something. Key to marketing is understanding peoples' core motivations, not just their interests. Successful marketing not only satisfies a need, it creates a need based on previously unthought-of potential. Effective marketers create a message that imbeds itself into peoples' minds, so that even when they are not feeling the need for the product, they feel a void that must be filled.

As a function, marketing includes disciplines like public relations, pricing, packaging, and distribution of a product or service. As a change-element, it is identifying the people to persuade. Perhaps the hardest part of marketing is taking your focus off your own needs/wants and seeing the existing and potential needs/wants of your prospective consumers. Needs/wants usually fall into three categories: 1) a problem that needs to be solved; 2) a changing situation that creates a need; and, 3) a want or need that has yet to be discovered. People generally want to buy on a concept first. For example, people who buy health food don't want it because it tastes good; they want it because of that better body and mind it can help to produce.

A good marketing plan begins with marketing research to identify the needs/wants and types of potential customers in your field, along with the opportunities therein.

"The aim of marketing is to know and understand the customer so well the product or service fits him and sells itself." ~ Peter Drucker

MARCH

BE EXCEPTIONAL

MARCH 1

I will put people first

Here's a quick question to see if you put people first: Was your most recent major decision (house, large purchase, job) made because you wanted it or because someone else wanted it? Are you a consensus decision-maker, insisting on agreement? Or are you a collaborator who seeks untapped opportunity that's best for everyone—like maybe combining a little business with pleasure on that vacation? How you arrive at decisions says a lot of about your consideration of others, and whether or not you are a good leader.

According to a two-year study by the Work Foundation in the United Kingdom, leaders who are both people and relationship-centered are far more likely to display outstanding performance. This study debunks the common assumption that people who make tough decisions irrespective of others are good leaders. Those who place relationships first manage people inclusively by "focusing on people, attitudes, and engagement," and by "co-creating vision and strategy," said Penny Tamkin, lead author of the study. If you want to get things done effectively, address the people issues first, says Tamkin. Personally developing others by challenging them and championing their endeavors produces the best results, as opposed to telling them to just get it done.

Respecting your fellow contributors is the first rule of success, and the best way to show this is by engaging them and considering their interests throughout the decision-making process and beyond. It's people who make the difference, from loved ones to customers to team members. Put them first, and expect good to happen.

"People are the gatekeepers of change."
~ Robert Kriegel, Sacred Cows Make the Best Burgers

"There is a magnet in your heart that will attract true friends. That magnet is unselfishness, thinking of others first; when you learn to live for others, they will live for you." ~ Paramahansa Yogananda

"A wise unselfishness is not a surrender of yourself to the wishes of anyone, but only to the best discoverable course of action." ~ David Seabury

MARCH 2

I will empower others

Those who keep power to themselves cannot reach their maximum potential. When we invest power in others, we trigger a surge of power analogous to plugging a cord into a socket. The result is a burst of energy that disperses creativity and production. Some try to protect their turf, a choice that often leads to defeatism. An empowering person invites participation into the greater vision of an endeavor. The highest form of empowerment is collaboration—two or more people working together to create something bigger than any individual contributor could ever devise on her own. Those who empower know when to lead by example, and when to step back and encourage others. Always, the needs of the team come first. Continuous improvement through learning is the mode of operation.

Are you in a position of authority? Make sure to limit the consolidation of power by breaking bigger tasks into smaller ones. Ensure that roles and responsibilities are shared and even interchanged once in awhile. Roles should be defined by talents, skills, and motivation, and not by jockeying for position. If someone doesn't have the necessary skill sets, provide the training that will stretch their abilities.

Just like that "plug in the socket," the energy of the team must circulate from person to person so that no one individual can claim to be the source of all knowing. Letting go of the reigns may be the biggest challenge, but it's not about you being ready—it's about your team being fully competent. If errors occur as a result of your delegation, use them as a learning experience in the spirit of continuous improvement. Stay positive.

"As we look ahead into the next century, leaders will be those who empower others." ~ Bill Gates

"The beauty of empowering others is that your own power is not diminished in the process." ~ Barbara Colorose

"An empowered organization is one in which individuals have the knowledge, skill, desire, and opportunity to personally succeed in a way that leads to collective organizational success." ~ Author Unknown

MARCH 3

I will know my purpose

The difference between a purpose and a dream or calling is that your purpose can mutate from situation to situation, whereas a dream or calling stays the same, barring any significant life-changing event. While there are as many variations as there are people, for the sake of learning, let's define your purpose as finding the reason you are in your current situation, and then doing what that situation requires.

Human nature wants some big driver, some reason for our being on this earth. The downside of this paradigm is that seemingly mundane tasks like washing laundry, making copies, or taking out the trash take up so much of our time they become mere nuisances—and there *can* be meaning in washing laundry! Your purpose is not based on the importance of what you do—it is about discovering and nurturing yourself, and helping meet others' needs. It's really that simple.

So when you wash those clothes, think about whom you are helping. While you wait for the cycle to finish, ponder nagging questions, or better yet—read a book. If you go to a coin-operated laundry, get to know your fellow launderers. Your purpose essentially is to grow and mature into the best *you* you can possibly be. If that's too simplistic for you, then you probably need to grow some patience.

As you grow into the person you want to be, you will naturally do what you always wanted to do. Human development is about changing the "have tos" of life into the "want tos." Said another way, as we become, therefore we are. Too existential? Maybe it's time to amend your nuts and bolts way of thinking.

Some of the best opportunities toward being the best version of you are found in the minutia of life. Discounting vast sums of our daily activities misses the nuances of life. Don't miss the opportunities life presents. Seek, grow, develop—and help others along the way.

"Any idea, plan, or purpose may be placed in the mind through repetition of thought." ~ Napoleon Hill

"As far as we can discern, the sole purpose of human existence is to kindle a light in the darkness of mere being." ~ Carl Jung

MARCH 4

I will eliminate the non-essentials

How much of your time is spent completing organizational tasks at the cost of doing important work? Time spent responding to social networks, attending meetings, paying bills, commuting, running errands, checking email and more could be eliminated or at least re-prioritized to free-up time for what's important.

Picture a world in which you are doing only that which you consider enjoyable. Is it possible? It is if you take back control of your time. Avoid or eliminate jobs that require administrative work. While this may result in lost income or business, it frees you to do more of what you love—and that could make you more effective at what you do. Try outsourcing tasks--perhaps using an answering service, hiring a temporary worker, using a cleaning or lawn service, or subcontracting work.

If advertising emails clutter your inbox, consider creating another email address for essential business communication, and then inform only your most essential key contacts of the change. Check emails only at certain times of the day—say once in the morning and once in the afternoon. And do not exceed an acceptable time for responding, say less than one hour each day. Consider using public transportation so that you can complete tasks while commuting. Place strict timelines on meetings with agendas and reject useless meetings where possible. Unsubscribe from newsletters, notifications, and clubs that are no longer important. Set up automatic-electronic payments for bills. Digitize paperwork. Schedule your shopping and other chores. Stop worrying about what you need to accomplish and just focus on doing a great job.

"Beside the noble art of getting things done, there is the noble art of leaving things undone. The wisdom of life consists in the elimination of non-essentials." ~ Lin Yutang

"Eliminating what is not wanted or needed is profitable in itself." ~ Phil Crosby

"Art is the elimination of the unnecessary." ~ Pablo Picasso

MARCH 5

I will develop my Emotional Intelligence

The study of Emotional Intelligence (EI) began with researchers Peter Salovey and John D. Mayer beginning in 1990, and was popularized by Daniel Goleman in his 1997 book of the same name (*Emotional Intelligence: Why It Can Matter More Than IQ*, Bantam). It refers to the ability to perceive, control and evaluate emotions.

According to these researchers there are four different factors of emotional intelligence: *the perception of emotion* (i.e., verbal and nonverbal signals such as body language), *the ability to reason using emotions* (responding emotionally to things to promote thinking), *the ability to understand emotion* (evaluating the cause of emotions such as knowing why someone is angry), and *the ability to manage emotions* (regulating emotions).

Our personal competence with emotions is comprised of our self-awareness and self-management skills—our ability to maintain awareness of our emotions and manage our behavior in response to them. Social competence is comprised of your social awareness and relationship management skills—your ability to understand other people's emotions, corresponding behaviors, and their motives in order to improve the quality of your relationships.

Your EI is associated with performance as in how it impacts your professional success. High EI corresponds with high performance and the converse is also true. EI can be developed via effective communication between the rational and emotional centers of the brain. You can train your brain through a discipline of keeping emotions under control through stress by putting yourself in the place of others and by being more open to their perspectives (showing empathy).

Sublimate your need for recognition in deference to others, remain open minded, deliberate through consciously analyzing something before responding, remain optimistic, and use effective communication skills to help understand the other person before responding. People with strong EI respond to situations in a constructive manner that assimilates the emotional needs of all concerned with the steps required to produce an effective outcome.

"If you do practice and train your attention to hover in the present, then you will build the internal capacity to do that as needed—at will and voluntarily." ~ Daniel Goleman

March 6

I will think BIG

Jared Young invited some people over to his house for a dinner party, and after clearing the dishes he pulled out his guitar, sat down, and starting entertaining his astounded guests. "Jared," one said, "you have the most amazing voice! You should be singing for thousands of people!" That one comment prompted Jared to form a band—and more than ten years later he has indeed sung for thousands of people. The courage to think BIG breeds power, opportunities, and amazing adventure.

If you have a product or service that others have validated through their encouragement or praise, then you owe it to yourself and the world to bring it to as many people and places as possible. Most people do not reach their full potential because they think too small. They'd rather play in the proverbial sandbox than envision a big, untapped island. That old saying "nothing ventured, nothing gained" holds true. Someone had told Jared that musicians don't make it as a full time career. He really should think more practically. Thankfully, Jared didn't listen. Sure, he held part-time jobs along the way, but he never gave up. A strong vision can overcome just about any obstacles.

Of course, all big dreams start small. The founders of Apple started in Steve Jobs's garage. But, they did something all big thinkers must do to succeed—they engaged others in their dream. Big success arises from tapping new talent to fill your own gaps. If you're a solo performer, don't let age stand in the way. Famed artist Grandma Moses (Anna Mary Robertson Moses) started painting in her seventies. During her last year of life, from age 100 to 101, she painted twenty-five pictures. Today, it is easier than ever to reach the masses easily. Think five or ten years down the road. What will your big picture look like? What obstacles, needs, and opportunities might you encounter along the way? Thinking ahead helps you plan accordingly. Big thinkers need big visions and big commitments.

"I like thinking big. If you're going to be thinking anything, you might as well think big." ~ Donald Trump

MARCH 7

I will focus

In this era where the whole world seems to have Attention Deficit Disorder, maintaining focus has become a daily challenge. Throughout modern times, great achievers have focused intensely on opportunities where others see nothing. This focus helped them eliminate wasted time and distractions. Most failed ventures die from being too bloated with busyness rather than from a starvation of ideas. Organizations suffer from doing too many things at the same time rather than doing too few things very well.

The same applies to individuals. Staying focused on the mission or the task at hand begins with clearing out all unnecessary distractions. Major drains include unhealthy relationships, a poor diet, and excess television or video games. Keep your goals central by making them as pop-ups on your computer monitor or as a printout kept in your wallet or purse. Measure your progress against goals routinely through a positive reinforcement system. Celebrate your successes with whatever little thing makes you feel good inside.

Replace bad habits with good ones, like exercise or a gluten-free, healthful diet that can stimulate your brain and cause increased focus. Brain foods include those rich in selenium like fish (or fish oil), spinach, blueberries, cherries, nuts and seeds, olive oil, avocados, eggs, cocoa, oysters, turmeric (the yellow spice found in many curries), foods rich in vitamin B, and even coffee. Avoid foods high in sugar, as these limit the brain's focus.

Surround yourself with people whose goals align with your own interests. Eliminate competing forces as much as possible, such as constant chit-chatters. If your mind starts to drift, take a break and recharge those batteries once in awhile.

Focus requires a concerted discipline to complete projects before moving on to new ones. If your attention still drifts after following these tips, consult a physician or find a new interest. You might just be bored.

"One reason so few of us achieve what we truly want is that we never direct our focus; we never concentrate our power. Most people dabble their way through life, never deciding to master anything in particular." ~ Tony Robbins

MARCH 8

I will do the hard things second

What's the first thing you do in the morning after you've had breakfast and get down to work? Is it your favorite thing to do, or least desirable? What about that challenging phone call that you dread? There's always tomorrow…right? Most will say that we should do the hard things first, but starting off the day with a taxing deed may not be the best way to set your emotional clock for the day. Instead, try first doing something that will make you feel really upbeat.

At the start of your day, fill your emotional tank with enough fuel to expend it on what is likely to drain it. However, *immediately* after doing that one thing that fills you up, do that one thing that is hardest. Most of the time what we dread is far less traumatic than we imagined it to be while it simmered, undone, in our mind.

Avoidance is one of the greatest causes of stress. When it comes to motivation, sometimes the tasks that pose the greatest risk can be deferred, like waiting for an appraisal before telling a client their house is thirty percent lower than they thought. The risk of delay needs to be assessed, because as a general rule bad news gets worse the longer it festers. In some rare cases a problem may naturally resolve itself in time, but don't count on it. It's usually best to do the hard things upfront, but always carefully consider how you will resolve a problem before confronting it. Imagine having that difficult discussion in advance in order to anticipate possible reactions. And then have faith in your abilities. You can do just about anything with the right attitude and commitment.

"Procrastination makes easy things hard, hard things harder." ~ Mason Cooley

"You may delay, but time will not." ~ Benjamin Franklin

"You cannot escape the responsibility of tomorrow by evading it today." ~ Abraham Lincoln

"Someday is not a day of the week." ~ Janet Dailey

MARCH 9

I will be that person others count on

Have you ever said you would do something and then didn't do it? That was a rhetorical question. Human beings are human. Perhaps you would have been better served by saying "no" to that request, since something done half-heartedly or with resentment often results in poor workmanship. Either way, not doing it or doing it poorly points to poor reliability.

Jesus offered this definition for reliability and integrity: "Let your 'Yes' be 'Yes,' and your 'No' be 'No' (Matthew 5:37). Trying to please everybody makes that definition impossible to meet. Spreading yourself too thin produces poor results.

Poor reliability does not always mean a person is deliberately careless. Unreliability may be caused by an overwhelming number of tasks or by a lack of organization. Being choosy as to what you can do or want to do is critical to managing your ability to get something done. To be reliable means that once a responsibility has been accepted, the accountable person must remain committed to its satisfactory completion—no ifs, ands, or buts about it. You're obligated. So be careful what you say "yes" to. It's better to decline something than to not do it well.

Once a responsibility is accepted, define the requirements to be met. Ill-defined expectations and tasks that cannot be objectively measured can lead to an unfair evaluation at task's end. You might think you've done a wonderful job, but if it isn't what the other person expected, as far as they're concerned you didn't satisfactorily complete the work. So be careful not to overcommit, but do clarify expectations before you commit. Get comfortable with saying 'no' when you know you lack the time or ability. Tell yourself it's OK to take a step back, and consider a less demanding role. It's all right to negotiate a postponement if your obligations will eventually ease and the other person agrees. Set yourself up for success.

"Simplicity is prerequisite for reliability." ~ Edsher Dijkstra

"Responsibility finds a way. Irresponsibility makes excuses."
~ Gene Bedley, National Educator of the Year

MARCH 10

I will perfect my craft, my art

Not many think of their work as a craft, except if you happen to work with your hands. However, if you think of your work as a masterpiece, then to do it right requires mastery. Just being competent today is not enough. You must invent something new by asking your customer what a perfect world for them looks like. Don't settle for just improving your customer's life with a product or service; find a way to offer something quintessential.

Though you may never find perfection, you can always seek after it through a healthful perspective of continuous improvement. Make it a goal to be the expert in your field. Excellence is accomplished through repetition, so it's not as much an act as it is a habit that forms through consistent practice. Each day represents a fresh chance to pursue mastery in what you already do by practicing the *10,000 Hour Rule*, which says that to master any non-trivial field requires 10,000 hours of dedicated practice and study. Sometimes this law is stated with "10 years" in place of "10,000 hours." Or, as an old saying puts it, "You have to write a million bad words before you can write a good one."

Besides studying your craft, the best way to perfect it is to teach it. "While we teach, we learn," said the Roman philosopher Seneca. Find an apprentice or someone to mentor-teach. Researchers have found that students enlisted to tutor others work harder to understand their subject, recall it more accurately, and apply it more effectively. While you are sharing your craft, ask your students what standard they think can be raised to distinguish your work from any others, and use this feedback to perfect your craft. Improvements are measured through customer emotions like "delighted" or "above and beyond" that come from exceeding expectations.

Benchmark with the thought leaders and visionaries in your industry to gain ideas and don't be afraid to invent a new craft if the old one won't be viable in twenty years. Be the master of your domain.

"We are what we repeatedly do. Excellence, then, is not an act but a habit." ~ Will Durant

"At first, the drudgery of mastering your craft is a prison—boring, slow, and with an awareness of how much time you'll have to put in. But somewhere along your prison sentence, you come to see the time you put into your work not as dull and meager, but as meaningful – and you realize that your prison has become your palace, your place of escape." ~ Jarod Kintz

MARCH 11

I will be above average

On a scale of one to ten, how would you rate yourself? Most of us would rate ourselves north of five, according to David Dunning, a psychologist at Cornell University who has studied what is called "illusory superiority" for years. This generous rating occurs because we tend to evaluate our intentions over our actual performance. According to Dunning, the most incompetent individuals are most likely to overestimate their skills. Top performers, on the other hand, assume their skills are commensurate with others and are therefore more likely to underrate themselves. Interestingly, Dunning notes, this tendency to overrate doesn't apply to Eastern cultures. This is possibly so because these cultures value self-improvement, while the West values self-esteem.

Illusionary superiority works most destructively for people in authority. The Workplace Arrogance Scale (WARS), developed by researchers at the University of Akron and Michigan State University, found that arrogant bosses often lead to increased employee turnover and an overall negative work atmosphere. Arrogant bosses, they found, are often more interested in proving their superiority, as opposed to improving work performance. The study found that these types of behaviors are more directly related with lower intelligence and self-esteem than in non-arrogant bosses. Overall research found that humility in a leader helped increase productivity and improve the work atmosphere of the organization.

The bottom-line for everyone, whether a boss or a contributor, is that humility works best. While striving to be above average is a noble goal, progress in reaching this goal is best evaluated not by ourselves, but by those whose lives we directly impact.

"We are just an advanced breed of monkeys on a minor planet of a very average star. But we can understand the Universe. That makes us something very special." ~ Stephen Hawking

"The healthiest competition occurs when average people win by putting above average effort." ~ Colin Powell

March 12

I will never be fully satisfied

In an interview on *CBS This Morning*, Bill Gates, the former CEO of Microsoft was asked whether he was happy with the company's innovations. Speaking of the current CEO, Gates answered: "Well, he and I are two of the most self-critical people you can imagine." Gates then proceeded to list a series of Microsoft accomplishments, and then said, "But is it enough? No, he (the current CEO) and I are not satisfied that in terms of, you know, breakthrough things, that we're doing everything possible." Gates said this about a company that has long held the record as the most valuable public company in the world. This begs the question: When is enough, enough? According to some of the most successful people on the planet, the answer is, "Never!"

Being satisfied with a job well done is a healthful attitude, but being satisfied that past achievement is satisfying enough, that there is no need to try harder, is the death knell of innovation. Self-critical people like Gates are always looking to improve, always asking themselves what they can do better. That is the distinctive mark of an innovator. Success to them is like a potato chip, you can't have just one. John Steinbeck called it a "capacity for appetite…that a whole heaven and earth of cake can't satisfy."

When you want to be the best at what you do, you can only outdo yourself. When you want to be the best that others can do, you need only do better than the best of them. Out-besting yourself is a far more attainable and more far reaching goal. You have control over yourself, and you are the only one who can improve upon your successes with the full knowledge of what it took to get there. Be your own best critic and you won't need to worry about the unfair criticism of others. You are committed to improvement, and that desire alone invariably will better your position. And that will lead to greater and greater achievements.

"I think we're having fun. I think our customers really like our products. And we're always trying to do better." ~ Steve Jobs

"One never notices what has been done; one can only see what remains to be done." ~ Marie Curie, Nobel Prize Winning Physicist

MARCH 13

I will accept rejection as a call for redirection

Les received a call from his boss to meet later that afternoon. "It's not good news. The company has decided to make some changes," the boss said. By evening Les found himself suddenly unemployed. News like that can be devastating. Any rejection creates a feeling of being unwanted, which then reduces self-esteem with thoughts such as 'you do not belong,' 'you are disliked,' or 'there is something wrong with you.'

But, rejection is a part of growing—be it in work or relationships. Rejection serves as a spotlight for redirection of our life toward something new, while illuminating areas in which we can develop. It sounds cliché, but you really cannot take the rejection too personally. Others typically reject us because either they have changed, or the situation in which we find ourselves has changed. You are simply at the affect of that change which could happen to anyone in your circumstance. We need to accept rejection as a normal part of life instead of thinking "it could never happen to me." Use that acceptance as motivation to improve yourself and to keep an eye toward future possibilities. Our sphere of influence really only includes our thoughts and actions, so any expectation that we can completely control the decisions around us is at best only partly delusional. Instead, focus on what you can do to move forward.

A forward-looking mindset includes answering questions such as: "What have I learned?" "What can I do to make my next step better than the previous one?" Before moving on, however, you need to determine why the rejection happened. Maybe there is something you need to improve, and if not, perhaps the relationship or situation in which you found yourself was not the right fit, in which case you don't want to jump back into a similar mistake.

Most importantly, realize that rejection is redirection, not recession. The more we learn from experience, the more equipped we are to tackle bigger and better opportunities.

"A rejection is nothing more than a necessary step in the pursuit of success." ~ Bo Bennett

"I think that you have to believe in your destiny; that you will succeed, you will meet a lot of rejection and it is not always a straight path, there will be detours—so enjoy the view." ~ Michael York

MARCH 14

I will be courageous

Wayne Miller was diagnosed with a rare form of bone cancer that made his bones on an x-ray look like Swiss cheese. His prognosis was at best around six months. Faced with imminent death, Wayne prayed God would spare his life until his son, Ian, grew to college age. Ian was six-years-old. Stretching that six months into twelve years called for a miracle. And, on Wayne's part, extreme courage to endure both the pain of the disease and the treatments needed to prolong his life for even a brief time—let alone twelve years.

Wayne's struggle testifies that courage means *risking being uncomfortable.* Whether it be cancer or some other life challenge, like Wayne we must be willing to *do that difficult thing.* Wayne spent nights thinking about others who had gone before him, and his purpose for pushing on. He took *one day at a time*, dealing with the small stuff—like going to chemotherapy. Anyone who is facing a daunting challenge must *do the small things first in preparation for the larger goal.* Finally, courage for Wayne, as for every other brave soul, means *stilling yourself, taking a deep breath*, and *jumping into the challenge without reservation*. These are the signatures of courage.

Like all courageous people, Wayne *followed his heart*, *persevered*, *followed the strength of his convictions*, *let go of the easy way*, and *suffered with dignity*, armed with his strong faith. After his miraculous twelve-year struggle with cancer, Wayne finally died. On the day of his funeral, Ian, Wayne's now eighteen-year-old son, went off to college. In case you forgot, Wayne's wish had been to see his son grow to college age.

Against all the odds and because of Wayne's courage and faith, he saw that wish come true. Courage is strength in the face of pain or grief or fear.

"Courage is being scared to death…and saddling up anyway." ~ John Wayne

"Courage is grace under pressure." ~ Ernest Hemingway

"You will never do anything in this world without courage. It is the greatest quality of the mind next to honor." ~ Aristotle

MARCH 15

I will not delay

Perhaps the surest way to *not* succeed is to procrastinate. Not only are procrastinators are their own worst enemy, they often harm others by undermining teamwork and by damaging relationships.

Two of the world's leading experts on procrastination, Joseph Ferrari, Ph.D., associate professor of psychology at DePaul University in Chicago, and Timothy Pychyl, Ph.D., associate professor of psychology at Carleton University in Ottawa Canada, explained reasons for this self-destructive behavior in a 2010 issue of *Psychology Today*. Twenty percent of the population identify themselves as chronic procrastinators, the doctors said, like last-minute Christmas shoppers, people who don't pay bills on time, or being chronically late for events.

The common perception says that procrastination is a problem of time management. It is not. Procrastinators *actively look* for distractions, like getting sidetracked with the Internet. These diversions serve as a way of regulating their emotions, such as the fear of failure. "I work better under pressure," they lie to themselves.

Dr. Ferrari identifies three basic types of procrastinators: 1) the arousal types that wait until the last minute for that thrilling rush; 2) the avoiders, who may be acting out of a fear of failure; and, 3) the decisional procrastinators, who simply cannot make a decision, thereby excusing them from responsibility for the outcome of decisions. According to the research, procrastinators *can* change their behavior with highly structured cognitive therapy, like creating deadlines, breaking tasks into smaller pieces, and making their work area as distraction free as possible.

Get started by attacking to-do lists. Keep your first priority in the front of your mind. Organize tasks in order of importance. Establish specific times when you can commit at least thirty minutes to getting things done. Are you ready? Don't wait—get started now!

"Nothing is so fatiguing as the eternal hanging on of an uncompleted task."
~ William James

"Putting off an easy thing makes it hard. Putting off a hard thing makes it impossible." ~ George Claude Lorimer

MARCH 16

I will be nice

What does it matter whether you're nice or mean? Maybe because success requires partnerships—people who'll help you develop your vision, give you a job, and introduce you to opportunities. On the personal side, only a masochist wants to associate with a mean person. People want positive, enthusiastic people around them—problem solvers, not problem creators.

Charles Dickens's character Ebenezer Scrooge lived a friendless life, until that fateful night when he recognized that inner disappointments had caused him to turn his resentment outward toward others. Only then were his eyes opened to the lonely death that would be his unless he turned his life around. Fortunately for Ebenezer, he made that choice and spent the rest of his days in acts of charity, done with a joyful heart.

We all have "Scrooge Days," when we want to say "bah humbug" to the world. Like Scrooge, we need to stop and consider the consequences of our actions, both to ourselves and others. Maybe we just need to go cool off.

Contrary to common myth, legendary Chicago Cubs baseball manager Leo Durocher never said, "Nice guys finish last." What he said, referring to the Philadelphia Phillies team, was, "They might be nice guys, but they're in last place." Many people in life's "first place"—CEOs, baseball coaches, and others—are actually nice people. If they weren't, they could not assemble the team needed to help them carry out their long-term vision. True, some mean people do find success, but, as Scrooge discovered, their demise is inevitable unless they turn things around. If you happen to have a lot of deep-seated anger, try to uncover the root cause. Unfortunately, many children who are abused grow up to be abusers. This sad irony can be broken by seeing the goodness in people and by realizing the benefits of returning good for wrongdoing. Nothing turns meanness around like an act of charity and kindness.

"Being nice to someone you dislike doesn't mean you're FAKE. It means you are mature enough to tolerate your dislike towards them." ~ Author Unknown

"A good character is the best tombstone. Those who loved you and were helped by you will remember you when forget-me-nots have withered. Carve your name on hearts, not on marble." ~ Charles H. Spurgeon

MARCH 17

I will make wise choices

Great leaders are often thought of as decisive, but decisiveness is not always the mark of greatness. Only *good* decisions merit a seal of approval. Quickly made judgments can be wrong or right, depending on the skill of the decider. Great decision-makers understand how to balance emotion with reason in determining what will constructively and positively influence themselves, those affected by the decision, their stakeholders or customers, and the organization as a whole.

Being able to accurately assess the tradeoffs between the positive influences of change and the possible downside to others, like stress and uncertainty, determines whether the impact is worth it or not. Knowing when to act, and when to wait—for additional data gathering or for the condition to be ripe—is critical to making good decisions. The tipping point for moving forward depends on managing the variables without becoming overwhelmed by too much information and too many advisors. Important to the process is making a list of desired outcomes and objectively assessing whether the consequence of a decision will produce those results.

Another checkpoint follows the Rotary International's Four-Way Test, which answers these questions: Is it the truth? Is it fair to all concerned? Will it build goodwill and better friendships? Will it be beneficial to all concerned? Another technique for making quick decisions is called *heuristics*, which means drawing up lists of "for" and "against," and going with the longer list.

Some of the best decision-makers rely on their gut thinking, a sense of peace that enough analysis has occurred. Trusting your intuition factors into this due diligence process that leads to an inner peace. That's when you know you've made a wise choice.

"If you chase two rabbits, both will escape." ~ Author Unknown

"The risk of a wrong decision is preferable to the terror of indecision." ~ Maimonides

"You will rarely make wise decisions if you surround yourself with fools." ~ Rasheed Ogunlaru

MARCH 18

I will negotiate collaboratively

Imagine you are famished at a party. Each person pitches in the same amount of money for pizza, but the problem is that collectively, you can only afford enough pizza for one slice per person—and you want at least three pieces! What can you do? For starters, think outside the (pizza) box. Consider a solution that creates a bigger pie. What if you went to the store and bought enough ingredients to create several huge pizzas? You could have fun making the pizzas together, and because it's cheaper to make your own, each person can have as much as they want. That is collaboration, which is the highest level of negotiation.

Collaboration creates something with others by producing an outcome that expands resources, instead of simply trying to divide the existing resources. Great negotiation doesn't try to divide resources. Rather it considers others as an integral part of the team, so that everyone wins or loses together by expanding the solution. Don't get caught in the trap of thinking that what's "on the table" is the only alternative. Sometimes you can ask for a little more, like when an airline offers a voucher for an overbooked flight, you might be able to negotiate a first class ticket or even an overnight hotel stay. You just need to ask. You probably won't get far if you're too pushy, but if you ask politely while showing empathy for the other person, expect good things to happen. If you lose your cool, appear overly anxious, bluff, or treat the other person rudely, expect bad things to happen.

The proverbial win-win of negotiation assumes an ongoing relationship, where both parties feel positive about the outcome. So make sure to set the right tone upfront by inviting the others to join you in finding a resolution that benefits all concerned. You must be sincere in wanting the best for everyone. Together, you win. Separate, you both stand to lose something. Make a bigger pie.

"Let us never negotiate out of fear. But let us never fear to negotiate." ~ John F. Kennedy

"Place a higher priority on discovering what a win looks like for the other person." ~ Harvey Robbins

MARCH 19

I will be a servant leader

What is servant leadership? A servant leader focuses on the needs of individuals—on the follower rather than the leader. Servant leadership uses core values that empower others to become more effective through skill building and support. In other words—it's servant first, leader second. Servant leaders are secure enough to share their power.

While the stereotypical leader commands respect through an autocratic type of management style, the servant leader *earns* respect, through an engaging style that promotes teamwork and shared ideas. There is an absence of competition between co-workers, resulting in greater productivity and creativity. Valuing team members earns the servant leader both position power and influence power. Because people tend to respect those who respect them, they trust the servant leader to serve their interests, the interests of the organization, and the customer foremost.

So-called leaders who view people as simply tools to achieve an end force people into a self-protective mode—impeding growth and stifling innovation. Servant leaders' personal security allows them to hire the best talent, including talent that exceeds their own abilities, so that together, the team can achieve more than the capacity of its leader. Autocratic leaders may feel more vulnerable because they lack the full support of their team, so their first priority in hiring is to demand loyalty first, even if the talent hired is less capable than others who interview.

Servant leaders tend to view their organization holistically. A culture of servant leadership also tends to be more decentralized because it empowers individuals within the organization to make decisions and grow talent organically.

What about you? Would you rather be a servant leader or an autocratic leader? Which one would you prefer as a supervisor?

"True leadership must be for the benefit of the followers, not to enrich the leader." ~ John C. Maxwell

"Outstanding leaders go out of their way to boost the self-esteem of their personnel. If people believe in themselves, it's amazing what they can accomplish." ~ Sam Walton

MARCH 20

I will effectively deal with a…holes

While the mere suggestion of this slang term for irritating or contemptible persons risks giving this PG rated book about success an R rating, it's a topic we all, at one time or another, confront. Those a…holes can show up anywhere—in corner offices, behind store counters, in traffic—anywhere we live and work. So knowing how to deal with them without sacrificing our own personal integrity is important.

The first rule is: Get away from them if at all possible. Being a jerk is contagious. It can infect you with anger and even spread to others around you. If distancing yourself is not possible, tactful confrontation should follow. Bullies especially thrive if unchallenged. However, there's a chance the jerk really doesn't see his/her behavior as offensive, or needs help to overcome bad habits—like drill sergeants who just need to realize that they're not in a platoon anymore. Always try to remain polite while limiting contact with the perpetrator. Returning fire with fire only burns both of you. To help control your emotions with difficult people, try removing yourself from a volatile situation. If that's not possible, mentally check out by turning your mind elsewhere while you regain your composure. If the jerk is deliberately trying to sabotage you, keep a record of his offenses in case Human Resources or legal authorities need to get involved. Since it's likely the jerk has offended others as well, it may be worthwhile to dialog with some of them—not to spread rumors, but to document that there are multiple grievances. Engage the Human Resources department, management, or a legal advisor as mediators to stop abuse when nastiness crosses the line into harassment.

Don't let a…holes damage your life. Chances are they are not happy people, and if you can't help them, leave them.

"Before you diagnose yourself with depression or low self-esteem, first make sure that you are not, in fact, just surrounded by a…holes." ~ William Gibson

"CEOs can talk and blab each day about culture, but the employees all know who the jerks are. They could name the jerks for you. It's just cultural. People just don't want to do it." ~ Jack Welch

MARCH 21

I will face my fears

There's useful fear—like the rush of adrenaline that causes you to avoid a speeding car, and there's destructive fear—like the trepidation that comes from anticipating a bad report. Just thinking about something that might happen represents most of what causes us anxiety. The problem arises when that fear holds us back from what we want to do.

The first step in overcoming a fear is to understand it. Try completing this sentence: I want ________, but I'm afraid ________. Once you've identified what's holding you back, mentally visualize yourself discarding the fear and achieving what you want. When it comes to future events, our brain's emotional processing cannot differentiate between what it imagines and what's actually happening in reality. You can trick your mind by trivializing the fear through your own rationalization. Try saying something like: *There are people suffering in hospitals all over the world who can't be helped, so why am I so worried? Really, why should I be afraid?*

Associating the fear with something positive can also help you get over the obstacle of facing it. For example, a fear of public speaking may be overcome by doing it for a worthy cause—like speaking at local clubs, churches, and other venues to raise money for a favorite charity. Take baby steps first in order to create some positive momentum. Keep your focus on what you want and you'll be more likely to get there, like a ball player who can only make contact with the ball when focusing on it. Let your eye move "off the ball" and onto your fear, and you're likely to miss your goal.

Now, try completing this sentence: I will overcome my fear of __________by doing: __________. That's the answer for overcoming your fear. Once you overcome one fear, go onto the next and celebrate along the way. Conquering fear is a one-step-at-a-time process.

"The greatest barrier to success is the fear of failure." ~ Sven Goran Eriksson

"Too many of us are not living our dreams because we are living our fears." ~ Les Brown

"Always do what you are afraid to do." ~ Ralph Waldo Emerson

MARCH 22

I will be tenacious

There is a wonderful song by Donnie McClurkin that inspires, especially when sung by a choir of children, as I once had the privilege of hearing: "We fall down (the name of the song), but we get up, we fall down, but we get up…for a saint is just a sinner who fell down, but we couldn't stay there, and got up." Tenacity is the ability to recover from misfortune, roll with the punches, and get up one more time. If you get up one more time than you fall down, you've succeeded.

Tenacious people tell themselves that defeat is never final—but neither is success. Life is an ebb and flow of rises and falls. The rollercoaster of our existence, between good days and bad days, should make us less dependent on good news (it won't last), and less devastated by bad news (it won't last). That's not a fatalistic viewpoint, but an outlook that says our present contentment need not depend on any one single occurrence, but on the summation of a life that keeps on moving forward. It's an outlook that let's us live a more tempered life, not rocked by momentary setbacks.

Relieve the stress of a trial by remembering that your attention to the negative situation only amplifies it. Focusing on self-perceived failures or faults only results in a spiraling effect. Instead, focus on the outcomes you want when you get up again, and let your attention amplify those positive places ahead of you. Successful people develop the mental toughness to keep going when the average person quits. View your setbacks as possibilities rather than grim reminders. Every time you fall down and rise again to overcome a setback, your tenacity grows stronger. You are standing tall, on your way up—that's the attitude to hang on to.

"I have not failed. I've just found 10,000 ways that won't work." ~ Thomas Edison

"People who soar are those who refuse to sit back, sigh and wish things would change. They neither complain of their lot nor passively dream of some distant ship coming in. Rather, they visualize in their minds that they are not quitters; they will not allow life's circumstances to push them down and hold them under." ~ Charles Swindoll

MARCH 23

I will stop trying to impress others

If you shop for clothes by designer label, go out to be seen in the hottest places in town, drive the latest status car—you're spending money to impress people. Is it worth it? I'm guessing you know the answer to that question. Being genuine means presenting your image in the same way for anyone, regardless of status or position. People are generally most comfortable with those who aren't trying to artificially impress them. That's not to say you shouldn't dress or behave appropriately for an interview or social function, it simply means you should always represent the real you—who you are on the inside.

Early in life, we form approval-seeking habits. We want to be liked, so we do what we think will impress the audience we want to be liked by. But who really needs all that stress? When you relax and let the true you shine, you'll end up impressing the people who matter. Those who aren't impressed are probably not the ones you want to be around anyway.

There's a lot to be said for living in the moment. Focus on your own intentions, without sizing up others around you, and you'll do fine. There's no need to be overly polite, overly apologetic, or defensive. Once you develop the habit of concentrating on your needs and just accept others for who they are, you'll relieve yourself of a tremendous burden. You don't need anyone else's approval!

"A man cannot be comfortable without his own approval." ~ Mark Twain

"Do not look for approval except for the consciousness of doing your best."
~ Andrew Carnegie

"The most splendid achievement of all is the constant striving to surpass yourself and to be worthy of your own approval." ~ Denis Waitley

MARCH 24

I will go the extra mile

A grocery store bagger packed an older man's purchases, starting with the cans first. The white-haired man was unshaven and dressed in clothes that were neatly pressed, despite faded slacks and two small holes in the shirt. All his food purchases were generic brand and all basic—no comfort foods. "Would you like some help in getting these to your car?" the boy asked. Without looking up the man nodded. As they walked, the boy pushed the cart with one hand. He saw that the old man struggled, his left leg dragging, so the boy steadied the man with his other hand.

The old man spoke not a word as the boy helped him into his car and finished loading the groceries. Just before closing the man's door, the boy pulled out a cloth, wetted it with water from his drinking bottle, and cleaned the man's very dirty windshield. "Can I do anything else for you, sir? Anything at all? I would be honored to help you." For the first time the man looked up, smiled, and nodded. "You have been kind to me, son," he said. He took out and handed the boy some money—what turned out to be a hundred dollar bill. "Now let me help you."

Researchers* have found that when a person gives more than expected, the receiver is more likely to be generous and give even more in return. The old saying, *one good deed deserves another*, should therefore be amended: One good deed deserves two in return. It's been proven time and again that going the extra mile results in exponential growth. So next time you're completing a transaction or deed, ask yourself what extra touch you can add.

"You can start right where you stand and apply the habit of going the extra mile by rendering more service and better service than you are now being paid for." ~ Napolean Hill

"If you expect your employees to go the extra mile for your customers, you must prove that you are willing to go the extra mile for them!" ~ Author Unknown

* The study was from researchers at the University of California and Harvard University and published in the Proceedings of the National Academy of Sciences.

MARCH 25

I will be faithful in the small things

After submitting her resignation as a receptionist for Molecular Design (MD) to pursue greater interests, Renee was approached by the CEO. "Please stay. I'll give you a better paying job," he said. "We'll find a more challenging position for you." How did Renee merit that kind of attention? She had worked late into the evening developing a sophisticated filing system for MD scientists. By her own admission, Renee wasn't a "detail-oriented person," but she made the extra effort to catalog all of the key information needed by each researcher so that they could easily reference it. She saw a gap and she filled it. It wasn't a sexy project. It wasn't even something she particularly enjoyed. But she took the initiative to meet a need, and took pride in doing it right. As a result, the CEO did not want to lose this employee. What's more, he was ready to reward her with greater responsibility. The moral of this story is: If you want more, you must be faithful in "the small stuff."

If you want to be seen as an original in a field of copycats, you must be reliable. You must do what nobody has done before you. Complete all of your job requirements—plus a little more. Seek to identify with these descriptions: true-to-your-word, trustworthy, dependable, and responsible.

Too many people these days feel they *deserve* something, even if it isn't merited. A person with a healthy attitude wants to earn what comes their way. They long for the satisfaction that comes with a job well done. Seek to be someone who does the job well, even if nobody recognizes it. You will, and you can sleep well at night knowing you gave it your best shot. If you've fallen short in the past, do not despair. It's never too late to start doing the right thing the next time. Be faithful in the small things.

"Be faithful in small things because it is in them that your strength lies." ~ Mother Teresa

"One sees great things from the valley; only small things from the peak."
~ G. K. Chesterton

"If you cannot do great things, do small things in a great way." ~ Napoleon Hill

MARCH 26

I will counter my strength

Are you the best at something? If so, congratulations! And watch out. A strength taken to the extreme becomes a glaring weakness. All too often, the bravado with which we may practice our unchecked strength steamrolls like a runaway locomotive, and ends up crashing. Instead of spending excess time capitalizing on your strength, you should develop a counter-strength.

A strong director who gets things done no matter what may be insensitive to others. As a counter-strength, that director learns to check-in with the emotions of others along the way—become *more sensitive.* A strong analyzer develops counter-strengths by looking at the big picture, and using intuition to make decisions.

If you don't learn to counter your strengths, you may become like a little dictator who steamrolls over others. Or you could become a pariah in your own field, like the all-too-many professional ballplayers whose unchecked drive has tempted them into the use of steroids.

Your default tendency always tugs you back to your strength, so don't worry about concentrating too much on a counter-strength. Seek to counter your strengths and surround yourself with a team of accountability partners—people who will tell it to you straight. Success breads a certain amount of arrogance that feeds our strengths, resulting in our potential demise. Certainly you should build on your strengths, but seek humility and a stronger devotion to your counter-strength so that you can become well rounded.

"The world breaks everyone, and afterward, some are strong at the broken places." ~ Ernest Hemingway

"There are two ways of exerting one's strength: one is pushing down, the other is pulling up." ~ Booker T. Washington

MARCH 27

I will take control over my finances

Money, or the lack of it, can cause tremendous stress, whether at home or in your business. Those who master their finances don't do it by coincidence. It takes planning, a reckoning of the life you want to live, and some discipline. The good news is that anyone can gain control over his finances. The key is to not just how much money you have, it's what you know about where it's coming from and where it needs to go.

The first step is to list out everything you buy, including all reoccurring costs, like bills, and occasional purchases. You can use a software program or just create a simple note on your smart phone and transfer it to your spreadsheet. Note what form of payment you used as well as the date and amount spent. Do this over a two to three month period and you can determine your weekly and monthly average spending. Use a budgeting application—there are lots of good ones out there—to get a clear picture of your income and outgo.

The next step is to decide how to better invest your money. Real estate, which is geographically and demographically dependent, can be a good investment if the market value increases. Use a "rent versus buy calculator" that you can source on the Internet to determine the best option for you. Retirement accounts are popular too. You can use the software calculator provided by your retirement account provider (they all have them) to determine a fair amount to deposit. Think about how much you will need to retire. Factor in a reasonable longevity and work backwards from there. If your employer matches a percent of your contribution, keep in mind that contributing the full amount that the company will match lowers your current income. Build an emergency savings fund to cover at least eight months' living expenses in the event of a job loss or some long-term medical issue. And, of course, pay off any protracted credit card balances by first paying off the cards with the highest interest rates. Finally, trust your common sense as to what and when to spend.

"Look everywhere you can to cut a little bit from your expenses. It will all add up to a meaningful sum." ~ Suze Orman

MARCH 28

I will live large without needing a large bank account

Living within your means shouldn't mean sacrificing your desire for the good life. Smart planning and shopping can keep you from spending over budget. You can find deals almost anywhere, including the "free stuff" offered through product introductions/promotions, contests, and even at work. If dining with guests, come to an arrangement for splitting the bill in *advance* of going to a restaurant, or consider a potluck at home for large parties. You can avoid an expensively stocked bar by offering one or two specialty drinks, such as wine or punch.

When you go on vacation, consider renting a condominium or house—major tourist destinations are full of them. Being flexible with your travel dates can provide you with cost-saving last-minute flights and hotel deals as well. Many budget travel websites offer special prices for travel within a short time-window. Some hotels discount their rooms a day or so before the arrival date. Airlines usually discount their flights if reservations are made at least two weeks in advance, and prices can be even lower if made at least a month in advance. Sign up for loyalty programs that can save big bucks.

At home, you don't need to hire high-priced contractors when you can do it yourself. Painting the walls can make a huge difference. Upgrading your kitchen with granite countertops is one of the most assured returns, or put in quality hardwood flooring in your living areas. Most stores will give you discounts on slightly used display models. If buying a new home, foreclosures and bank-owned homes represent some of the best potential savings. Instead of buying artwork at galleries, try auctions or art fairs where you can find relatively affordable works by unknown artists. When buying electronics, stores often discount their current devices once the new technology is introduced. Look for clothes that are not classified as "designer" or are out of season, or find out which stores offer annual or semi-annual sales. Designer brand outlet stores often have end of season sales for leftovers. Maintaining all of your things in good condition keeps you living large.

"A vision not lived remains only a dream…"
~ Terrill Welch, from "Your Blooming Success!" article

"You only live once, but if you do it right, once is enough." ~ Mae West

MARCH 29

I will change my routine by replacing bad habits

Without habits we would have to invent life every day. So they're not all bad. In fact, the mind's tendency toward regimen alleviates many of life's stresses. Both good and bad behaviors send pleasure or pain impulses to the brain that help it decide if the resulting experience should become a habit.

When damaging habits keep looping within the brain, a new routine must be established to essentially short-circuit the existing signal/temptation. Dieters wishing to lose weight can adopt new routines of eating and exercising that can preempt old eating habits. Trainers use this technique of masking bad habits by overlapping old responses with new stimuli, like rewarding runners each time they increase their distance or finish time.

The key is to create incremental wins that gradually rewire the brain. Changing bad to good involves discovering the root cause of the habit in the first place. Knuckle cracking, for example, may be a response to bad news. Janet L. Wolfe, Ph.D., a clinical psychologist in New York City and author of several books including the series *What to Do When He Has a Headache* (Hyperion, Penguin), suggests keeping a log to help establish a baseline. "Put down the antecedents, the emotions surrounding the knuckle cracking and what goes through your head when you crack your knuckles," she says. "This will make your bad habit more conscious."

The next phase of retraining the brain is to replace the bad habit with the new one. Wolfe says about knuckle cracking, "Try getting your hands in a position where you won't be able to crack your knuckles." Maybe doodle or stroke your sleeve. Start with small wins, and work your way to a new routine.

"Successful people are simply those with successful habits." ~ Brian Tracy

"A nail is driven out by another nail. Habit is overcome by habit." ~ Desiderius Erasmus

"First we form habits, then they form us. Conquer your bad habits or they will conquer you." ~ Rob Gilbert

MARCH 30

I will make the customer my boss

Have you ever asked for help in a store, only to get this response: "Sorry I can't help you." How does that make you feel? In today's marketplace, increasingly saturated with multiple product and service choices that on the surface appear the same, we need help seeing the difference. Customer service is becoming more important than product or price. Service and product designers who succeed in the future will need to change their paradigm from trying to fit customers to products, to making products and services fitted to the customer. To shift current thinking, the drivers of today's decision makers must change. Customers essentially want value for their purchase, whereas providers want a return. Companies are often motivated to drive returns for their shareholders.

In the early twentieth century, the mantra was "The Customer is King." That shifted to a share and profit-driven focus toward the late 1900s and into the 21st century. Future success will demand that the customer create the rules by which the provider exists. The days of centralized control are finished, driven largely by a global media that shares customer feedback in real time. That is why service-based companies thrive, and organization-centric companies do not. The new model considers the individual, their market demographic, trends, and multi-dynamic preferences, and produces a solution tailored to their progressive requisites.

Companies like Nordstrom and Wal-Mart understand these dynamics. The emerging customer-centricity is catering to the overall customer experience, making the customer king once again by making him or her feel good about their purchase. A customer focus trains everyone to serve the customer with comprehensive support. If you want to succeed, let the person on the buying end of your transaction make the ultimate decision.

"There is only one boss. The customer. And he can fire everybody in the company from the chairman on down, simply by spending his money somewhere else." ~ Sam Walton

"Do what you do so well that they will want to see it again and bring their friends." ~ Walt Disney

MARCH 31

I will manage stress

One of the best ways to promote your own overall health is through good stress management. Stress comes in several forms: 1) *Acute Stress*, the most common form, a short-term type that can be either positive (a brief thrill, like riding a rollercoaster) or can cause unhealthful anxiety (dealing with road rage); 2) *Episodic Acute Stress* that occurs when acute stress becomes a constant way of living, creating a life of disorder and confusion (the type of stress related to people who are always immersed in drama and/or absentmindedness); or 3) *Chronic Stress*—the type that seems inescapable, like that from an extremely oppressive job or a bad relationship. It's a type of stress that can lead to mental collapse.

In times of chronic stress our body cannot relax and physical symptoms may occur, beginning with headaches and an increased vulnerability to colds. Left unresolved, chronic stress can lead to more serious health problems like depression, diabetes, or heart disease. It's been estimated that as much as ninety percent of all ailments resulting in doctor visits are stress related.

Eating right, getting enough sleep, regular exercise, and maintaining a healthy attitude are all activities that can lower stress. Relieve tension through deep breathing, meditation, journaling, and using positive imagery. We cannot avoid acute stress all the time, however good time management and organization can help. If a job or relationship is causing chronic stress that cannot be resolved, you might need to make a change. If you are experiencing chronic stress, you may need to seek professional help as you could have a stress-related disorder that requires medications or other treatments. Seek to maintain an outlook that says things will get better, and with your commitment, they will.

"The greatest weapon against stress is our ability to choose one thought over another." ~ William James

"It's not stress that kills us, it is our reaction to it." ~ Hans Selye

"Besides the noble art of getting things done, there is a nobler art of leaving things undone." ~ Lin Yutang

APRIL

VALUE YOURSELF AND OTHERS

APRIL 1

I will be a lie detector

Did you know that if you wrinkle your nose too much it will grow into the size of an Idaho potato? Haha—April fool's! Not true. But people do sometimes lie, and it's important for us to be able to detect that lie to keep from becoming a victim of it. The deception techniques used by police and forensic psychologists can be useful.

People who lie typically use expressions that are stiff and contained, with few hand movements except to scratch behind the ear or touching the nose. They keep their movements tight to their body and avoid eye contact. Their gestures and emotions are usually irregular, with delayed emotional responses that stop abruptly. The liar, for example, may hear a joke, but then laugh well after the joke has passed. Expressions and movements will not match verbal utterances, like smiling after saying, "It's a gloomy day outside." When someone is faking it, their expressions are confined to the mouth as opposed to the full-face (eyes, jaw and forehead do not move). While confident people are overt, those who feel guilty become defensive, and may turn their body or head away from the other person as a form of avoidance. Dishonest people look for obstacles to place between themselves and the other person, like tables, cups, or other objects.

If you ask, "Did you have a satisfying lunch across the street?" the liar might respond, "Yes, I had a satisfying lunch across the street," repeating your words verbatim. Statements using contractions, like "I don't think so," are usually more truthful than "I do not think so." Liars avoid direct statements but might also over-speak, adding unnecessary details. They do not like pauses and may leave out pronouns or speak with a monotone, talking softly and mumbling at times, using improper grammar in a jumbled manner. While changing the subject relieves the liar, it may often confuse the honest person who wants to keep on topic.

The best way to judge someone's honesty is to compare their normal behavior to the current behavior, because not everyone who exhibits these kinds of behaviors is lying. Buyer beware.

"No man has a good enough memory to be a successful liar." ~ Abraham Lincoln

APRIL 2

I will put everything in its place

You've heard it said before: A place for everything and everything in its place. This notion implies that every item should be neatly returned to its rightful place after use. Test yourself to see if you follow the "everything in its place rule": you have five minutes to find the following: a paperclip, a tape measure or ruler, a measuring cup, and a comb. Did you pass?

What items are constantly out of place in your home or workspace? Maybe they need a new, more logical location. Michele Connolly, the *Get Organized Wizard*, uses these principles for storage: 1) Keep similar things together, like all winter accessories, including gloves, scarves, etc., in the same drawer; all flashlights and light-bulbs together; all paperwork in one filing cabinet. 2) Match frequency of use to accessibility of place. Suitcases, for instance, can be stored on a high shelf if you're not a frequent traveler. The important factor is to assign a permanent place for everything you own. If things work together, they should go together—toothpaste and toothbrush; buckets and brooms; scissors, tape, and stapler.

Place wastebaskets in each room. Discard unused or damaged goods. Place a broom, plunger, and dustpan in each bathroom. Set your computer's calendar alarm for dates you need to remember. Make standing appointments. Place tomorrow's outfit on a hook outside your closet door. Make a portable cosmetics bag. Create an "emergency" box in the car trunk supplied with umbrella, paper towels, plastic bags. Sort your day by action, not project. Check phone and email messages only twice a day. Get everything off your desk that you don't need every day. Place oldest papers first on top of your stack. For the household, keep one credit card per grownup. Create only one folder/container for all receipts. Ask your creditors to shift their due dates so you can lump them together. Beware of nostalgia clutter, and weed out your wardrobe frequently. Stick to a schedule and remember to place yourself only where you need to be.

"A place for everything, everything in its place." ~ Benjamin Franklin

APRIL 3

I will communicate effectively

Effective communication includes a variety of verbal and nonverbal skills, such as active listening, speaking clearly, and interpersonal relationships. Listening is as critical as speaking. It's far more than just hearing and understanding information being expressed, but involves empathizing with the speakers' feelings about their subject. Strong eye contact and genuine acknowledgements, like nodding and smiling, make the speaker feel understood—and that establishes a strong connection between you. By saying something like, "I understand how that would make you feel…," the speaker senses you truly understand them. Additionally, it gives him an opportunity to confirm or amend your interpretation. For free-flowiong discussion, it's important that each participant feels secure enough to openly express her feelings and opinions. This includes not passing immediate judgment. Acknowledge the other's statements by clarifying his information ("So what I heard you say is….") without feeling obligated to agree with it.

You will further gain favor from the other person by keeping your focus on the speaker (no texting!) and by not interrupting. Maintain an open posture (arms uncrossed, open stance, sitting forward) to set the other person at ease and convey interest. Matching your words and tone to your body language helps establish honesty. Avoid laughing, for instance, if you are saying something serious.

Stand tall with your shoulders back, good eye contact, and a firm but not hurtful handshake. That conveys confidence. If everything about you says sincerity, openness, and trust—you will be effective.

"To effectively communicate, we must realize that we are all different in the way we perceive the world and use this understanding as a guide to our communication with others." ~ Tony Robbins

"Say what you mean, and mean what you say, but don't say it mean!" ~ Lisa Johnson

"The trouble with talking too fast is you may say something you haven't thought of yet." ~ Ann Landers

APRIL 4

I will believe in my ability to get better

Jerry joined a healthcare manufacturing company after spending nine years as a nurse. He found the transition from clinic to industry difficult. Instead of focusing on patient care, his new job as an associate marketing manager involved analyzing data and dealing with peoples' competing agendas. Over several years, Jerry felt he had become stagnant in his position. Others received promotions before him. He heard positive comments about those who passed over him, like "He's a natural leader" or "She's exceptionally intelligent." Jerry rarely received a compliment. Frustrated and demotivated, he felt as though he wasn't putting forth his full potential,. "I'm just not good at analytics," he concluded.

Believing that success depends only on ability can lead to disabling insecurity. When others start passing us over, we start believing we are destined to fail. That then triggers a self-fulfilling prophecy, and eventually we stop trying. Conversely, studies demonstrate that people who believe in their ability to grow not only succeed more, but they also are more motivated, deal more efficiently with challenges, and experience more job satisfaction, along with less anxiety. Similarly, those who ask themselves who, rather than what, they want to become, also tend to succeed more. Their view of life as a journey in discovering new skills allows them to overcome the fear of change.

Eventually Jerry stopped paying attention to what people said about others and started following a development plan that included charting his progress against his goals. Before long, Jerry was promoted. So the next time you catch yourself thinking, "I am no good at this," remind yourself that you're just not good at it *yet*.

"Without continual growth and progress, such words as improvement, achievement, and success have no meaning." ~ Benjamin Franklin

"Formal education will make you a living; self-education will make you a fortune." ~ Jim Rohn

APRIL 5

I will remain optimistic

It was a mostly positive review, but that one criticism ruined your day. Worse, it stuck with you months later. Sound familiar? As humans we tend to accentuate the negatives. Psychologists call it negativity bias. Our selective memory harbors negative encounters more than positive ones because they provoke more intense reactions, which makes us more timid and less willing to take risks.

Thankfully, we can take steps to overcome our negative propensity, so we can escape the disease of pessimism without having to ascribe to that worn-out axiom of believing the "glass half full."

Several experts suggest we review past accomplishments. Remembering what we've done well in the past gives us hope for the future. Gratitude also has a powerful influence on your thinking. It not only makes you feel better, but it turns your focus outward, to the positive. There's no need to ignore problems, but think of them instead as challenges—or better yet opportunities. Your brain will subconsciously replace the paradigm of failure, evoked by the word "problem," with a more encouraging outlook. Psychologists have also found that humor and just being silly replaces negative impulses with a more childlike optimism.

When one depressed businessman decided to join a comedy club, he discovered that his disposition changed dramatically in the process. Or there's the teacher who dresses up as a clown and entertains kids at a children's hospital. It's like a game in which you make a habit of actively searching for the positive side in everything. Looking for the good around you awakens you to reasons for being optimistic by moving attention from the dark side of life. Replace words like "things will *never* get better," to "it will be better *tomorrow*." If you act like an optimistic person, your mind accepts that as your reality. Also, people are attracted to your brighter outlook in life and will respond with more encouragement back to you. Our attitude toward life determines others' attitude toward us.

"A pessimist sees the difficulty in every opportunity; an optimist sees the opportunity in every difficulty." ~ Winston Churchill

APRIL 6

I will take a break

Thinking of ways in which to be more productive? Work through lunch, concentrate more, because the longer you work the more you'll get done. That's the way, correct? BZZZ – Wrong! New research tells us you should heed your inner alarm clock and take a break. Even brief intermissions can significantly improve one's ability to focus on a task for longer periods of time. Scientists say that after a certain period of time your cognition decreases and your performance begins to decline. Some researchers explain that this "vigilance decrement," as they term it, results from a drop in one's "attentional resources." University of Illinois psychology professor Dr. Alejandro Lieras, who led the recent study, describes the brain's tendency to stop registering a sight, feeling, or sound if a stimulus remains constant over time. For example, over time most people lose awareness of the soft music playing in the background of a store. Lieras says the body becomes "habituated" to stimuli, such as looking at a fixed object in one's peripheral vision until that object completely disappears from view. "Constant stimulation is registered by our brains as unimportant, to the point that the brain erases it from our awareness," Lieras said.

Studies like this one point to the need for people to stop feeling guilty about taking a break to detach from their work and reinvigorate their internal resources. So if your mind starts wandering, take a walk or do some other movement. Don't just go from one sedentary position to another. Watch out for that other extreme, of course. Too many breaks can cause procrastination.

So the next time your boss says you have to work through break time, tell her about these latest studies. Or better yet, invite her to go for a walk with you.

"Doing nothing is better than being busy doing nothing." ~ Lao Tzu

"There is more to life than increasing its speed." ~ Mahatma Gandhi

"The really idle man gets nowhere. The perpetually busy man does not get much further." ~ Sir H. Ogilvie

APRIL 7

I will practice my faith

Whether you celebrate Easter, Yom Kippur, Ramadan, or no religious observances, faith is a vital part of anyone's life. Even atheists must have faith in themselves, or they will struggle with their motive to achieve success. The process begins with finding your faith entity, which by simple definition is the arbiter of your truth: that driving force or being that defines for you what's right or wrong, and the reason for your life.

Some of us say our reason for living is a person—someone we love. But most describe God as our focus of worship. The vast majority of people in the world, almost ninety percent by most surveys, practice some form of religion, with Christianity representing thirty-four percent of the world's population, followed by Islam at twenty-two percent. Only eleven percent classify themselves as non-religious (nine-point-forty-two percent) or atheist (two percent).

Faith, by definition, is "complete trust or confidence in someone or something." Do you desire to reach beyond yourself? If so, who best fits that definition for you? Faith offers comfort during hard times. A respected study conducted over a six-year period among 4,000 persons aged sixty-five years and over asked about their health problems and whether respondents prayed, meditated, or read the Bible.

According to a Garnett News Service article, researchers discovered that those seniors who said they rarely or never prayed ran about a fifty-percent greater risk of dying earlier than those seniors who prayed at least once a month. While this study is not in and of itself conclusive, other studies confirm that faith and prayer lead to more satisfying lives. If you are feeling alone or isolated, faith can provide the assurance that you can triumph over it. Believing does not deny your ability to reason, rather it complements your mind's finite ability – it gives you something or someone beyond yourself to hold onto.

"Ask, and it will be given you; seek, and you will find; knock, and it will be opened to you: For every one that asks receives; and he that seeks finds; and to him that knocks it will be opened." ~ Jesus

"The Christian does not think God will love us because we are good, but that God will make us good because he loves us." ~ C.S. Lewis

APRIL 8

I will confess

Lisa sat in her office not knowing what to say. Since she'd been on this job, it was clear that her general manager, Dean, did not like her. Maybe she came off too strong for the "good ol' boy network," or maybe she'd, well, outsmarted him one time too many. Abused as a child, Lisa found that Dean's bullish behavior reminded her a little of her father.

To avoid punishment, she often lied to her dad. Eventually lying became a normal way of life. She lied on her résumé to get her present job, falsely noting an MBA she'd never received. Finally, the lying got to her. She didn't want to live that way anymore. "I was not entirely honest in getting this job," Lisa told Dean. "I do not have an MBA. I'm ready to accept the consequences." Dean's response surprised Lisa. "You know, I don't have an MBA either. I appreciate your honesty Lisa. Don't worry. This won't affect you position here." From that point forward their working relationship improved dramatically. Today, Lisa lives a more transparent life.

Two things happen when we give voice to failings: it lessons their power over us by releasing those secrets that fester within the destructive privacy of our mind, and it resets our thinking. We get to begin again. The pathway for change is open before us. Confession realigns what we know to be right with what *is* right, readjusting our world. So in a sense, it is chiropractic for the soul. Releasing the heavy burden of a false persona mitigates any negative consequences that may result from a misrepresentation.

Eventually, someone accepts you for who you are, and not for why you think others should accept you. If the confession reveals a mistake or moral failure, counseling and the healing balm of time may help set things right again.

"A confession has to be part of your new life." ~ Ludwig Wittgenstein

"Confess you were wrong yesterday; it will show you are wise today." ~ Proverb

"Confession, alas, is the new handshake." ~ Richard D. Rosen

APRIL 9

I will value who I am

According to The Self-Esteem Institute, fear and anxiety are the cornerstones of low self-esteem. The Institute's Dr. Sorensen explains that panic attacks are often mistaken for "self-esteem attacks," caused when a person perceives she has done or said something insensitive, inappropriate, stupid, or ridiculous. Wishing she could just disappear, the person experiencing the self-esteem attack may try to escape by faking an illness, escaping without a word, or just being completely silent to avoid notice. Paranoia sets-in when the person going through the attack believes everyone witnessed her mistake, and is thinking negatively about her.

Because people with low self-esteem are fearful of rejection, self-confidence and assertiveness are depleted. Gossiping, hinting at something to gain their way and other passive aggressive manipulative behavior are common behaviors. Work becomes a place of security, causing low self-esteem sufferers to stay in jobs even when the compensation is poor.

The cure begins by surrounding yourself with people who encourage you without defining your worth. Don't put too much stock in what people say or do. They're projecting their own reality—not yours. Find something you do well, and stick with it. Escape isolation by volunteering, joining a club, or finding an organization that let's you showcase your talent. Become aware of your thoughts and beliefs, including what you tell yourself. Do your thoughts line up with the facts? Turn your mind toward constructive thoughts. Forgive yourself. Replace "should-have" and "could-have" statements with words like, "I can do this." Remind yourself of what you've done well. Practice affirming your value, and your confidence and sense of well-being will skyrocket.

"Until you value yourself, you won't value your time. Until you value your time, you will not do anything with it." ~ M. Scott Peck

APRIL 10

I will start something new

Why does everything have to be "new"? What's the matter with the "old," anyway? There may be nothing wrong with the old, but if things stayed the same forever, life would get pretty dull after awhile. "New" can be as small as a new hobby, or as large as a new job. "New" can alleviate boredom, but it can also be scary. We like our routines. Doing something out of the ordinary could result in fear and anxiety.

To enter the new, we need to realize the difference between simply existing and living life to the fullest. To simply exist is to live on autopilot, doing the "same ol' same ol'" with little variation. Living life to the fullest means trying new things, stretching your boundaries, and even doing something spontaneous or crazy once in awhile.

Those who think things are "just fine the way they are" may be the most in need of something new. Kickstart new thinking by spending time with some of the adventurers in your circle. Truly afraid to try new things? Professional counseling can also help. Like walking or learning to rollerskate, getting started may be a little wobbly at first. So take baby steps with the slightly familiar, get to know the new thing slowly, and don't expect perfection the first time out. Let people know you're a beginner. Ask them to be kind and not judge too harshly—and that includes you! Surround yourself with encouragers and praise yourself for taking a chance on "new." And whatever you do—have fun!

"We keep moving forward, opening new doors, and doing new things, because we're curious and curiosity keeps leading us down new paths." ~ Walt Disney

"Maybe it's not about trying to fix something broken. Maybe it's about starting over and creating something better." ~ Author Unknown

"If you never did you should. These things are fun and fun is good." ~ Dr. Seuss

APRIL 11

I will not allow sorrow to disable me

If you have ever grieved a death, said goodbye to someone you wouldn't see for a long time or ever again, ended a relationship or sent a son or daughter off to college, you know sorrow. Left unhealed, the pain of loss can debilitate every area of life. While denial may be tempting, it's far healthier to accept those feelings, and to go through the grieving process in a deliberate manner.

Therese Rando, Ph.D. and grief expert, says those things that are important in our life should be remembered and kept in a very special place in our heart and mind. Consider where you would like to keep those memories. Visualize keeping your loved one in a special place in your heart, maybe even keep a container filled with treasured photographs and mementos. It's natural to feel pain, so don't cover it up with keeping busy or simply getting away.

"To enrich your present and future life without forgetting your past," Rando says, take what you gained from your loved one, along with your renewed sense of self and a different way of interrelating with the world. A part of our lifestyle will pass with the departure, so we need to also grieve the loss of shared activities and communion just as much as the physical loss. It can take a few months for it all to sink in, so be patient with yourself.

For most people, the hardest part of loss is what to do with the love they felt for the one who left. You can continue loving someone long after they're gone, and in fact that love should be a comfort as your thoughts and memories reconnect you to the joys the two of you shared. Use the past to nurture you while continuing the journey.

"The grief within me has its own heartbeat. It has its own life, its own song. Part of me wants to resist the rhythms of my grief, yet as I surrender to the song, I learn to listen deep within myself." ~ Alan Wolfel

"Every day my love for you grows higher, deeper, wider, stronger…It grows and grows until it touches the tip of where you are and comes back to me in the loving memory of you, and my heart melts with that love and grows even more." ~ Maureen Hunter

APRIL 12

I will be a problem solver

Problems come in two varieties: 1) glaring problems that are readily apparent to most persons; and, 2) underlying problems that appear hidden and cause erosion. The first would be something like a leaky faucet; the second, faulty plumbing that could eventually lead to a flood. One requires an immediate fix, the other corrective action. It's a little like plugging the hole versus getting to the root of the problem. Sometimes you just have to fix it to survive, but ultimately, you'll need a lasting solution.

Digging deeper to uncover the root cause involves analyzing the problem before identifying possible solutions. Selecting the best solutions requires an earnest evaluation of what will have the most permanent effect. Once the best solution is agreed on, the next stop is to implement it. That requires an action plan. Most people fail because they go for temporary fixes. Or they skip a step in the problem-solving process: 1) discover the root problem, 2) analyze its cause, 3) determine and evaluate potential solutions, 4) choose the best and most practical solution, 5) allocate resources needed for implementing the solution, 6) correct the problem, and 7) evaluate the results (has it worked).

Resolving any problem involves both analytical and creative skills. A logical and methodical approach is best if you need to draw on technical expertise (the plumbing example). For resolving more nuanced problems, like coworkers who don't get along, creative or "lateral thinking" is best. Always apply the seven-step plan, and you'll be known as a problem solver.

"The measure of success is not whether you have a tough problem to deal with, but whether it is the same problem you had last year."
~ John Foster Dulles, Former US Secretary of State

"Erroneous assumptions can be disastrous." ~ Peter Drucker

"You don't drown by falling in the water; you drown by staying there."
~ Edwin Louis Cole

"Price is what you pay. Value is what you get." - Warren Buffet.

APRIL 13

I will see what's incomprehensible

Read the following sentence: FINDING FACTS IN THE FACE OF CONFUSING THEORIES BORN OUT OF CONFLICTING SOURCES ONLY BEFUDDLES PEOPLE OF FANCY WHO FIND IT DIFFICULT TO DISCERN FACTS FROM THE MYTH OF FANTASY. How many f's do you count in that sentence? If you counted thirteen you would be almost correct. Most people do not perceive the letter f in the word of, and there were four of them. So, the answer is seventeen.

Such is the deceptiveness of the brain, which cannot always match truth with perception. Throughout history, several formerly perceived "truths" have been debunked with fact. The earth was perceived as flat, bloodletting was thought to cure disease, and the smallest particle was thought to be the atom. Humans (let alone pigs) could not fly until the Wright Brothers invented the first plane. In the 17th century, astronomical theory was based on the assumption that the earth was the center of the universe. Then astronomer Galileo Galilei proposed a new idea that the sun was the center of the universe. For thousands of years, scaling Mount Everest was considered impossible. Since 1953, people have been climbing it without even using additional oxygen.

We cannot see the reality of what appears impossible until we establish the impossible as our destination. In order to go beyond what has already been done, to attain new discoveries, we need to transition from an inward state of mind to an outward focus. Mind-determined visions allow new ideas to energize our consciousness with new aspirations. To achieve the previously unknown, we need to forge within ourselves the will to achieve quality outcomes, based on what is incomprehensible—and not just what we think is true. This requires a malleable attitude that adds never before observed inputs and receives stimuli for creative thinking, and the ability to set impossible goals connected to multiple related outputs to achieve them. Impossibilities grow into possibilities and then mature as new realities for those who dare to try.

"Women, like men, should try to do the impossible, and when they fail, their failure should be a challenge to others." ~ Amelia Earhart

APRIL 14

I will integrate my life with my work

Common thought in work-life balance is that time dedicated to work is compensated by an equal amount of time dedicated to all other activities and relationships outside of work. This concept was birthed from the idea that work demands encroach upon family relationships, recreation, and other personal concerns. Said another way, work and the rest of life compete against each other. Research now reveals that work-life integration, not work-life separation, leads to a more satisfying life.

A vital aspect of integrating work-life involves the extent to which we are willing to blend work and personal tasks. People who see life as *Work First* permit work to interfere with personal life. The *Family First* crowd, on the other hand, allows personal life to infringe on work. Then there are the *Dividers*, who separate the tasks for work and personal life into clearly divided schedules. Finally, there are the *Alternators*, who schedule time between work and personal life by switching back and forth, such as seasonal workers.

The beginning point of integrating work-life is to discover your style. If you prefer a job that doesn't require you to take any work home, you are probably a *Divider,* someone who prefers a scheduled work environment. A *Family First* person may feel that an onsite day care center is important. Don't think in terms of balancing life with work, which can never be fully achieved. Instead think of integrating the two, by negotiating or finding positions you can control to best fit your style, such as a virtual work environment for *Family First* persons or an office position for the *Work First* person. A fulfilled life achieves the proper amount of control to fit one's work-life integration by creating an environment that meets their primary needs. If you can control your environment to integrate your needs, you will find greater satisfaction.

"You will never find time for anything. If you want time you must make it."
~ Charles Buxton

"I've learned that you can't have everything and do everything at the same time." ~ Oprah Winfrey

APRIL 15

I will go out on a limb

You may not want to dive out of an airplane at 20,000 feet, but there are plenty of other opportunities to take risks without endangering your life. Some equate risk-taking with reckless abandonment, but successful risk takers say absolutely not! In fact, almost all of them insist that before entering uncharted territory, you need to establish boundaries. Determine the point or factor that will cause you to stop. Top poker players know when to go home and when to stay. They understand that the higher the uncertainty, the higher the risk. So the key is to reduce uncertainty by taking calculated risks when the upside outweighs the downside.

Playing out a risk in your mind assesses all the variables, imagining all that could possibly go wrong or right when making a decision. When it feels comfortable and familiar from playing out the different scenarios in your mind, the timing may be right. Of course, it's almost impossible to remove all of the nervousness that naturally occurs with a bold move, so the rule of thumb is to not risk everything. To avoid becoming stretched too thin, risk only small amounts of your resources. The old saying, "never put all your eggs in one basket" is old for a reason—experts agree it's true! The chance of losing it all is just too high. Think about what's most important to you, and factor in the consequences to you and your loved ones by using plain common sense. For example, if buying another franchise territory will jeopardize your ability to pay the mortgage, it probably isn't a good idea.

Most successful risk takers only assume one risky adventure at a time. If all of the stars align for that one opportunity (and even when a few minor ones don't), shoot for the moon. The longer you procrastinate, the greater the likelihood you will never act. Don't let the moon get out of reach.

"Progress always involves risks. You can't steal second base and keep your foot on first." ~ Fred B. Wilcox

"Why not go out on a limb? Isn't that where the fruit is?" ~ Frank Scully

APRIL 16

I will demonstrate determination and commitment

No other human power can match determination and commitment. Some of the most accomplished persons, as well as some of the most challenged strugglers, demonstrate great determination. Twenty-four year old Greg suffered from brain damage with hydrocephalus (brain fluid). His face contorted as he strained out each word. Greg loved art. While working at a craft store during the day, he took as many art classes as his meager salary would afford him, and took meticulous notes. No one gave Greg much notice, until one day he handed out postcards in class announcing an exhibit in a prestigious gallery—featuring *his* artwork. Greg had become a success while no one noticed! His story is a classic one of determination translated into willpower. Greg demonstrated the conviction to master his passion, regardless of the consequences. He didn't strive to be successful or well-known, he just wanted to be the best artist he could possibly be, and the rest took care of itself.

Determination gives birth to persistence as its heart and soul. It turns passion into reality that forces continuous action, and then commitment keeps you there. One person like Greg could accomplish more than a hundred other students who were just interested in art. Greg had pit bull determination, ready to grab onto his passion and never let go.

Passion, determination and commitment will propel you to succeed, like Greg. It's the proverbial "fire in the belly" that cannot be extinguished.

"Gold medals aren't really made of gold. They're made of sweat, determination, and a hard-to-find alloy called guts." ~ Dan Gable

"The quality of a person's life is in direct proportion to their commitment to excellence, regardless of their chosen field of endeavor." ~ Vince Lombardi

APRIL 17

I will build up treasures of joy, not money

During periods of joyfulness, physiological and biochemical changes take place that infuse within us a sense of well being, transforming negative outlooks on life. A joyful attitude soothes even the most sorrowful of occasions. In the purest sense, joy is not an emotion. It is not the same as happiness. More than simply the end result of something pleasant, joy is an attitude of the heart. Truth be told, it is joy—not money—that motivates people to work more efficiently.

According to a study by researchers at the University of Iowa, many employees find greater motivation from a sense of attachment and belonging to a group of co-workers—feelings that bring joy—than they do from money. Chances are the one who chooses money over joy will always strive for more. Joy lets us live in the moment. It centers us with an abundant attitude toward work and life, which in turn tends to attract more abundance in life—including money.

Learning to be content in whatever situation you find yourself calls for an indwelling joy. People who enjoy what they do tend to work harder and produce more. People who are tied to money lose some of their freedom. They may stay at a job they hate, for instance, so that they can earn more money, believing that will make them happy. It's a vicious cycle. We buy more to cheer us up, then have to work at joyless jobs to pay for it all. And it starts all over again.

Verne Teyler gave up a high paying job at E.F. Hutton to begin a home for foster kids. Thirty years later Mr. and Mrs. Teyler are two of the most joyful people on earth. Gaining joy doesn't meaning quitting your job, but it does require a change in attitude. The question is: for whom or what do you work? The answer will tell you if it's worth it. Love, people, God, joy, freedom—all of these are good reasons. Money, not so much.

"Joy is not in things; it is in us." ~ Richard Wagner

"I slept and dreamt that life was joy. I awoke and saw that life was service. I acted and behold, service was joy." ~ Rabindranath Tagore

April 18

I will do what others don't want to do

Wayne H. Huizenga, son of Dutch immigrants, grew up in the Chicago area during the 1940s. After marrying, Wayne and his wife moved to Florida, where Wayne went to work for a garbage collection service. In 1962, after learning the business, he bought a truck and $500 worth of clients from a rubbish service. That was Wayne's first move in what became Waste Management, Inc., the largest waste collection and processing firm in the world, serving some twenty million customers, with revenues of over fourteen billion dollars. And it all started with a dirty job of collecting trash. There must have been days when Wayne wished to be a doctor or lawyer or follow some other wealth-producing path, but he started doing what just about everyone else didn't want to do. That was Wayne's key to success, and it can be yours as well.

Your story may not involve collecting garbage, but it may be about a difficult or lowly task that no one is willing or able to complete. Maybe it's about something that needs to be fixed, or someone who needs help in a hard time. Doing what no one else wants to do doesn't demean us, it elevates others' opinions of us. People see us as a team player, a go-getter, an initiator—someone ready to do whatever it takes to get the job done, including the less desirable things.

The staircase to success still starts at the bottom step. Progress works from the base upward. Whatever keeps most people from doing a thing may be universal, but we can overcome our reservations by taking that first step, and then trusting ourselves to get the job done. Even if we've failed, we at least tried; and, that speaks volumes in terms of our character, strength, and fortitude. And no one can say we did nothing.

"Faith is taking the first step even when you don't see the whole staircase." ~ Martin Luther King, Jr.

"It's the little details that are vital. Little things make big things happen." ~ John Wooden

"Only a life lived for others is a life worthwhile." ~ Albert Einstein

APRIL 19

I will be tactfully assertive

Being treated fairly is not always a given. Sometimes you need to stand up for your rights and beliefs, without being hostile toward others. Tactful assertiveness means adroitly and justly expressing your feelings, opinions, and needs in order to strengthen relationships, reduce stress, and obtain an effective resolution. Assertiveness should not be confused with aggressiveness, which is defined as being self-centered, arrogant, and inconsiderate. Instead, a polite but assertive refusal to accept unfair or excessive requests from others will prevent you from becoming overwhelmed and frustrated.

Being nice is one thing, but when you suppress your needs in order "not to cause trouble," you may be allowing a greedy or dominant person to take advantage of you, and only reinforces negative, self-centered behaviors. Researchers suggest several approaches toward a healthful state of tactful assertiveness.

The first step is to realize when you've been overly passive or compliant, and to recognize your rights as an individual. If you can't say "no" when someone asks you for a favor, you have trouble disagreeing during a meeting, or your spouse or children are controlling your life, you need to assert yourself.

Begin by telling the other person very factually what they've done to upset you. Avoid general accusations such as, "You never listen to me," by using specifics like, "When I asked you to clean your room before ten o'clock, you watched TV instead." Make the other person aware of the consequence of their neglect: "Because your room wasn't cleaned, we won't be able to go to the game this afternoon." Be open about how you feel, but don't get emotional. Make eye contact, be firm but pleasant, stand or sit-up straight, and focus positively on what can help both of you reach your goals. Start your sentences with "I" instead of "You," so you don't come across as attacking. Saying "I was affected by…" shows honesty and accountability, and avoids blame. Ask questions to gain a complete understanding. The goal is to reach a mutually beneficial win-win.

"You don't get harmony when everybody sings the same note." ~ Doug Floyd

APRIL 20

I will maximize my time

Each of us has twenty-four hours in a day, but it's just not enough to get things done. Still others seem able to get everything they need accomplished, no problem. What's the difference? For one, effective time managers set goals to know where they're going and what needs to be done in order of priority. That requires discipline, but after practice it can become a normal routine. Prioritizing tasks is essential.

Without assigning each activity in order of importance, we can work hard without necessarily being smart about it. Even a to-do list can be ineffective if it's not listed in order of highest valued tasks from first to last. If there's a deadline of today, and if there's a personal loss if it doesn't get done, it shoots right to the top. Postponing a task should only be done if another more important and more urgently needed task takes its place.

Procrastination is a lethal temptress. If you are a constant procrastinator, ask yourself the tough questions—are you afraid to fail, are you avoiding something? Keep yourself on track by considering the consequences of postponement. If interruptions consistently interfere with your ability to complete things, determine which urgent matters actually require your attention, and decide if they can be scheduled, such as setting up a meeting, delegating, or managing in some other way. If an interruption exceeds the level of importance of your top priorities, deal with it at that time.

Developing and keeping a schedule factors in not only planned activities, but also inevitable interruptions. With only twenty-four hours in a day, do your activities in order: 1) goals and commitments first; 2) do the things you want to do, but don't have to do, second; 3) do your small work third; 4) do your chit-chat or idle entertaining things last. Don't go onto the next set of tasks until you've completed the first. This way you'll master your time.

"The key is not spending time, but in investing it." ~ Stephen R. Covey

"It's not enough to be busy, so are the ants. The question is, what are we busy about?" ~ Henry Thoreau

APRIL 21

I will stay positive

It's not easy to stay positive after being hit with challenges of all kinds, but experts say we can train ourselves to change our thoughts from negative to positive. Researchers have documented that staying positive is healthy. People who've consciously remembered at least once a week things for which they are grateful experienced fewer physical complaints than those who did not. Pessimistic people increased their risk of dying by nearly twenty-percent over a thirty-year period. The good news is that people obsessed with negative thoughts were able to transform their unhealthy habits, and their brain activity changed with the transformation.

We know that to remain positive we must practice an "attitude of gratitude." We can do so by keeping a journal, reaching out to thank others, being still and focusing on pleasant surroundings, and sharing good experiences. Studies show that people who share good news about a pleasant experience enjoy it even more. Focusing on the positive is essential to develop a pattern of positive thinking. Instead of dreading the future, imagine a future where your dreams come true. When challenges arise, project a positive outcome for the situation.

It's equally important to suppress any negative thinking. In a study of performers, those obsessed with fear of failure performed worse than those who were distracted from their worries. Ask yourself if your concern will be important a year from now. If not, why waste valuable time on it? Distract yourself by watching a movie, exercising, or reading. Cognitive-behavioral therapy helps reverse negative thoughts by challenging the validity of the thought: are you really a poor communicator or is it just your imagination? Take solace that your previous accomplishments predict a greater likelihood that you can do it again. If you've failed, don't use that as an excuse to falsely reason you'll fail again. Instead, learn from the mistake. Play devil's advocate with yourself by reversing negative expectations with a positive projection. And don't read too much into a situation. If that person hasn't called yet, maybe it's because he is just too busy.

"Some people grumble that roses have thorns; I am grateful that thorns have roses." ~ Alphonse Karr

APRIL 22

I will get the monkey off my back

One of Harvard Business Review's best-selling reprints ever was a December 1974 publication entitled, *Management Time: Who's Got the Monkey?* It helps to answer the question as to why managers are typically running out of time while their subordinates are typically running out of work. Too many managers, the article concluded, tend to assume the burden of figuring out their subordinates' problems for them. If Jimmy can't figure out how to operate an accounting system, the manager feels obligated to either teach him or figure out a way for Jimmy to learn it. In that scenario, which one carries the monkey on his back—Jimmy or his manager? By trying to solve Jimmy's problem for him, the manager is carrying the monkey. If the manager simply told Jimmy he would have to come-up with a solution on his own using the resources available to him, the manager would have kept the monkey on Jimmy's back, eliminating one more time-drain.

Monkeys are the distractions of extra work or tasks. They prevent you from completing your important goals. As soon as we accept someone else's responsibility, we take the monkey. It can be anything from a lost file to a frustrated customer to a simple request for help from a friend.

The first lesson in keeping the monkey from leaping on your back is to just say "no." If you are a people pleaser who always wants to take care of others, practice being more assertive. When someone asks you to do something, rather than just doing it, ask them to explain more about the task and what's involved, and then challenge them to come-up with a solution on their own as an opportunity for growth. If the monkey is from your manager, try to explain what you're already working on. See if you can't postpone the monkey, in order to do what's top on your list of priorities. Don't give-in. Use tactful assertiveness.

"He who is carried on another's back does not appreciate how far off the town is." ~ African Proverb

"The price of greatness is responsibility." ~ Winston Churchill

APRIL 23

I will coach others effectively

Every successful person has gotten where they are in large part thanks to coaches. Coaches can be mentors, parents, managers, and friends. Coaching involves listening, observing, evaluating, encouraging, supporting, and advising. It is a process that promotes learning and development, leading to improved performance. Effective coaches possess the knowledge and understanding of who they are coaching, their needs, and the appropriate skills and techniques that will motivate them to succeed. They build a relationship of mutual trust and define clear objectives for each training session.

No coaching can move forward unless the other person agrees they need to improve their performance. Sometimes the coach needs to cite specific examples of that need in order to gain acceptance. Once you're on the same page, ask the person to identify her own solutions by avoiding the temptation to jump in with your own. Help her to choose her option and encourage her choice for moving forward. Remain empathic with her frustrations or excuses without feeling compelled to agree. Rather than simply saying, "You did a good job," provide timely feedback with specific comments like, "I really liked the way you asked questions first and actively listened." Rather than judging, act as an observer by noting what you've seen or heard, as in, "I noticed that you jumped into selling the benefits before gaining agreement." Remember to use a genuine and friendly tone of voice.

Most people have a negative bias toward criticism, so use the "Rule of Four." Don't force it, but ease into the conversation at least four positive things he has accomplished along with the one area needing improvement. People will naturally want to improve if they feel recognized and appreciated. Keeping the coaching upbeat goes a long way toward realizing the end goal.

"All coaching is, is taking a player where he can't take himself." ~ Bill McCartney

"Make sure that the team members know they are working with you, not for you." ~ John Wooden

APRIL 24

I will make deadlines irrelevant

Don't worry so much about deadlines; just do the job as quickly and as efficiently as possible. That's the modus operandi of the "get it done" mentality—and it works. It begins with defining expectations upfront. What is the reporting mechanism (verbal, written, email, information required) and what is the absolute deadline? For more than one assignment, the priority of each must be clearly delineated and agreed upon. If you are the delegator of the task, make sure you follow the same steps you'd expect of the one to whom you are making demands. The deliverables must be clearly stated. What is the desired outcome? Include as many specific details as possible. Converting compliance to commitment is not only agreeing to the expectations, but also taking ownership of them. Consider the responsibility as mine. The onus is not just on the one giving it.

The second step to "do it now" is by creating a sense of urgency, thereby making the deadline irrelevant. If it's a high priority, negotiate other tasks to a later date. W. Clement Stone, founder of an insurance empire that grew to one of the largest in the world, made all his employees recite the same phrase over and over at the start of each workday, "Do it now!" Make that your mantra each day.

Here's a method for getting it done: Once you've thoroughly completed all your agreed upon requirements for a task, including assembling the necessary information, click on an imaginary two-minute timer to make a confirmed decision. The same goes for multiple priorities. Once you've made an informed decision, do it. Research shows that the best leaders have a high tolerance for ambiguity, because they are able to act boldly without overanalyzing. Use the vast majority of your time for taking action, not for decision making. In the professional world, experience and thoroughness take a back seat to accomplishment. Delivering or exceeding the expected results means everything. Deadlines establish a parameter, but the deadline usually means the least acceptable timeline. Those who excel will generally complete tasks well before the deadline and have enough time to spare to volunteer for other responsibilities that will further elevate their value in the organization.

"Don't make excuses for why you can't get it done.
Focus on all the reasons why you must do it." ~ Author Unknown

APRIL 25

I will be charismatic

Let's face it. If there were twenty strangers in a room, the most charismatic one would meet with the most approval. Charismatic people actually make you feel different. Maybe you don't see yourself as a charming person who turns heads at every corner. What is it they do differently? Charismatic people possess an exceptional ability to connect emotionally, using their voice and their expressions. It's been documented that highly charismatic people even use more muscles in their face. Their mood is infectious because they practice three essential skills: mirroring, matching and leading.

Mirroring is reflecting the behaviors of the other person. Relaxed posture is met with relaxed posture, and so forth. *Matching* the other person's gestures and mannerisms establishes a rapport with them, allowing us to *lead* that person through a subconscious reaction. For example, say after mirroring their behavior and picking-up on a connection, we ask if the person would like to do something. That's *leading*. Research also shows that some people are just naturally charismatic—"transmitters of emotion."

Even if you're not a natural "transmitter," you can still train others to feel your emotions. A warm smile usually elicits a smile in return in the same way that an angry expression can infect another person with anger. Charismatic people actually take this a step further. They can tune into the subconscious mind as easily as they relate to the conscious mind. For example, asking someone to hand them something is a direct appeal to the conscious mind. In saying that a certain situation will make the person *feel stress*, the charismatic person is leading the subconscious mind. That's called the power of suggestion. Empathy plays a large role in charisma, but so do skills that physically relate to both the conscious and subconscious. You can ask for something, for example, but if like a hypnotist you suggest that doing that something will cause the other person to relate to an emotion or experience, you are transmitting emotion to that person, thereby increasing your charisma. It's all about influencing the emotions through both subtle and direct persuasion.

"Charm is the quality in others that makes us more satisfied with ourselves." ~ Henri Frederic Ameil

APRIL 26

I will keep it simple

Ever heard of the KISS Principle: **K**eep **I**t **S**imple **S**tupid? It's a foundational principle by which successful marketing and sales people present ideas that will resonate with their target prospects. New concepts, products, and ideas that are communicated using language that is familiar *only* to the presenter often elicit a confused or negative response. When these same messages are then presented using simple, clearly understood terminology, the natural reaction is: "Why didn't you just say so in the first place?"

Because we know our subject matter so well, we can be tempted to speak either over someone's head or in a way that loses their attention. A plumber is an expert in plumbing. A product specialist is expert in their product. The plumber speaking to the customer should not reference a problem due to a "revent pipe"; rather he should talk about "a pipe that connects with a waste pipe." Every profession has its "jargon," and using it within the profession is expected. But when speaking to those outside your area of expertise, keep it simple.

Keeping a discussion strictly relevant to the other person's interests prevents discussion burnout. If someone cannot relate to a discussion point, or if they are not interested in hearing about the history or details of something, their attention will quickly fade. The human attention span is at best two to five minutes times the person's age, and usually no more than twenty minutes for the average adult. The situation largely determines attention span. For example, a doctor who has one minute in between patients will have an attention span of no more than one minute. Regardless of how long we have to capture someone's interest or attention, the best principle is to be concise and relevant. In other words, Keep It Simple, SMARTY.

"Keep it simple." ~ Alfred Eisenstaedt

"Simplicity means the achievement of maximum effect with minimum means." ~ Dr. Koichi Kawana

APRIL 27

I will balance my focus on results with my focus on people

Two extremes can be found in the workplace: those who focus on pampering co-workers with every privilege possible, even if their results are consistently below standards; and, those who focus on performance, while considering people as little more than chess pieces in a game of winning at all costs. Neither extreme works well in an organization.

Academic research suggests that results-focused leaders drive employee performance to achieve goals, albeit with a tendency to be impersonal. They tend to deliver on productivity, but the lack of human attention can lead to high turnover and low morale. People-focused leaders are considered to be thoughtful, and tend to build others' confidence and abilities. This type of leadership delivers a high degree of satisfaction within the organization, but efficiency may be compromised in favor of treating low performers fairly.

Distinguished leadership embraces both a people and a results orientation. Neither should be mutually exclusive. A high degree of social awareness and a commitment to others' well-being, coupled with a dedication to managing performance against goals will produce an effective and successful outcome in the workplace.

Healthy organizations integrate learning into their culture in a way that is strategic and drives both individual performance and business results. Focus on designing strategic plans with both personal and organizational goals in a *learning environment* engages people to deliver. Since execution is even more important than strategy, a strong leader creates team motivation *and* connects peoples' actions to the organizational goals so that each person understands how their role fits within the whole. This creates a healthy learning organization that is both people *and* results oriented.

"Thoughts lead to feelings. Feelings lead to actions. Actions lead to results." ~ T. Harv Eker

"Leadership is the process of social influence in which one person can enlist the aid and support of others in the accomplishment of a common task." ~ M. Chemers

APRIL 28

I will build my network

In order to find a job, get new business or advance your position in today's world, building a network is crucial. That old adage, "it's not what you know, it's who you know," is not far from the truth. Networking involves creating a list of people you know and exchanging ideas, referrals, and contacts. It's a give and take relationship, with an equal weighting for both. According to Debbie Campbell, Senior Consultant for outsourcing giant Right Management, you should participate in networking groups like professional associations, networking events, groups that meet routinely to exchange professional relationships, and online networks like LinkedIn.

For job hunters, the best approach is to meet or talk with people in your network. Says Campbell, "If someone tells me they had three introductory phone interviews that week, and another person tells me they met with one influential person in their network that same week, I would say that the person who met with that key person in their network had a more successful week." The key is to remain visible by getting out and connecting with people.

Building relationships is the primary objective, and to develop deeper relationships it takes some investment of time and effort, before you start asking for favors. The people in your network have to get to know you and what you have to offer before they'll trust you enough to enter into a collaboration. That can involve meeting with them in settings other than business. Get to know people outside of your industry and interests as well. You never know what influencers may expand your opportunities in new and improved ways.

Never ask for something from someone you've just met. The important takeaway is that networking is about building deeper relationships. Favors will happen naturally if you've developed those relationships. Always give as much as you can, understanding that you may get what you want in the long term. Be the go-to person, not the I-want person. Reaching out to a well-developed connection should be comfortable and mutually rewarding.

"The richest people in the world look for and build networks, everyone else looks for work." ~ Robert Kiyosaki

APRIL 29

I will do what gives me energy

Some things give us energy, and some things suck the energy right out of us. We can't do our best if we are surrounded by a lot of negative energy, such as mean or overly needy people or toxic environments that replace our natural vigor with fatigue. Some people are natural naysayers. When you approach them with a spring in your step that says you want to do something, they look at you like you're in a clown outfit.

Some people get a charge out of others' failures. You can decide to plug into their negativism or unplug yourself from those kinds of people. Tell yourself, "I will succeed no matter what others say. I will not allow my aspirations to be someone's exasperation." Avoid the drain influencers whenever and wherever possible. Tell them you will not be able to spend as much time with them because of a project, a craft class—anything that serves as a suitable replacement to your normal interactions. Just get rid of negative friends.

Ultimately, we cannot control all our external events, but we can control our reaction to them. We can also use relaxing methods like prayer or meditation, soothing music, and exercise. Throw out anything you associate with people who have hurt you so you won't be constantly reminded of them. Find a new job or a new position or a different department if the workplace is a constant drain. Try to surround yourself with positive people. Make a list of the energy fillers, or energy suckers in your life. Then start planning your life around the energy fillers, and start eliminating as many of the energy suckers as possible.

It's OK to let go of the things that cause you to power down, because success happens when you charge your batteries through positive experiences and people. In the words of Aulus Cornelius Celsus (ca 25 BC – ca 50), a Roman encyclopaedist:

"Live in rooms full of light; avoid heavy food; be moderate in the drinking of wine; take a massage, baths, exercise, and gymnastics; fight insomnia with gentle rocking or the sound of running water; change surroundings and take long journeys; strictly avoid frightening ideas; indulge in cheerful conversation and amusements; listen to music." ~ Aulus Cornelius Celsus

APRIL 30

I will interview well

You just received a call to interview for what seems like a terrific job—now what? The next step is researching the company. Gather as much background information as possible. You may be asked questions about the company, and being able answer from an informed standpoint adds credibility to your overall impression.

Prepare in advance answers to some of the most common questions: 1) "Why are you interested in this position and why do you want to change jobs, or why were you let go?" 2) What were your responsibilities? 3) What were your greatest challenges, and how did you handle them? 4) What did you like and dislike about your current/previous position? 5) What is your greatest strength and weakness? 6) What have you learned from your mistakes? 6) What was your most significant accomplishment/failure in this position? 7) What was it like working for your supervisor? 8) What problems have you experienced at work and with your manager? Be honest and concise with your answers. Don't ramble on with unnecessary details.

A common technique used by companies is called Behavior Based Interviewing. Questions are tailored to determine future performance based on the candidate's answers to how they handled past performance. Beyond simple questions about your background, the questioner asks you to provide a detailed explanation as to how you handled certain responsibilities, your objective, your process for achieving the result, and the outcome.

Preparing for this kind of interview requires that you think through situations that have demonstrated your success in practicing the skills and values you consider as strengths. Emphasize how your assets can benefit the company.

On the day of the interview show up about ten minutes early. Bring extra copies of your résumé. Keep breath mints on hand, take a deep breath, and try to remain as calm as possible. Answer honestly, but don't focus on the negatives. After the interview, follow-up with a thank you note.

"So many people out there have no idea what they want to do for a living, but they think that by going on job interviews they'll magically figure it out. If you're not sure, that message comes out loud and clear in the interview." ~ Todd Bermont

MAY

THE ONE AND ONLY YOU

MAY 1

I will show mercy

Barbara, a company vice president, berated people with her short temper. Since her authority covered most of the company, those subject to her outbursts felt powerless to do anything about it. She hadn't always been this abrupt. It was just over the past two months that Barbara's direct style had become nearly tyrannical. Morale fell to an abysmal level, and the CEO seemed clueless.

Jean, a customer service representative about four ranks beneath Barbara, became sensitive to Barbara's increasing isolation within the department. Once a meticulous dresser, Barbara arrived wearing mismatched colors and with disheveled hair. The office "water cooler" talks centered on how best to get rid of Barbara. The vitriol toward her increased almost daily—except for Jean, who decided enough was enough. She walked into Barbara's office uninvited, closed the door, and said, "What's going on, Barbara? You have really been difficult recently and I just want to help you if I can."

As if she'd been waiting for an invitation, Barbara let it all out. Her husband was having an affair, and she had just discovered it about two months ago. "Barbara, you must be devastated," Jean said as Barbara nodded. Jean gave her a hug and said, "I'll do anything to support you through this time, Barbara. I've got your back." Barbara's attitude began to change for the positive. She and Jean became friends and gradually the department's morale rose again, all because Jean showed Barbara mercy.

We all need mercy, because we all stumble. Instead of judging Barbara's behavior, Jean confronted the problem. Whenever someone hurts us, we have a choice to either use up our energy for retaliation or for resolution. We can't do both. People are grumpy for a reason, and sometimes an offer to listen and to help is just the right solution for turning them around.

"May we not succumb to thoughts of violence and revenge today, but rather to thoughts of mercy and compassion. We are to love our enemies that they might be returned to their right minds." ~ M. Williamson

MAY 2

I will live a life of integrity

Integrity is more than simply doing the right thing; it's about demonstrating the quality of character that can withstand the pressures to act otherwise. At his funeral, World War II veteran and dockworker turned senior executive Robert William Kay received numerous homages testifying to his life of integrity. In war, Robert's unflinching heroism helped save a fellow soldier after a Kamikaze attack. In work, he refused temptations to bend the truth when mistakes were made by his company, and despite some unpopular decisions, Robert's hard work paid off with a series of promotions. There are some ways in which this youthful man built his life of integrity over the years that can apply to all of us.

First, he was honest with himself and others. He questioned his own motives, and rarely excused his mistakes. Second, he sought the wise counsel of executives and experts who were in positions that Robert wanted to achieve. Third, Robert had great interpersonal skills, but he wasn't a devout people pleaser. His long-term vision of what needed to be done outweighed short-term opportunities to just get along. During hard times, his faith served as his foundation. When Robert made a mistake, he was the first to admit it. He even joked about his shortcomings. Fourth, Robert was a man of integrity, acting with the same character, whether seen or unseen. Those who knew Robert during all walks of his life said the same thing about him—he was not perfect, but he was the same to everyone he met. Finally, Robert taught all of us who knew him that integrity comes to those who earnestly search their past, and who genuinely commit to changing those behaviors that must be aligned to the moral principles that define good character.

Robert wasn't the same person at eighteen years of age that he was on the date of his death at eighty-five. He lived a life of continual growth and development toward a goal of being good; and, although none of us are always good, striving for goodness in everything is a noble endeavor.

"The foundation stones for a balanced success are honesty, character, integrity, faith, love and loyalty." ~ Zig Ziglar

MAY 3

I will never let possessions own me

It's just stuff! Granted, some of it is really nice stuff, but none of our material possessions have any lasting value. One man tried. He owned a cherry-condition 1957 convertible Cadillac that he religiously cared for each day of his life. Not a scratch could be found on the car because, in order to maintain the car's almost perfect condition, he rarely drove it. In his will, this wealthy man stipulated that he wanted to be buried with his 1957 Cadillac.

To accommodate his wish, the digging crew dug a hole large enough to fit the car and the man, who was conveniently placed in the driver's seat per his final wish, unable to go anywhere. Ironically, he was also unaware that his spotless car was eventually covered in dirt as the crew filled-in the grave. Too bad he didn't quite realize that the most valuable things in life—God, family, friends, love, respect, giving and knowledge—don't cost any money, and that the return on investing in these things can endure for generations following our passing.

Things like cars, houses and most other tangibles are liabilities. They take money out of your pocket each month. Our goal should be to surround ourselves with people and things that give us true value. Certainly we should enjoy what brings us happiness, but our possessions should be weighed carefully. *Am I doing what's best for myself, or just seeking the approval of others? Is what I own preventing me from investing in more lasting and more important treasures?*

Instead of spending money on things, consider spending it on experiences and understanding. When we spend money and time just to feel a certain way, like status or self-worth, maybe the possession has started to possess us. Consider instead a thing's functionality. Disown your possessions and reinvest that time and energy into valuable relationships. The perfect balance would be to have *just enough* of something but not too much. Those who live with this combination are the most contented persons.

"Anything you cannot relinquish when it has outlived its usefulness possesses you, and in this materialistic age a great many of us are possessed by our possessions." ~ Peace Pilgrim

MAY 4

I will have a harmonious passion

Is doing what you love, and loving what you do enough? What if the passion consumes your time to the point you can do little else? What if someone has a passion for something destructive? According to "Ruminations and Flow: Why do People With a More Harmonious Passion Experience Higher Wellbeing?," a report in the *Journal of Happiness Studies*, the answer lies with the type of passion. Basically, it says that an "obsessive passion" is bad for you, but a "harmonious passion" is good for you. Co-author Robert J. Vallerand explains that a harmonious passion can be controlled.

A teacher may love her work, but must be careful not to let it dominate her life, thus creating an unhealthful work-life balance. Obsessive passions are those that become addictive, such as an online stock trader who consistently borrows large sums of money to gamble on a few risky stocks. The practice of more harmonious passions, the study concluded, leads to greater wellbeing. Those with an obsessive passion tended to reflect on their passion while engaging in some other activity. In other words, they think about it constantly.

One of the ways to ensure a harmonious passion without the downside of it consuming you, is to surround yourself with people who can inspire your success while holding you accountable. Friends and coworkers can prevent you from going off-track while encouraging you through the tough times. Also, test the outcomes. A healthful harmonious passion gives you energy, boosts your confidence, and naturally fuels your perseverance to move forward despite the obstacles. A harmonious passion that leads to a more harmonious life in all of your important areas is good to follow.

"Passion is energy. Feel the power that comes from focusing on what excites you." ~ Oprah Winfrey

"If passion drives you, let reason hold the reins." ~ Benjamin Franklin

"Never let your persistence and passion turn into stubbornness and ignorance." ~ Anthony J. D'Angelo

MAY 5

I will demonstrate strong interpersonal skills

Let's all just get along. That's easy to say, but how do we do it? Even the most talented people in the world can fail if their social skills are subpar. Thankfully, there are proven skills to make people really like you, and anyone can learn them. Generally persuasive people convey two key impressions—warmth and grit. Notice how those who genuinely care about you elicit a warm feeling in return? People who display genuine caring coupled with the courage and strength of character to get things done usually merit some degree of admiration.

What do the people you like have in common? Chances are they have a positive outlook on life. People like to be around pleasant people. Second, likeable people take a sincere interest in others. Ask about others' interests and accomplishments. Encourage them and make them feel valued. People who feel valued are likely to value you too. Find out what's happening in their lives. Know the names of spouses and children. Keep a calendar of birthdays to send them a greeting, and be aware of other important occasions.

When you're speaking to someone, give them your full attention—eye contact, no texting. Ask for their opinions to show that you value their input. When speaking to someone, reflect and acknowledge their comments to show that you are listening. For example, you might say something like, "I really hear your passion behind this project" (that's reflective language, as in "I hear you,") or, "I understand your concern over the timeline" (show empathy). Try to be thoughtful with your communications, and interject a little (appropriate) humor once in awhile to ease feelings.

Much of relationship is about creating an inviting and supportive environment. Those who treat everyone with the same respect, from the CEO to the assistant, usually earn mutual respect. People generally don't appreciate gossipers (even if they listen to them), but they do appreciate someone who recognizes others. When conflicts arise—and they *will*—try to facilitate some reconciliation. People often appreciate the peacemaker. Finally, keep your emotions on an even-keel by demonstrating good judgment and sound wisdom. Heck, you might even be able to run for mayor!

"You can make more friends in two months by becoming really interested in other people than you can in two years by trying to get other people interested in you." ~ Dale Carnegie

MAY 6

I will be loyal

U.S. Navy SEALS are the elite branch of the U.S. Navy's principal special operations force. When a tough assignment is required, military experts know to rely on them as their first option, as they did when eliminating the threat of terrorist Osama bin Laden. Their training entails extraordinarily severe physical and mental punishment. Their mission success rate is one of the best of any organization. What drives their uncompromising determination and success? It is the Navy SEAL Creed: "My loyalty to Country and Team is beyond reproach."

In an age when loyalty in corporations and among employees is low, we would do well to consider the SEAL's primary reasons for their unparalleled success as declared by their Creed. It is summed-up in one overriding principle: We either succeed together or we fail together—there are no individual heroes and no one gets left behind. If a person makes a mistake, it is addressed behind closed doors and not publicly, such as in a meeting. In other words, praise publicly and criticize privately. Loyalty is built on trust. If someone knows you've "got their back," and that you will be open and transparent with them, they learn to trust you. It is earned each day when we put the welfare of our team, our partners, our relationships and our customers ahead of our own self-serving interests.

Harvard Business School author Frederick Reichheld discovered *Loyalty-Based Management*, which is based on valuing employees, customers, and investors. It's a way to predict with pinpoint accuracy the future growth and profits of any company. Those who improved retention loyalty by just five percentage points, such as Lexus (the market leader in customer loyalty), realized a doubling of their company's profits. Loyalty to others breeds success in almost every facet of our day-to-day operations. In fact, loyalty generates an exceptional return on investment.

"Loyalty means nothing unless it has at its heart the absolute principle of self-sacrifice." ~ Woodrow Wilson

"Leadership is a two-way street, loyalty up and loyalty down." ~ Grace Murray Hopper

MAY 7

I will develop a sense of urgency

What is the most critical factor for creating success? Some would say good habits. Many claim it's being a leader. Still others say it's hard work. While these are key factors, when it comes to getting things done, developing a sense of urgency ranks at the very top.

People and organizations overwhelmed with responsibilities and sixty-hour workweeks find it difficult to cut through the myriad of decisions to get the most essential things done. People who represent a sense of urgency to others can cut through the red tape and make it happen. Decisions tend to vacillate or percolate until the status quo takes over—that is, until someone who imparts urgency drives the process forward to completion.

If you want to make things happen, your skill in adapting others to your objective is key. Begin by evaluating what decisions have been simmering on your mental stove for a while, and make a sixty-minute decision to implement your decision *now*. When others see you as being decisive, it engages them to act as well. This includes getting tasks or reports done for others that have been sitting for too long.

Likewise, ask yourself what responsibilities from others are due to you. Try moving up the due date or quickening the process by making what's owed you move to the top of the other person's to-do list—without sounding too pushy. It can be tricky, but try it by saying something like: "I fully trust in your ability to make it happen because I believe in your skills and abilities!" Establish a deadline and challenge others to beat that deadline if at all possible by offering a reward for doing so.

Urgency is a state of mind. Instead of accepting the status quo, ask yourself and others why something can't be done better, and sooner. We tend to accomplish what we expect of others and ourselves. An ever-present attitude of getting it done urgently inspires the will to accomplish something vigorously and expeditiously.

"Without a sense of urgency, desire loses its value." ~ Jim Rohn

MAY 8

I will nurture my friendships

Ever heard the saying, "you can't make an old friend"? Some friends come and go from our lives. Some last a lifetime. All of them color a life of success with indelible imprints. Without them, all the riches in the world would not matter. But friendships require as much, if not more, nurturing than our careers. Social networks and new technologies like Facebook, LinkedIn, email, and texting have made staying in touch a bit easier in recent years, but true friendships require that personal touch that comes from a phone call or a note of encouragement. Recognizing important events with a call or a card tells someone they're special. Forgetting them sends the opposite message. Sometimes the most impactful thing you can do is a simple call or note like this: "I just wanted to say 'hi' and to tell you how much you are appreciated and how proud I am of you."

Don't wait for an occasion or a favor to contact your friends. In our busy world, sometimes we only think of reaching out to a friend when we need something. There should be a balance between encouraging them and satisfying our need for something from them. Ask your friend what you can do for them. Offer to babysit, or surprise them with a treat or gift. Knowing him like you do, occasionally give your friend what he really wants—something homemade, a new recipe, or tickets to his favorite entertainment.

Friendships center around honest communication, so if there's a problem, don't avoid it. Resolving differences actually strengthens friendships. Settle disagreements with forgiveness and a future focus, as in "from now on I will _____," or "next time I will not _____." Determine what both of you can do to build a better future, based on what you learned about your mistakes. Put the emphasis on what *you* will do. The foundation of a strong friendship is constructed of consistently positive discourse.

"A friend is one who knows you and loves you just the same." ~ Elbert Hubbard

"It is one of the blessings of old friends that you can afford to be stupid with them." ~ Ralph Waldo Emerson

MAY 9

I will always keep playing

Who says adults have to give up swing sets and toys? Allowing the little kid inside you to play primes the imagination. Play also increases productivity, job satisfaction, and well-being. Studies have also shown that introducing play into the workplace decreases stress, absenteeism, and health related costs.

Several years ago a popular and effective management system using fun activities was introduced by John Christensen called The FISH! Philosophy. It was inspired by the energizing work culture at Seattle's Pike Place Fish Market, where workers joke around and throw fish at each other before packaging them for customers. FISH! centers on basic four principles: 1) *Be There*, as being emotionally present for people; 2) *Play* by tapping into your natural creativity; 3) *Make Their Day* by finding ways to serve or delight people for the sheer sake of being the person who you want to be; and 4) *Choose Your Attitude*, which means taking responsibility for what life throws at you. The paradigm shift is that work can be fun and that attitudes can be improved by changing peoples' motives.

Many work environments that practice the FISH! philosophy introduced toys into the environment—like scooters, funny hats, and squishy balls that encouraged workers to release their innovative juices. Placing things like Play-Doh and other toys in meetings, believe it or not, actually increased peoples' attention span. Some eclectic companies in the high-tech and biotech industries have allowed pets to come to work, and encouraged a casual work environment where people could take off their shoes. As a result, people enjoyed coming to work more, and they maintained a more focused and creative approach, thereby increasing productivity. The lesson here is that being a kid again once in awhile can boost your energy and make you a better performer. It's OK to play. Really. It's even *necessary* to have fun in order to boost your success!

"You're never too old to do goofy stuff."
~ Ward Cleaver, from the TV show Leave it to Beaver

"You will find more happiness growing down than up." ~ Author Unknown

MAY 10

I will develop patience

"I want patience, and I want it now!" Have you ever been around people who seem to stoke crises? Impatient people may be successful in the short-term, but eventually their impetuous nature leads to burnout and resentment. Success is about trial and error, like a researcher who devises a plan and finally reaches a successful outcome on the tenth try. If that same researcher were to become impatient and give up after only three attempts, his work will fail. Developing patience involves going through trials and persevering, recognizing why we became impatient, and forgiving ourselves when we mess-up. Critical thoughts make us more impatient, so we have to show mercy both to others and to ourselves.

Experts in patience-therapy suggest that we train ourselves by trying to achieve little wins before tackling the bigger pet peeves, such as diverting our attention when waiting in line or playing soothing music in traffic congestion. Impatient urges are difficult to overcome. We have to relinquish our position as judge, and not look to those we may view as enjoying more success—like that spoiled former college roommate who is now a wealthy executive.

We need to understand what triggers our anger and irritations, and then realize our feelings of discomfort *can* be overcome. Trials that steel our character and forge greater patience may come from the outside, but it's our inner mindset that allows them to become a source of intolerance. *We* allow the annoyance, not the outside situation. Some psychologists try to re-train the mind by asking their patients to recognize when the bubbling-up effect of irritation begins to boil over. Rather than immediately trying to fix the problem, we need to uncover what caused the episode of impatience. Some people become hurt and then start telling themselves a story about how a delay or unfairness will wreak havoc. It's better to say something like: "Sure, this makes me feel uncomfortable, but I can get through it"; or, "So I made a mistake. I can live with my flaws." Just think how much easier life would be with patience.

"We could never learn to be brave and patient, if there were only joy in the world." ~ Helen Keller

MAY 11

I will be self-disciplined

After interviewing with several companies, junior military officer Joel received several job offers. He accepted one to become a sales person for a large company. Having succeeded in every endeavor he faced since Little League baseball, Joel had graduated top of his class. He was a sure bet to succeed. A little over one month after starting the job, Joel went AWOL. His manager couldn't find him. Finally Joel called his supervisor and said he just couldn't do the job. He had been so accustomed to following a rigid schedule with well-defined rules that he couldn't cope with the independence of being a sales person who had to manage everything by himself. Joel lacked self-discipline. He required some selective training to create new habits of thought and action.

Developing self-discipline starts with harnessing the power of routine. It involves acting according to thought patterns instead of responding to how you feel. For example, allocating a specific time each day of the week for tasks, and not diverting from that schedule is a trained way of thinking. This kind of discipline forces you to go the gym instead of watching that TV show, or to say "no" to that extra bowl of ice cream. It's a constant awareness of what you are doing in comparison to what you must do. It takes time and commitment. If you struggle with commitment, start tracking your progress. People tend to respect what they inspect.

Self-discipline is a little like having a Vince Lombardi or some other internal coach inside of you, reminding you of what you need to do and encouraging you along the way. Almost all successful people think with a long-term perspective. They can delay immediate gratification for the sake of longer term payoffs, so they can achieve their goals. This means doing the hard things first—like eating your vegetables before dessert. Contrary to popular belief, people who are self-disciplined actually enjoy life more. Remember how good you felt after accomplishing a task that once daunted you? Let that memory reframe your resistance. Think of the task as enjoyable, and you're more likely to do it.

"Discipline enables you to think first and act second." ~ Joyce Meyer

MAY 12

I will make cost irrelevant

What's the number one reason why individuals and companies fail to sell and market their products? Answer: they fail to make the cost of their product irrelevant. That may sound a little like an oxymoron, because shouldn't everyone be concerned with the cost of something? Well, yes, the consumer should make sure a product is affordable, but their reason for buying should have less to do its cost and more to do with its benefits. In fact, only ten to fifteen percent of prospects put price first. More often than not, concerns over cost are related not to the price of an item but to its usefulness in comparison to its cost.

If price is mentioned as a reason for not buying a service or product, the first step toward addressing this concern is to uncover why it is a concern. For example, say you are going on a ski vacation in Colorado and you live in Florida, so you need to buy a warm jacket for skiing, but since you'll only use the jacket for one week a year, you don't want to pay too much for it. Cost in that case is only a valid concern if the jacket will keep you from freezing, as opposed to a thinner one that might ruin your vacation. But in order to sell their product, the sales person and manufacturer have to believe in the superiority of their product.

Sales and marketing people fail to sell their product if they do not resolutely believe in the value of it. Value is worth a premium if the benefits outweigh the cost, and customers believe this. Otherwise, why buy bottled water rather than just getting it from the tap? You get the point. It's different if someone genuinely doesn't have the money to purchase an item, but in that case they wouldn't likely be in the market for it. If a prospect hyper-focuses on price, they don't believe in the value. Take the time to ask the right questions. Discuss the cost-versus-benefit based on what the customer needs, and break down the actual costs if necessary. That $200 quality jacket might cost out to only $28.57 per recreational day and would contribute to a more comfortable vacation. It all centers on perceived value. As Jim Rembach said, "When cost is number one in importance, you've already lost."

"When you can't compete on cost, compete on quality." ~ James Dyson

"Joy has not cost." ~ Marianne Williamson

MAY 13

I will use the power of compartmentalization

Strangely enough, the concept of compartmentalization was introduced to America during the scandal involving President Bill Clinton's indiscretion with White House intern Monica Lewinsky. It was said that Clinton used this psychological tool (subconsciously) to manage the stress that resulted from separating this dalliance from the myriad of presidential responsibilities around him. Military training uses compartmentalization to ward off the stresses of warfare.

The process of compartmentalization places two or more conflicting thoughts, beliefs, values, or activities of one's life in separate mental boxes. Hence, the compartmentalizer believes their topics have nothing to do with each other, thus eliminating any internal conflict that might arise should the opposing worlds come in contact with each other. Used positively, compartmentalizing can prevent someone from bleeding over a negative (a bad day at the office) into a positive (caring for a loved one). It allows you to be pleasant at home without carrying over your bad mood from the office.

Here is how you retrain your thinking to accomplish this compartmentalization: 1) isolate the stimulus from your response (don't react impulsively); 2) defer the problem (if it's not an emergency, you can deal with it later); 3) take a break (get away, try to relax, breathe deeply, stretch); 4) mentally deposit your concerns (leave worries behind when you physically leave a place); and 5) keep relationships separate (if the boss is the problem, don't let it affect your relationships at home). Think of it as a warehouse where you can place your problems in a box, store them elsewhere, and deal with them when your mind is clearer. Compartmentalization works well for short-term fixes in the midst of an inflamed non-emergency. Over the long-term it's best not to suppress emotions too long. After all, most problems need to be resolved. But compartmentalization offers those with enough self-discipline a solution for getting through the initial shock of a situation, so the emotions don't invade other parts of their life.

"I was proud when (my wife) Nellie told an interviewer, 'I never could tell whether John had a good practice or a bad practice, because he never brought it home.'" ~ John Wooden

MAY 14

I will resolve conflicts

Conflict happens when two people express different views. Armed with the proper skills, we can all learn to resolve conflict. There are basically two types: 1) *Inflamed Conflict* – where someone expresses anger or frustration and needs to calm down; and, 2) *Situational Conflict* – where someone's concerns or desires simply differ from another person's.

The way to resolve *Inflamed Conflict* is to first calm the angry person down. Use the skill of *reflective response*—restate the person's concern to let them know you've heard and understood their feelings. For example, you might say: "I feel your frustration over not receiving a merit increase." This begins to mentally disarm the inflamed person, who might respond: "Yeah, I'm really upset that everyone else got a raise and I didn't!" Next you recognize the emotional impact with a *sympathetic acknowledgement*: "And that left you with a *feeling* of unfairness." Gradually, the angry person's outrage is being defused. The resolver can enter into *Situational Conflict* resolution by then focusing on a rational solution.

The first step toward resolution is to recognize that people have different conflict styles, based on their level of assertiveness and cooperativeness, so it's important to offer a solution based on the other person's style. Some people want to just *"win"* (high assertiveness, low cooperativeness) while others want an *accommodating* solution (low assertiveness, high cooperativeness); and, still others want to *compromise* (moderate assertiveness and cooperativeness) or *collaborate* (high assertiveness, high cooperativeness).

Finally, there are the *avoiders* (low assertiveness, low cooperativeness). Finding the right balance relies on assessing the other person and offering a solution that matches their style with yours. If Sally is a compromiser, her conflict resolution would offer a fifty-fifty split. Joe, the collaborator, is looking for an "out-of-the-box" solution. As the resolver, you need to reconcile your own style with the needs of the other person in order to achieve a resolution that works for both of you.

"No pressure, no diamonds." ~ Mary Case

"An apology is the superglue of life. It can repair just about anything." ~ Lynn Johnston

MAY 15

I will keep my hands and nose clean

"Keeping one's hands clean" is an eighteenth-century English phrase that essentially means "stay out of trouble." In an age of just getting ahead at all costs, many believe their good name and reputation depend more on what's concealed than what's revealed. To some, power means hiding mistakes and then blaming someone else. There was a day when just being respectful and doing your job was enough to be rewarded in the corporate culture. Sadly, some cultures have devolved into an environment of ruthless competition. They no longer recognize the nobility of doing the right thing.

Thanks to technological advancements like computers, the Internet, and smartphones, the 9-to-5 workday belongs in the museum under "history," right along with "lifetime employment." One rule that has survived the test of time is that of being a good team player. That's how you keep your hands and nose clean today. In most companies, the administrative or personal assistants know more about the inside scoop than even the coworker or boss's spouses. You need to spend just a few minutes getting to know them, and respecting their position.

Assistants are the gateways to understanding the organization's comings and goings, and they carry news to their supervisor more quickly than any email or text message. They can tell you who said what, who knows what, and what you need to do in order to be a valued part of the team. Once you get beyond the assistant, start recognizing those who play an influential role within the organization, whether it's a power position or not. These typically are people who have been around for a long time, and can tell you what has worked, and what or whom you should avoid. They remember the pitfalls that have caused the demise of good people who stumbled and fell in the wrong direction. You'll want to become friends with these invaluable information resources. They can often support your efforts in ways you could have never imagined. Ted was a mid-level manager who had served in the company for twenty-six years and happened to be an influential confidant of the CEO. People like Ted can help support your perception in the company as a "valuable team player."

"Keep your nose out of another's mess." ~ Author Unknown

MAY 16

I will find the best in others

Humans tend to define themselves by their intentions, and others by their actions. We tend to be forgiving of our faults and assume others to be unfair, harmful, or mean when they offend our rules. Changing this tendency to judge others is not easy. In his bestseller, *The Greatest Salesman in the World* (Bantam Books, 1968, 1983), Og Mandino suggested that we should walk up to a person and inwardly say "I love you." This, he said, would help transform our attitude toward them to an instant positive. Consciously valuing others causes us to humanize them, opening conversation and leading to greater understanding and appreciation of one another.

It's easier to dislike a stranger than someone we know. Pay special attention to what that person has done to help others. Asking about family members usually reveals a soft spot that can soften your own attitude toward that person. Helping them even in something small can turn a person's attitude toward you into more of a positive, and it's always easier to like someone who likes you. That old saying, "to have a friend you need to be a friend" applies to seeing the best in people.

Expectations also play a key role in defining relationships. While these expectations may prove correct over the long-term, in the short-term they only create an internal battle of trying to outthink the other person, which can lead toward a hostile impression. Focus instead on meeting your own needs and consider the other person as a mostly blank slate without any expectation. When we meet our own needs, we feel more positive about ourselves, and we tend to think more positively about others. Seeing others in a positive light is usually a reflection from our own life. So take care of yourself, and look on the bright side.

"When we seek to discover the best in others, we somehow bring out the best in ourselves." ~ William Arthur Ward

"If you look for the worst in people and expect to find it, you surely will." ~ Abraham Lincoln

MAY 17

I will never lose hope

As children, we dreamt big dreams on the world's stage. Then as we grew to know our limitations, our dreams shrunk. Reality tends to do that to our hopes and dreams. We get bigger, but they get smaller. There was one eight-year-old boy who never saw his stage shrink.

Jimmy lay in his hospital bed in Hinsdale, Illinois, after several rounds of chemotherapy. His sunken eyes telegraphed kindness—and hope. Jimmy wanted to someday be a famous evangelist like Billy Graham. A fifteen-year-old orderly, with his own grand plan to someday be a doctor, asked Jimmy, "So what do you want to be when you grow-up?" He had not thought that the boy would probably never grow-up. "I want to share the love of God with hundreds of people," Jimmy answered. They spent hours talking about baseball and things. "Do you know God?" Jimmy finally asked the orderly. "Sure, doesn't everybody know about God?" Jimmy pressed on. He didn't mean to just know *about* God. He wanted to know if the orderly knew God on a personal basis, "like a friend." The orderly finally confessed that no, he didn't know God that way. So Jimmy proceeded to share the "Good News" with the orderly.

Something about Jimmy's innocent sincerity changed the orderly. He prayed with Jimmy to receive Jesus Christ as his Lord. At the age of eight Jimmy died. Thousands packed the church auditorium for his memorial service, including the orderly. Many shared their experiences with the boy they called "amazingly kind," "loving," "generous," and "always hopeful." Jimmy loved talking about God, they recalled. Indeed, many came to know God through Jimmy—even kids from his school. After hearing so many stories and meeting so many people who, like he, had come to their faith through Jimmy, the orderly realized Jimmy's dream *had* come true. The boy had probably evangelized hundreds during his short lifetime, and continued to do so even on the day of his memorial service. The young orderly grew up to become an evangelist. Jimmy's stage never shrunk, and he never lost his hope.

"We must accept finite disappointment, but never lose infinite hope." ~ Martin Luther King, Jr.

MAY 18

I will compete against myself

A sense of competition must be inbred as part of our primitive instinct to achieve predominance. Most think of competition as trying to best a person or team. But what if we lived alone on an island? Would our sense of competition diminish? Would we only be consumed with survival? No, because as humans our propensity is to create value. Our loftiest tendency is not to survive, or to compare ourselves with anyone else (as it is with competition). Our loftiest instinct is to do better, to be somebody.

Unlike animals, if alone on an island we would not stop at simply surviving. We would be compelled to set higher standards for ourselves—to build a better home, or to create a better place. Our nature is to set the bar a little higher than before. That drive comes *not* from a need to do better than someone else, it is to do better, period. When we compete against someone else, our standard becomes that person. When we compete against our self, there is no standard. The sky's the limit. We seek something that no one has ever achieved before. Think from a reference point of boundless abundance, that you can achieve more than your surroundings appear to offer.

The win-lose scenario of competing against someone or something establishes an endpoint that stops creativity. A race toward greater discovery with no end in sight offers boundless possibilities. Bill Gates once described his philosophy as driving a bus at full throttle, with no need to look through the rearview mirror because competition was irrelevant. It was all about the next adventure, the new frontier. Competition against others adds a pressure to win that often stops the flow of inspiration. It may be fun in sports, but it doesn't work well as a way of living or for breakthrough advancements. Competing against yourself is more than just self-improvement; it's about tapping into your potential and the resources to pioneer greater opportunities.

"A man's reach must exceed his grasp or what's a heaven for?" ~ Robert Browning

MAY 19

I will not use excuses

Walt Disney once wrote about what he called the four C's of success: curiosity, courage, confidence, and constancy. Even if all four are practiced, there is one overriding fault that will sink any efforts—that of making excuses. Both conscious and subconscious excuses can undermine the best of intentions. The first and most common one is, "I'm just not qualified." Was the gangly state senator from Illinois, Abe Lincoln, qualified to save the United States of America? Was the young part-time employee with one semester of college, Steve Jobs, qualified to revolutionize the personal computer world? Once you face the truth about this excuse, you'll realize that that it is a façade for your ego's fear of failure. But, that's what life is all about—stretching your abilities in the world of the unknown. Just go for it. Find an area that matches your passion with your talents and launch into the unknown.

The second most common excuse is, "I can't afford to do it." You may not have a million dollars to invest in some venture, but companies like Nordstrom, Dell, Mattel, and Whole Foods started with next to nothing, and there are thousands of other examples as well. What's lacking is not money, it's your limited understanding of your limitless capabilities. You can do just about anything with the right connections and sheer determination. If more money is required, seek some partners or investors, or if it's a recurring problem, read *The Energy of Money: A Spiritual Guide to Financial and Personal Fulfillment* (Wellspring/Ballentine, 1999), by Maria Nemeth. Don't play the "woe is poor little me" game anymore.

The third biggest excuse is, "What if it doesn't work out?" Who says failure is permanent? Not only is failure temporary to those who possess the four C's, it is necessary. High achievers like Albert Einstein and Bill Gates learned from their failures. Without them, they would have never discovered something greater. When excuses prevent you from moving forward, the simple response is just say "no."

"An excuse is a skin of a reason stuffed with a lie." ~ Billy Sunday

"Excuses are the nails used to build a house of failure." ~ Don Wilder and Bill Rechin

MAY 20

I will use effective body language

Ever heard of the warning, "don't get on his bad side?" Research now confirms that people do have a preferred side, though they may not be aware of it. You can tell when you're standing or sitting on someone's good (or bad) side by their gestures: wrinkled nose (disgust), crow's-feet around the eyes (happiness), lip corner pulled in and back on one side of the face (contempt), or a solid touch to your forearm (a sign of rapport). See how they react to you standing on either side, and if you want to ingratiate yourself to that person, stay on his good side.

In her bestseller book, *You Say More Than You Think* (Three Rivers Press, 2010), body language expert Janine Driver says that the new body language requires asking high gain questions, such as those that begin with "how," in order to baseline that person's behavior before you add meaning to any of their nonverbals. One of Driver's assertions is called "The Belly Button Rule," which states that people face their belly button toward others they like, admire, and trust, and that you should always point your belly button toward the person you most want to influence positively, especially when you shake his or her hand. The other key body indicator, believe it or not, involves your nether region, or what Driver refers to as your "naughty bits." Directing that portion of the body in a wide stance (six to ten inches apart), toward the other person, along with hands at sides, on hips, or with only the thumbs in pockets (other fingers are showing) denotes confidence.

Gestures can be altered based on how you wish to be perceived, such as reaching your palms down to exhibit power, or facing your palms up to establish rapport with another person which displays honesty and openness. Holding those palms apart so that they face each other, as though holding a basketball, evokes passion and authority, while holding fingertips together simply connotes authority (minus the passion). When that steeple position turns into the two index fingers pointing outward, it can tell the other person you don't like what he or she is doing or saying.

Managing your body language to reflect the attitude you wish to convey establishes your personal brand with the other person. Establishing an effective connection with someone should always be demonstrated with respect. Fifty percent of our happiness comes from doing something for others – in other words, caring. That happens with the right attitude, and when your attitude is right your body language will be right.

"The most important thing in communication is hearing what isn't said." ~ Peter Drucker

MAY 21

I will develop a good sense of humor

Science has revealed that a good sense of humor provides a unique internal restoration that actually cleanses and relaxes our organs. This explains why we feel better after a good laugh. Some are born comedians, other need to learn. But the good news is that a good sense of humor *can* be developed. It begins by smiling more. For a lot of us, it's about giving ourselves permission to laugh. Laugh at yourself the next time you trip over a crack or knock over those papers. Make faces at yourself in the mirror while brushing your teeth. Flap your ears, roll your eyes, and crinkle your nose until your silliness makes you chuckle. Humor is all about adopting a lighter attitude toward life, and when we do, the whole paradigm of what's serious and what's not will shift around you.

The key is to find out what things make you laugh. Discover what TV shows, books, or comics make you laugh out loud and take regular doses of that medicine. Treat yourself to comedy nights by renting a funny movie or going to a comedy show. Remember embarrassing or simply hilarious times in your life that can open your mind to life's natural comedy.

Cartoonists and comedians work by exaggerating situations. Doing the same from our vantage point can help us develop a humorous perspective. Using humorous techniques to diffuse inflamed circumstances can help in times of confrontation. If someone or something makes you angry, try responding with humor instead of hostility. Next time someone criticizes your appearance, say, "Wow, you'd make a great motivational speaker." Swap funny stories or experiences with friends or coworkers on a regular basis and pretty soon they'll start giving you impromptu material for jokes. It boils down to this—we need to create a more humorous environment around us. It's as easy as posting funny cartoons or sayings at work and at home. Laughter heals.

"You can turn painful situations around through laughter. If you can find humor in anything, even poverty, you can survive it." ~ Bill Cosby

May 22

I will be interdependent

The new paradigm for success in relationships and in the work environment is interdependence, in which we achieve something that cannot be achieved independently. Most in Western society practice either independence—"I'll do it my way"—or dependence—"The company will take care of me." Another, even less healthy, type of relationship is called *co*dependence, in which we give someone else power over our self-esteem.

Interdependence is about making allies, forming collaborative partnerships. It's about creating mutually beneficial connections that share power over our welfare and our purpose. Developing interdependence encourages cooperation and resolution by replacing the competition and conflict that often results from states of dependence and codependence. A key ingredient of productive relationships is what Johnson and Johnson (1975) called positive interdependence, which many consider today as the essential quality for cooperative groups. It begins with each person in the relationship believing that their personal success is integral to the success of the others in a group. The paradigm shift results when the individual sees the others in the group as indispensable to their own goals.

Experts have determined that the positive emotions that come from people being able to earnestly rely upon each other result in better information processing and more mutually beneficial performance. In order to arrive at this mindset, we must realize that other people will help us accomplish more than we could ever do alone. Remember—shared success is multiplied; shared failure is reduced failure. Once we give up some of our personal power for the benefit of the relationship or team, we increase our collective power several-fold. Interdependence is a collaborative value that develops when a person commits to a sense of community in the workforce, or a sense of bonding in a relationship. We all win or lose together, and we can do more together than apart.

"We are here to awaken from the illusion of our separateness." – Thich Nhat Hanh

"The way you get to know yourself is by the expression on other people's faces." ~ Gil Scott Heron

MAY 23

I will grow where I'm planted

United States Marine Corps lieutenant general Martin Steele served on several special intelligence projects that merited his stellar reputation as a leader in both the military, and as a corporate leadership trainer. He has served presidents, and has functioned as a dignitary who communicated sensitive messages between countries like China and the United States.

One day while speaking to a group at Johnson & Johnson Corporation, General Steele articulated an enlightening message prefaced with this often spoken statement: "Grow where you're planted." Many, he said, find themselves feeling restricted by the confines of their work environment, or other limitations in their life, so people find themselves looking for some other place where the "grass appears greener." The principle of making the best with what you have doesn't preclude anyone from making a change. It just means that today, now, each of us must make the best of our present opportunities.

General Steele recounted his experiences in warfare, stuck in battle with nowhere else to go, and he and his soldiers having to fight their way out of a trap. In the workplace as well, he said, people can feel trapped, and the only alternative is to do what you can to succeed with where and what you're given.

No matter where you are, with whom you share your life, what you do, or what your age, we all need to make the best of our situation. Growing where you're planted means giving your best in the here and now. Stay focused. Grow your abilities to do more and be more and to reach new heights of success. There will be a better place for you in the future. It starts with what happens inside of you now.

"Most successful men have not achieved their distinction by having some new talent or opportunity presented to them. They have developed the opportunity that was at hand." ~ Bruce Barton

"Do what you can, with what you have, where you are." ~ Theodore Roosevelt

"Success seems to be largely a matter of hanging on after others have let go." ~ William Feather

May 24

I will stop worrying

There's the good kind of worry, that prompts you to solve a problem with action, and the bad kind, that consumes the mind with "what ifs," often imagining the worst case scenario. It's the bad kind of worry that sidetracks our productive thought processes with useless conjecture. Because we can think that our worries have sometimes helped us discover a solution or prevent harm, our minds have been partially conditioned to continue worrying, even though the vast majority of the time the worries are proven unmerited.

Excessive worrying causes anxiety, which can lead to more worrying, until this vicious cycle causes some of our worries to come true. Telling yourself to stop doesn't always work if you have an anxiety problem. So try giving yourself permission to worry—but at a later time. By postponing the worry, say by writing it down, you can forget about it for now. While your mind is "tricked" into thinking you haven't given-up on worrying, you are meanwhile breaking the habit of worrying in the present moment. It often works. You won't stop worrying if you think it benefits you, so it's healthful to differentiate the *flight-or-fight* response (good worry) from the *worst-can-happen* response (bad worry). Most chronic worriers are controllers who cannot deal well with uncertainty. If a problem truly exists, work through the problem resolution process. But if uncertainty is the problem, then the illusion that worrying will make you safer must be debunked. Worrying doesn't predict certainty, which runs counter to the controller's mindset.

We need to challenge the validity of worry at every occasion by looking for the reasons behind it. Perhaps people are making you anxious, in which case try to spend less time with these people. Eliminate whatever condition or situation feeds your worry. One way to counter worry is to consciously refute its validity or find a different place that will starve worry of its energy.

"Rule number one is, don't sweat the small stuff. Rule number two is, it's all small stuff." ~ Robert Eliot

MAY 25

I will discover why I was created

Your passions and talents direct you to your calling, but there is another step needed to experience success in life. You must discover the problem(s) you are tailored to solve. There is something in the world that really bothers you. It's not a mere annoyance, but a grating, gnawing problem that eats away at your ability to enjoy life. Perhaps it's some terrible injustice, like world hunger, or disease, or the lack of good education in high schools. Everyone with a purpose (that's you and me) needs to undo what bothers us the most. A truly inspired oncologist must eradicate the problem of cancer whenever possible. A dedicated criminal attorney must work to ensure that people are not treated unjustly. An inspired children's caseworker must prevent the problem of abuse. A devoted librarian must solve the problem of illiteracy.

Your passion leads you to your vocation, whereas that intolerable problem leads you toward your mission in life. You need not dedicate your career toward solving that problem. You may instead volunteer or do something else without receiving an income. But you *must* do it. You were created to solve a problem, and your satisfaction in life depends on your success in finding that significant problem and solving it. Most successful people look outside of themselves and find a problem, which eventually defines their life. Rather than developing themselves first and then leading a life, they are called by a problem, and that calling gradually forms their development. Sometimes it's a tragedy. A family member may have been the victim of a violent crime, which compelled a relative to become a police officer. Or some problem that prevented a person from attaining a goal may serve as their driving force for correcting that problem. When a problem becomes a blood-fueled living force that boils over into consistent anger or frustration, not solving it would be tantamount to being disloyal to yourself.

So finding your intolerable problem and making it your life's work to solve that problem is the best way toward satisfying the purpose for which you were created.

"A sum can be put right: but only by going back till you find the error and working it afresh from that point, never by simply going on." ~ C.S. Lewis

MAY 26

I will be slow to correct and quick to commend

Whether you are a basketball fan or not, aficionados of character and leadership appreciate a man who exemplified these qualities both on and off the court. Revered UCLA basketball head coach John Wooden (the "Wizard of Westwood") won seven NCAA national championships in a row for a total of ten top finishes in a twelve-year period—an unprecedented achievement. His teams won a record eighty-eight consecutive games, and he was named national coach of the year six times. After retirement, Wooden received the Presidential Medal of Freedom, the nation's highest civilian honor.

Throughout his life Wooden espoused his values during lectures, interviews, and through his writings until his death just ten days shy of his 100th birthday. Asked to explain his success, Wooden once commented that he was "slow to correct and quick to commend." He was a stickler for details, spending hours with his players to perfect their play down to the minutia, even as to how they dressed for a game, but his patience was unparalleled.

Andre McCarter, the point guard on Wooden's final championship in 1975, sometimes clashed with his head coach, but grew to love the man. McCarter, whose swagger moves like crossover dribbles and behind-the-back passes failed to impress the no-nonsense coach, told of how Wooden's criticism upset him so much that he stormed into the coach's office one day to complain. "He starts digging in his drawer and I'm thinking, 'What do you have to dig for?'...You know, I'm hot about it," McCarter said. "Then he pulls out these statistics he keeps and says to me, 'That play you made, we've been keeping statistics on 2-on-1s and the percentage of what you did is around 70 or 72 percent. If you make the straight, basic pass, it'll be like 98 percent."

Wooden's methodical and matter-of-fact approach disarmed McCarter, who couldn't argue with the coach's pinpoint rationale. Over the years, players on Wooden's teams commented on Coach's factual approach to criticism, always offset with an abundance of encouragement that endeared his players to him. Wooden's patient coaching motivated his players to an extraordinary level of success well beyond their natural talent.

"Be slow to criticize and quick to commend." ~ John Wooden

MAY 27

I will be a strong public speaker

The ability to speak clearly, convincingly, and confidently in front of an audience, regardless of its size, is one of the most vital skills to develop. Effective speakers present themselves as confident, comfortable (with themselves), and charismatic. Being able to speak with these characteristics can persuade your listeners in almost any way to advance your cause and your career.

The first step toward being an effective speaker is to understand your interpersonal skills, how you best connect with others, and what other skills you need to improve. Accentuate your positives. If you are skilled at analyzing data, make sure you're incorporating several meaningful patterns of data into your presentation. The book *StrengthsFinder 2.0* (Tom Rath, Gallup Press 2007) is an excellent resource for discovering your skills.

The second step is to master your message. Through researching your material and your audience, outlining your presentation, and practicing, you will instill confidence within yourself. Enhance your effectiveness through storytelling. Your audience needs to connect with you, and presenting relatable stories that connect on an emotional and personal level inspires a positive response from them. To make that connection, you need to know the audience. Do they like high energy, or are they looking for bottom line results?

Third is to engage the audience through effective presentation skills: 1) pause after important points to highlight your message; 2) maintain eye focus on each audience participant for three to five seconds before moving on to the next person. It makes people believe you are speaking only to them; 3) move around and be animated (fifty-five percent of how people perceive you is through body language, thirty-eight percent by your voice, and only seven percent by your words); 4) show enthusiasm and smile. If your audience feels like you are enjoying the experience, they are more likely to appreciate it. Public speaking is about effective content and connection.

"You can speak well if your tongue can deliver the message of your heart." ~ John Ford

MAY 28

I will be a critical thinker

Over the course of a day we are exposed to hundreds of pieces of information—so much it can all easily overwhelm our capacity to assimilate and prioritize it. It is therefore absolutely critical to be able to quickly evaluate the information, decipher it into "valuable" versus "unnecessary" categories and analyze the relevance and content of what is deemed valuable. Then you can relate what's valuable and new to corresponding information, leading toward a productive outcome. Competent critical thinking skills will distinguish you from the average person in this day and age.

Critical thinking means not taking reporting at face value, but using your critical skills to assess the evidence and consider the implications of information, based on its value and affect. You must apply criteria to your decision making in order to determine the conditions that must be met for you to judge whether the information is relevant and believable. For example, engage in "what-if" thinking: "If we do this in response to the information, how will it affect our ability to perform?" Choose a critical problem and systematically think through the information's likely impact: How relevant is it to solving the problem?

How a problem or situation is defined determines not only how we feel about it, but also what information is crucial, how we should act upon it, and the implications it will have on us. Because each situation can be defined in more than one way, critical thinking is about finding the best way. To do that, we must be able to spot false assumptions (all the people I see have two legs, so all humans must have two legs). And it must be challenging: "How can I be wrong? Is there a better solution?" Make it a habit to require evidence for the information you receive. Consider the source as well. How reliable is that person or that research? Ask yourself what bias may have factored into the reporting (the sales manager may have under-forecasted in order to exceed quota). Effective critical thinking factors in the myriad of possibilities based on an objective or a problem to be solved. If you can prioritize your objectives and potential problems, you can then assess what information will best help achieve the solution.

"It is the mark of an educated mind to be able to entertain a thought without accepting it." ~ Aristotle

MAY 29

I will perfect my writing skills

Jackie spent hours preparing a detailed report for her boss. "If you can save us at least ten percent on our operational costs," the boss said, "I can't see any reason why you won't get that senior title." When Jackie submitted the report, her boss was so delighted with the eighteen percent savings that he copied it to all members of the board. Following the next board meeting, Jackie's boss entered her office with a frown saying, "Everyone liked your analyses, Jackie, but quite honestly your writing was sloppy. I didn't see it but others caught several misspellings and grammatical mistakes." Jackie didn't get the promotion. Correct grammar, punctuation, and spelling are key in written communications.

The best way to improve your writing skills is to simply write often. This helps you learn different syntaxes and it builds confidence. Have your friends and family give you feedback on your writing. There are also some tactical ways to prevent mistakes like Jackie's. Before submitting any communications, including email, re-read it. If it's really important, ask someone with good critiquing skills to look it over as well. Don't just assume automated spelling and grammar checkers will catch errors, such as using "their" when it should be "there." Read your writing out loud to hear how it sounds to the reader—or better yet, have someone else read it aloud in your presence. Reading books and magazine articles trains your mind to recognize what good writing looks like. Brush up on proper grammar through the web and other sources.

Some of the rules have changed over the years, but some have remained constant—like following a preposition with a noun and never with a verb. If you want to be a really effective writer, add some creativity into your communications. Instead of saying, "The equipment is very old," you might say, "Our first generation copying machine prints out almost as much scrap paper as it does usable copies." Make effective writing a priority in order to better succeed.

"Write. Rewrite. When not writing or rewriting, read. I know of no shortcuts." ~ Larry L. King

"You have brilliant ideas, but if you can't get them across, your ideas won't get you anywhere." ~ Lee Iacocca

MAY 30

I will relax

Stress not only kills, it leads to poor decision-making, ineffective thinking, and broken relationships. So by relaxing, we can improve all three areas. The idea that it's all work and no relaxation in order to get ahead, with no time to enjoy the benefits, isn't truly "success" anyway.

Taking daily time for relaxation allows you to face even the most grueling crises with your wits intact and enough energy to remain productive for the long-term. Physically relaxing your body interrupts and reverses the stress response. It halts the negative feedback cycle that signals a tension-causing physical stress response to the brain. To alleviate this response, try some breathing exercises. Slowly inhale through your nose and count to five in your head. Then to a count of eight, slowly exhale through your mouth. Repeat this several times. Exercise can also decrease "stress hormones" and increase your body's "mood-boosting" endorphins, besides taking your mind off your problems. An easy exercise is to tense each of your muscles, from the face to the foot. Inhale, tense the muscles, count eight seconds, then exhale and completely relax the tensed muscles.

Just getting alone helps you relax. Don't forget that you'll need to relax yourself emotionally as well. Negative statements from others tend to erode our feeling of self-worth and can lead to tension. So we need to counter these imprinted thoughts with our own self-talk. Replace statements like, "I can't deal with this," with "I can" and "I will." Think on those things for which you are thankful. Do something different to break away from your current stress situation. Take a walk in the park. Reframe your problems with something that evokes a positive image. See a problem as an opportunity, a weakness as a strength, or unkindness as a lack of understanding. Do whatever it takes to relieve the stress: get organized, become more assertive, take a vacation, maintain a balanced lifestyle, or find the hidden rewards and recognitions in your job. You need to make relaxing a priority in your life.

"The mark of a successful man is one that has spent an entire day on the bank of a river without feeling guilty about it." ~ Author Unknown

MAY 31

I will research what I need to know

An uninformed decision is an unnecessary risk. It's important that we have at least a threshold of knowledge before jumping into something. Nobody can be expected to know all, or even a small fraction of all there is to know. Even within your field of expertise, chances are you could know a lot more about what you do. You don't need to know everything, but you should be able to expeditiously and easily find out what more you need to know. That means learning to conduct online research and tap other sources, like subject experts.

There are over eighty billion web pages published, most of which are worthless. To successfully get through to the useful ones, you must use effective filtering tools. If your research requires highly credible facts and figures, you need to scrutinize every resource. If you want more opinion-based information, then you have more latitude in perusing different sources. Blogs like Consumer Reports are good places to solicit differing opinions. Topical discussion forums and commercial sites like About.com are good resources, as well.

For accurate, factual information avoid the opinion blogs. Your research should focus on experts, academics, and professionals with high credibility. Research academic journals, government publications (like USA.gov), scientific and medical sites like WebMD.com and Scirus.com, and objective non-government sites like Consumer Watch. Reliable search engines include Wikipedia, Internet Public Library, Google, Ask.com, and Invisible Web. A knowledge-driven (non-commercial) site like Surfwax can help with purist reearch; Scirus is good for scientific research; and the US Government Library of Congress can source a wide range of historical information.

Be careful with personal and commercial web pages that are promoting an agenda. Pages with advertisements may represent a bias that can influence facts. Commercial sites can provide useful data, but be wary of surveys that are heavily slanted. Of course, there are numerous other non-Internet research tools—from personal surveys, interviews, and talking with customers and businesses, to trade publications, bookstores, and libraries. The key is to gain enough information to make an informed decision without burying yourself in it all. Good luck!

"If we knew what it was we were doing, it would not be called research, would it?" ~ Albert Einstein

JUNE

TIME TO RE-ENERGIZE

JUNE 1

I will believe that nothing is impossible

The legendary Audrey Hepburn, whose very presence evoked confidence and allure, observed a strange twist in the word "impossible" when she said: "Nothing is impossible, the word itself says, 'I'm possible!'" Even if you don't believe that nothing's impossible, at least the attitude that "all things are possible" will transcend many of the roadblocks along your way. One might even say that to believe the impossible gives birth to the creative genius that drives people like Audrey Hepburn, Albert Einstein, Thomas Edison, The Wright Brothers, Steve Jobs, and even those whose discoveries have yet to defy the seemingly impossible.

Creativity is the invention that has never been tested, the role that has yet to be played, the idea that has yet to form. Who could have imagined in the early days of humankind that we could fly, or that light could be captured in a bulb, or that hundreds could talk in the same instant of time while speaking in different countries? Even typists in the early twentieth century would be stunned to consider a computer that would open sites into millions of households at the touch of a button. All of these inventions began with the belief in something that others viewed as impossible.

Creating the impossible starts with an unbridled imagination sparked by a vision. Any of us can tap into this creativity to solve the present view of impossibility. What can you make possible at your creative core? Maybe it has something to do with finding a better way, or a widget that makes life easier. Or perhaps your imagination takes you to a world without hunger, a cure for cancer, or peace around the globe. Creativity for the artist causes them to create a picture they didn't even realize was in their imagination. Just starting to create can birth a new idea, which leads to another thought, until something unfathomable turns into reality. What seemingly impossible obstacle is holding you back? Perhaps it simply starts with overcoming a fear. You may need to just walk out the door. Whatever it is, overcoming your "impossible" can start today.

"It always seems impossible until it's done." ~ Nelson Mandela

"We would accomplish many more things if we did not think of them as impossible." ~ Vince Lombardi

JUNE 2

I will accept trials

No one wants to struggle, but we all contend with the downsides of life. Many believe that failure and struggle go together. But thanks to research conducted by James Heckman, an economist at the University of Chicago and winner of the Nobel Prize for economics, we're learning that this is not necessarily true. In studying the reasons for both success and failure, Mr. Heckman assembled economists and psychologists to identify which skills and traits lead to success, and how they develop in childhood. Common knowledge was that intelligence best predicted success. However, according to an article published in the *Wall Street Journal*, economists, psychologists, educators, and neuroscientists determined that personality and behavioral characteristics influence success in life more than previously thought. Cognition, this group found, was not necessarily the number one determinant. They also discovered that qualities like self-control, curiosity, conscientiousness and persistence may be even stronger contributors to success.

While all of these traits can be developed, they are, unlike knowledge, forged through life experiences. Most of them, like persistence and self-confidence, result from life's trials that serve to strengthen us if handled correctly. Those who live a sheltered or over-protected life eventually face difficulty in practicing self-control. They tend to give-up more easily and their conscientiousness toward others may also be compromised.

Our natural instinct as parents is to protect our children and to personally avoid struggles whenever possible. But we need to allow a measure of failure so that our children—and even we—can better learn how to triumph over life's trials. Self-confidence, persistence, and mental strength are learned through struggles. Our key takeaway is to allow and even embrace challenges, as they forge within us those skills that will lead toward future success. In so doing, we must also discern how much adversity is too much, and when to intervene or back away from a challenge—and that requires wisdom.

"Success is not measured by what you accomplish, but by the opposition you have encountered, and the courage with which you have maintained the struggle against overwhelming odds." ~ Orison Swett Marden

JUNE 3

I will be conscientious in my life

Textbooks define "conscientious" as: *Wishing to do what is right, especially to do one's work or duty well and thoroughly*. Who would not want to hire someone who lived by that definition? According to the article in the Journal of Research in Personality, "What do Conscientious People Do? Development and Validation of the Behavioral Indicators of Conscientious (BIC)," related behavioral traits would include orderliness, industriousness, impulse control, reliability, and conventionality. These traits are also considered universally desirable.

According to the BIC study, those traits rated most contrary to conscientiousness included avoiding work, impulsivity (buying something on whim), being antisocial (littering), procrastination, not being punctual, laziness, and lack of responsibility (breaking a promise). All of these characteristics predict a person will *not* be successful.

Conscientious people tend to work hard, are clean and tidy, and they follow the rules. They think before acting and are organized. Conscientious people tend to write down important dates, comb their hair, polish their shoes, and stand up straight. People on the reverse end tend to exceed their credit limit, cancel plans, curse, oversleep, watch more television, and break promises. These behaviors are not necessarily related to personality, as different personalities can demonstrate the same behavioral traits. This fact indicates that the positive traits of conscientiousness can be trained or developed. It begins with a self-disciplined commitment to accomplish the characteristics described for a conscientious person by thinking that you *can* achieve them, even though you may feel otherwise. Retraining yourself is a state of mind in which you cannot see yourself as anything other than the person you desire to be. When you believe that you can be that person, you will find that instead of your mind closing to the task, it begins to open you to its inevitability. Once you decide you *will* do it, the transition from wishful thinking to reality is underway.

"Life's most persistent and urgent question is,
'What are you doing for others?'" ~ Martin Luther King, Jr.

June 4

I will be a person of curiosity

What makes you curious? Do you find outer space fascinating? Perhaps you stay awake at night wondering about relationships, and what makes them tick. Those things that spark our curiosity tend to serve as our primary drivers and motivators. They are not observations; rather curiosity compels us to delve into research for finding answers, and this compulsion impacts both our personal and our business lives. There are simple curiosities that serve more as fleeting desires to know more, like wanting to know more about the American Civil War, and, then there are complex curiosities that can drive a lifetime of discovery, like the career scientist who wants to treat multiple sclerosis. And then there are life-transforming curiosities, like wanting to know the meaning of life, or how to discover God.

Curiosity within us sparks discovery, it feeds meaning, it helps direct our paths, and it may even define our careers and our approach to life in general. The antithesis is being bored and stagnant. Because curiosity leads us to learn more and do more, the lack of it can result in an unfulfilled life. To develop our curiosity, we must tap into that inner child who always wants to know the hows and whys. That type of thinking triggers a chain of causation: what causes that, and what's the meaning behind this, and how can that make life better? Getting to the root cause of a curiosity—like what causes obesity, or what causes people to fail—can lead to the solution.

Author and speaker Bruce Wilkinson went through this exercise of curiosity to uncover the reasons why people in Africa were unable to feed themselves. He determined that a permanent solution would never arrive until these people could irrigate their crops, so he started a movement to engage others in an irrigation project throughout Africa. This is the type of positive outcome than can arise from a robust curiosity about things. It begins with a nagging question that won't go away, and it ends with an answer that can't be dismissed without doing it.

"The important thing is not to stop questioning. Curiosity has its own reason for existing." ~ Albert Einstein

"Curiosity is one of the most permanent and certain characteristics of a vigorous intellect." ~ Sam Johnson

JUNE 5

I will learn new words (each day) and new languages

We live in an ever-increasingly global community, with new terminologies, more complex ideas, greater liberties with language and a growing need to more effectively express ourselves, both to people who speak our native language and those who do not. The term "mesofact" refers to a fact that is slowly evolving over time. For example, the term "managed care" might have one meaning at first, but gradually evolves into a more defined meaning as new healthcare laws emerge. Tech words are especially evolving. Ever heard of a "Mi-Fi"? It's a new version of a wireless network, and one that may be common knowledge before this book is published. That's how fast new words and terms are making their way into our language.

There are also a growing number of slang words and abbreviations, like "deleb" (a popular celebrity who has died but is still popular on the Internet, like Michael Jackson) and "dis," which means to act or speak in a disrespectful way. Young people are great at making up new terms that somehow go viral in their community. Of course, there are words in the English language that are rarely heard anymore, but that can be more descriptive, as with the word loquacious (which means *very* talkative) and ameliorate (which means improve). Some of these terms serve only to confuse people who have never heard of them, but if your are a professional or an academic, they can come in handy by improving others' respect for your intellect and education. On the other hand, none of us wants to be speaking with someone who consistently uses a word or words we cannot understand, forcing us to either ask them to explain what they mean (in other words, 'dumb it down'), or to miss their point all-together.

Words from foreign languages are finding their way more and more into our native communications. In parts of the United States, Spanish words like hola (hi) and gracias (thank you) are spoken as routinely as their English counterparts. When speaking with people using a foreign tongue, knowing at least some of their words and proper grammar use often elicits a higher level of appreciation from them. So if you haven't committed on a regular basis to learn new words, or to learn a new language (or at least the basic terms commonly used in a foreign language), start today—tener exito.

"The limits of my language are the limits of my world." ~ Ludwig Wittgenstein

JUNE 6

I will practice self-control

In the 1960s, Stanford University launched a now-often-cited study of the effect of instant gratification. Researcher Michael Mischel, in conducting a longitudinal study, offered two marshmallows each to hungry four year olds, but instructed them to wait while he left to presumably complete an errand. Those who waited fifteen or twenty minutes for the experimenter to return—about a third of the children—were able to control their impulses. Other kids ate their marshmallows before the researcher even left the room. All in all, two-thirds did not wait for Mischel to return, as they had been instructed. Years later, after the children graduated from high school, the follow-up research exposed dramatic findings. The group that resisted grabbing the marshmallow exhibited more of these characteristics: a positive attitude, persistence in the face of trials, self-motivation, self-assertiveness, and the ability to delay gratification in pursuit of their goals. They also produced more positive outcomes: successful marriages, greater career satisfaction, higher incomes, superior health, and generally more fulfilling lives. This group also scored 210 points higher on their SAT exams.

Those who grabbed the marshmallows without waiting were more troubled, mistrustful, indecisive, stubborn, and less self-confident. Trouble in sublimating impulses impeded their ability to achieve long-range goals, as revealed by broken marriages, inferior health, and low job satisfaction. Many in the field of psychology contend that people with poor impulse control suffer from "weak ego boundaries," a term coined by Sigmund Freud. According to this theory, people unable to control themselves may possess an unbalanced id (the pleasure principle) that exceeds the ability of one's ego to control it.

Dr. Kentaro Fujita of Ohio State University says we can improve self-control by focusing on the ultimate or long-term goal. That involves seeing the big picture. Use abstract reasoning to avoid thinking about the specific details of a situation (the marshmallows). Focus instead on how one's actions fit into an overall framework. Being philosophical about life helps develop self-control.

"Discipline is remembering what you want." ~ David Campbell

JUNE 7

I will tell the truth

To Tell the Truth was an amusing television game show popular in the 1950s. The basic premise consisted of a panel of four celebrities trying to correctly identify a contestant from a choice of three possibilities. Usually the contestant held a unique occupation, or represented some exemplary accomplishment. The other two masqueraders would make-up lies, while the real person could only tell the truth. After a certain time, the panel would vote as to whom they believed, and then the host would say, "Will the real (person's name) please stand up." Besides the sheer entertainment, the show revealed how difficult it can be to discern lies from truth. Even more difficult is to tell the truth, all of the time.

Have you ever lied when someone asked you, "How do I look?" to keep from offending them? How many people can you confide in, people you know will keep your confidence? The world is full of liars, including…at times…maybe…well, OK, all but you and me. Telling the truth in hard situations is a trained discipline. Using that example of someone who asks how they look, a way to answer honestly might be, "Do you really want me to tell the truth or do you want me to tell you what you want to hear?"

Practicing telling the truth is the single most liberating thing you can do for your life. It relieves burdens you never knew existed. Here's a dare: be brutally honest for the next seventy-two hours. No little white lies, no false flattery, and no innocent excuses. It's harder than it seems. You can't tell that person that you didn't get his email in time, when you know you did. That signature fish dish your husband is so proud of (but you hate)? No more chewing your pasta in silence. It's time to admit you truly "don't love it." That friend who says she lost five pounds and still looks eight months pregnant? No more, "Congratulations, you look great!"

The more we practice, the easier it gets. Well, actually, that's a lie. Telling the truth all of the time is a constant and not-so-easy discipline. But in the long run you'll gain energy and peace of mind. A 2004 Temple University School of Medicine study discovered that lying uses more brain effort than telling the truth. It's the ones who hear the truth that may prickle.

"Truth is beautiful, without doubt; but so are lies." ~ Ralph Waldo Emerson

JUNE 8

I will invest my earnings wisely

With all of the choices out there, how do you know where to best invest your hard-earned savings? You need to know both your options and what degree of risk you will tolerate. Conservative investors may place most of their money in a certificate of deposit and keep it there. More risky investors like to get involved with the stock market. One of the best ways to grow your money it to invest in tax-deferred accounts, where earnings are reinvested without tax penalties, allowing you to gain more from your investment money. The sooner you begin to save this way, the more growth you will experience. If your employer offers a 401(k), sign-up for it and start contributing two to five percent per pay period in order to assess the impact on your paycheck. You can always make adjustments later. Remember that this type of investment is pre-tax, which lowers your taxable income and may even increase your after-tax earnings. Another option is to make contributions to an Individual Retirement Account (IRA), which allows you to deduct the contribution from your income taxes. A Roth IRA is not tax deductible, but once money goes into this account it grows tax-free and is never taxed thereafter. The advantage of a Roth is that you can withdraw contributions you make before retirement without a penalty.

Real estate investments vary based on appreciation in the area and whether you create a cash flow income from tenant rent money. Foreclosures represent one of the best opportunities to increase property value, but first you will need to secure funding that does not tap into your home's equity.

The key is to consider diversifying your investments. Placing your entire nest egg into the stock market is probably not the best idea, nor is any one place. One of the biggest mistakes people make is rushing into an investment. You don't want to wait too long to make a decision, but taking your time and completing the necessary due diligence to choose the right option for you will save both time and money in the long-term. You may want to consult with a financial planner for advice, but keep in mind that they charge fees or commissions. If you do consult with an expert, pick someone with a lot of experience who comes highly recommended. Once you've made your decision, you will need to track the investments that are providing you with the greatest returns, so that you can make adjustments based on the changing market conditions. You will enjoy the benefits of having your earnings work for you.

"Money is like manure. You have to spread it around or it smells." ~ J. Paul Getty

JUNE 9

I will be a good citizen and neighbor

One Saturday afternoon, Martha, a widow who lived alone, looked out her window to check on the sound of a lawnmower just outside her window. Her eyes lit up and her mouth spread into a wide grin as she observed her neighbor mowing her lawn while his son trimmed her trees. A man who daily crossed the Bay Bridge heading to work in San Francisco made it a habit to pay the toll for the car behind him, every other Monday, much to the delight of its driver. Each year and throughout our land, people practice good citizenship—whether by working philanthropically, being considerate of others, obeying rules and laws, participating in a community service project, or by simply doing a favor for their neighbors or a stranger.

Being a good citizen begins with a heart attitude that expresses itself through caring and generosity. It also starts by maintaining a clean and presentable home. A good citizen is trustworthy and follows the rules by respecting the rights of others. Volunteering is a great example of good citizenship, as are simple tasks like recycling and depositing leftovers into trash receptacles. Good citizenship involves an eye for safety, such as walking on the sidewalk and obeying street signs and markings. It means taking care of public places like libraries, schools, and restrooms, knowing that others who come after you will need to use or clean them.

Someone who is a good neighbor to visitors and tourists shows good manners and a respect for differences. They care for the less fortunate, and give of themselves and their time through acts such as donating blood, calling 911 in the event of an emergency, and helping the elderly and disabled with groceries and other routine tasks. The good neighbor shows dignity and respect for people, no matter what social or economic status or racial class they belong to.

Being a good citizen includes voting and supporting others' basic human rights. Whatever specific examples we might use, being a good neighbor and citizen is always about helping others, our communities and our nation. Today and every day, make a pledge to practice good citizenship wherever you may go.

"Let us at all times remember that all American citizens are brothers of a common country, and should dwell together in bonds of fraternal feeling." ~ Abraham Lincoln

JUNE 10

I will practice honoring others

Throughout history, honor has been a reoccurring theme in life and literature. Shakespeare wrote prolifically about honor and human nature's quest to achieve it. America's Founding Fathers pledged to each other their "sacred honor." The practice of upholding honor remained a central driving force in the early history of the United States of America. Today in many circles the word "honor" seems like an archaic term, without much clear definition to most. When you give honor to people, you open them to your influence in powerful ways, though you would be hard pressed to find any current literature about it. Perhaps that's why so many people think "chivalry is dead." Just ask any woman about the last time a man opened the passenger door for them. The fact remains that when we honor people with our actions and decisions, we open the other person's attitude to respond favorably toward us. We honor people when we show them complete respect. An honorable person considers the value of a person to be worthy of that respect regardless of their bias.

Often people practice what is called "confirmation bias"—the tendency to find things that support our bias, either good or bad—toward someone or something. If we believe someone's bad, we focus on their bad traits.

The truth is that there exists both good and bad in everyone. Honor should not be withheld simply because someone appears unworthy from a bias standpoint. When we honor people, they tend to live up to the way we treat them. We honor people by valuing them and the things they value, even when they don't deserve it. Leaders who wish to gain their followers respect must honor them with some declaration of their value, such as saying, "I am privileged to have someone of your caliber on the team." Dishonoring someone by demeaning their value closes that person, and also closes our influence with them. One of the simplest ways to honor someone is to simply be courteous enough to listen to their needs and to show appreciation for their opinion and efforts. If someone makes an error, criticize the behavior, not the person. People who feel valued are more loyal, more energized, and more productive. Honor is one of the most effective ways to succeed.

"Who sows virtue reaps honor." ~ Leonardo da Vinci

JUNE 11

I will be proactive

Life just doesn't happen to us. We make the choices that define it. We choose whether to be happy, or sad, or to respond with fear or courage. We also choose whether to be successful or not. One of the greatest choices we can make in order to be successful is to be proactive. That means taking responsibility for our actions. Proactive people don't blame others; they don't blame their physical or mental impairments, or their conditions in life. Unlike reactive people who depend on their circumstances and others to determine their choices, proactive people choose their response to the conditions and people around them. To the person who doubts their ability, they say, "I can get this done." They say, "I will finish this project," after a disaster wipes out their previous work.

Reactive people doubt their own abilities. They succumb to trials that impede their efforts. In other words, reactive people choose to live according to the dictates around them. After a while, they begin to live down to the low expectations of others. They show up late to appointments, they do mediocre work, and they quit things before they are finished—all because they choose to gravitate toward the inevitable failings around them. Reactive people are, by their own choice, at the mercy of external influences—like a change in company ownership, poor weather, a bad economy, or the threat of disaster.

Instead of concerning themselves with influences for which they have no control, proactive people center their attention on those things they *can* influence—their work, their health, their time, and their attitude. Proactive people anticipate the conditions around them so they can choose their actions. However, they do not depend on these conditions to manage their response. Instead, they imagine new ideas and solutions in advance of obstacles turning into roadblocks. They choose a long-term solution based on where they want to end-up, not on where the situation will take them. Proactive people are not just idle observers waiting for life to happen to them, they are consistently involving themselves in the creative process to plan for the future. They don't just react—they control their actions.

"I say if it's going to be done, let's do it. Let's not put it in the hands of fate. Let's not put it in the hands of someone who doesn't know me. I know me best. Then take a breath and go ahead." ~ Anita Baker

JUNE 12

I will express my appreciation

"Care for more coffee?" Adriana asked. "No, thank you," answered the man sitting with his wife at the booth. Adriana asked if he was finished with the roast turkey lunch, even though nothing remained on the plate. The man patted his jacket, and slowly began to place it over his pressed white shirt. The dark circles under Adriana's eyes testified of her working back-to-back shifts. Before she could remove his plate the man gently patted her arm and, with a smile, said, "I just want to tell you that I appreciate how you kept checking in with me to see if I needed more coffee. And I appreciated your pleasant smile. You've been a wonderful waitress and I expect you are a very kind person to everyone." Adriana's smile turned into a Cheshire cat grin. She stood taller, said "Thank you," and went on to have the most wonderful day.

Expressing appreciation can make someone's day. If we really thought about it, we would probably admit that we don't give or hear expressions of gratefulness as often as we should. All it takes is saying "thank you" and telling people what was so special about what they did. Adriana's customer stated some very specific compliments—her checking-in and her smiles—and then made a polite generalization that her actions likely reflected her character. People like hearing specifics. It helps them know *why* they are special. Then the general compliment just tops if off.

Appreciation is the spark of courtesy, generosity, gratitude, and concern that ignites that "warmth in the soul" feeling in others. It's one of the best ways in which to positively influence the attitudes and behaviors of those who receive it. It can come in the form of a nod, a smile, a thankful word, a card, a gift, or a helping hand. The key is to look for every opportunity to thank someone—from the waitress, to the clerk, to your boss for supporting your efforts. Look for as many opportunities to express your appreciation as there are occasions that deserve it. Appreciation is a soothing salve for the heart, and one of the best benefits is that it makes both the giver and the receiver feel better.

"Let us be grateful to people who make us happy; they are the charming gardeners who make our souls blossom." ~ Marcel Proust

JUNE 13

I will follow-up with people

Good follow-up may be one of the most neglected success factors in life. Many people we meet professionally or casually just do not merit a follow-up. We don't have time to circle back with everyone we meet. However, everyone we meet should fall into one of two categories: Contributors or Relaters.

Relaters are friends, family members, acquaintances, and long-time professional relationships that are sustained without the need for any motivation. Follow-up with these people is only occasional or as needed. Contributors are people whose support must be nurtured or developed in order to elicit something in return. Timely feedback must be maintained with these people in order to build a sense of urgency to get something done (preferably to your advantage). For example, a sales call with a potential customer should receive a prompt follow-up, as should the regular customer who is in need of critical assistance.

Those with whom you interview should always receive a follow-up email or (preferably) a note within a day or two. Follow-up to Contributors should add value to the recipient, such as a way in which you can help them, or provide useful resources to them. This builds trust and credibility, and the more value you can provide to someone, the more likely they are to support your needs. If you can't help them in the immediate, then at least communicate a plan of action for doing so. For example, you might say to a client that you don't have any information about their area of interest now, but you will conduct thorough research for some available options. Make sure to establish expectations with your Contributor as to the timeline for follow-up. Ask them how soon or by what date they would like to receive something so that you are both aligned.

A good idea is to make a list of important Contributors, noting things that would be useful or helpful for them, in order to keep their needs top of mind. Timely feedback is an easy way of differentiating yourself from your competition, and it can be as easy as a quick telephone call or email to confirm a service, next-step, or delivery. Don't take for granted that a Contributor will contact you. Be proactive and contact them first.

"Success comes from taking the initiative and following up…" ~ Tony Robbins

JUNE 14

I will be prepared

The founder of the Boy Scouts of America, Lord Baden-Powell, was once asked what the Scout's motto of "Be Prepared" meant. "Be prepared for what?" the questioner asked. "Why, for any old thing," said Baden-Powell. Sure, the Scouts learn first aid and rescue, but Baden-Powell wasn't thinking of just emergencies. He also meant to live happily and without regret, knowing that you have done your best. That's the meaning behind Be Prepared.

How often do you meet a situation, thinking "nobody prepared me for this?" In fact, no one can be prepared for everything life presents. We just need to do our best and believe that everything will work out in the end. As is espoused in the Scout training and much other professional training, we need to be ready in mind and body for any struggles, and to meet with courage whatever challenges may come our way. There is nothing that you might face that you can't find some way to handle. But you first need to believe in yourself. When we believe in ourselves, we find the strength to act on our values in the best interests of everyone involved.

If you don't posses enough self-esteem to think that way, you need to develop a strong base of support with other people who can encourage you and build-up your self-confidence. Everyone needs a listening ear, a helping hand, and sound advice to resolve whatever problems come our way. If you are a loner, there's still no reason why you can't find like-minded people who will understand and respect you enough to accommodate your personality. The key is to experience as much in life with enough of a foundation of support to deal with any situation. As we put ourselves out there to experience all life has to offer, we learn to deal with the various situations that can cause different reactions and emotions, and those experiences strengthen our ability to take on even weightier challenges that will in turn build our self-confidence.

Life always presents the unexpected. We can try to anticipate and prepare for some challenges, but the vast majority will require the kind of training that results from just going through life. So the next time someone asks you to try something new, do it. You'll be prepared, with an even higher threshold for the next new venture.

"Life belongs to the living, and he who lives must be prepared for changes." ~ JohannWolfgang von Goethe

JUNE 15

I will confront injustice

A life of sincere satisfaction cannot coexist with injustice in its midst. Abraham Lincoln could not deem his presidency a success without abolishing slavery. The people of the United States could not be content with an emerging prosperity in the wake of Hitler's devastation and holocaust. All people of good conscience cannot ignore injustices no matter how large or small, whether on a global scale or in the classroom.

Perhaps your life doesn't include any menacing atrocities, but invariably we all run across injustices, and when they happen, we cannot be at peace without at least attempting to right them. You've probably heard the Hebrew word "shalom," which is often translated as "peace." Shalom purposely means to offer a pledge for another's well-being. It implies that to attain peace we must place the needs of others above our own needs. If someone is suffering from an abusive co-worker who is enjoying the admiration of their peers, there is no shalom or justice, and therefore no peace.

Martin Luther King Jr. once said, "True peace is not merely the absence of tension—it is the presence of justice." The Hebrew word for justice, *zedakah*, does not mean retribution or punishment, or getting even. It means righteousness, insisting on doing what's right. When someone gets treated unfairly, at home, at work, or in a public or private setting, people who insist on zedakah practice true courage and leadership.

So the next time you hear someone unfairly putting down another through gossip or subversion, confront his or her injustice. Or seek someone in authority who can help you right the wrong. If someone commits a wrongful act, don't always let it slide. In the face of wrong, we must be careful to choose our battles wisely. But when someone is being mentally or physically harmed by another's unfair treatment, we must do something constructive in order to help stem its effect. We can also help right the injustices of societies through organizations that fight poverty and abuse. Change happens when ordinary people do what they can to stop injustice—and that change always happens with taking action now.

"Injustice anywhere is a threat to justice everywhere." ~ Martin Luther King, Jr.

JUNE 16

I will learn about international customs

The world is becoming more global than ever before. As the world shrinks we need to expand our understanding of the unique customs of other cultures in order to effectively communicate and do business with each other. Certain practices can save you from embarrassment. For example, Americans typically believe that looking someone in the eyes demonstrates confidence. In Asian cultures, such as Japan and China, intense eye contact with a superior is typically not appropriate. Avoiding looking someone in the eye is usually interpreted as being polite or respectful. Staring at a superior in Asian, Latin American, and African cultures is seen as a sign of disrespect. In most Middle Eastern cultures, especially amongst Muslims, direct contact between opposite genders is not appropriate.

There also exist some common rules of conduct that are specific to certain countries. In Germany never discuss business matters during a meal—only before or after. In Mexico, business is more commonly conducted during lunch than dinner. In Russia, placing your hands in your pockets is considered rude. In Japan, it is courteous to bring a small gift to a meeting and present it to the senior member of the team. In most Asian countries, a business card should be presented with two hands, accompanied by a small bow.

In Arab and some Asian countries you should never present a business card with your left hand, as this hand is used for personal hygiene. In certain parts of Latin America, such as Brazil, the okay sign is considered rude. In parts of the Middle East, such as Egypt, it is considered rude not to accept tea or coffee if it is offered. Shaking hands is mostly universal, however in most countries (including the U.S.), never initiate a handshake with someone of a higher status. Let them approach you first. In the Arab world, touching women in western dress is forbidden. In certain countries like Morocco, when at social functions it is customary to shake hands starting with the person to your right first before moving to the left. In some Asian countries like South Korea the elderly are highly revered, so it is polite to greet any older people first. Keep in mind that cultures can change, so keep up to date.

"No culture can live if it attempts to be exclusive." ~ Mahatma Gandhi

JUNE 17

I will practice excellent telephone skills

The phone rings. It's your success calling. That's the attitude professionals need to imbed in their way of thinking whenever a call arrives. Even at home, seeing your phone as a reflection of your personality, or at the office as your brand, can inspire you to communicate more professionally. When someone never gets an answer from the phone, our standard of responsiveness is compromised. When you think of the phone as a reflection on you, you are more likely to speak with confidence than irritability when answering the phone or placing a call. People generally form an impression of you during the first thirty seconds of a call and their lasting impression is formed during the final thirty seconds.

So before you answer or place the call, take a deep breath in. Let your energy exhale out when you answer the phone. Psyche yourself up to speak confidently and positively. Your tone inflection should vary (no monotone), with peaks and valleys in your voice to maintain and show interest. Give your name and position if it's a company related call. A "thank you for calling" is always a nice way to open your response. Make sure not to speak too quickly, as a calm and deliberate voice typically elicits a more ready state from the other person.

If you are initiating the phone conversation, develop a plan for what you will discuss prior to the call. You might ask a question to set the tone, such as asking the person how their day is going. Use good listening skills by acknowledging their comments with an occasional "aha" or an "oh." Be sincere, addressing the other person's questions quickly and politely. Your focus should always be on what the other person is saying or needing. Avoid jumping into your own agenda before their issues are addressed. Take notes if possible, and confirm what's been said with a, "What I'm hearing you say is ________" type of restatement to clarify important points. Use the final thirty seconds to thank them for the call, reviewing issues or concerns and how you will address them. Thank them for their support. Stay positive. How the caller feels at the end of a conversation will determine whether they will speak with you longer or return for a follow-up phone conversation.

"The telephone is a good way to talk to people without having to offer them a drink." ~ Fran Lebowitz

JUNE 18

I will be accountable

It takes a lot of courage for someone to openly accept full responsibility for his or her failures in a public setting without being forced. Accepting responsibility is one of the most difficult and necessary factors for anyone who wants other people to respect them. Acknowledging our errors instead of blaming others demonstrates maturity and leadership. Everyone makes mistakes, but the real proof of our character is reflected in how we react to them.

When someone sincerely apologizes, we know he or she is placing honesty above personal comfort. Not only is it inspiring, it increases the legitimacy of the confessor. Leaders who encourage this level of transparency among their followers actually build stronger cultures of loyalty, camaraderie, and innovation. Indeed, people respect those brave enough to fess-up, and it makes them feel more comfortable in signing-up for whatever that person has to offer. Leaders who are courageous enough to admit their own faults impart the same level of courage to others, which makes others feel like the leader's got their backs. It is a sign of confidence and humility that is contagious to everyone around them.

A useful way to hold yourself accountable is through accountability partners—people you know who are not afraid to tell you when you've gone astray. Keep an annual planner, even if it's in pencil, to see what goals you've accomplished and those you did not. See where you can correct mistakes to improve your performance. Get comfortable with saying, "I'm sorry," and don't pass off your explanation by speaking in the third person. Say for example, "I'm sorry that I didn't follow-through on my promise," instead of "You know, when someone is pressed for time, it's hard to get everything done." Don't make excuses, like, "If only I hadn't gotten all of these last minute projects." Own-up to a failure, even if the circumstances were against you, by allowing the apology to stand on its own. Then tell the wronged person how you will make it right, and make sure to do it as promised and on schedule. It will probably feel unnerving at first, but once you've done it you will feel much better—and so will others.

"A body of men holding themselves accountable to nobody ought not to be trusted by anybody." ~ Thomas Paine

JUNE 19

I will expand my vision

We all live within our own isolated worlds, however successful people understand that expanding one's outlook helps create a larger view of the possibilities available to them. The more people, places, and experiences we can include in our envisioning, the better. Broadening our horizon doesn't have to be as complicated as planning a trip to some distant land. It can be as simple as networking with others or retreating to a relaxing environment.

Just by expanding our visual horizon, we can extend our range of thinking beyond the parameters of our normal thought processes. When we get stuck in a rut, the creative juices tend to dry up. That's because left to our limited environment, we fail to see the possibilities. We can't expand our vision without first expanding our view beyond just our self. Our vision needs to include the larger context of the world around us.

Bob Buford did this after creating a successful cable company. He wanted to do more than just make money, so he developed *Halftime* as a way to help people invest the second half of their life by helping others through charitable work. In order to expand its influence, he wrote a book about this organization. Today, *Halftime* engages thousands of successful people in philanthropic efforts around the world.

As it was with Bob, expanding your vision requires an awareness of the needs not just within your own community, but also in the communities around you. Just by using your current skills and abilities, you can make a broader impact. *Halftime* helps successful homebuilders in the U.S. build housing units in Africa, and it facilitates doctors practicing medicine where no hospitals exist. The more we expand the scope and understanding of what's around us, the better we can identify a grander vision that can positively influence even more people. That's the definition of multiplying success—continually helping others to succeed.

"All successful people are big dreamers. They imagine what their future could be, ideal in every respect, and then they work every day toward their distant vision, that goal or purpose." ~ Brian Tracy

JUNE 20

I will plan to win

Do you ever feel on overload with all the cares and responsibilities that keep coming? Do unfinished tasks keep you awake at night? Time management is one of the most necessary and often neglected skills in life. Thankfully, you can regain control over your life through some proven techniques, even if your organizational skills are not very strong.

Winston Churchill coined the phrase: "Fail to plan, plan to fail." Planning each day with a calendar and a prioritized list of tasks is a good way to keep interruptions from interfering with our best intentions. One of the best ways to keep on target is to learn the skill of "just saying no." We all need to remain faithful to our goals and deadlines. Granted, some last-minute tasks can legitimately overrule our top priorities (such as a boss's urgent requests), but these should be the exceptions and not the routine. Feel free to turn off the phone, close the door, or go someplace offsite to devote full attention to your most important work. Much of our wasted time involves fixing or redoing tasks, like that paper with misspellings that need correcting. "Do the job right the first time" should always play in the back of your mind in order to consistently produce quality work that won't consume your time with circling back. Another timewaster is leaving emails in your in-box—organize them in file folders. If a project is too large to complete within a reasonable time, try breaking it into smaller tasks. Then either delegate some of them or negotiate some type of shared responsibility with your team.

Think creatively of ways in which you might be able to complete tasks using empty time, such as taking public transportation to read or complete reports. Make sure to get enough sleep, eat right, exercise, and take enough breaks to improve your concentration and your efficiency to do more in less time. Good time managers are often thought of as multitaskers, but this isn't usually true. Doing several tasks at once can decrease productivity. Instead, give your full attention to each task before moving onto the next. It's OK to slow down in order to process and plan your work. Winning the day requires a mindful plan that completes one task at a time.

"Ordinary people think merely of spending time.
Great people think of using it." ~ Author Unknown

JUNE 21

I will teach others

We've all heard the phrase, "the best way to learn something is to teach it to someone else." Why not apply that to your own career? If you want to learn about communication styles, write an article about it. If you want to perfect your jujitsu, offer to teach those in your neighborhood. Interested in perfecting your leadership skills? Start a workshop.

By teaching others, we not only benefit those we teach, we also develop stronger interpersonal skills by learning to interface with a wide variety of people. People have different learning styles just as they have different behavioral styles. Visual learners learn with pictures and images. Aural learners prefer sounds and music. Verbal learners prefer words in speech and writing. Logical learners gain from reasoning and the use of systems. Social learners benefit from being with other people in groups. Solitary learners work best alone using self-study. And physical learners learn best from using their body, hands, and their sense of touch. When we modify our teaching style to accommodate how others learn, we also improve our own adaptation and organizational skills. Teaching forces us to create a specific context in which to communicate effectively. The research we will uncover while preparing our lesson exposes us to new ideas as we uncover the latest thinking and best practices in the field. Once we start teaching, our performance starts to peak and we identify instant opportunities and approaches that can grow our own understanding. In the process, others will challenge our expertise, which can either stretch our knowledge and skills, or validate them.

Helping someone else become competent or better forces us to be the best rendition of ourselves, and that can build self-confidence and personal credibility with others. It also introduces us to new people and builds our network. One cautionary word about teaching: avoid being too vague or theoretical. People respond to practical applications. That's why word pictures and real-life stories help students to apply principles and skills to their own situations. A person learns when it becomes relevant to them, and only after they start practicing in their own life what they were taught.

"Tell me and I forget. Teach me and I remember. Involve me and I learn." ~ Benjamin Franklin

JUNE 22

I will treat people as if they were what they ought to be

For most of her career, Sheila was shunned by others. She saw life through smoky-colored glasses. Her posture drooped from years of carrying the burdens of the world on her shoulder. Give her a glass half full, and she would say it was three-quarters empty. Invariably, Sheila would read on her work evaluation comments like, "You need to be a better team player." None of her bosses knew what to do with Sheila, except get her out of their department as soon as possible.

One day a new supervisor arrived in the department. He met with Sheila and soon discovered the same negative behaviors all others did. Only he responded to Sheila differently. "You're an organizer, Sheila," he said. "I see you as someone who can make things happen. I believe you're just the person I need. We should plan a team-building event for the department, and I can't think of anyone else I'd rather have as chief planner. Will you do it?" Sheila lifted her shoulders for the first time—perhaps since she'd been a child—and said with a hint of enthusiasm, "Yes." To everyone's surprise—except her supervisor's—Sheila produced a spectacular event.

After everyone finished their afternoon treat, Sheila's supervisor asked her to give a speech to the team. She'd never given a speech before, but again she rose to the occasion and forced a few words: "I know I haven't been the most involved person here. It's hard...well, you know when you don't feel that people...what I really want to say is, thanks for letting me do this." Before she could utter another strained word, everyone began clapping and cheering for Sheila. Her grin revealed teeth no one had ever seen before. Afterwards, at least three people came up to invite her to a future lunch. During cleanup, Sheila's supervisor came up to her and said, "I knew all along you'd do a great job. You're a winner, Sheila. You're just the person I need in our department." Sheila went on to be a strong performer in the department, thanks to one person who treated her as she ought to be.

Who is your Sheila? Whose life can you help turn around today, simply by believing in them?

"Treat people as if they were what they ought to be and you help them become what they are capable of becoming." ~ Goethe

JUNE 23

I will not place success as my target

Failure is in our future. It's inevitable, so stop worrying about it. Investing all your efforts to eliminate or minimize failure will not contribute one iota to your success. That's because success changes with different expectations, and the possibility for failure accompanies each one. Dispel the myth that success should be your target.

Most of the time we base success on what it can give us—whether that's status, material things, or a lifestyle. When external things serve as our stimulus to succeed, we can be left feeling empty. When our driving force comes from within ourselves, we feel more secure, stronger. So focusing only on what imbues within us genuine joy, confidence, and security will help us get to where we want to be now—not in the future. We need to remain center-focused in the present so that we're not continually seeking after something that may never come to pass.

Once you get there, you need to stop worrying about what you can't do, and start establishing confidence in what you are right now, in this moment, ready and able to do. Doubting yourself is a useless feeling that prevents you from taking action. Confidence instills in us a positive self-image that says, sure, you will do things that are wrong, but you will not allow the downside of trying something to keep you from taking significant action right now. Success is a very subjective and variable objective. Working to build your self-confidence is an attainable and strengthening exercise. That should be your goal.

The outcome of building confidence is likely to lead to also obtaining some of your external desires. So how do you build self-confidence? Forget what others expect of you, and just do what you feel driven to do. Many of the expectations we perceive are simply made-up expectations. They're what we believe others expect of us. So use your own strengths and values to make a decision, without the constraints of wondering how it will turn out. Your success is not what others think, or how it looks. It's what you believe.

"Giving people self-confidence is by far the most important thing that I can do. Because then they will act." ~ Jack Welch

JUNE 24

I will stop waiting

If you could travel back in time to this present time, what would you do differently? Judy and Verne Teyler asked themselves that question while Verne worked as a top executive at E.F. Hutton. Inspired by their passion for children, they acquired a 100-acre ranch in Castro Valley, California. They became foster parents, determined to teach, house, and find placements for abandoned and abused children. Almost thirty years later, over one thousand children have found nurturing homes through their Hosanna Homes ministry. This amazing couple did not wait for the opportunity to follow their passion. Like many who have successfully redefined their lives, they got real with themselves.

Author Po Bronson writes about defining the "New Era," wherein those who thrive do so because they focus on the question of who they really are, instantly connecting that to work they truly love. In his article "Choosing What To Do With Your Life," Bronson recounts the story of a catfish farmer who used to be an investment broker, an academic-turned-chef, and a Harvard MBA who found his calling as a police officer. These examples of people who stopped waiting and started living out what they truly love give testimony to the fact that all of us can do the same.

The average person spends from forty to sixty minutes a day waiting, usually for fairly unimportant things—such as another person to show-up, or a ride to arrive. But the average person also regrets waiting to do what is most important for themselves—to live a life true to themselves.

Over time, those who endlessly wait for tomorrows waste their todays—until they casually accept their situation as inevitable. They become resigned to what seems normal or inevitable. Just as fresh food left too long will rot, so too our dreams will spoil over time if not applied as reality, and after awhile we will be left wondering, *if I could do it over again, what would I do differently?* Once you've got the answer, the response must be to do it!

"The journey of a thousand miles begins with a single step." ~ Lao Tzu

"When you were born, you cried and the world rejoiced. Live your life in such a manner that when you die the world cries and you rejoice." ~ Native American saying

JUNE 25

I will take a walk in the park

Walking and other types of moderate exercise can help reduce stress and elevate our mood, especially if done in a calm and inspiring location. It releases endorphins that make you feel relaxed and happier. After only a ten-minute walk, your body temperature increases, triggering this response. So taking a quick walk before an important meeting or a jog before going to work can help put you in a better frame of mind.

You don't have to be a triathlete to enjoy the benefits of physical activity. Think of how churning water in a pool keeps it from getting stagnant with germs. The same principle applies to your own circulatory system. The more body movement you cause by way of just about any physical activity, the more effectively your body can fight off disease and make you feel better overall. Exercise causes multiple benefits. It can even increase your confidence level by distracting your attention away from stress-induced activities and onto other healthy brain stimulating responses.

Our bodies release adrenaline as a stress hormone, and exercise is understood by the body as a form of stress. By inducing the adrenal glands to release cortisol and adrenaline, exercise initiates a positive stress response, increasing blood flow, glucose availability, and voluntary muscle activity. Negative stress induced by such things as anxiety can release high levels of these stress hormones for extended periods of time causing heart disease, sleep problems, depression, memory impairment, and even obesity. Anticipation, like preparing for an important meeting or a job interview can manifest this type of negative stress, as can worries that result from not being able to rest after a project has been finished. Taking a walk, going for a run, or exercising at the gym resets hormone levels when followed by some form of relaxation. Even stretching exercises can get the blood flowing at a positive level.

If you do these things before a stressful encounter like that important meeting, you'll feel calmer and better able to formulate those ideas and responses more quickly. It's a win-win.

"Follow your dreams, work hard, practice and persevere. Make sure you eat a variety of foods, get plenty of exercise and maintain a healthy lifestyle." ~ Sasha Cohen

JUNE 26

I will read a book a month

Here's a fact: the most successful and influential people read books. They even reread books. People who read engage their thinking process more efficiently than those who use simple observation, like watching television or other less mind stirring activities.

One of the most healthful habits of successful people is a consistent diet of reading. Reading success books allows you to learn from people who have observed or experienced the level of success that you desire. For just a few dollars, you can avail yourself of years of time-tested wisdom.

It's true that we tend to become what we think about, and reading forces us to think about new ideas and approaches. With self-help books we can become vicariously successful. By reading about success, we get inspired, and success tends to happen. Consider the authors and experts of books you read as some of your closest friends, since you spend hours with them in print or via your digital notebook. When you read, it's just you and them having a mental conversation. Chances are that few of your other friends and associates can match the experience or factual evidence you will find in a book that packs years of knowledge into two hundred or so pages. If you're human, you've probably received some bad advice in the past from others. But few will complain they've received bad advice in a book.

Reputable authors spend countless hours pouring over their material, researching information, and fact checking it before going to publication. By the time laudable books reach our hands, several other eyes have scrutinized the material and checked everything down to the grammatical context.

With so much wasted time in our lives, spending just a few hours each week reading a book is a great way to begin a new adventure while increasing your knowledge and skills.

"A man only learns in two ways, one by reading, and the other by association with smarter people." ~ Will Rogers

JUNE 27

I will not try to suppress my bad habits

What are your goals? Do you want to lose weight, quit smoking, or turn your bad temper into patience? Rather than concentrating on the bad habits, plan how you will replace them with good ones. Attempting to push a negative thought or a bad habit out of your consciousness can actually bring it back even more powerfully.

Our minds seem at times to work against us. We want to get a good night's sleep, but thoughts keep racing through our head. We want to stop that craving for sweets, but pictures of chocolate fudge sundaes dance in our minds. The typical response is to try to forget about whatever's nagging us. However, psychological research has found that this approach can actually make the condition worse.

Professor Daniel Wegner and his colleagues initially researched the effects of thought suppression in 1987. Participants were asked to try not to think about a white bear for five minutes, then for the following five minutes to think about a white bear. Throughout the process, they were asked to articulate their thoughts, and to ring a bell each time they thought of a white bear. Those who tried to suppress their thoughts rang the bell almost twice as often as participants in a control group. Other researchers have confirmed Wegner's findings, such that this phenomenon is now called the "post-suppression rebound effect." This principle is particularly pronounced when people attempt to suppress their emotions. Trying to suppress depressing thoughts or bad memories can actually double psychological distress. Apparently our minds initiate an unconscious monitoring process to check if we are continuing to think about what we are trying not to think about—a sad twist of irony. Anything that remotely seems like the suppressed idea triggers the mind's looping response.

So the key is to give up trying to repress negative thoughts. If you want to change your ways, ask yourself, "What can I do instead?" For example, if you're trying to lose weight, devise a plan that when you have that craving, you'll go for a walk or do something active as a form of replacement therapy to stave off a reoccurrence of the habit. Eventually, if you remain committed, your bad habit will start declining until it vanishes completely.

"Once you replace negative thoughts with positive ones, you'll start having positive results." ~ Willie Nelson

JUNE 28

I will be the challenger

In the best-selling book *The Challenger Sale: Taking Control of the Customer Conversation* (Dixon and Adamson, Portfolio Hardcover, 2011), a survey of over 6,000 sales people revealed that sales representatives can be categorized into one of five profiles: 1) The Hard Worker; 2) The Problem Solver; 3) The Challenger; 4) The Relationship Builder; and, 5) The Lone Wolf. Each of the profiles was found to demonstrate only average performance, with the exception of one that consistently outperforms—The Challenger. Challengers are different, in that instead of just focusing on building customer relationships, they tend to push the customer's thinking by exposing generally overlooked problems. Challengers then introduce new solutions to their customers' newly surfaced problems. They target accounts whose needs are still undefined. They also target buyers who are skeptical, but can be considered as change agents (called "Mobilizers"), versus targeting what the authors term as friendly "Talkers."

The basic premise is that customers no longer need sales people in the conventional sense, where sales reps diagnose customer needs, tailor their product's benefits to those needs, and sell them better solutions than their competitors. In today's world, companies are usually defining solutions for themselves, thanks to more advanced procurement teams and consultants who provide a superabundance of data. So successful sales people must generate new demands in a world of resistant, risk-averse customers. Challengers exhibit a profound knowledge of the customer's business and they use that insight to push the customer's thinking, as well as to instruct them about innovative ways in which their company can compete more effectively. Essentially, the challenger is focused on pushing the customer out of their comfort zone through a value-based or solutions-oriented approach.

The key is to try to control the business decision process with tactful assertiveness and empathy for the customer while transitioning the dialogue from simply cost to real value. What sets the most successful providers apart from those who are unsuccessful is not so much the quality or features of their products, but the new insights they provide to customers that will either make them more profitable or save them money in ways they would have never thought possible. Customers will return your value proposition with loyalty when you teach them something. Their paradigm has shifted to a new value you can give.

"Don't be afraid to challenge the pros, even in their own backyard." ~ Colin Powell

JUNE 29

I will build my social business acumen

To get ahead in the era of social media, professionals need to be well-versed in the various modalities, and be able to critically read and assess them in the same way that they currently access a paper or a presentation, according to the *Institute of the Future* report. The report also says that you will need to be comfortable creating and presenting your own visual information using social media.

The changing dynamics of the future information age are analogous to the time before word processing programs made the use of layouts and the knowledge of fonts available to everyday workers. Before these user-friendly innovations, training in complex programs was required to do even the simplest tasks. As interactive and visually stimulating presentations become the norm, professionals will need more sophisticated skills in order to use the latest tools to engage and influence their audiences.

Key to success in social media is engineering platforms where people can interact with each other. This is a powerful opportunity for individuals and companies to create and promote their own brands by creating an "online culture" around their products. It begins by establishing a universal language that consumers will use when talking about their preferred products.

Google is a perfect example of how a product name can assume a common vernacular in the cyberspace (we "Google" information), just as Kleenex dominated the branding language for facial tissue through conventional marketing tools of old. Second, establishing common goals that people will pursue within the social engines is key to driving support for a brand or campaign. For example, one author solicited ideas for her book on gluten free recipes using Twitter, and continued dialoguing with her gluten-free respondents until her book was published. Many of her followers ordered her new book.

These types of interactions that are aligned to brand strengths foster consumer loyalty, especially when coupled with rewards (the author conducted a contest for the best submission). Social media presentations and interactions are growing in excess of forty percent annually, according to The International Data Corporation. It's the future.

"Social Media is about sociology and psychology more than technology." ~ Brian Solis

JUNE 30

I will focus on being a "black belt"

As CEO of General Electric in the mid-1980s, Jack Welch made famous a set of tools and strategies for process improvement called *Six Sigma*. This hugely successful program improves the quality of process outputs by identifying and removing the cause of errors (defects) and by standardizing business processes using a set of quality management methods like statistical analyses, and by using experts in these complex methods. These experts on process improvement are called "Black Belts," and they basically exhibit certain essential qualities that can be applied by anyone in business. Those who want their Black Belt must be self-motivated and positive.

Sometimes in the work environment you will need to be a cheerleader, as well as a customer advocate. Both external and internal (employee) customers must be the final judges as to the product or service quality, and the Black Belt must insist on understanding the customer needs in order to eliminate the process variations that can cause periodic failures. By nature, Black Belts are effective change agents through coaching, training, and mentoring others. Instead of simply trying to improve quality, Black Belts can challenge paradigms because of their acute understanding of how businesses can lead their markets versus simply tweaking existing operations. An understanding of the project scope, needs, resources, timelines, and possibilities is essential, but a Black Belt needn't be a statistician or engineer by degree. However, the process driven Black Belt must possess some technical aptitude in order to format and analyze data so that he or she can determine process gaps and areas for improvement. Producing quantifiable financial results for the client is job number one for any Black Belt, but above all he or she must demonstrate strong leadership, influencing, team, and motivational skills.

If you possess all of these qualifications, you could be a Black Belt—but keep in mind that there is a rigid certification requirement that must be completed online and/or in the classroom. Mid- to larger companies are increasingly seeking experts in process management, if you are so inclined to become a Black Belt.

"Quality in a service or product is not what you put into it. It is what the client or customer gets out of it." ~ Peter Drucker

JULY

STAY CONNECTED

JULY 1

I will meditate each day

At the University of Massachusetts, a study headed by Dr. Richard J. Davidson measured the brain effects of those who practiced meditation versus those who did not over a fifty-six day period. MRIs of both groups showed that those who meditated daily actually shrunk their amygdala, a small mass of gray matter deep inside the cerebral hemisphere that drives disturbing emotions like stress. Another study by Professor Elizabeth Blackburn, a Nobel Prize winner in Physiology or Medicine, discovered that regular meditators, over a period of time, experience more telomerase activity, an enzymatic process that preserves the length of telomeres across cell divisions in stem cells. It is thought to play a role in the proliferation and therefore immortality of cells. When telomeres drop below a critical length, the cell can no longer divide properly and eventually dies. The study by Dr. Blackburn is the first to link positive well-being and longevity to higher telomerase as a direct result of meditation.

Meditation is a restful awareness response that occurs from breathing deeply and slowly in personal silence, accompanied with a mindful state of essentially "decluttering" the brain. Simply stilling oneself has been shown to increase normal blood flow and prevent blood clotting. Some meditate by repetitively humming to themselves sounds like "om," or listening to the nature sounds, or by using a prayer language.

Simply changing what we think doesn't produce that positive meditative state. Rather, positive meditation pauses the mind. Try it by getting alone and then inhaling deeply through your nostrils, while at the same time relaxing your belly muscles. Feel as though the belly is filling with air. Fill up the middle of your chest. Feel your chest and rib cage expand. Hold the breath for a moment, then begin to exhale as slowly as possible. As the air is slowly let out, relax your chest and rib cage. Begin to pull your belly in to force out the remaining breath. Close your eyes and concentrate on your breathing. Relax your face and mind. Let everything go. Hum to yourself quietly while doing this for about ten minutes in the morning, and for about ten minutes after you return from work.

"Meditation dissolves the mind. It erases itself. Throws the ego out on its brittle ass." ~ Tony Robbins

JULY 2

I will be happy

In a recent study do you know what people listed as their number one personal pleasure? No, it's not what you think. They described shopping as what gives them the greatest pleasure. Now, don't just go out and start shopping. There's more to happiness than making yourself poorer.

Physicians at the Chopra Center in Carlsbad, California have actually devised what they call the "Happiness Formula," or: H = S + C + V. S is the "set point" in the brain, involving our basic life attitude. Do we see the problems or opportunities in life? S, says Chopra, accounts for about forty percent of our daily happiness. C stands for our condition—our living conditions, but mostly our physical condition. If we are poor but win the lottery, for example, we may be happy for a brief time, but eventually we'll return to S, the set point. C, then, represents about ten to fifteen percent of our daily happiness. Finally, V represents our voluntary choices. If we fill our time with pleasurable activities only—like shopping, eating, creativity, sex, etc.—our happiness again is temporary. More meaningful, longer lasting choices include using your creativity and making others happy.

By making conscious choices to improve yourself and your environment, or by simply being more mindful, you can change your condition (C). You can increase voluntary (V) satisfaction by noticing your strengths, ridding yourself of resentment, forgiving yourself and others, and becoming more grateful. We should act, say the researchers, as if this is our first day and our last day. Consider life as an adventure, without worrying about the outcome. We can have questions, but we must also be comfortable with uncertainty—without needing all the answers. Chopra calls this "just living the questions." Knowing yourself is the key, as well as perceiving your reality as beyond the conditions in which you find yourself. Suffering because we don't know what is real or we are grasping for what's not real, or because we fear impermanence or death, can be mitigated simply by just being in the present and by being confident in who you are.

"Happiness often sneaks in through a door you didn't know you left open."
~ John Barrymore

"Most folks are as happy as they make up their minds to be." ~ Abraham Lincoln

JULY 3

I will know my mind and body type

For centuries people have been classifying themselves into to all kinds of categories. In *The Tipping Point*, author Malcolm Gladwell described society's "doers" as Connectors (networkers), Mavens (information specialists), or Salesmen (persuaders). What's called Constitutional Typing, one of the oldest philosophies of health maintenance, aligns nature's elements of space, air, fire, water, and earth with three basic constitutional types: Vatas (who reflect the qualities of air and water), Pittas (who reflect the qualities of fire and water), and Kaphas (who reflect the qualities of earth and water). A Vata resembles the wind, in that they are open, ready to go, spontaneous, adaptable, creative, move and talk quickly, resist routine, are good communicators and welcome new experiences. Pittas demonstrate a fiery nature that makes things happen, follows through, easily makes decisions, leads, is precise, friendly, judging, and task-oriented. A Kapha is grounded, and solid in nature. They love routine, don't like change, are process-oriented, calm, content, steady, loyal, and consistent.

Kaphas would be the ones to say "whatever," and in a competition would invite the other person to "go ahead of me." In a stress situation, Pittas would tend to blame the other person, or send one of those nuclear emails that get everyone else riled. They tend to obsess about themselves. Vatas tend to blame themselves, as in "What have I done wrong?" Under stress they look introspectively.

Which type are you? It's important to balance your type in all situations. If you're a Vata, find things that will ground you, such as establishing a to-do list or a schedule, and be easy on yourself when there's a conflict. You Pitta-types become angry, irritable, and excessively critical when you're imbalanced, so work on delegating responsibility, relaxing, and trusting in others. If you're a Kapha, it's time to move out of your comfort zone by letting go of those things that don't serve you anymore and push yourself to try new things. An imbalanced Kapha will become needy, attached, overly protective, and dull. An imbalanced Vata's overactive mind will cause anxiety, worry, and insomnia. All types must be careful not to allow their strengths to move to the extreme, by balancing their natural propensity with a complementary approach to life.

"Self-knowledge is the beginning of self-improvement." ~ *Baltasar Gracian*

JULY 4

I will prioritize System-2 thinking

"A bat and ball cost $1.10. The bat costs one dollar more than the ball. How much does the ball cost?" More than likely an amount popped into your head, and chances are that figure was ten cents. If you came up with that amount, you just followed the law of least effort by using System-1 thinking.

If you had used System-2 thinking to check your answer, your thinking might have followed this line of thought: "If the ball costs ten cents, then the total cost will be $1.20" (10 cents for the ball and $1.10 for the bat). You still would not be correct because together they only cost $1.10, so you would have further used System 2 to perform the math a little more carefully, and you would have found that the correct answer is five cents. Don't worry if you got the answer wrong. University students with average grades gave the intuitive (System-1 type) incorrect answer in excess of eighty percent. This example was given in Daniel Kahneman's thought-provoking book *Thinking, Fast and Slow* (Farrar, Straus and Giroux, 2011).

In this book, the Nobel Prize-winning psychologist explains thinking as comprising two modes or systems. Slow thinking (System 2) is the system that we generally consider as thought in the strictest sense—deliberate, conscious—as when we consider what to eat, what stocks to buy, etc. By contrast, System-1 thinking is automatic and unconscious, and is intended as a means of protection (i.e., fight or flight) by surveying the environment and processing incoming stimuli at lightning speed. If we allow System-1 thinking to prevail, we can make snap decisions that factor in preprogrammed bias, which can lead to incorrect reasoning, such as when answering the bat-and-ball quiz incorrectly.

System-1 thinking can cause us to hold on to stocks too long for fear of loss (because of a bias against losses) even when the potential upside is higher. It can incorrectly frame an effect, such as when doctors tended to advise surgery to patients *less often* when the doctors were informed of a mortality rate of 10%, and advised their patients to undergo surgery *more often* when these same doctors were informed of a survival rate of 90%, even though the statistics are the same.

Even when facts are presented, System-1 thinking can overlook them unless System-2 thinking takes over, in which case a more reasoned and more accurate approach can be taken. So avoid snap decisions whenever possible. Allow for thoughtful deliberation in order to engage System-2 thinking, so that you can make calculated decisions based on reasoning and not just pre-conceived assumptions.

"The important thing is not to stop questioning." - Albert Einstein

JULY 5

I will tell only clean jokes in public

A group of professional men and women sat at tables during dinnertime after a long meeting day to await their meals. The president came up with a "brilliant" idea to break the ice. He asked that each person tell a joke, starting with his. One by one, each person told a joke until one man decided to share a dirty joke, which offended most of the women and several of the men in the group. The moral of this true story: if you have to tell joke, at least make it a clean one. In order to give you some material, here are twenty good, or at least decent, ones:

1) I poured root beer into a square cup. Now I just have beer. 2) Why did the scarecrow win an award? He was outstanding in his field. 3) Why do chicken coops have two doors? Because if they had four it would be a chicken sedan. 4) What do you get when you put a piano down a mineshaft? A flat miner. 5) What did the buffalo say to his son when he dropped him off at school?...Bison. 6) What do you call a fake noodle? An impasta. 7) I once worked at a fire hydrant factory. You couldn't park anywhere near it. 8) Doctor: "I am not exactly sure of the cause. I think it could be due to alcohol." Patient: "That's OK, I will come back when you are sober." 9) What's red and bad for your teeth? A brick. 10) I told my friend that she drew her eyebrows on too high. She looked surprised. 11) What do you call a zebra that has been given an uppercut by Chuck Norris? A giraffe. 12) Why did the chicken cross the road only halfway? She wanted to lay it on the line. 13) What do you get when you cross a chicken and a pit bull? Just the pit bull. 14) Why don't cats play poker in the jungle? Too many cheetahs. 15) Knock, Knock! Who's there? Ya. Ya who? What are you getting so excited about? 16) Knock, Knock! Who's there? Vera. Vera who? Vera few people think these jokes are funny! 17) What's the difference between a shower curtain and a piece of toilet paper? Response: "I don't know." Answer: So you're the one. 18) What time does Sean Connery arrive at Wimbledon? Tennish. 19) I never wanted to believe that my dad was stealing from his job as a road worker, but when I got home, all the signs were there. 20) Who is the roundest knight at King Arthur's table? Sir Cumference.

"The difficult thing with quotes on the Internet is verifying them." ~ Abraham Lincoln

JULY 6

I will adapt

The popular line of thought is to be different. While that holds true for many advances, like innovation, sometimes it's best to be like others. In his blockbuster book, *Swim with the Sharks Without Being Eaten Alive* (MJF Books, 2005), Harvey Mackay reveals the key to surviving with the sharks is to become like one of them. If a shark recognizes a fish or some other food source, it will eat it. But sharks do not eat other sharks.

Being willing to adapt your behavior increases your ability to communicate and build relationships with other people. But few actually practice adaptability. Perhaps that's because, as research shows, people view themselves as more versatile than they truly are. In order to develop the skill of adaptability, you must first practice empathy, tolerance, and respect for the other person. Empathy is the most important contributor to adaptability, which is essentially feeling how the other person feels, or "walking in their shoes." Strong empathy for another person usually leads to greater respect for them, and a higher tolerance for their faults. If we feel the need to compete with someone else, or if we feel it must be "my way or the highway," then prepare to be attacked by the sharks. If you are attacked or rejected, don't give-up. Being adaptable requires that you bounce back from rejection to suggest alternative ways in which to work together.

Remember that people respond positively to those who maintain a positive attitude in finding ways to accommodate their style and agenda. People respond favorably to those who can offer a collaborative approach in attending to *their* needs. Telltale signs are always given off by people to alert us as to whether they are receptive, bored, or irritated. The adaptable person must be perceptive in reading these signals, and to adjust their response accordingly. The ability to self-correct behavior is a key need in developing adaptability. If something isn't working, change course. "It's not all about me,' says the adaptable person. 'It's about us." Understand the other person's behavioral style and their mind-body style in order to match your behaviors to their preferred style. For example, when dealing with a Driver-Pitta, you'll want to show respect and speak concisely in support of their efforts. When you do, *you* win.

"All failure is failure to adapt, all success is successful adaptation." ~ Max McKeown

JULY 7

I will grow younger

Who knew that the fountain of youth *is* possible! We all know that the way we see aging is changing. Fifty is the new forty, as they say, and so on, rolling the clock back a little more each decade. As it turns out, several studies have revealed the brain's elasticity, and that interactive activities benefit the brain the most. While we know this happens with new learning, studies also show that we can reprogram our brain to function through brain exercises. One way that's growing in popularity uses video-like games produced by companies such as Advanced Brain Technologies, Nintendo and PositScience, to name a few.

We can all improve our memories by focusing attention on details, using facts in conversation, associating something new with what you already know, and through visualization—like drawing or writing down what you see. And then there's our body, which requires an adequate amount of sleep, deep-meditative rest, good nutrition, and regular as well as intense exercising.

New research found that just thirty minutes of high intensity exercise a week—a total exercise time of seventy-five minutes including warm-up and cool-down—could lower blood sugar levels for up to twenty-four hours after exercise. Other studies have demonstrated that intense exercise every other day (aerobic activity at least three times a week) actually stabilizes, if not reduces, the aging process. As to nutrition, the best advice is to include a variety of healthful foods (vegetables, fruits, legumes, fish, grains, dairy—even dark chocolate), at least two to three liters of water daily, and listening to the hunger and satiety in your body.

Stay away from red meats and processed foods. High Vitamin A foods like spinach and mangoes can reverse sun damaged skin. Vitamin D is vital for your memory, skin, heart, bones, and arteries, and it helps fight off cancer. However, seventy-five percent of people don't get enough of it. Getting enough vitamin D daily (1,000 mg; 1,200 after age sixty) can make your "real age" nine-point-four years younger, according to an expert committee in the Institute of Medicine. The so-called MIDAS study found that taking Omega-3 DHA supplements took three years off the brain. Attitude plays a key role in getting and staying younger—like not taking yourself too seriously, breaking habitual negative thoughts, and consciously "letting go" (the beginning of The Lord's Prayer, "Thy will be done…," is a wonderful way surrender your cares). Staying young is all about stimulating the brain, reducing stress, eating and drinking right, using the right herbs and supplements, exercising, meditating, and having a good attitude.

"To remain young while growing old is the highest blessing." ~ German Proverb

JULY 8

I will use my inner pharmacy

It's been said that the mind can trick us, but the body never lies. Psychologists use cognitive therapy to redirect dysfunctional thinking and behavior that has been influenced by an unhealthy limbic system, that part of the brain that is responsible for our emotional life and for forming memories. Cognitive therapy taps into the prefrontal cortex, which is located just behind the forehead and is the part of the brain that has been implicated in planning complex, cognitive behavior, decision making, and moderating social behavior. It's the prefrontal cortex that allows us to work toward defined goals, but it's our experiences and choices that can influence the brain to act in accordance with our desires. How we experience the world influences hormones and other chemicals in the body. Our awareness of the world around us is achieved by balancing the mind through our senses.

The thalamus or center of the brain causes visceral reactions and is the gateway to our senses such as sound, touch, sight, taste and smell. Sounds represent a powerful sense that can produce an accentuated resonance, such as when vibrations at the same frequency double the magnitude of the resonance. This explains why some singers can break glass through their reverberations. Functional MRI's show that natural sounds, music, and meditation sounds cause vibrations that deactivate the limbic system and turns on a parasympathetic response with the effect of relaxing us. That same relaxation can occur via massage therapy. Gently massaging the forehead, the ears, the sinus, the chin, the arms, hands, fingers, chest, abdomen, legs and feet can cause the potentiation of nerves within the body that improve feelings.

Our four emotional needs for attention, affection, appreciation, and acceptance can be met through touch, which can also detoxify tissues, calm the mind, and enhance our immune system. Sight can positively influence our mind, as when we get out and view the beauty of nature. Earth tones tend to ground us, cool, soft colors calm us, and bright, bold colors invigorate us. Taste represents our most direct relationship to the body. Tastes and smells like chocolate slow down brain waves and reduce stress. Smell affects memory and instinct (used by animals to detect danger). Aromatherapy helps with neuro-associative conditioning, especially lavender, which has been shown to reduce pain (Hadi 2011). When we manage our senses, we manage our body and mind for success.

"Nourishing yourself in a way that helps you blossom in the direction you want to go is attainable, and you are worth the effort." ~ Deborah Day, author of Be Happy Now!

JULY 9

I will eat my way to success

You are what you eat, states the proverb. Someone once responded to that by saying it must be true, because they ate large sums of nuts! When you consider that the body always metabolizes food, it's plausible that food could actually be medicine. It all centers on metabolism. Lighter foods leave you feeling better, heavier foods weigh you down. An ancient proverb says, "When diet is wrong, medicine is of no use. When diet is correct, medicine is of no need."

Sweets such as grains, pasta, breads, nuts, fruits, and sugar produce carbohydrates, fats, and proteins. We all need to watch the sugars, or the "glycemic index" of these foods. The glycemic index is a number representing the ability of food, relative to glucose (the body's natural sugar), to increase the level of glucose in the blood. Sucrose (table sugar) has the highest index, meaning that it is the worst kind of sugar, followed by high fructose corn syrup (like agave nectar), honey, and fructose (the best kind of sugar, found in fruits). The problem with excessive sugars is that they affect the brain so that the body doesn't feel full even if it *is* full, which causes weight gain. Low glycemic foods like legumes and vegetables are metabolized more effectively. Any genetically engineered foods should be avoided. Some monosaturated and polyunsaturated fats are good, like olive oil (not cooked to burning), avocado, flaxseed (ground), and fish. Saturated animal and plant fats (coconut, palm) are best in moderation if not eliminated. To enhance digestion, don't overeat, reduce ice-cold food and beverages (room temperature is best), and sip water with your meals (don't gulp). Fresh ginger is also good for digestion. To reduce gas and bloating, cinnamon, mint, and chamomile are good sources.

As a rule, listen to your appetite. Eat only when you are hungry, and eat all seven natural colors of foods. Red and blue foods help fight cancer and are anti-inflammatory, as do orange foods that are also anti-bacterial and support immune health. Yellow foods do likewise and promote eye and skin health. Greens do all of these as well as help the heart and liver. White/tan foods also help promote hormone balance. Make sure to include in your diet the powerhouse foods like berries, walnuts, broccoli, artichokes, kefir/yogurt, and flaxseed. Avoid frozen, unnatural, nuked, and canned foods. In other words, eat real, natural foods that will waste if not digested soon. Your body and mind will thank you.

"If you don't take care of you body, where are you going to live?" ~ Author Unknown

JULY 10

I will stay calm in a crisis

You've checked voicemail and your boss wants to see you immediately because the company is facing a recall of its product. Your job is on the line. Your adrenaline shoots higher and faster than a shooting star. What do you do? The first rule of handling a crisis is to think before you act. Many people respond with "fight or flight," which is the body's instinctual response to a perceived threat or attack. The most effective crisis managers have already prepared for that moment, because they've followed their Girl Scout troop leader's teaching to always be prepared, and they've also followed their mother's advice to count to ten before acting.

Many times the crisis is either not as big as you first imagined or it clears on its own. Given that the damage has already occurred, it's best to consider the options and how you can move forward with corrective action. If you've properly prepared, that feeling of knowing what to do will give you a sense of control and direction. Now take deep breaths to slow down the mental and emotional body.

One of the biggest challenges in a crisis is finding perspective. In crisis our emotions tend to take over, compounding the fears and elevating the worst-case scenario as a playback in your mind. You need to remind yourself of how brave and capable you are to handle the crisis. Confidence and courage go hand in hand, so give yourself a pep talk before going into battle. Visualize the success you will have after the crisis is over—what will the glowing reports say—then identify the steps you need to take to get there. Crisis often invites chaos, so you need to counter that with focused center-mindedness. Don't allow yourself to be caught-up in thinking about what-ifs or future consequences.

Hospital emergency workers and combat soldiers are trained in the skill of mindfulness by setting aside their feelings and thoughts to focus on the moment and what is the most important next step. You can practice this the next time you wash the car by focusing solely on the car, or only on the carpet the next time you vacuum. Remember, the time to start preparing for a crisis is well before the crisis hits. So start planning for it now.

"When written in Chinese, the word 'crisis' is composed of two characters. One represents danger and the other represents opportunity." ~ John F. Kennedy

JULY 11

I will start journaling

"Dear Journal: I feel like I can't share this with anyone. I'm beginning to hate my life because of all of the stress from…" Do you journal? If not, starting a successful habit of five to ten minutes of daily journaling can take the initial jolt out of the intensity of your days.

When people say or do things that are hurtful to us, we tend to repress those hurtful feelings for fear of overreacting, or we feel a loss of self-esteem in doing so. Bottling up these emotions causes increased risk for serious illnesses, such as heart disease and cancer. Studies at Southern Methodist University of Texas have shown that individuals who were encouraged and supported to express their emotions demonstrated an improvement in the function of their immune system. These people visited their physicians less often than those who did not express their feelings. Experts have also found that journaling represents one of the most convenient and effective ways to express many of the emotions we tend to push down until they explode into something more serious. If you feel like even the slightest negative comment could push you over the edge, then you're probably at the point where your perception of what's going on around you is distorted by these pent-up emotions. Journaling has been proven as a successful way to give these repressed feelings an outlet so that they don't take over our lives and well-being.

Just grabbing a pen and notebook and writing about the disappointments and hurts in our daily lives helps eliminate our tendency to suppress our feelings. According to clinical psychologist Thomas Conte Manheim, who specializes in the treatment of anxiety and depression, "Writing down our feelings is a therapeutic way of expression and reflection on our day. When we journal, we are able to tease out of ourselves the deeper meaning of our lives and make sense of the hurt by reflection." He explains that when we process these emotions through our mind through journaling, the toxicity is released, preventing harm to both ourselves and others. According to research, people who journal report sleeping better and having a more positive outlook on life.

"A page of my journal is like a cup of portable soup. A little may be diffused into a considerable portion." ~ James Boswell

JULY 12

I will not major on the minors

An effective CEO of a successful healthcare company found himself in a tough predicament. A drug that could potentially save thousands of lives from certain death had not performed in six patients who were part of a final stage clinical trial. The CEO had banked the future of his company on the success of this one potential blockbuster. Most of the pharmaceuticals manufactured by his company were sold to raise funds for further research and development in order to expand the potential use of the new drug. Now, the clinical trial appeared in jeopardy because a few patients experienced negligible results from the drug. To save the company, the CEO mastered all of his resources to focus the entire effort on finding a solution to the existing problem. He needed to decide whether to terminate the clinical study, or to continue and find a solution to the apparent failure of the drug. Weeks of late night strategy sessions took place. Hundreds of thousands of dollars were spent retesting the drug formulation, analyzing data, benchmarking with other studies, and shifting resources to save the company's future.

Meanwhile, the CFO of the company was frantically trying to account for all of the changes. He decided to use some off-balance accounting to pay for some of the company's transactions. He also shifted some funds into places that were suspect, but nobody paid attention. The CEO was preoccupied with finding a solution to problems with the clinical trials. One day, the CEO opened his newspaper and was shocked to see a front page article about his company. The reporter detailed a series of what he termed "illegal or at best manipulative" financial practices. Soon thereafter, the federal regulatory agency investigated the company and found some serious discrepancies in the accounting. Three years later the company filed for bankruptcy.

The CEO learned a painful lesson throughout the process. He learned that when we hyper-focus on a problem in exclusion to more important issues, by *not* covering all the bases, the outcome can be devastating. As it turned-out, the drug was sold and developed successfully. The company, however, failed. And by most accounts, so did the CEO. It's important to major in majors.

"The key is not to prioritize what's on
your schedule, but to schedule your priorities." ~ Stephen Covey

JULY 13

I will respect the differences between men and women

Jane married Joe in large part because he was the strong, silent type. Twenty years later Jane complained that Joe didn't talk to her enough. Joe did talk when Jane shared a problem with him, but he always provided advice instead of just listening, which is all Jane wanted out of the conversation. So she felt unheard in that situation.

Sound familiar? Men and women are different—duh. Just as Joe needs to participate more in conversation, Jane needs to understand that just because Joe wants to solve her problems instead of just listening to them, it doesn't mean he doesn't care. In fact, Joe's offer of a solution indicates that he *is* listening. In the 1970s, it was politically incorrect to mention sex differences. But thinking that men and women are the same ignores the needs of women and just perpetuates the male norm that has dominated society for eons. Sexual tensions still unfortunately enter into male/female relationships, both socially and to a lesser extent (because of professional conduct) in the workplace.

Men have a harder time keeping friendships with women platonic, according to a study published in *Scientific American.* This study showed that men attracted to women tend to assume that the woman feels the same, when she doesn't. Females were far less attracted to their male friends in the study. So when it comes to male/female relationships, there are a lot of mixed signals. In the workplace, women tend to see problems holistically, whereas men are linear and narrower in their problem solving, says Keith Merron, a specialist in gender diversity. Both perspectives are needed. Women are better team players because of their supportive tendencies and higher level of compassion, according to a study on gender bias by a New York research group, whereas men were judged better at delegating and managing up. Which is higher in assertiveness? Surprise! According to a 2005 Caliper study, women leaders scored significantly higher than male leaders, and they were also shown as more persuasive. That's because according to the authors, women were able to "read situations accurately and take information from all sides." The key takeaway from our differences is that both sexes complement each other, and we need to understand this.

"A man does what he can; a woman does what a man cannot." ~ *Isabel Allende, Ines of My Soul*

JULY 14

I will take the forty-day challenge

Dave tried to start a consulting business, but quit after one year because he could not source enough clients to support him. He joined a men's breakfast club, but soon tired of getting up early on a Saturday morning, so he quit going. He set a goal of running a marathon, but after straining to just reach the five-mile mark, he gave-up. This was the pattern of Dave's life story, until one day when he decided to take an art class in Mendocino, California. He was mesmerized by his eighty-year-old teacher's abstract paintings that fetched thousands of dollars.

One day, because of some house repair, Dave's teacher asked her students to enter through the rear door. Dave saw lying against the walls of the back room at least fifteen landscape paintings so realistic looking you could almost walk into the scene. As the group assembled in the teacher's studio, Dave inquired as to the artist for those paintings. "I painted them," answered the teacher. "But they are so different than your abstract paintings," he said. The teacher smiled and said, "For almost all of my life I painted those kinds of landscapes. I have at least two hundred that never sold, and the ones I did sell went for almost less than what they cost to make. Then when I turned seventy, I just gave up and starting painting whatever came to mind, and now you see the results."

The lesson in this story (and the artist's story *is* true) is that it may sometimes take a lifetime of rejection and faded dreams, but if we keep on trying and eventually develop the courage to just let go and do what we were born to do, success can happen.

Here's the challenge to you: For the next forty days pick a goal or project that is important to you—it can even be something you've failed at in the past. Commit to acting on that goal *each day* for the next forty days. Don't quit, no matter what happens. At the end of forty days, see if others will affirm the work that you have produced. That should give you the answer as to whether your goal or project has the legs to stand on its own. Remember that it can take only one breakthrough to turn a failure into a success. Try abandoning yourself to your talent and dream.

"Life's real failure is when you do not realize how close you were to success when you gave up." ~ The Universe

JULY 15

I will use the key intrinsic motivators

Telling people, "You're just lucky you have a job" certainly does not qualify as motivation. Neither does using intimidation. Good leaders help people motivate themselves, as reinforced by Daniel Pink in *Drive: The Surprising Truth About What Motivates Us* (Riverhead Hardcover, 2009). Pink notes research about what's called the self-determination theory, which "...argues that we have three innate psychological needs—competence, autonomy, and relatedness. When these needs are satisfied, we're motivated, productive and happy. When they're thwarted, our motivation, productivity and happiness plummet."

The old paradigm is to offer rewards in order to create motivation. The new paradigm is to pay attention to what stimulates a person to be their best, and then give that to them. Sure, not paying someone enough money can de-motivate him or her, but it's more than money that turns people into self-motivators. Self-motivation occurs when we give someone the tools they need to succeed and when we involve that person in decisions. When rewards are given, they should be based on achievement of realistic performance goals that stretch the person's ability using both verbal and non-verbal praise such as, "I believe in your ability to take on this assignment even though it's a challenging, and I'll support you all the way." When someone feels totally involved and supported in an activity they run on autopilot, and there are certain factors that leaders can give a person to help them reach that readiness state. Those would be a sense of control, a level of challenge together with the skills to succeed, an elimination of competing goals (allowing the person to focus), and the freedom to move at will. The self-motivator also needs to feel positive about their team, and anything that gives him or her a good feeling about their performance and confidence will ignite their mojo.

Competence is an intrinsic motivator, and leaders can instill this feeling with positive feedback that tells them specifically what they are doing well and why, by giving them tasks that play to their strength, and by conveying to their followers that what they are doing is important and meaningful. They will respond by becoming the "go-to" person for their mastery, which will motivate them even further.

"Be patient with yourself. Self-growth is tender...
There is no greater investment." ~ Stephen Covey

JULY 16

I will understand basic accounting skills

Successful executives must understand everything about the business they oversee. One of the most important aspects of managing a business is accounting. It can make the difference between profitability and bankruptcy.

The first principle of accounting is to understand the basic accounting equation which is used to detect errors in bookkeeping and is determined: Assets = Liabilities + Shareholders' Equity. An "asset," by this accounting definition, refers to the property owned by the company. "Liabilities" refer to the debt owed by the company. "Shareholders' equity" refers to the money left over as profit and interest payments for investors. Knowing this formula allows executives to conduct informed reviews with their financial managers. Companies like Enron were guilty for "cooking the books." Executives immediately claimed their innocence because they said they were not aware this was happening. However, ignorance is not an excuse when you're at the top.

Understanding the basic accounting software can give you an idea as to how your business finances are balanced in order to know the company's financial picture. When speaking with your accountant, ask for the balance sheet reconciliations to verify account balances and activity. Reconciliations are generally performed in accordance with company policies and procedures. Your accountant will use the reconciliation sheet to identify and correct errors and material misstatements. Executives can ask for reports that reflect activity, such as depreciation schedules (tracks capitalized items and their depreciation), accounts receivable and accounts payable aging reports (a statement that records the number of debtors and the amounts they owe), and depreciation schedules (outlines the depreciation allowances). All executives should view the basic income statement (shows the company's revenues and expenses during a particular period) and the balance sheet (a statement of assets, liabilities, and capital of a business at a point in time) in order to understand the fundamental economic performance of the company. Your accountant will create various spreadsheets to report and analyze the financial business data per your request. The general ledger is the core of your company's financial records and should be reviewed routinely. Keeping abreast of the financial stability of your company is critical to the success of any business leader.

"The only way to get out of the "Rat Race" is to prove your proficiency at both accounting and investing, arguably two of the most difficult subjects to master." ~ Robert Kiyosaki, author of Rich Dad Poor Dad bestselling series of books

JULY 17

I will project an attitude of gratitude

Developing an attitude of gratitude can make the difference between success and a negative situation. Just a few expressive words can make you the person people want to be around. It's all about sounding the right tone. Developing the ability to align your thoughts and feelings with your actions is the key. Your thoughts can train your feelings that send out what are commonly referred to as positive vibes. Feel gratitude for every act of giving by another person, and you'll attract others to you. If you feel entitled or dismissive, you will attract negative feelings like resentment, anger, and regret.

The problem that most of us face is controlling our emotions so that we can project the attitudes that will elicit the reactions we desire. Fixing your thoughts on things like what is right, true, lovely, admirable, pure, and honorable places you in the correct frame of mind to attract similarly positive responses from others. Once you've trained your thoughts and feelings, expressing gratitude becomes a natural process of being in a state of thankfulness. When you feel thankful and develop thoughts of gratitude, you are intentionally projecting those thoughts to people around you. This is what we commonly refer to as the Law of Attraction.

The way in which we think and the thoughts we hold most strongly in our minds have a profound effect on our lives in almost every way. What's called "thought energy" is sending the right "vibe" that will resonate to the other person, thereby causing the same response. Positive feelings and thoughts will elicit a positive response, just as an attitude of gratitude will elicit positive feelings.

Gratitude extracts positive feelings such as joy, positivism, excitement, and love. Not only will an attitude of gratitude create the positive responses you desire, but expressing gratitude also makes you feel satisfied. Anytime you find yourself in a negative situation you can quickly turn your feelings around by developing gratitude. Feeling genuinely thankful is a failsafe way to achieve joy and realize your desire for success.

"Choosing to be positive and having a grateful attitude is going to determine how you're going to live your life." ~ Joel Osteen

JULY 18

I will develop peace of mind

The hurries and worries of this fast-paced world can perpetuate a chaotic state in our mind that causes us to think, "When will it ever end?" The hectic nature of life leads to mind overload and disharmony, yet a peaceful mind is vital to our effectiveness. The human mind tends to over-rationalize or overthink situations. Einstein, one of the most brilliant and productive minds in recent history, actually discounted the value of rational thinking when he declared, "I never came upon any of my discoveries through the process of rational thinking." He used a more intuitive approach to problems. Our intuition provides us with instant answers so that the mind needn't over-think circumstances. Einstein acknowledged as much when he said, "The only valuable thing is intuition."

There's another sensing and decision-making facet of our mind, and that's what some call the heart or soul. Our mind-soul connection is a built-in "right-o-meter" that helps regulate our ability to do the right thing. The heart or soul is where our core values and principles reside. The saying "be true to yourself" relates directly to following the yearnings, cautions, desires, and promptings of the heart. Peace of mind often follows a heart-felt decision to do something even if it contradicts our rational and intuitive thinking. That's because as our core regulator, the heart can determine what's truly best for us.

Another practical technique for returning our peace of mind is to move all of our responsibilities out of our mind by recording them externally and then breaking them into actionable work items. This proven technique, devised by David Allen and called *Getting Things Done* (GTD), allows us to focus attention on taking action, rather than recalling what actions needs to be taken. You can use digital tools like *Lotus Notes*, *The Brain*, or *Microsoft Office*. Or you can simply use good old-fashioned paper to take notes. The in-basket is what Allen says is a must for creating a "parking lot" for catchall items.

Meditation is a long-recognized method for restoring peace of mind. Get alone in a quiet place and simply be still for several minutes while trying to empty your mind of all but the most tranquil sounds and visualizations. Peace of mind is all about stopping the frenzy in our midst.

"You'll never find peace of mind until you listen to your heart." ~ *George Michael*

JULY 19

I will stop trying to always be right

Would you rather be right all of the time or have more joy in your life? Sadly, most people unintentionally choose to be right over their own happiness. Though our egos seem to demand it, the need to always be right shortens life and damages relationships and our own success. All you need to do is engage in a political discussion with someone of the opposite persuasion to understand the power of people's need to be right. Consider those you know who hold their convictions so rigidly that they constantly judge, ridicule, complain, and ultimately become depressed due to their need to be right, and to make others wrong. Left to the ego's control, most people would risk even their most important relationships.

The need to be viewed as right by one or both partners is ranked as one of the top reasons why marriages fail. Not to be confused with trying to do the right thing, which is typically selfless, the propensity toward being right enters into almost every disagreement. Whether it's as trivial as placing the toilet tissue right side up, or as impactful as which social stance to endorse, we need to ask ourselves if being right is worth chewing our nails down to the core or sacrificing important relationships.

The next time you feel the need to be right, try just letting it go. Allow the other person to feel that they are right. Then notice how challenged that makes you feel. Letting go and letting others believe they are right is probably one of the most difficult things to do, so strong is the hold our ego has over us. But after some practice in mastering your ego (versus it controlling you), you'll start realizing the advantages—fewer arguments, less tension, more joy, and greater success. What's more, when people around you see that you are not constantly insisting that you are right, they will be more apt to engage you in conversation. You become more approachable.

After you've established a habit of not always insisting on being right, others may respond in kind. It makes others more amenable to your point of view, thus increasing your influence with them. You just need to be patient and work on yourself first. So start taking over your ego, act with deference toward others, and observe how much more joy you'll experience in life!

"It's much easier to forgive others for being wrong than it is for being right." ~ Author Unknown

JULY 20

I will run effective meetings

Have you ever sat in a meeting and wondered "why am I here?" Are some meetings big time wasters? Bad meetings drag on forever, seem pointless, and leave us feeling like we just watched paint dry. Great meetings give us energy and direction. So what's the difference? A lot of meeting facilitators want a brainstorming meeting with lots of free flowing ideas, but unless you're soliciting some creative ideas for a new promotion or ad campaign, these usually don't work well. A lack of structure usually produces unproductive results.

Effective meetings usually contain three ingredients: 1) they achieve a meeting objective based on a structured agenda and process; 2) they do not go over their allotted time and are as brief as possible; and 3) they engage participants in such a way that they feel they've been valuable contributors in developing a well-defined action plan. If the meeting is for problem solving, ask the participants to come prepared with some viable solutions. To prevent timewasters, use your agenda as your time guide. If you're running a planning meeting, make sure that people from different departments have the same understanding as to the meeting objectives, and that they all agree to the purpose for calling the meeting.

Retreats or long-term planning meetings should include all of the key stakeholders to ensure the desired deliverables. If high-level executives and their staff are both present, allow the executives to share their visions with all of the employees to discuss implementation plans, improvements, and any changes that should be made. For brainstorming or creative meetings, construct some time guidelines so that the free flowing discussion does not ramble on. Bringing Play-Doh, squishy balls, and other toys can actually encourage more creativity and focus during the meeting. For any meeting over two hours, make sure there are plenty of drinks, especially water, and healthy snacks.

To prepare for the meeting, consider what the top priorities are to be covered, establish your desired result, make sure the right participants (decision makers and influencers) are there, establish the meeting order, define how much time will be spent on each topic, and create an inviting meeting space. Then keep the meeting on track.

"Meetings are a symptom of bad organization. The fewer meetings the better."
~ Peter Drucker

JULY 21

I will figure out why I haven't succeeded

Have you faced consistent failures in meeting your goals? Perhaps you run into the same lack of success in your career over and over? Same people problems, same challenges…nothing seems to be working for you? If you consistently fail at tasks and relationships, perhaps you subconsciously believe that you are not up to the job or that you are not good enough, or that you're destined to fail. It's also possible there's an important lesson you have not learned yet, and you won't be able to move forward until you get it right. Your subconscious could now be programmed to fail.

Time to take a breather. Your previous failures *can* turn into your future successes. Just because you failed yesterday doesn't mean you can't succeed today. You may need to start with a smaller goal, or find a more well-fitted position, or you may need to change your attitude toward a particular type of person with whom you've been having consistent problems. The key is to find out why you've been failing, and then consciously commit to changing whatever attitude or behaviors are holding you back. If your goals are too large or unrealistic, start smaller and be more practical. Establish a goal you positively know you can accomplish within a short period of time. Once you've accomplished it, celebrate your success. You've done it! Set another short-term goal and immediately dive into it. Keep doing this and each time, stretch your goal to further challenge yourself. As you meet your goals, remind yourself that you are a successful person. Your subconscious mind will be transformed in the process to believe that you can meet you goals, you can alter your attitude, and you can make the decisions that will lead to success.

Remember that life is a continual forward adventure, not a sprint, and you can always change course to get on the right track for you. Succeeding in little ways, no matter how insignificant they may seem to you, will motivate you to achieve greater goals and to realize larger visions. Don't allow your self-doubts to drown out the truth that you will not fail in the end—you will gain the victory. The only way we fail is to quit. Start making the change you need now to begin again with smaller wins, and work your way up to consistent success.

"Your past does not equal your future." ~ Tony Robbins

JULY 22

I will stop complaining

Complaining destroys happiness. It steals your energy and the drive needed to discover your success in life by robbing you of your highest potential. No one wins by complaining, period. So what is there to complain about? Your job, your relationship, the economy, the weather, your home, your neighbors. The possibilities are endless. The key is to get out of the gutter of complaining that drains your energy, and to spring into the possibilities a positive change in attitude can bring. When we complain, our attention is focused on the negatives. But nothing changes by complaining, so what good is it?

If your situation leaves you feeling stuck, the immediate solution is to focus on the positives of your life. Reality is pretty much how we define it. The glass can be viewed as empty, or it can be viewed as a receptacle waiting for your favorite drink. Ask yourself why you are complaining. Maybe you are telling yourself that you're not good enough, or perhaps you are protecting yourself from disappointment. If things go wrong, that would make you right. Maybe complaining is a front for not taking a risk, going for our dream. Perhaps it's a way of seeking attention or sympathy from others. It could be an excuse for not correcting something within yourself by using other's faults to excuse you from changing.

Once you identify the reason(s) for your complaining, start disciplining yourself to stop the complaint before verbalizing it. Think about the positives and see compassion for others' failings. Focus on the things for which to be grateful. Assess your current situation by defining your reality and taking action to make it better—making lemonade out of lemons. Let go of what's out of your control and decide to thrive within your environment. When you stop complaining, all of that wasted energy can be routed to more productive outcomes. You release the power to tap into your full potential. The opposites of complaining are applauding and approving, which leads to contentment and happiness. That, and a fresh start.

"Complaining not only ruins everybody else's day, it ruins the complainer's day, too. The more we complain, the more unhappy we get." ~ Dennis Prager

JULY 23

I will be an idea person

Doesn't it sound great to be known as an idea person? Easier said than done, perhaps, because it involves a number of skills and habits. First, you need to be an inquirer. Learn about people's experiences and insights. Are you always committed to continuous improvement in your work and areas of interest? If so, you may be an ideal candidate for employers who are increasingly seeking idea people to fill a creative void—one of the fastest growing needs in the workplace. A true idea person can find ways to fit that square peg into a round hole. They think like Thomas Edison who said that ideas are waiting to be discovered. "Idea people" scan their environment for new ways of doing things as naturally as breathing air.

Idea people are open to new ideas from others and from a diversity of places, like museums, books, offbeat locales, and people outside of their normal acquaintances. Do you seek out projects outside of your normal areas of expertise? Idea people do that, plus they spend dedicated time each day seeking out new ideas and investing their time with sources that give them the greatest return of ideas—like thought or opinion leaders, creative people, innovators, and leaders. Idea people track their observations through journaling or recordings. They exhibit a high level of empathy for their co-workers, customers, and personal relationships. They seek out ways in which to better understand what creates value for them, what needs or wants are unmet.

Hearing others ideas is core to being an idea person, and this can be accomplished through simple "water-cooler conversations," or at the cafeteria. Creative solutions from the idea person often need to be enacted quickly, so having a ready-made source of ideas is important. Idea persons can disseminate ideas through blogging, tweeting, discussion groups, or in writing, and by testing concepts with others in order to focus on the ones with the greatest viability or priority.

All of these ways in which idea persons go idea hunting depend on dedicating time every day to learning and observing the world around them, as well as circulating and developing their ideas with others. It's a forced habit that taps into the limitless ideas around us. We have an idea shortage today, so the idea person can make a huge impact in their world. Success comes from ideas, so tap into your limitless abundance of sources and means to make them a reality.

"Ideas can be life-changing. Sometimes all you need to open the door is just one more good idea." ~ Jim Rohn

JULY 24

I will say it straight, simple and with a smile

It seemed to Jenny that she did not get a minute of sleep last night. Thoughts of how she would end her three-year relationship with Anthony kept playing in her mind, like a looping crying scene from a movie. She wanted to marry and he did not. Surely enough time had elapsed for him to know whether she was the one. Since he couldn't make-up his mind, she would. She waited on a bench in the park, which now seemed a bit sadistic since it was the same bench on which they first met. But at the time it seemed like a fitting place for closure. Around the curve, Anthony emerged from behind a tree carrying a flower in his hand. He sat down next to her extending the yellow daffodil with the giddiness of a five-year old—her favorite flower. She hurriedly tucked the flower behind her with an awkward smile, sat-up tall, and cleared her throat. "Thank you," she said. Anthony's face tightened as he tilted his head in that befuddled look she'd seen too often.

"It's been three years since we met on this bench," Jenny said, "and you say that you love me, but not enough to get married." Jenny relaxed her face and broke a more genuine smile this time. "So I'm going to end our relationship as lovers, Anthony. That's the best for you and me and I'm not going to change my decision, not now, not ever." Anthony tucked his head and closed his eyes, and nodded. She was right. It was time to let go.

How many times do we approach the awkwardness of a moment with drawn out sentences, fumbling our words in a vain attempt to comfort the receiver from the harshness of a situation? We struggle with just the right sound, the right expression, and the right approach, and an hour later we still haven't communicated our precise meaning. People tend to process messages better if spoken with kindness and directness. They know exactly what you mean, and can clarify their processing with you based on the facts, not conjecture. After a simple, straight message conveyed with a genuine smile, the other person can digest the message from a point of clarity, not confusion. Most people appreciate honesty, even if it's harsh, if it comes from someone who shows that they truly care about them. Try it the next time you speak with someone. They'll appreciate your doing so.

"Live simply, love generously, care deeply, speak kindly, leave the rest to God." ~ Ronald Reagan

JULY 25

I will connect with others using Emotion Coaching

When we criticize or coach someone, whether it is our child or a direct report, emotions invariably take center stage. However, all too often we fail to connect with the other person because they are too consumed in dealing with their own emotions. So the message can get lost, or the person can become resentful, and we do more harm than good. Telling someone they need to do something differently requires a thoughtful approach.

Emotion Coaching starts by connecting to the other person's feelings, and recognizing their emotional response. There are five connecting emotions that open a person's receptivity: love, kindness, compassion, empathy, and composure. People who feel these emotions from you are more apt to listen and understand your message. Conversely, the disconnecting emotions are: antipathy, meanness, indifference, harshness, apathy, and agitation. Use the connecting emotions when speaking anything of importance to another, and avoid the disconnecting emotions.

Remember that emotional moments can be opportunities for teaching, so don't respond to an upsetting emotional reaction with a disconnecting emotion. Keep your connection going. Then listen to the other person. Keep your eyes focused on theirs, lean forward, and let them know that you've heard what they have said by acknowledging their sentiment, not just their words. Avoid judging the other's emotions. If you maintain emotional connectedness, you will have the opportunity to coach the other person only after their emotions have calmed, and they have acknowledged back to you that they are receptive to what you are saying.

Only after the other person is feeling understood should you proceed to the solutions part of your conversation. Too often coaches and parents try to immediately jump into fix-it mode. That opportunity will arise when the student is ready to learn, and not just when you are ready to teach or coach. Encourage emotional expression, but set limits on what behavior is acceptable. And don't expect instant results. Your job after offering a critique and some solutions is to support the other person by catching them doing things right, and praising them.

"Your intellect may be confused, but your emotions will never lie to you." ~ *Roger Ebert*

JULY 26

I will honor marriage

Romance in the workplace is not new. However, studies have shown that it has increased in the last fifty years with the influx of women into the labor force. Additionally the average number of hours spent at work has increased since the 1980s. The combination of a more gender-diverse workforce and more time spent at work has had the effect of giving birth to more emotions that can birth romance between co-workers and between subordinates and their supervisor. Some organizations have workplace romance and fraternization policies, but for the most part, people are left on their own to determine what relationships are acceptable, and which may cross the line.

One type of relationship in particular has done more to cause harm both at home and at work than any other, and that is workplace affairs between two separately married persons or between a single person and a married person. Fidelity may seem old-fashioned in some circles, but it keeps the office gossip from spreading. And it prevents more serious repercussions, such as accusations of unfairness, that can impede work progress. Even romance between two unmarried persons in the workplace can have a detrimental affect.

Family issues, namely divorce and marital problems, are the number one cause for loss in productivity. According to a report by the Corporation Research Council, "Social science research shows that marriage is an important social good that benefits employers, employees, and their children." Studies showed that most people valued a happy marriage above satisfying work, a big income, and even good health. People whose marriage is healthy were found to be more productive. Tips for strengthening your marriage include banishing divorce from your consideration, honoring and respecting your partner, healthy communication that is open and honest, giving each other the space each wants, sharing financial expectations and standings, taking care of your health, courting each other (date nights), quickness to forgive, and seeking professional counsel if needed. Given the research and just common sense, we would all do best to honor marriages, both our own and those of others.

"A successful marriage requires falling in love many times, always with the same person." ~ Author Unknown

JULY 27

I will use good email etiquette

Have you ever received one of those nuclear emails from someone that blows your top? Not only are those emails bad for the receiver, but they can also jeopardize the sender, because emails may be used as incriminating documents in complaints and in a court of law. Don't use email to resolve an inflamed situation, and don't use it as an excuse to avoid personal contact. Emotional issues should be dealt with face to face. Be aware that email at work is not private—it is considered company property and can be retrieved. Always assume that email over the Internet is not secure, and keep in mind that your email can be forwarded to unintended recipients.

Always keep email messages brief and to the point, concentrating on just one subject per email if at all possible. Check grammar and spelling before sending your email, especially if it is going to an external customer. Sloppiness is a poor reflection on you and your company. Avoid using all caps, as this connotes anger or irritation. Conversely, using all lowercase letters appears lazy. For emphasis use bold formatting and avoid special graphics, because not everyone can display them. When copying others, don't use BCC to keep others from seeing whom you copied—this looks suspicious. Do use BCC when sending to a large distribution list, so that recipients won't see a long list of names. Avoid overusing CCs by copying only people who are directly involved with the subject matter. Don't change the wording in a forwarded message. The sender should approve posting a group message that was sent only to you first. Use "reply all" only when sending information that is relevant to all of those copied.

People tend to get irritated receiving email they don't need. Only use the email's content description within the subject—don't say things like "hi" or "just me." You can note that the email is long or urgent in the subject field to give the reader advance notice. As a general rule avoid forwarding jokes, junk mail, or chain letters.

Check with your IT department before alerting others to a possible virus to confirm whether it is accurate. Remember that email cannot convey verbal nuances, so it's easy to misread the tone of an email. Avoid sarcasm or off-color remarks. You can use emoticons, but only sparingly and directly corresponding to the tone of the message. When you place your signature at the end, make sure to include all of your contact information.

"Etiquette means behaving yourself a little better than is absolutely essential." ~ Will Cuppy

July 28

I will use professional conduct

Professional conduct does not only apply to professionals. It applies to anyone in the workforce. We can usually spot those who consistently demonstrate good conduct, and it can help you to advance your career and most certainly will keep you out of trouble.

So what are the traits you must demonstrate in order to exhibit professionalism? As a general rule, conduct yourself in the same way that you admire conduct in others. Be punctual, and don't consistently abuse break times since being late reflects poorly on your attitude toward work. Don't be in a foul mood. You need to separate the problems at home from the mood you display at work, and if work causes you to feel irritated, step away or talk through your issue in a constructive manner, and by all means don't offload your emotions onto someone in the work environment. Swearing, cussing, or backstabbing should not be tolerated in the workplace, especially in front of those who may be offended by it. As a rule of thumb, don't use any language you would not use in front of your high school English teacher.

Workplace harassment can be considered as any language, gestures, or inferences that might be construed as demeaning, offensive, derogatory, or abusive. This applies to sexual harassment as well when anything of that nature is related to a person of different gender or sexual persuasion—especially if the harassment is sexually charged. As to dress, follow any dress code within the workplace, and if none exists, then mirror the norm and make sure your clothes are clean and well maintained. Revealing clothing is inappropriate. Shorts and tank tops are generally not condoned on weekdays unless specifically stated by management. Also a wrinkled shirt and crumpled sports jacket will not reflect a professional appearance anymore than ripped jeans. Good professional conduct means being sensitive to others and not spoiling the work environment with detrimental behaviors like gossiping and put-downs. Reserve your verbal frustrations for a relative or best friend. Being helpful to those in need is also a part of good conduct and demonstrates good teamwork. Stay positive, and if you see a problem, try to do something constructive about it using common sense.

"A professional is someone who can do his best work when he doesn't feel like it." ~ Alistair Cooke

JULY 29

I will grow in wisdom

We live in an over-communicated world with information bombarding us almost non-stop. Yet are we experiencing fewer problems? T.S. Eliot posed the question: "Where is the wisdom we have lost in knowledge? Where is the knowledge we have lost in information?" We've *got* knowledge. We *need* more wisdom. There's a big difference between the two.

Knowledge is the accumulation of information and skills acquired through experience and education. Wisdom mediates that knowledge toward the achievement of a sound decision that results in the common good. In other words, wisdom makes you do the right thing. Given the choice between hiring a highly educated intelligent person who only *sometimes* does what's right for the organization, or hiring someone with moderate education and intelligence who *always* does what's right for everyone involved, which would you choose? Most would choose the wiser of the two. However, it's harder to find wise people than it is knowledgeable ones. That's because wisdom is more difficult to develop than knowledge.

Wisdom grows as we learn from the mistakes we make through taking risks. Jeff Foxworthy puts it this way: "Wisdom equals knowledge plus scars." Here's how you develop wisdom: When you see a problem in your or someone else's life, ask yourself why something went wrong. Figure it out. The answer will bring you greater wisdom. A successful life is comprised of a series of course corrections that add up to making more improved decisions. If we can take our ego and emotions out during our decision-making process to figure out the right thing to do, and then proceed with what must be done, we live more according to our values and wisdom.

See the big picture so that you can place yourself in the correct position relative to everything around you. Remain teachable and humble, so that you can maintain an outward focus in learning more than the sum of your understanding. Ask yourself, what have I learned that would make me do things differently? Then apply that newfound wisdom to action. You are building a foundation of wisdom, and that is worth more than any formal education can provide.

"Some of the best lessons we ever learn we learn from our mistakes and failures. The error of the past is the wisdom of the future." ~ Tryon Edwards

JULY 30

I will do my good deed for the day

When you woke up today, what's the first thing that came to your mind? Did you think about doing a good deed? If you're like most, your first thoughts were about the essentials of the day. Still, even if it is your hundredth thought of the day, consider doing something nice today, because that old saying is true: "Do good, feel good." How about giving someone an honest compliment today? Go up to that person you know who's having a hard day and say something like, "I just wanted to tell you that without your _______, our success would not have happened." Sometimes the hardest people to compliment are the ones closest to us. So make it a point to give at least three compliments to that loved one.

There are plenty of other very doable ideas for you to achieve your good deed today. Maybe you can buy coffee for the person in line behind you; smile and say hello to a stranger; hold the door for someone; do someone else's chore; send an ecard to someone just to cheer them; offer to give someone a ride; let someone go ahead of you in line or in traffic; email someone you admire and tell them why; cook a meal for your family; share a book; write a thank you note to a waiter; buy flowers for a loved one; become an organ donor through DonateLife.net; leave your mail carrier or trash pick-up service a thank you note; bake some cookies and give them out in your workplace; write a note to the boss of someone who helped you; send a card to someone in the military overseas.

Start a conversation with a co-worker you don't yet know; visit someone in a nursing home who doesn't get visitors; drop off a toy or game at a hospital or homeless shelter; invite someone who is alone over for dinner; put a quarter in a parking meter that has expired; drop off a pie or flowers at your neighbor's house; drop some coins in an area where children play; donate your favorite book to a hospital; offer to babysit; donate clothes to Goodwill; write anonymous post-its notes of encouragement for strangers to find; pick-up trash around the neighborhood; buy a homeless person a hot meal; make someone's bed; treat yourself!

"A good deed is never lost. He who sows courtesy reaps friendship; he who plants kindness, gathers love; pleasure bestowed on a grateful mind was never sterile, but generally gratitude begets reward." ~ St. Basil

JULY 31

I will be a good parent

Parenting is one of the toughest jobs you'll ever love. Even if you don't have any biological or adopted children, you can serve as a foster parent, regardless of your age. Because children often model the behavior of their parents, being a great parent begins with being a better person. Your kids are always watching you. So take care of yourself, and be careful not to overcompensate for your children by forcefully imposing your dreams upon them, or overdoing things for your child just because you never had "this or that" as a child. Your job is simply to love and to guide them. Children are born with behavior that needs correcting, and as parents that's what we do. But it's important to remember that they are young, and they do not have the benefit of your experience. Think about how you feel when someone corrects or picks on you. Then ask yourself: *can I be a little more patient or gentle?*

Make sure your kids always feel safe. Remind them through your words and actions that you love them, that they are needed, and they are thought about. You can never be too loving. Staying involved in your child's life, both mentally and physically, requires hard work, sacrifice and reprioritizing at times to accommodate what your child needs to do—but it's important, so make sure you do it. Remember, one approach does not fit all ages. A two-year-old who says "no" requires a different response than a fifteen-year-old who argues with you. Consider the physical as well as the emotional needs (are they getting enough sleep?; are there problems at school?). Rules are important, and it's equally important that these rules be clearly explained and consistent in their enforcement. At the same time you want to nurture your child's independence by balancing the limits you set for them with the self-control they must be allowed to develop.

Experts tell us we should avoid harsh discipline imposed in anger—time-outs are good for children and parents alike. Carefully explain your decisions to your children and respect their opinions, because children will treat others just as you treat them. All in all, if you have a good relationship with your child he or she will turn out just fine.

"As your kids grow they may forget what you said, but won't forget how you made them feel." ~ Kevin Heath

AUGUST

LOOK FOR CREATIVE SOLUTIONS

AUGUST 1

I will overcome obstacles

Feeling overwhelmed with work and family drama? Perhaps it's time to gain a little more control over the shifting demands in your life. Obstacles can be viewed in one of two ways—as either negatives or as opportunities for personal growth. Nothing develops without the challenge of overcoming obstacles. Athletes push themselves to reach higher and more challenging levels of endurance, just as professionals need to stretch their abilities by overcoming the hurdles that lie in their way. By remaining disciplined, purposeful, and meaningful, the obstacles in life will strengthen your abilities and you will improve your wisdom and maturity. There are two types of obstacles: the external kind that come from people and situations, and the internal kind that arise from feelings of self-doubt. External obstacles can be internalized and seen as either roadblocks to leap over or as an insurmountable behemoth. Left unchallenged, they cause defeatism.

Remember that success comes in "cans" and defeat comes in "can'ts." So internalize your declarations by saying things like, "I can overcome this and go on to victory," or "I will prevail." Eliminate the "not" part of will-not, cannot, have-not or do-not in your inner-speech and make a believer out of yourself. Maintaining a positive can-do attitude is the key to overcoming obstacles.

One of the best ways to maintain a positive approach is to measure your success in overcoming them. Keep a log of each obstacle and record your success at conquering them. After a while, you'll notice a positive trend as your achievements keep increasing, and this will instill within you much more confidence in your ability to succeed in the future. It takes practice. But with each victory you will gain increased confidence. Think of it this way: if we didn't have obstacles and weren't forced to navigate a new direction either over or around them, we would never discover our very best. Too few obstacles stunt our growth, limit our strength, and prevent wisdom from happening. Too many can break us. So find a way to reframe your obstacles as opportunities. Even laugh about them—"Here goes another one. Been there, done that!" Surround yourself with other positive can-do people, exercise, and sleep well. Your triumph is certain to happen!

"The way I look at it, if you want the rainbow, you gotta put up with the rain." ~ Dolly Parton

AUGUST 2

I will commit to a lasting marriage

There are different opinions about what makes a happy marriage, but it's the one you hadn't thought about that may be the saving one for you. We know, for example, that a man's primary need in a relationship is respect, and that a woman's primary need is to feel loved. Let's consider what some of the most enduring marriage partners have to say about what's kept them together.

A survey of partners across the country who had been married for thirty-plus years asked them how they stayed together. What ranked as the most often given reason? The answer: they may have thought of killing each other, but never seriously considered divorce as an option. These long-term couples remained committed to finding solutions for even their most heated arguments. They focused on the next period in their relationship rather than the immediate threat.

Commitment ranked as the number one reason why marriages last, and the one quality that is lacking most in today's marriages. The top reasons given for leaving a partner, even for those who have remained committed, were abuse, infidelity, and unresolved addiction. Indeed, no one should be at the constant affect of any of these destructive habits. Research found that while marriage can be a bed of roses, it invariably includes a few thorns. Tempers can erupt over a tube of toothpaste pressed in the middle, or some unmet expectation, but couples who accept their partner's peculiarities were found to be most satisfied.

Couples who expected perfection were the least satisfied. These statistics testify to the fact that marriage is hard work, but always worth the effort—and communication is the key. Those who maintain respect for their partner through open and honest communication created a more trusting relationship. Mutual respect and unselfishness were the two biggest reasons for flourishing marriages. Partners couldn't get too mired in their own selfish wants. Those who wanted a fifty-fifty split in getting their way didn't succeed as well as those who would settle for forty-sixty, with each agreeing to offer the most to the other. These couples put *we* first, themselves second. Successful marriage partners also valued time for each other. Sparking the romance involved planned dates to keep the flames burning. Making time to create treasured memories cemented lasting love.

"A successful marriage is an edifice that must be rebuilt every day." ~ *Andre Maurois*

AUGUST 3

I will be a good conversationalist

They are the entertaining and engaging ones at the dinner, party, or any social event at which you attend. Great conversationalists can make a huge difference at influencing the positive opinions of others. How can you improve your conversation skills? Most people start by talking about themselves, but showing interest in others from the start of a conversation is more involving and appreciated. So ask general and non-threatening questions of someone you've met for the first time, such as where they live, what they enjoying doing, or the latest movie they've seen. For people you know better, you can ask about their aspirations or their most challenging obstacles.

Remember to keep your comments modest and positive. Don't launch into a rendition of your accomplishments or mention the sad state of affairs in the world. People respond favorably to those who are humble, positive, and who express interest in them. That's why good listeners make the best conversationalists, because listening makes people feel that you want to know about them. When someone brings up a topic or situation, don't just move on to the next subject. Ask follow-up questions such as, "So how did that make you feel?" or "How did you react to that?" or "Tell me more."

Dale Carnegie once said the best way to be likeable is to be interested in the other person. Likeable conversationalists are terrific at bringing up shared experiences with their counterparts, such as saying, "Whatever happened to _____?" or "What you said reminds me when we _____." Look for opportunities to pay someone a sincere compliment. If they got a new hairstyle, say something like "That really complements your look," or when they mention an accomplishment, congratulate them. Don't forget to remain a little playful and humorous if the discussion hasn't turned serious.

Self-deprecating stories tend to be the safest form of humor, such as telling someone about a personal mishap or a silly misstep. Always make sure to laugh at others' funny stories, but never ruin their punch lines or interrupt their conversations. Keep up to date on topical issues such as current events or popular entertainment, but don't bring up controversial subjects. Also, don't hog the conversation. Just relax and enjoy yourself.

"Confidence contributes more to conversation than wit." ~ Francis de La Rochefoucauld.

August 4

I will create a good résumé

Whether or not you're actively looking for a job, you should always keep an up-to-date résumé on file. To create a great one, make sure it is concise, well organized, free of typos/misspellings, coherent, and easy to read. Résumés with the biggest impact emphasize *specific* accomplishments. Don't just say you are good at increasing sales; tell them you increased sales by fifty-three percent, or that you managed a product that ranked second out of fifteen categories in the first two years. Prioritize the content of your résumé so that your most important and relevant information is at the top, with your most outstanding accomplishments listed at the top of each position. If you are applying for a specific type of job, incorporate the same keywords that appear in the job description into your résumé, tailored to the position you want. You can use a résumé template as a starting point, then add your information to the template. Edit it to personalize your résumé by highlighting key skills and abilities. Make sure to include only relevant job experience. If your résumé is overstated or full of fluff, most hiring managers will assume you are not qualified for the position.

One of the biggest mistakes résumé writers make is spreading themselves too thin. Remember, you are creating a clear and concise story about yourself. So focus on your top three skills and sharpen your message. Avoid listing things that most people can do (such as using the Internet or MSWord). This detracts from your useful skills. An easy-to-read format is also important. Include all of your contact information in the heading, using bold print to highlight your strongest achievements and bullets to list out details. If you are interested in more than one type of position that requires different skills, create a different résumé for each one. Again, the more you can tailor your résumé to the position you're seeking, the better. The best résumés tell a story that demonstrates what you can do for the organization—not what the company can give you. Verbiage like 'company XYZ is just what I'm looking for' is not as effective as stating, 'my unique skills and experience have prepared me to excel in launching your new product.' Choosing your words carefully will entice an employer to want more.

"I am very detail-oreinted." ~ Applicant Unknown (misspelling is intentional)

AUGUST 5

I will not be anxious about anything

Forty million people suffer from the frightening physical and mental symptoms of anxiety. Are you one of them? There is hope, even for those, like most of us, who experience only anxious occasional bouts. For chronic or long-term anxiety, of course, you should see a doctor. However, there's a more comprehensive approach to enhance your level of success in dealing with the problem.

Regular exercise is not only good for you physically, it releases endorphins that promote a general sense of well-being. Even just three to four sessions per week of moderate intensity exercise has shown significant benefits. Dehydration can cause fatigue, which can trigger anxiety, so drink lots of water. Complex carbohydrates, such as those found in foods like grains, legumes, vegetables and root tubers, fiber (i.e., nuts, seeds, bran), and select fruits (like blueberries, bananas, and cantaloupe), help to maintain your energy and suppress anxiety. One and a-half to two cups of fruit daily is recommended by the U.S. Department of Agriculture. Minimize caffeine and alcohol intake to two to four caffeinated and alcoholic drinks a week.

Healthy relationships are also key to coping with anxiety. A supportive network of friends and relatives can help you to find healthful alternatives to some of your stress factors. People who make you feel down, guilty, or who are insensitive to your anxiety struggles are best relegated to infrequent contacts, or perhaps even eliminated if possible. Making such decisions can be the most difficult part of your healing process, but certainly one of the most important.

Please don't allow anxieties to back you into a corner. Getting out of your comfort zone helps inoculate you against anxiety. It may be challenging, but it's key to developing your self-confidence. Taking at least one risk each week helps stretch your boundaries and tackle even more difficult situations in the future. Most of the time what we worry about never happens, so recording your worries helps you identify the level at which you are overestimating your fears. Very few things are actually catastrophic.

"Concentration is a fine antidote to anxiety." ~ Jack Nicklaus

AUGUST 6

I will plan my retirement

The average American spends twenty years in retirement, according to the United States Department of Labor. That makes planning for it one of the best investments of your time. Job number one is to save as much as can for those years. Try to increase the amount you save each month if possible.

Begin a plan by knowing your retirement needs. Experts say you need about seventy-percent of your pre-retirement income, and for low earners that figure reaches ninety-percent or more in order to maintain your standard of living after you stop working. Meanwhile your expenses will be the same, if not more, because of increased health risks. Paying off major debts like your home loan as quickly as possible helps reduce your cash-flow drains. The best savings plan is through your employer's 401(k) plan, if they have one. Maximizing these contributions may lower your taxes and your company may match or contribute more to your savings. Fewer and fewer companies today are offering pension plans, but if yours does, consider the risk if you leave that company. Also find out if you are entitled to your spouse's plan.

Diversifying your investments creates a hedge against changing economic conditions, but the most important key is to *not* touch your retirement savings if at all possible. If you do, you'll lose principal and interest and you may lose tax benefits, or have to pay withdrawal penalties. If you change jobs, leave your savings in your previous retirement plan, or roll them over to an Individual Retirement Account (IRA) or your new employer's plan if it's more advantageous. You can place up to $5,000 a year into an IRA, and you can contribute even more if you are age fifty or older (check for changing limits). You can set your IRA up so that a contributing amount is automatically deducted from your checking or savings account. Social Security pays benefits that are on average equal to about forty-percent of what you earned before retirement (check for changes). You can estimate your benefits using the retirement estimator on the Social Security Administration's website. If you have any further questions, ask for advice.

As Star Trek's Mr. Spock would say, "Live long and prosper!" (minus the exclamation point, of course, for the emotionless Vulcan Spock).

"Don't simply retire from something; have something to retire to."
~ Harry Emerson Fosdick

AUGUST 7

I will have at my fingertips interesting facts

Want to impress someone with your base of knowledge? Here are some interesting facts that can, if nothing else, provide you with topics for idle chatter:

1) The President of the USA receives about 500 death threats every month. 2) The Hungarian psychologist Laszlo Polgar wrote a book on how to raise a genius and raised three geniuses (all daughters) himself. 3) McDonald's first bookkeeper at first worked for free, but ended up with shares worth over $28 million. 4) Cracking your knuckles doesn't hurt you or cause arthritis; the sound you hear is just gas bubbles bursting. 5) In 1970, Sesame Street was banned in Mississippi because of its racially integrated cast. 6) Humans could theoretically survive on just potatoes and butter. 7) Anatidaephobia is the fear that somewhere in the world there is a duck watching you. 8) It's impossible to hum while plugging your nose. 9) Four is the only number that has the same amount of letters as its actual value. 10) You're more likely to die on your way to buy a lottery ticket than you are to actually win the lottery. 11) If you touch your tongue while yawning, it can stop the yawn. 12) Women speak about 7,000 words a day and the average man just over 2,000. 13) Jellyfish evaporate in the sun since they are ninety-eight percent water. 14) When you laugh while being tickled, you are actually experiencing a form of panic. 15) Yawning is contagious. Even thinking about yawning is enough. 16) Those stars and colors you see when you rub your eyes are called phosphenes. 17) The total weight of all the ants on Earth is about the same as the weight of all humans on the earth. 18) Grapes explode when you place them in the microwave. 19) In Japan, they grow square watermelons. 20) Kissing someone for one minute burns about two-point-six calories. 21) It cost seven million dollars to build the Titanic and 200 million to make a film about it. 22) Two-percent of Earth's people have red hair. 23) 'Dreamt' is the only word in the English language that ends in the letters 'mt.' 24) Dysania is the state of finding it hard to get out of bed in the morning. 25) A seashell next to your ear is the sound of your blood surging, not the ocean. 26) At least forty-five-percent of Americans are unaware that the sun is a star. 27) Oysters can change genders back and forth. 28) The Bible is the number one most shoplifted book of all time. 29) According to suicide statistics, Monday has the preferred day for self-destruction. 30) People who laugh a lot are healthier than those who don't. 31) Tabasco sauce takes over three years to make.

"Facts are to the mind what food is to the body." ~ Edmund Burke

AUGUST 8

I will grow my intellect

Yes, it is possible to grow your intellect, and no, you don't have to lose brainpower as you age. A strong mind typically results in a better job, more income, and improved mental health. Common research has discovered that we use only one-third of the brain, so the key is to engage the other two-thirds.

The research linking physical and mental health continues to grow. A Cambridge University study showed that jogging just a couple of times a week stimulates the brain. After a few days of running, tests revealed that several hundred thousand new brain cells had grown in a part of the brain linked to the formation and recall of memories. Vigorous exercise actually helps release a protein called "noggin" that helps counter another protein called bone morphogenetic protein, thus stimulating an increase in the division of brain stem cells. This keeps the brain active and quick, and could possibly prevent the onset of age-related brain malfunctions such as dementia. After that exercise, taking a nap was also shown to benefit the memory. An hour nap in the afternoon boosts the brain's ability to learn new facts and applications. Those in the study who stay awake all day could not process information as well, thus leading the researchers to suggest regular napping may help to head off degenerative mental diseases.

The brain requires significant amounts of nutrients, complex stimulation, oxygen, water, and exercise, so monitor your intake of all of these. Excessive sugars have been shown to cause cellular damage. Mental exercises like word puzzles can help as can "tricking" the brain by using your non-dominant hand, which develops different neuropathways that can access untapped parts of the brain. Experts also suggest that long controlled breaths not only create a greater oxygen intake for the brain, but they also signal to the brain that air is plentiful so that it can focus on complex tasks. Research published in the journal *Neuron* found that an increase of magnesium (Mg) in the brain could help learning in humans regardless of age. Foods rich in Mg include vegetables like spinach and broccoli. Vitamin D (which we get from the sun and from oily fish) also kept the brain active and could improve information processing. Learning of any kind is healthy.

"It is better to have a fair intellect that is well used than a powerful one that is idle." ~ Bryant H. McGill

AUGUST 9

I will develop my key relationships

We've all heard the saying, "it's not what you know but who you know." But that's only partly true. Knowing who can help you reach your goals is only the first step. Developing those key relationships is the second and most important step. It's key that we cultivate credibility and trust in our relationships with others, as this comment once made by the vice president of a company about a person two levels beneath his position demonstrates: "I would trust Anderson with my kids." Now that's trust!

In the professional world, those types of relationships are built on helping others achieve *their* success. That may not appear like a normal action toward a person whose position is higher than your own. After all, why do they need *your* help? People in positions of authority need to feel supported, and sometimes they need help to get them toward their goals. "How can I help you today?" may be enough to initiate a conversation that begins the process. So it's not just what you know or who you know—it's how well you know them, how much support they feel from you, and how influential they are with the people who will influence *your* future.

Not everyone who can help you achieve your goals is in a senior position. Sometimes we need to look for what author Malcolm Gladwell (*The Tipping Point,* Back Bay Books, 2002) calls "hub-like, nodal, super connectors," who are basically the matchmakers in the professional world. They are the networkers of our age. The better-connected people are, the more they succeed if those connections are developed, as in the case of Anderson, whose VP would allow him to babysit his children.

Professional mobility allows people to develop relationships of respect that can be "graded" according to the level of support one feels from the other. When people feel safe and supported, they don't have to concern themselves with survival tasks. They let down their guard, and so they're more likely to help others succeed. Trusting relationships, even those that are not close, tend to bear out positives for the one who is trusted. As human beings we want success for those who desire our own success.

"When we give cheerfully and accept gratefully, everyone is blessed." ~ Maya Angelou

AUGUST 10

I will focus on one big important thing

"Jack of all trades, master of none" is a figure of speech referring to someone who is competent with many skills but not outstanding in any particular one. The debate between who is more effective—the generalist or the master—has gone on for a long time. While a base of understanding across a wide range of subjects is important in order to be prepared for life's variable circumstances, the masters of that "one big thing" tend to better succeed in the long term.

Jim Collins, author of the best seller *Good to Great: Why Some Companies Make the Leap...And Others Don't* (HarperBusiness, 2001), references this phenomenon in what he calls "The Hedgehog Concept." Using a parable of a hedgehog and a fox, he asserts that the fox knows many things, whereas the hedgehog knows one big thing. Great companies, Collins writes, were built, by and large, by "hedgehogs." They were the ones better able to focus on one big important thing that made their companies great. Sometimes it takes brilliant insight to see through all the confusion and hold onto that one, simple, unique thing that gives you the advantage.

So how do you find *your* one big thing? Collins suggests the concept of three interlocking circles, representing 1) what you are passionate about, 2) what you can make money at, and 3) what you can be the best at. At the intersection of these three things lies your winning target. Equally important is to realize the things you can never be the best at, and avoid them if possible. When you measure your success in a business, identify your profit in terms of only one factor—such as users of your product, units sold, number of customers, etc. In other words, clearly define your success. That one big thing you are mastering could be a product, a service, or a skill that makes you absolutely the best in your field. Ask yourself this question: What is it that people continually ask me to do?

Sometimes your failures force you to your one big thing. In 1931, Samuel Morse became frustrated because his life's desire to become a painter, even traveling to Paris to perfect his craft, seemed to be failing. His preacher father told him, "Attend to one thing at a time. The steady and undissipated attention to one object is the sure mark of a superior genius." Samuel Morse heeded his father's advise, gave up painting, and went on to discover the telegraph.

"Concentrate... The sun's rays do not burn until brought to a focus." ~ Alexander Graham Bell

AUGUST 11

I will reflect

Imagine yourself directing traffic in the middle of a busy intersection. Seven intersecting roads and lines of traffic are coming at you, and it's pouring down rain. That's your life, isn't it? You have to direct oncoming traffic from several different directions. The roads represent the different pathways in your life. The cars and trucks represent the people, products, and services you need to direct in a flow that gets them where they need to be. The rain represents the changing climate conditions that can affect your attitude, abilities, and decisions. You are in a constant state of directing traffic. It never seems to end. That's why you need to carve "think time" out of your busy schedule, to engage in dedicated, productive reflection.

The information age that has birthed technologies at a faster rate than anytime in history has overwhelmed our ability to think clearly. Thoughtful consideration has been replaced with this hurried human impulse we all have toward taking action, even at the risk of taking the wrong action. The classic way of thinking is that we have to just get things done. The myth is that we can multi-task effectively, but the brain doesn't work maximally when rushed. We need to pause.

Have you ever taken a time-out in the morning just to wonder? Time to consider the trends that are happening in the world, in your environment, or in your industry? Over time, that dedicated pondering allows your subconscious to bubble-up an idea that could lead to a breakthrough. Unplug yourself from the computer for a while and you might be surprised at how refreshing it can be. Stop the outside interruptions that can take several minutes to recover from, and try not to interrupt others so much. Getting to breakthrough requires dedicated reflective time.

All too often companies reflect on situations only after a disaster happens. Say a recall is forced on a business. At a post mortem meeting of the directors, they assess what went wrong. Why can't we conduct those deliberations upfront? Think through the different possibilities, the potential downsides and upsides, before they happen. That requires dedicated time each day to either individually or collectively create opportunity, instead of deconstructing misfortune based on rash decisions.

"Life is a mirror and will reflect back to the thinker what he thinks into it."
~ Ernest Holmes

AUGUST 12

I will be results-driven

You hear it a lot in the work environment, but what does being results-driven really mean? It's one part setting and meeting goals (the tactical part), and one part impulse to achieve a purpose (the desire part). You can't have one without the other if you want to maintain that drive to succeed.

Setting and meeting goals is the easier of the two parts. You need to establish a realistic list of goals, not a wish list of just what you want to accomplish. The desire part reveals itself in that gut feeling that comes from knowing yourself. Understand what drives you and what best fits with your lifestyle and abilities. For example, setting a goal for finishing a new project within a week when you've got five others going is probably not a good idea. Neither is taking on an accounting assignment when you're an artist at heart. Find the right fit that will sustain your momentum for the long-term. This means taking on something that's realistic. If you agree to build a house in three weeks when it takes you over a week to even draw up the architectural plans, you need to redefine the goal. You need to believe in your ability and desire to attain a goal before you can be successful at it. Most goals wither toward the middle or end stages because the inspiration dries-up.

Don't let your ambition to succeed override your desire for the project itself. Why you set a goal is more important than what you will do to achieve it, so make sure the goal is what truly motivates you. Once you've decided the goal fits with your "sweet-spot," the tactical part requires that you establish only goals that can be measured. This is where the desire part turns into the tactical part. Just saying you want something to look better doesn't mean it *will* look better. Specific timeframes for completion of each phase must be included with a specific answer as to what the finished product will look like. Will it return twenty-percent more profit, will it have three parts instead of two? Next you need to laser focus on the goal. Don't allow distractions or procrastination to interfere with your *daily* plan of action, which must include specific tasks.

Finally, consistently reevaluate your goals to ensure that life's changes have not also changed your desires. Change may be a constant, but unless your desires are steady, the results will suffer.

"Nothing great was ever achieved without enthusiasm." ~ Ralph Waldo Emerson

AUGUST 13

I will improve my execution skills

Effective execution continues to be one of the biggest problems facing people who need to get things done. The July-August 2010 edition of the Harvard Business Review survey of 1,075 readers found that the most significant execution obstacles facing organizations were those associated with making strategy meaningful to those responsible for getting things done. Once the strategic plans had been developed, executing them through aligning jobs to the strategy was among the biggest obstacles to fulfillment. Management apparently is not clear enough in relaying the strategy to their employees. Employees don't have the foggiest idea as to what the strategy is, or how they fit into the overall scheme. The need to simply and clearly communicate the strategy through a systematic approach seems to be the key to more effective execution.

In the mid-1990s, the diabetes company LifeScan decided all employees would be trained in a Quality Improvement Process (QIP)—all meaning everyone. Part of the indoctrination was that everyone also had to complete training on the company's values statement, requiring each person to commit those values to memory so that everyone was speaking the same language of quality and values. Upper management met mid-year to establish the company's five to seven strategic plans that were then communicated to employees at a winter meeting. These plans were the basis for determining a company-wide bonus program that paid on the number of goals met.

The next step involved management meeting with their teams to develop department objectives and action plans directly related to the five to seven strategic plans, the results of which were up-reported to senior management. Each person's merit pay was linked to the achievement of these objectives, as measured by well-defined criteria for productivity. The execution strategy always remained linked to the all-embracing five to seven strategic plans that were funneled down to each individual's own personal set of objectives so that everyone was operating from the same general benchmark.

As a result of this strategy, LifeScan rose from obscurity to the number one position in its market. The basics for outstanding execution: 1) clear goals for everyone in the organization and buy-in to the overall strategy; 2) a means for measuring progress toward these goals on a regular basis; and 3) clear accountability for that progress—improved execution skills.

"Strategy gets you on the playing field, but execution pays the bills." ~ Gordon Eubanks

AUGUST 14

I will develop my empathy skills

Ask the majority of counselors and even psychologists to identify the most common reason for frustration between people and you will discover none bigger than the inability to feel empathy in a relationship. Empathy is the ability to accurately place yourself in someone else's "skin"—to understand feelings and perceptions from another's point of view. Unlike sympathy, which affected by another's s feelings and perceptions, empathy heals. It removes distance between people.

So how do you develop empathy? First, you need to imagine yourself in the other person's place. Immerse yourself in their environment and feel their emotions, especially their pains. Ask them how they feel, and why they feel that way, in order to confirm your understanding. Put aside your personal agenda and just listen to them, without judging. Relate their feelings to similar situations in your own life that elicited the same types of emotions.

Be careful in your empathy not to become an enabler of the other person. In other words, you must use good emotional intelligence to clarify your own personhood. Make sure you don't become overly entangled with the other person, or you may take his or her feelings too personally. You'll need to get in touch with your own emotions and biases first, so you can distinguish between different emotions from a somewhat objective point of view.

One of the biggest challenges in communicating empathy is when you don't feel it toward another person, because of some bad experience or anger toward them. It takes time and practice to remove these barriers, beginning with recognizing the other person's right to be heard. Some of the hardest people to love are the most damaged. Your responsibility in developing your empathy skills is to identify the "why" of someone's feelings, without the need to determine whether their feelings or even their negative behaviors are justified.

"When you listen with empathy to another person,
you give that person psychological air." ~ Stephen Covey

AUGUST 15

I will strive after something transformational

There's a market principle that never changes: products succeed when enough people consider a product's value greater than their contentment living without it, such that the provider realizes a sustainable profit. The same principle applies to services as well. So what makes a product or service a true game-changer—one that actually transforms peoples' gold standard for a particular industry? It follows the same market principle, but in a market space that has yet to be identified.

In his top selling book, *The Innovator's Dilemma: The Revolutionary Book That Will Change the Way You Do Business* (HarperBusiness, 2011), author Clayton M. Christensen calls these game-changing innovations "disruptive technologies" that upset the existing "order of things" in a specific industry. The typical process tries to improve features and benefits that appeal to customers who will then be discontented enough with their current product to acquire the new one. Over time, the game-changing innovation slowly erodes the incumbent's position by appealing to subliminal needs yet to be discovered by customers. Only fellow innovators will choose to embrace the new concept. Early adopters or trendsetters will lead the revolution to purchase the new product, followed by the early majority, then the late majority, and eventually the "laggards." This is called the "innovation adoption lifecycle."

According to Christensen's theory, incumbents generally don't react to these game-changers (or "disruptive technology") until it's too late. Indeed, incumbents are too focused on tweaking their product to fit their existing manufacturing, branding, and talent. Some are too large to make wholesale changes, and others determine that the market is too small or niche to justify a reinvestment of resources. However, small markets grow into large markets when general discontentment grows, a viral influx of people want the "latest and greatest," and when cost versus want crosses the threshold of a plurality of people. That's where you come in.

What product or service can you provide that will make a significant number of people discontented with the status quo? Or what organization can you join that is committed to the next big game-changer?

"Whatever the mind can conceive and believe, the mind can achieve." ~ Mark Twain

AUGUST 16

I will be genuine

One of the greatest teachers of success, Dale Carnegie, wrote an overnight success back in 1936 that's considered even today as one of the all-time best for its teachings on dealing with people—*How to Win Friends and Influence People*. Carnegie wrote about how to make people like you, and suggested ways to win people over to your thinking. But his pervasive theme is that if the intent is manipulation, none of the lessons will work. The word "genuine" appears throughout his writings as the foundation for winning over people. The takeaway is that over the long-haul, only with honesty and authenticity will we be able to influence people.

Most people are pretty adept at detecting if someone is genuine or "fake," meaning that they are behaving unnaturally. Unfortunately for them, most phony people don't realize that others can recognize their fake behavior. So the key to true influence is to "get real." When someone asks you for your opinion on a subject, be honest about the way you feel. Avoid telling her what you think she wants to hear. Just imagine that she will know whether you're telling the truth or not. So why not be honest?

We all need to accept ourselves for who we are, so strive to know yourself and be as transparent with others as possible. Insecurity causes us to be fake. Accepting yourself is more likely to make others like you. And if they don't, so what? So-called friends gained through deceit are not really true friends at all. "To err is human," the saying goes, but in addition to forgiveness being "divine," admitting our mistakes and flaws—and even laughing at them—is absolutely supernatural!

Fitting in should never be our goal. Instead we should just accept people as they are and do the same in return for ourselves. Mean what you say, and say what you mean. Trying to guess what somebody wants to hear is a game with no winners. Sincere compliments and smiles are great, but flattery only turns people off. Better than compliments is trying to help the other person. Genuine people are caring, and when we make people happy, the favor is always returned with a feel-good response. Don't try to appease others by accepting invitations or projects that you will later regret. It's OK to politely turn down an invitation to the opera if that's not your thing. Just be the one and only, original, genuine you.

"Be yourself. Everyone else is taken." ~ Author Unknown

AUGUST 17

I will take safety precautions

Jenny exited the elevator to the underground parking lot after another successful meeting that ran late into the evening. At age thirty-two with a Wharton MBA, recently promoted to a senior marketing post, Jenny was on top of the world—until someone from its underside forced her down. The rapist had waited for his prey in the poorly lit garage, and sadly Jenny was his most vulnerable victim. Thankfully, Jenny survived and recovered, but her story serves as a warning for anyone to take precautions in order to remain safe. Please consider these general safety tips:

First, be aware of your surroundings during periods when you may be less alert and more vulnerable to an attack—when you are tired, upset, sick, or if you have been drinking. If someone tries to snatch your purse, let it go. Most injuries from robberies occur when people resist giving up their valuables.

Learn self-defense techniques. If an attacker is attempting to choke you and you feel his arm coming from behind you, drop your chin to your chest and put up your arm on the inside of your attacker. Then drop your body and use your elbow to strike his solar plexus, which is the area at the top of the stomach just below the center of the rib cage. You can then use your hand or elbow to strike the groin area several times. You can also pull your left hip behind your attacker's right hip so that your leg is behind his. Using your left arm, elbow your attacker in the throat or face and, using your arm, push your attacker backwards over your leg.

If the attacker places a knife against your throat, take both hands and pull his wrist down while sinking your body into his inside armpit. With your hands still on his wrist move the knife toward his body making him stab himself.

Other techniques include smashing his nose with a palm strike, gouging his eyes using your fingers or smashing his windpipe with your hand. You can strike his groin with your knee or the ball of your foot. Driving your heel in a downward motion to his knee is also effective. Scream. Take a martial arts class like Aikido, Judo, or Krav Maga, which relies on simple brute force. Have your keys in hand as you approach your car. Always lock your doors. Check your backseat and floor before entering. Park in well-lighted areas. Trust your instincts. Always play it safe!

"Safety doesn't happen by accident." ~ *Author Unknown*

AUGUST 18

I will dedicate time for recreation

Jack and José think about recreation differently. Their skills sets, experience, and abilities are roughly the same. However, Jack, the archetypal workaholic, hasn't taken a vacation in over three years and rarely takes time out to recreate, whereas José takes regular vacations and remains active in sports and other forms of recreation. Which is the more productive of the two? The answer is José.

In addition to helping you lead a more interesting life, recreation is important because of the many health, social, work and educational benefits it can provide. Even the word "re-create" itself implies that something in our normal routine needs to be replenished. The most basic recreation can release the pent-up energy that is needed for us to perform at maximum capacity. For example, some people will tell you that watching TV is wasted time, or that it destroys brain cells. But guess what? Your brain cells *need* to rest in order to maintain health. And if TV reduces stress and creates a more positive environment, especially if you can share some laughter with others, you will reinvigorate your brain.

Relaxation is important for health. Our bodies tend toward sickness if we go non-stop all of the time. Sleep regenerates the mind, but even sitting still and consciously taking a time-out can do roughly the same. Lie in bed for a few minutes and listen to the pleasant sounds outside. Doing so can actually reduce your blood pressure by calming your mind. Once you get outside, segment out some time during the day or week to participate in some kind of group activity—a sport, a chess club, a movie, or theater production. The relationships you build from these mutually beneficial group activities develop a non-stress community with which you can build your social networks and talk about more relaxing topics. Just getting outside, even if it's for a few minutes in the sun, gets you out of the inside air with its disgusting pollutants—from insect pieces to airborne germs. The sun's vitamin D boosts your immune system.

Think of recreation as mental refreshment that can take many forms from reading, just lying on a couch, exercising, taking a long cruise, or camping. You need to get out of your normal life. Even God rested on the seventh day!

"People who cannot find time for recreation (will)... sooner or later find time for illness." ~ J. Wannamaker

AUGUST 19

I will choose my memories

Have you ever felt so distraught over a situation, or so stressed about a work gone bad that you would give just about anything for someone to give you a gentle hug and tell your everything would be OK? Wouldn't it be great if someone could just express their unconditional acceptance to you and erase all of the insecurities and fears that come with failure and disappointment? So often we get caught up in the reasons for our anxiety and trying to be perfect at winning all of the time that we lash out at ourselves emotionally, falsely believing we can never be good enough. Those awful memories resurrect themselves at the most hurtful times.

Memories are complicated. Some encourage us, while others make us mournful. Some create comforting mental playbacks, while others appear more like a horror show. Memories place in context the whole of our lives as reminders of the opportunities in our midst. Each moment is a snapshot to be taken advantage of before being placed in our memory bank. When we recall memories that bring sadness to our heart, we can either allow them to make us bitter, or we can recall how we became stronger as a result of the sad event. When you remember times you felt abandoned or that you failed, you can throw yourself a pity party—or you can envision God or a friend hugging you, reminding you that you are loved, and that you are never alone.

Choose to remember your times of joy and victories—the ones that invoke a tender smile. Every time a negative memory pops into your head, cover it up with a pleasant one. If a bad memory about work sneaks in, counter it with a time when you succeeded, and then stay there for as long as you like. Make this a constant discipline so that only the good memories will be accepted by your psyche.

If you need to learn something from a painful memory, project what you would do differently and imagine a new memory in which you have learned your lesson and have accomplished what you wished. You may not have control over each and every memory, but you do have control as to what to do with those memories. Memories are a cathartic vehicle for the mind to process our life's experiences. They help us to make sense of it all. Be selective which ones you will entertain, and then move on.

"Take care of all of your memories. For you cannot relive them." ~ Bob Dylan

AUGUST 20

I will be a mentor to someone

There's an intrinsic reward people gain from helping others, but mentorships—and the commitments they involve—require a sincere desire to utilize your position or your life experiences to help others advance. You can't help everyone, but you can find someone who is passionate about what they want to do yet lacks the skills or abilities you have developed. That is your prime candidate for mentorship. Pay it forward by finding someone new to a role whose position and goals flow naturally into the skills, experience, and attributes you've developed over the years. In addition to professional interests, there are a few other factors to consider for a successful mentorship.

It's important that you find a good fit in terms of personalities and personal values. For example, if your protégé lives to work but work/life balance matters to you, this fundamental philosophical difference might hinder a successful partnership. Determine how much time you are willing to commit to the relationship and make that clear to your mentee. Show your protégé what to do, give them examples, and then observe them doing the task so that you can coach them. Discourage any kind of "just show me what to do" mentality.

When pointing out areas that need improvement, always focus on the mentee's behavior—never their character—by explaining how you handled certain situations, so that the mentee can start thinking about how she will handle similar situations. Provide the benefit of your knowledge and experience while keeping in mind that every situation will be different because of your unique attributes. Always encourage positive professional behavior openly and confront negative behavior in private.

Mentorship is about challenging mentees to grow by giving them opportunities they would not normally have at their level. Being a positive role model is richly rewarding, but it requires a genuine interest in your mentee as an individual. A manager cannot always step into that role without appearing to show favoritism, so that's where you can come in to share your experience and insights. Be open to share stories of what made you successful, while sharing your mistakes and failures as well, so that your mentee can learn to recognize potential challenges and develop their own resilience. You will be glad you did it.

"Mentoring is a brain to pick, an ear to listen, and a push in the right direction." ~ John Crosby

AUGUST 21

I will "think and grow rich"

More than seventy years ago, the iconic author Napoleon Hill wrote *Think and Grow Rich.* Over 15 million copies later, the principles in this book are as relevant today as they were back then. Why? Because the fundamentals for success have not changed much. Hill contends that wealth creation is a product of the mind, combining reasoning, tenacity, and imagination. His guaranteed recipe for success, what he called "uniqueness," we now call innovation.

One ingredient in Hill's formula is rarely referenced in today's literature, and that is the underpinning concept of morality that integrates spiritual values with one's ability to grow rich. Hill's famous principled quote, "what the mind of man can conceive and believe, it can achieve," was qualified with man's willingness to be humble in starting from a lowly or mediocre position—something today's culture eschews largely because of the need to preserve a sense of pride. Connecting to a higher state of consciousness, not simply a higher status, constituted the realm of innovation.

Hill references a story where Thomas Edison retreated to his basement to simply "receive" his ideas. Thus, he posited, thinking beyond the current boundaries of understood reality could free the mind to comprehend far-reaching possibilities. Hill called this concept "Infinite Intelligence," where like a radio receiver we could just tune into the subconscious, which would then telegraph ideas into some universal space of knowledge, and essentially boomerang back as our "circumstances." This is how we can determine our success: by speaking our intent to our subconscious, which will manifest our physical activities to achieve that goal. Hill speaks of prayer as a means for connecting the infinite possibilities with our desire to manifest something yet to be discovered. Today we might call that wishful thinking, but to the icons of success then (Edison, Ford, and eventually Einstein) it was a common practice. Hill would define "rich" in terms of family harmony, quality of friendships, good work relationships, and spiritual peace. He also believed that great leaders (citing several examples) need to learn to serve before they can achieve positions of authority. His central message that wealth is non-material is hard for a needs-based society to grasp, especially in modern circles. However, its timeless message of attributing success to "spiritual" or ethereal abilities is testified by the fact that thousands of people continue to read about Hill's works even today.

"The way of success is the way of continuous pursuit of knowledge."
~ Napoleon Hill, Think and Grow Rich

AUGUST 22

I will form thoughts to creativity

Some of the greatest opinion leaders in the area of success have focused on the science of thought. Visualization is one long accepted means toward forming thought to creation, by passing from a competitive mindset to a creative way of thinking. The process begins with a clear image of what you wish to do, own, or become. The factory of creativity from your mind to actualization involves allowing your vision to stew during long periods of contemplation and self-affirmation.

Norman Vincent Peale espoused this approach in his writings about the power of positive thinking—replacing thoughts of impossibility, unlikelihood, and improbability with thoughts of possibility, certainty, and positivity. Some call this will power, but the translation from one's will to making it happen comes from returning added value to each person with whom you carry forth a transaction. For example, at a successful Panera's restaurant in California, the manager hired Joe as "The Cookie Man," who goes around the store offering free cookies. The manager thought that creating added value would increased customer loyalty, and indeed it has happened.

Everything we create begins with a thought. "I think, therefore I am," said Descartes. There are two thought paradigms: one that deals with what exists now, and the other that deals with what is possible. Consider the story of the two shoe sales people who were sent to an island. One told his company that since no one on the island wore shoes, there was no possibility to make sales there. The other called his store and said, "Send as many shoes as possible. We're going to be rich!"

Appearances can be deceiving, but the truth never lies. So focusing our thinking on the truth, regardless of appearances, is the first step toward success. The second step is to affirm our thoughts through positive reinforcement. The third step is to create value for our idea, and the fourth and final step is to form our thoughts through an expectation that our actions will invariably succeed, despite the multiple paths that may be required to eventually attain the desired outcome.

"Change your thoughts and you change your world." ~ Norman Vincent Peale

AUGUST 23

I will take care of the three parts of myself

Some define the soul as the spirit, and some define the soul as the human psyche or mind. For the sake of argument, let's say that each of us is composed of three parts: body, soul (psyche), and spirit. The body is our housing unit, what some call "the flesh." The soul is our arbiter of truth, our "moral compass," or what some term our "conscious." The spirit is that eternal part of our being that defies most definitions. Its reality is evidenced through what are called Near Death Experiences (NDE's), where scientists have studied unconscious people who claim to have had similar experiences, like seeing a brilliant light, a tunnel, rushing sounds, peace and painlessness. The brain cannot create images while unconscious. Even if it did, an individual would not be able to remember such clear, lucid memories. So NDE research tends to validate humankinds' spiritual component. Some may have also heard about the theory that the body loses twenty-one grams—thought to be the weight of the soul— after we die. Although more controversial, this concept joins the body of evidence that we are not simply organic beings.

That said, the alignment of our physical, soul, and spiritual needs is required to achieve complete success. The body is nourished through food, water, and stimulation. The soul, or conscience, is nourished by doing the right thing—or what is morally correct. The spirit is nourished through spiritual connectedness, as with God.

To achieve total satisfaction, all three needs must be met. Of course, we all know that not taking care of our bodies can produce sickness. Corruption of the soul also sickens us in producing that nagging feeling we are doing something wrong, also known as a "troubled conscious." Most people admit that feeling spiritually deprived—having no hope for life after death, no belief in God, or a crisis or lack of faith—leaves them feeling incomplete, or at least less hopeful. Hopelessness is usually a spiritual form of sickness.

So in order to be truly successful, we need to address the needs of all three parts—by feeding ourselves a healthful diet, by exercising, through leading a disciplined life of doing what's right, and by spiritual connectedness.

"Problems are spiritual lessons from God—spiritual lessons to be learned."
~ Tony Robbins

AUGUST 24

I will aspire toward meaning

We all start as blank canvasses, without any imprints on the world, as creations soon to realize that we are in the world and need to do something about that. Then ambition takes over as we grow into young adults. The ego takes center stage as we try to outperform each other. Our identity focuses on "me"—how people think of me, based on what I do and what I have. This period of time in which our mindset is ego driven tends to separate us from people in our world, as the attention is on "me" and "them."

At some point the human tendency is to look beyond the ego or selfish desires to a more altruistic perspective of unselfish concern for, or devotion to, the welfare of others. That's when we fulfill our destiny as a person with meaning, by changing our thought pattern from a "me and them" perspective to a "we and us" perspective. Finding true meaning exists in seeing ourselves as interdependent, and then attending to the needs of those who are struggling, hurting, or just in need of help. An "us" perspective cannot feel complete unless the people around us are made whole as well—like a body that can't feel better until the throbbing toe it stubbed stops hurting. This kind of thinking overrides the ego by focusing on making life better for others, which invariably makes our life better as well.

In order to give your life meaning, continually ask others, "How can I serve you?" As humans living on the same planet at the same time, such a question affirms our interconnectedness at the same time it reveals our influence and absolves us of attending to our ego's selfish wants.

"There is no exercise better for the heart than reaching down and lifting people up." ~ John Holmes

AUGUST 25

I will not be the victim of injustice

Every day, we balance our lives between two compulsions that consistently sound in our minds. The first pushes us to work diligently, to maintain our focus on the immediate task before us, and to finish it well before moving onto the next one. The other compulsion speaks to our desire for comfort. It tells us that we can put things off until tomorrow. Zone out for a while. Watch TV, surf the Web, or simply take a break. Disappointment or the feeling of unfairness may be fueling a desire to just give-up. It could be that someone else received recognition that we deserved, or perhaps a less qualified person was promoted to a position that should have gone to us.

In life we will face bias, injustice, and downright foolishness—these are inevitable and mostly out of our control. We can choose whether to feel the resentment that feeds the compulsion to give-up, or press forward and decide to shove the unfairness into the waste bin. The healthiest response would be to use the unfairness as a motivator, showing that you are more than capable and worthy.

Young Walt Disney could have used his unjust firing by a newspaper editor as an excuse to become angry and give-up. The editor said Disney, "lacked imagination and had no good ideas." Instead, Walt used that editor's analysis as motivation for creating the most imaginative company of its time. A young Abraham Lincoln went to war as a captain and was demoted to private, but instead of giving up he used that unfairness as an opportunity to study harder, grow, and develop his leadership skills until he ultimately became one of the greatest leaders in American history.

Consider what excuses you may have used. Why did you decide to agree with the low expectations of others, or even of yourself? Mentally determine a different statement in your mind that makes you responsible and places you in control of your situation and your future. Finally, don't accept excuses—not from yourself and not from others. Excuses only demean our value. Stay until the work is finished, and when it's polished just right to reflect your abilities and skills.

"An excuse is worse than a lie, for an excuse is a lie, guarded." ~ Alexander Pope

AUGUST 26

I will create a lasting legacy

If you quit on your dream, how will you ever know if you'd have succeeded? Maybe just a little more time or effort is all it would take for the dream to come true. It could happen tomorrow, or ten years from now. No one really knows. What separates many successful people from those who failed is simply that they never quit. Quitting was removed from their list of options, erased from their vocabulary—even if it meant the realization of their dreams would only benefit the next generation, or even later. When they reached their dream, they created a new one, a new reason for going forward.

Consider Galileo Galilei, the Italian physicist who invented the telescope, allowing both himself and others to discover the galaxies. Galileo was largely criticized, and even accused of heresy by Pope Urban VIII, who placed him on house arrest until his death. The famous painter Vincent Van Gogh's 2,000 pieces of art were never discovered until after his death—and today they are worth millions (his Portrait of Dr. Gachet, alone, was valued recently at $134 million). Many of these unheralded achievers followed their dreams knowing full well that their dedication might never be recognized. But they never quit. They were willing to leave a legacy for others.

We don't know when our breakthrough will happen. So don't guarantee failure by quitting now. You can develop, adapt, and change, but don't stop. Be content with a legacy for those who may follow after you. Create an inheritance built upon the foundation of your efforts. Just like a farmer who plants a crop knowing he'll never taste its fruit, a legacy is a gift you leave behind without any expectation of a return. The values and life lessons you impart to those around you can benefit countless others. Just make sure your legacy is a labor of love, not a chore. It's all about giving back, as psychologist Erik Erikson so poignantly said, "I am what survives of me." Success should not only be motivated by the desire to accomplish something through a "never quit attitude," but also by the desire to share it with others.

"The legacy we leave is part of the ongoing foundations of life." ~ Jim Rohn

AUGUST 27

I will never be good enough, but…

It seems almost heretical to believe that we should never wish to be "good enough" in the society of successful people, where reaching the pinnacle of achievement is the goal. But here's what striving to be good enough does to people—it keeps them in a perpetual state of *not* having arrived.

Ask yourself this question: "Who or what will measure when or whether you are good enough?" Will it be someone who says you have to satisfy his or her requirements, or is it a rule that says to be the best you must finish first? Let's be clear as to who defines if and when you have arrived. The second question is: "What *is* good enough?" Let's be clear as to what that means. The third question is: "What will I gain from being good enough?" Is it a promotion, a medal, a sense of pride, or a satisfaction in helping the team? Let's also be clear as to the reward, and whether that reward is good enough to satisfy us. Is it money, status, or just the satisfaction of a job well done?

After answering those questions consider whether any of the answers suffice for measuring your worth. The fact is that no one is good enough to please anyone all of the time. No accomplishment is good enough if you want to be the very best. The best athletes never score all of the time. The best professionals never meet their goals without fail. No accomplishment or reward lasts forever. Every victory eventually gets filed in history. The fact remains that we can never be "good enough" to have arrived at our perfect or best station in life. Life is dynamic. We win and we lose. We succeed and we fail. So not being "good enough" is OK—as long as we maintain a healthy mindset of continuous improvement that enjoys the journey as much as the destination. We will not be good enough to attain the very best in the world, perhaps not even within our community, because the best has yet to be determined. But we can reach new heights of personal success. Try answering this question: What is your favorite accomplishment? "The next one," is the refrain of the person with a healthy attitude. We may never be "good enough"…but we can always become better than before. Ask yourself: "What can I do the next time around to demonstrate my newfound understanding?"

"We cannot become what we want to be by remaining what we are." ~ Max DePree

AUGUST 28

I will not fear success

After sixteen years in a large corporation serving as an analyst and in various low level management positions, Lynda arrived at a personal revelation. Over the course of her career, she had observed several promotions of people similarly or even less qualified than she. "Why?" she asked herself. After much introspection, Lynda realized that she feared success. Lynda felt she really didn't belong with the "high and mighty." She belonged in her place, she thought. Her circle of friends might even resent her applying for higher-level positions, and she certainly didn't want to lose the acceptance of her peers.

Lynda also discovered this about herself: she'd heard it was lonely at the top, and she didn't want that. Success would make her different, and she liked being normal. Eventually she realized this fear, like the others, was just an irrational idea about success. Also, whenever Lynda pictured herself in positions of greater challenge, fears of being in the spotlight highlighted her lack of self-confidence. Her thick New Jersey accent and use of some slang words didn't quite fit the image of an executive, and she didn't want to embarrass herself. Staying unnoticed was safer, Lynda thought. Leaving her comfort zone would be difficult.

Lynda's final revelation was that she was afraid of the hard work that would follow moving to a more challenging position. The truth was that she was always a hard worker, and as both a mother and a leader she could help to advance a healthier approach to balancing work and life. Armed with the realization that all her fears were irrational and were simply holding her back, Lynda decided to apply for a position as vice president. "What the heck," she said. "At least that will let them know I'm interested in progressing within the company." To her shock, two weeks later, Lynda was offered the promotion!

Take Lynda's example to heart, and don't allow fear of success to hold *you* back. Personal growth only happens when we stretch ourselves to take on greater challenges. Once you recognize your fears—and their falseness—the next step is to jump into opportunity without hesitation. You may even hear yourself say, "Why didn't I do this before?"

"Do what you fear most and you control fear." ~ Tom Hopkins

AUGUST 29

I will discount my false beliefs

False beliefs are deceptions you maintain about about yourself or about something. An example of a false belief could be, "I'm too old to do that job." False beliefs stifle our potential, stunt our personal growth, and prevent our success. In order to succeed, you must understand these false beliefs and eliminate them. If they continue unabated, they can ruin your life. Don't let that happen.

All of us have been brainwashed to some extent, somewhat like a trained animal that cannot break free of its surroundings because it assumes danger lurks outside its confines. Society imbues within our mind certain lies that over time can seem true—sayings like, "I can't quit that bad habit. I'd relapse anyway"; "I'm not good enough to deserve that"; "The economy is just too bad for me to be able to succeed"; "I'm too out of shape to lose weight now"; "I'm not smart enough"; "I'm just unlucky at those sorts of things." When we internalize false beliefs, either through what others say or through our own self-speak, eventually they wear on us like heavy chains. They can become so heavy, they cause us to just give-up. Almost all of them are baseless, so we need to break the chains.

Ben was told by several students, "No one passes Professor Gorski's class." But Ben wanted to take the class, so he asked the students about their experience with the professor. It turned out none of them had taken Gorski's class, nor did they know of anyone who had taken his class! This story tells us that we need to test others' opinions before making them our own. Even if Dr. Gorski indeed flunked most of his students, that didn't mean Ben would fail.

We all have unique abilities and skills. What doesn't work for one person may work for you. The incident of failure by others does not preclude you from experiencing success, given the same opportunity. Even our bodies are different, so a diet or health plan that fails for one person may work for you. Feel free to challenge your beliefs, especially if they are holding you back. Here's one belief that's false regardless of your situation, and that one is "you cannot succeed." Of course you can succeed! You just need to know the truth about yourself and your conditions. It's time to shed those false beliefs, and live a successful life based on truth.

"If you think you can do a thing or think you can't do a thing, you're right."
~ Henry Ford

AUGUST 30

I will have an internal locus of control

The term *locus of control* was first introduced in the 1950s by psychologist Julian Rotter. It refers to a person's foundational belief system about the influences that affect their life's outcome. According to Rotter's theory, there are two classifications of people: those with internal locus of control and those with external locus of control. The most successful people tend to be internal, whereas those with an external locus of control tend to be more negative about the world and their standing in it. Those with an internal locus of control believe they are essentially responsible for the outcomes in their lives. They display the characteristic of self-reliance and believe that no external influence can prevent their success. Only they can do that.

Research reveals that people with an internal locus of control tend to be more successful because they remain committed to a goal while earnestly believing they will attain it. These studies also show that men tend to be more internally focused, and that people tend to become more internally focused as they age. On the flip side, those with an external locus of control believe that influences outside of themselves invariably affect their ability to succeed. These people tend to believe their future depends on arbitrary influences such as luck, providence, or society. Because those with an external locus of control believe they have very little control over their future, they tend to place less effort into their work and projects. Therefore, as the research confirms, they perform less successfully in their career and in school than those with an internal locus of control.

People with a strong internal locus of control tend to be very achievement-oriented. To develop an internal locus of control, recognize that you always have a choice. Set goals for yourself and take note that achieving these goals allows you to control what happens in your life, which build self-confidence. Make a concerted effort to be more decisive, and to improve your problem solving skills in order to build confidence that you can control what happens. Be careful not to say to yourself things like, "There's nothing I can do" or "I have no choice." Remind yourself that you do have a choice, and that you have control in making your own choices regardless of what others do.

"Make a decision, make it with confidence, and the world will be yours."
~ Jaren L. Davis

AUGUST 31

I will develop my learning skills

Developing effective learning skills is essential for success in any field. How we learn is as important as what we learn in order to grasp ideas, and we tend to learn based on our learning style.

One of the most widely used models of learning styles is the *Index of Learning Styles,* developed by Richard Fielder and Linda Silverman in the late 1980s and that Fielder revised in 2002. According to this model, the learning styles are: Sensory (learners prefer practical information – the facts); Intuitive (learners prefer conceptual information – meaning); Visual (learners prefer graphs, pictures and diagrams); Verbal (learners prefer to hear or read information); Active (learners prefer to manipulate objects – hands on); Reflective (learners prefer to evaluate and analyze options – figuring it out); Sequential (learners prefer to put together details in order to see how the big picture emerges); Global (learners prefer holistic and systematic approaches – see the big picture first and then fill in the details).

Once you understand your learning style, you can begin to stretch beyond your preference and develop a more balanced approach to learning. The key is balance. Staying with just one style limits your ability to take in new information and assimilate it quickly and accurately. For example, if you are a sensory learner, seek out opportunities to learn theoretical information and then use facts to evaluate these theories. Reflective learners can over-think something at the risk of doing nothing, so practice making practical decisions—be decisive. Visual learners can practice note taking and look for opportunities to explain information using words. As a global learner you easily grasp the big picture, but you risk missing some key details, so take time to ask for explanations. Sequential learners can easily break down problems, so they need to slow down and occasionally consider the "big picture." Sensory-intuitive learners need both plain facts and general concepts. Active-Reflective learners should evaluate and analyze, along with using experiential learning. Take time to learn your preferred style and force yourself to break out of your comfort zone. Once you do, you'll be pleased at how much more you can learn and apply in life.

"Whoever ceases to be a student has never been a student." ~ George Iles

SEPTEMBER

EXCEED EXPECTATIONS

SEPTEMBER 1

I will identify my Key Success Factors

With all of the competing demands in our life, it is becoming increasingly more difficult to identify what's most important. That's where knowing your Key Success Factors (KSFs) can help. KSFs are the most important areas of activity in your life that must be performed satisfactorily if you are going to meet your goals. They create a focal point for both yourself and your team in order to accurately measure success, and to help you execute important strategies.

First, you need to identify the select key areas where activities must be on target for your project or goal to succeed. If the results in these areas are not fully realized, your success and that of your team will be compromised. KSFs focus on what's "mission critical" on any project or mission. For example, say one of your strategic goals is to increase your number of customers by twenty-percent. The corresponding Key Success Factor might be to increase your competitive advantage versus other similar products in order to attract more customers. Another goal might be to create a new service to attract more customers. The corresponding KSF might be to find new services through current providers.

After identifying your KSFs you should prioritize them by level of importance as they relate to your mission (which might be to become the number one provider of ______ in your area). Once the mission is established, align your strategic goals (increasing sales by twenty- percent), with the essentials for achieving them. Those essentials will be your KSFs. Next prioritize your KSFs and focus on the top three to five. Make sure to routinely measure your success against your KSFs and reevaluate them to ensure they remain relevant in the face of changes.

Though KSFs may be more challenging to measure than goals which have set timelines and values, assigning some milestone for achievement will help keep you on track. Key Success Factors are the critical components of your success. By identifying them ahead of a project or endeavor, you will help to ensure that your efforts are well focused and that you are dedicating the right resources in the right places. As long as they are continually monitored, KSFs keep teams and individuals "on the same page" and committed toward common goals.

"Goals allow you to control the direction of change in your favor." ~ Brian Tracy

SEPTEMBER 2

I will make good decisions when faced with options

Imagine your boss just placed you in charge of the due diligence team responsible for evaluating whether a product acquisition makes sense for the company. You've identified a list of criteria to determine whether the potential new product fits with the organization's overall portfolio. You could decide to pass on buying the new product because it is expensive, but you don't want to make your decision on price alone. Other factors to be considered are the quality of the product, patent protection, forecasted growth potential, and the ability to modify either the existing product or the current marketing plan to make it more appealing.

So how can you make the best decision given all of these variables? Analyzing and prioritizing each one may be the key, by first listing all your options and the factors that will go into your decision making for each one. You then rate/rank each option-factor and weight them by relative importance. Score each option from one (meaning completely unimportant) to five (meaning critically important) —you can have options with the same level of importance. Now multiply each of your scores by the ranking of importance you gave to each one. This may help you to distinguish which options hold more importance than you originally thought.

Your go/no-go decision will then assess the impact of your top two to three options, which is best evaluated by the team. Brainstorm these top options affected by the decision relative to the organizational and market impact. Identify all of the areas impacted by your decision, and how they will be affected, listing out the possible negative and positive impacts of the decision. You will need to determine whether to go ahead, given the negative consequences it will cause and their related costs.

Place your decision in a series of "what if" scenarios to determine if the negatives you are considering will actually happen. Consider any "knock-out" factors, such as the company going bankrupt because of your decisions, or layoffs that may occur. Speak with the accounting department so that they can conduct a cash flow forecast to check the financial viability of your decision. Then go with your decision based on the summary assessment from each of these methods. Chances are great you'll make the right decision!

"Waiting hurts…But not knowing which decisions to take can… be the most painful." ~ José Harris

SEPTEMBER 3

I will create a personal goal statement

A young woman was asked to define her personal goal statement. "To be successful," she answered. "So what does success look like to you?" the interviewer asked. "Money and independence," she said. Next the woman was asked how much money she wanted to make, and from whom or what she desired independence. Finally after drilling down to specifics, the twenty-one-year-old established her goal statement: "By the time I am twenty-three, I want to be debt free, live in a nice two-bedroom apartment in North L.A., and be able to give my parents a nice vacation by working forty hours a week as a fitness instructor." Finally, she had a goal.

A personal goal statement is a *specific* plan of action you will take in one or more areas of your life—such as relationship goals, financial goals or career goals. It should be measureable, with deadlines and quantifiable numbers (such as zero debt) by which to absolutely determine its achievement. Desires such as "I want to be a happier person" are not goals, they are hopes. Goal statements should include a clear plan of action, such as getting up at 6:00 each morning or exercising every other day for one hour. All goals should define a beginning and an end with frequent progress assessments, affirmations for doing a good job, and a date on which to evaluate whether the goal has been met. Personal goal statements establish what you want to achieve in the areas of faith, home, health, career, and leisure.

Those who establish and regularly monitor both long-term as well as short-term goals have been found to stay motivated and exhibit greater self-confidence. According to a study by Dr. Laura Cartensen at Stanford University, personal goal setting maximizes positive emotions. Try establishing your personal goal statement, and start realizing a more purposeful life that brings joy.

"A goal is a dream with a deadline." ~ Napoleon Hill

"Our business in life is not to get ahead of other people, but to get ahead of ourselves." ~ Maltbie D. Malock

SEPTEMBER 4

I will manage my boss

Les was an acknowledged genius, and by most standards, a very effective executive. Les was not, however, a good manager of people. Tyler was promoted into a position reporting to Les. Tyler had an excellent track record. Twelve months after he started reporting to Les, Tyler was fired. What happened? Tyler did not effectively manage his boss. Tyler never thought he needed to "manage up," and as a result he never tried to see things from his Les's perspective.

To "manage up" you need to know whether your boss is detail-oriented or outcome-oriented to fit his or her style. Know when and how often the boss would like to be approached. Another mistake Tyler made was not sending background information ahead of meetings. Like most bosses, Les didn't want a huge data dump; he wanted Tyler to analyze and filter data and to present actionable information to him. On a couple of occasions, Tyler did not back-up his resource requests with enough justifications, which made Tyler appear less credible. Tyler's frustration caused him to complain about his boss with others—which undermines any ability to manage up. Instead of supporting Les in doing what he was good at doing, Tyler downplayed his boss's strengths and emphasized his weaknesses.

Maintaining positive communications is key to managing your boss. Keeping him updated on what you're doing is important, and make sure not to complain every time he sees you. Occasionally express some sincere appreciation to your boss, and ask him if there's anything you can do to improve your performance. Show that you are on top of things by taking responsibility, and coming up with options so that both of you can make informed decisions. Let the boss know exactly what is needed from his side.

If problems occur, prepare a sound plan to correct the root cause and to prevent future such problems. Make sure that your boss is never blindsided with information, especially when he meets with upper management. Make sure that information about your area comes mainly from you, not others, and make an effort to bring good news to your boss so that he can associate you with a positive mental image. Managing your boss is an important skill that will benefit your career and performance.

"The best time to start thinking about your retirement is before the boss does." ~ Author Unknown

SEPTEMBER 5

I will create my job satisfaction

Unless you're a professional athlete or superstar, your work may not exactly feel like a paid vacation. Dreams are one thing; practicality is another. Thankfully job satisfaction doesn't have to be confined to dream jobs. At the core of being satisfied are your attitude and expectations. If you consider your work as a job or even as a career, your reward comes in the form of compensation, status, influence, or position. If you consider it a passion, your efforts define your satisfaction.

Developing passion for what you do involves being honest about your strengths and weaknesses, and then trying to fit them to something that values your current skills. Even if you're in a position that doesn't fully tap your abilities, your attitude could change that. A positive attitude that sees the potential for variety in current circumstances can make all the difference. Whether we admit it or not, we all flourish within a dynamic environment. If you don't find yourself there yet, try asking for new opportunities, set the bar higher for your performance, mentor someone, or use your time to develop and strengthen your skills. Don't allow boredom to take over. Create the position to which you aspire. Ask for it. Volunteer for something more stimulating, get involved with special task forces, and if those don't work, take an extended leave and redesign your career as a passion and not just a job.

Your attitude leads the way to your future possibilities. Reframe your thinking by seeing a problem as a chance to shine. Recognize your feelings of sameness as confirmation that you've achieved enough success to move-on, or move forward. Look at setbacks as times to learn and change direction. In other words, be an optimist. No matter what it may feel like, the truth is you are never trapped in a position. You can change direction at any time, update your résumé, consistently check employment trends and opportunities, or contact people in places you'd enjoy working.

No one can succeed without finding purpose in what they're doing. Even if your job isn't your ideal, there is something or someone who can benefit from what you have to offer. The most tedious of jobs can turn into works of satisfaction and purpose if you can find that hidden need that only you can fill.

"Satisfaction lies in the effort, not in the attainment, full effort is full victory." ~ *Mahatma Gandhi*

SEPTEMBER 6

I will adapt my leadership style

You've just hired a top talent. Before leaving for an out-of-state meeting, you give him the information needed to perform a specific task that needs to get done. When you return later that week, you find he not only hasn't accomplished what you had asked him to do, he didn't even get started. He lacked the confidence. How can you avoid situations like this?

Situational Leadership®, developed by experts Paul Hersey and Ken Blanchard, matches a leader's style to the maturity of the person or group they are leading. The theory categorizes leadership styles as: Telling (S1) – telling reports what to do, and how to do it; Selling (S2) – leaders still provide direction, but they moreover "sell" their message to get the person/team onboard; Participating (S3) – focuses more on the relationship and less on direction, sharing decision-making responsibilities; and Delegating (S4) – passes most of the responsibility onto the follower/group, and is less involved in decisions.

Maturity of the follower also fits into four levels: M1s – lack the knowledge, skills, or confidence to work on their own; M2s – willing to perform a task, but still lack the skills to succeed; M3s –ready and willing to perform a task, more skilled than M2s, but still not confident in their abilities; and M4s – able to work on their own, have high confidence, commitment and strong skills. The Hersey-Blanchard model matches each leadership style to each maturity level, so that an M1 would require an S1 style (telling/directing); an M2 would require an S2 style (selling/coaching); an M3 would require an S3 style (participating/supporting); and an M4 would require an S4 style (delegating).

In the example of the new hire, the leader should have used an S1 style (telling/directing) before he left town, because, despite the new hire's talent, he was less mature in his knowledge of the company and its culture, so he required more direction. If the follower had been a long-term successful contributor with the company, the appropriate leadership style would likely have been S4 (delegating). Someone promoted to a new position, may have a high level of skills and excitement, yet lack some initial confidence. In that instance an S3 (participating/supporting) style involving teaching/coaching where necessary, would be most effective while still largely leaving the employee to make their own decisions. Adapt your style to the situation and the individual.

"You manage things; you lead people." ~ Rear Admiral Grace Murray Hopper

SEPTEMBER 7

I will put things in perspective

When you're feeling like the weight of the world is sitting right on top of your shoulders, when things become too overwhelming and it seems like your challenges are never-ending, consider the universe around you. How magnificent its creator must be to envision it! Allow your cares to drift into the eternity in which we exist, and discover God's infinite ability to carry you through your current state of affairs.

Ponder the fact that we are standing on a planet that's revolving at a speed of 900 miles an hour, and orbiting the sun at ninety miles a second. All that we can perceive on this planet, plus all the stars that we can see, move a million miles a day. Our galaxy alone contains a hundred billion stars, measuring 100,000 light years side to side. Our planet measures 30,000 light years from its galactic central point, which means we go around every 200 billion years. To top it off, our galaxy is only one-millionth of this spectacular expanding universe. Some estimates peg that expansion at twelve million miles a minute. Our Milky Way galaxy is rotating at 225 kilometers per second, and darting through the universe at an estimated 305 kilometers per second. These figures added together mean that you're racing through space at around 530 kilometers, or 330 miles per second. So in one minute, you've traveled almost 20,000 kilometers, or more than 12,000 miles. A beam of light you see from an exploding star is only an illusion of one that actually happened millions of years ago.

If you could imagine yourself poised on the edge of a black hole (that immeasurable non-material energy that represents almost eighty-percent of our universe), you would be suspended indefinitely, without movement, neither losing energy nor gaining it; and, in this static state time would be standing still—and you would be living in the realm of eternity!

Now just consider how fleeting your worries are in the endless scheme of time, how infinitesimal your problems are compared to the vast expanse of the universe in which you live. This is your world. You are so important to live in the midst of it with boundless possibilities! You are part of a wondrous universe—as its most amazing creation!

"That deep emotional conviction of the presence of a superior reasoning power, which is revealed in the incomprehensible universe, forms my idea of God." ~ Albert Einstein

SEPTEMBER 8

I will know how to manage massive projects

You've just inherited a project that a mere mortal would appear unable to complete. You're neither Superman nor Superwoman, but you don't need to be—you can manage it quite well without any superpowers. How do you accomplish this Herculean task, you ask?

The key is to break it into smaller chunks that can be managed more effectively. You first define clearly what you are delivering. You then need to break these deliverables into manageable pieces, to make it simpler and clearer. For example, if you're remodeling a house, break down the different project tasks into categories such as kitchen, flooring, electrical and plumbing, and so forth. After doing this, prioritize each of the subtasks. For example, before adding kitchen utilities, you will need to tear out the existing flooring and repaint the walls before laying the new flooring.

If you're involved in a collaborative project at work, assign team members to each subtask and create timelines and expectations based on your deliverables. In order to ensure that everyone is contributing to the larger project outcome, show each member the final plans and what the end result should look like. As the project manager overseeing a team of people, you need to make sure that you don't become overwhelmed with competing deadlines, so alternate target dates. If that's not possible, allocate time for reviewing the project details and for possible delays. The key functionality you need is to construct a hierarchy of all deliverables, which is called a "work breakdown structure." For example, if you are working on a project to upgrade technologies, establish reviews with each subproject team so that you can orchestrate the blending of each one's progress with the others. Ask them how, who, when, and where things will be done by drilling down to the most fundamental parts of the work breakdown structure, called "work packages." Each subproject team should be clear on what the outcome looks like when it is done in delivering their respective work packages. Always keep the subproject teams focused on the central outcome, as in how does this fit with the desired big picture. When all of the deliverables are complete and the outcome meets with your pre-defined requirements, you've accomplished what may have seemed impossible. Congratulations!

"After two weeks of working on a project, you know whether it will work or not."
~ Bill Budge

SEPTEMBER 9

I will deliver products and services that delight customers

Your efforts so far to break away from the pack have been weighed down by a profit-centered mindset that say you need to design a product that meets the basic needs of customers at a fair cost-to-benefit ratio. What attributes will give your product preeminent status?

In the 1980s, Dr. Noriaki Kano introduced a model to change that paradigm. The Kano Model Analysis is a technique for deciding which features in a product or service will actually delight your customers. According to the Kano Model, a product or service can have three types of properties: 1) Threshold Attributes 2) Performance Attributes, and, 3) Excitement Attributes.

Threshold attributes must be provided to meet the customers' satisfaction. Their absence would cause immediate dissatisfaction, but would not necessarily make the customer happy. An example of Threshold Attribute would a television with good screen resolution and variable settings.

Most products and services compete at the Performance Attribute level, which are also called product differentiation features. On a TV, a Performance Attribute might be an extended warranty, or the ability to convert signal formats from a DVD player to produce even more striking colors.

Excitement Attributes are offerings that people don't expect, but which delight them. In the TV, a breakthrough technology would truly resemble real life in 4D, including surround sounds, or free giveaways such as headsets or a video module. Customer satisfaction rises exponentially when these features are offered at a price they can afford.

The key for using this Kano tool is to categorize your ideas into the three types of Attributes. Make sure you meet the Threshold Attributes first, and then the Performance Attributes. Finally, brainstorm the Excitement Attributes and think of how you can incorporate these into your product or service. Let your customers and prospects do the categorization of your ideas for you. Find out what they're willing to pay in order for you to create a good profit.

"I want to put a ding in the Universe." ~ Steve Jobs

SEPTEMBER 10

I will live in a place that improves my quality of life

Don't allow random influences to determine where you live, like where you grew up or went to school. Instead, find a place where you can fit in. Rebecca Ryan, CEO of Next Generation Consulting, says: "Where you live is more important than where you work because a mortgage and your kids' school are more long-term than the job you have." When deciding where to live, think about the place as much as the challenge you'll get from a job, advises Richard Florida, author of *The Rise of the Creative Class* (Basic Books, 2004), although he says these two are "not as important as relationships with family and friends." So place the consideration of relationships at the top of where you want to be.

Then think about the kinds of activities you enjoy and how much weather and the location's overall environment will affect those activities. Start by making a list of all the things you like to do. If you're an outdoors person, Manhattan or downtown Los Angeles may not be your place. But you might enjoy living in the Northwest or the San Diego area. Since jobs will more than likely change now and then, you'll also want to consider the flexibility of your career. If you want to pursue a career in entertainment, then L.A. or New York City may provide you with more opportunities. However, moving to places that reflect your values (think conservative/liberal, spiritual life, family life) and non-work interests (Colorado skiing, big city theater) allows you to move among careers without having to relocate away from relationships and interests.

Overall quality of life matters most. This includes keeping your commute short. "You think you are moving out to the suburbs because it's better for your kids, but in some cities, you're never going to see your kids because you're always in your car," says Wendy Walters, founder of the blog *All About Cities*. Consider also that expensive areas limit your flexibility if you're on a limited budget, and can place you at an economic disadvantage compared to others in your community. Consider all of the infrastructure needs of yourself and those with whom you live—such as public transit (if you don't want to drive very much), good health care (especially if you are later in life or have health issues), and good schools (for the kids). Where you live is key to your success.

"Love the life you live, live the life you love." ~ Bob Marley

SEPTEMBER 11

I will get my mojo back

Do you feel like you have lost your mojo? Have those feelings of boundless energy and that drive to achieve your goals vanished? Your first step is to ask yourself why. Identify the momentum killers in your life. Maybe you need a change, or maybe you need some physical stimulation. Something as small as shifting your office or workspace may help. Try shaking things up by doing something different. Maybe that usual meeting place could change. You could even change your goals. It's amazing the big difference even small changes can make. Sometimes our myopic thinking just makes us stale. Hiring a personal coach can help you gain a fresh perspective.

Or maybe there's a physical reason you've lost that mojo. Make sure you're getting enough sleep. In addition to refreshing your body, sleep gives your brain the ability to process all of the information you've received. Aim for eight to nine hours of sleep by going to bed before 11 p.m. and avoiding stimulants like caffeine and alcohol that can decrease REM (for rapid eye movement)—the deeper, restorative stage of sleep. Exercise serves as a great rejuvenator. It stimulates circulation and oxygenation, and elevates your mood by increasing endorphins and enkephalins. Exercise improves elimination, keeping bodily toxins from building up. The more oxygen in your body, the more energy you create. Besides exercise, vitamin C-rich foods have been shown to increase circulation—by up to thirty-six-percent, according to a study of diabetics reported in the *Journal of Clinical Investigation.* Also, natural blood thinners like ginger, garlic, and cinnamon increase blood circulation. A high intake of essential fatty acids such as those found in fish, nuts, and green, leafy vegetables improves the blood's ability to carry oxygen.

Just getting out in the sun can help to revitalize you. Sunlight contains Vitamin D that supports digestion and helps your body's utilization of sugar, helping to maintain the insulin balance that is key to sustaining your energy. Try to get out in the sun at least fifteen minutes each day without sunglasses. UV light received through the eyes promotes serotonin (which lifts your mood) and increases melatonin production needed for quality sleep. How we take care of ourselves determines how much energy we can spend on the things that matter most.

"One way to keep momentum going is to have constantly greater goals." ~ Michael Korda

SEPTEMBER 12

I will fail forward

If you're not succeeding, maybe you need to fail more often. Thomas Watson, founder of IBM, recommended that an important route to success was to "double your failure rate." The key to "failing forward" is to learn from mistakes and do a better job next time.

What may be holding you back is the sometimes false idea that achieving most of your objectives constitutes success. In baseball, a batting average over .300 is good, meaning that the batter fails two-thirds of the time. Legendary hitter Ty Cobb's .366 career batting average ranks first in the history of major league baseball, which means that he failed to get a hit sixty-three-percent of the time he faced a pitcher. According to one study, the vast majority of small businesses (sixty-four-percent) fail within a ten-year period. It's that one major success that defines many of those who finally succeed big-time.

If we stretch ourselves and expand our goals, we can't avoid the possibility of failure. Even when we achieve success, often there's a delayed response before others recognize it. In the election of 1860, Abraham Lincoln received only thirty-nine-percent of the popular vote—the second lowest percentage of anyone ever elected to the presidency. Both North and South newspapers were filled with suggestions for violence against Lincoln, but he was later recognized as one of the greatest United States presidents. Victorious people like Lincoln keep their eyes on the horizon, their mind on the mission, their attitude on the positives, and their perspective on a critical view toward failing forward. The successful person says something like, "Going forward, I will now _________ (do better)."

The major difference between achievers and just average performers is that achievers respond to failure with the conviction to try even harder the next time. They accept responsibility for their failures without taking it too personally, and they are able to put the past in the past. Often the difference between failure and success is just one more or a different ingredient, a little extra effort, or a smidgen of advice. We need to learn from all our experiences, whether good or bad, because failure is the teacher of progress. So the next time you try something, remember: fail early, fail thoughtfully, and fail forward.

"It's fine to celebrate success but it is more important to heed the lessons of failure." ~ Bill Gates

SEPTEMBER 13

I will negotiate "no"

Can you negotiate your way out of a situation that's not right for you? Negotiation is really about reaching agreement while finding a mutually beneficial solution. But when the answer is no, it can be unsettling. Too often we just give-up and accommodate the other person in order to keep things friendly.

In the book *Getting to Yes: Negotiating Agreement without Giving In* (Penguin Books, 2011), authors Roger Fisher and William Ury suggest that in order to effectively negotiate we need to separate the people from the problem by focusing on interests, not positions. Define objective standards as the criteria for making the decision. When you're already maxed and someone wants you to take on another project, you need to remain assertive by saying "no" through effective negotiation. Perhaps you could negotiate a lighter workload—which would get you to "yes"—or redefine your role and responsibilities as an opportunity to move forward. You have plenty of options, but just saying "no" may be the most challenging.

So the key is to say "no" to the task, but "yes" to the person at the same time. Begin by explaining your reason for saying "no" so that it's clear whether just the timing is wrong, or whether there are other prohibitive factors. If someone understands your justification, they're more likely to agree with it, or at least they are less apt to become confrontational. Next, think through different ways for the other person's needs to be met. Consider other resources and areas of flexibility by searching for common interests to achieve the primary end-goal.

Gaining the other person's trust is central to any negotiation process. You do that through genuinely trying to understand their needs, assuring them you respect them enough to want to work through a solution that will get them to where they want to be. Say something like, "I'm sorry, I know you need to get this done and I want to help you. At the same time I'm committed to a project this week and don't have time to do a good job for you right now. But I have a couple of other ideas. Jane is anxious to develop her skills in this area. Would you like me to show the project scope to her so that she can take this on? Or I can do this in about two weeks if you like." Look for that proverbial win-win.

"Diplomacy is the art of letting someone else have your way." ~ Sir David Frost

September 14

I will eliminate excess drama in my life

Your teenage daughter calls you and screams, "I want to DIE!" After listening to her long diatribe, you discover the real reason behind her frantic call: she had an argument with her boyfriend and according to her, they are "breaking up." How do you bring her down to earth without raising your blood pressure? Try reminding her that life is comprised of millions of moments, and that her moment of angst now will eventually fade into the future where this situation will probably not even be a memory.

We all have to take on one thing at a time in order to stay sane, and we need to place our instant frustrations in the context of countless moments. In truth, only a miniscule number of them will be remembered. Many of us take on too many responsibilities, and we conceptualize passing problems as having long term repercussions. As a result, we end up emotionally strained.

Human nature appears to be addicted to chaos and frenzy. Perhaps this has something to do with too many communication modes and messages—from television to smartphones to the Internet—that bombard us with sensory overload. Since we have been exposed to chaos for most of our lives, in a perverted way we may be drawn to its familiarity. It presents us with the quandary of desiring calm while being attracted to constant excitement, even if it's detrimental to our health.

There is hope. The treatment requires honesty with ourselves and others, and some behavioral modification. Much of our drama comes from not resolving conflict that should be dealt with the moment it occurs. After agreeing to disagree or agree, consider it settled. The other cause of drama comes from not dealing with needs when we should be meeting those needs. People whose lives seem to be filled with drama and who are often anticipating the worst-case scenario may simply fail to be proactive or place things in the right perspective. These failures affect our relationships with others, bleeding over to financial matters, family issues, dating issues, and work issues. To cut down on the drama, eliminate procrastination. Or change your perspective and refuse to feed into other people's drama. Listen without reacting and be straight and clear.

"When you are not honoring the present moment by allowing it to be, you are creating drama." ~ E. Tolle

SEPTEMBER 15

I will use social connections to succeed

Social media sites like Facebook, Twitter and LinkedIn have become part of the national psyche, yet business leaders are still struggling as to how to use these transformative technologies to their advantage. It makes one wonder—which familiar companies will be around in the future, and which yet undiscovered ones will take their place?

In just ten years time, forty-percent of the Fortune 500 was replaced. Electronic superpowers like J.C Penny and Circuit City closed many of their retail stores because of erosion in their business to other technology sources, in part due to a plan that failed to recognize the power of the emerging social marketplace. In his book *What's the Future of Business: Changing the Way Businesses Create Experiences* (Wiley, 2013), futurist Brian Solis presents a clear path for how businesses can create consumer experiences instead of the usual way of marketing and servicing their products. The great distinguisher, he says, between online influence and online popularity, is that the connected consumer will share negative experiences much more often than positive ones within their circle of influence. Understanding his three principles of influence— reach, resonance, and relevance—Solis says, are key to creaing a market-changing consumer experience. He says, "The future of business is about creating experiences, products, programs and processes that evoke splendor and rekindle meaningful and sincere interaction and growth. At the center of this evolution—or (r)evolution—is the experience."

The emerging social climate demands that successful companies create, rather than simply respond to, experiences. "Social media," Solis says, "is about social science not technology." His definition of social science includes understanding "the journey (customers and stakeholders) take to make decisions" by asking the questions: "Do you know what customers or stakeholders expect or the challenges they face? Are you familiar with how they connect and communicate and why?" The future of business boils down to shared experiences—what people sense as they experience your product over time and how they feel supported given what's called the future generation's "digital lifestyle," which lives and breathes in social networks.

"The power of social media is it forces necessary change." ~ *Erik Qualman*

SEPTEMBER 16

I will get buy-in from others

"It was a good day," Judi thought to herself when her idea for reorganizing the department got approved by upper management. But that was almost one year ago. Today, Judi's department has missed meeting four of its five strategic goals after three key contributors resigned. "It was a bad year," Judi thought to herself. After deconstructing what happened, Judi realized she had failed to gain buy-in from several key stakeholders within the reorganization. Judi got what she wanted short term, but in the long run the team became demoralized and demotivated.

People today are seeking a purpose for their work that should be stated by their leadership, which begins by telling them the "why" of what's happening. That's not happening in many cultures. According to the Gallup-Healthways Well Being Index, fifty-two-percent of the U.S. workforce described themselves as not engaged, which Gallup estimates costing companies $300 billion annually. Whereas executives are mainly concerned with financial performance and business strategies, employees are focused on less tangible factors: frequent communications, access to leadership, and the organization's values or beliefs—all facets of the organization's culture. These factors help to create buy-in, and without at least the key stakeholders being on board, any initiative is at risk of failure. People in general do not like to feel railroaded or disenfranchised. They want to be part of the decision-making process, or at least they want to feel that they are. This starts with the change-maker or the leader explaining the purpose for what's being considered. Defining the rationale (giving clarity), reinforcing core beliefs, inviting others to look at the big picture, and asking for input and suggestions establishes connection between the change-maker and the people at the affect of the final decision. It's key that leadership connect with their followers on a personal level.

People will buy in if they know they're cared for, that they will be helped, and that leadership is trustworthy. Respect for decisions is earned through involvement, not edicts. When people join leadership in genuinely owning the responsibility for the organization's success, teamwork and commitment naturally happen.

"If you would win a man to your cause, first convince him that you are a sincere friend." ~ Abraham Lincoln

SEPTEMBER 17

I will wisely choose my battles

Conflict happens frequently, because, as Isaac Newton discovered, for every force there is an equal and opposite force. You may be tempted to battle through each of these conflicts, but most experts agree that choosing your battles wisely is a better way to live. According to Dr. Richard Carlson, author of *Don't Sweat the Small Stuff* (Hyperion, 1996), "Often we allow ourselves to get all worked up about things that, upon closer examination, aren't really that big a deal. We focus on little problems and concerns and blow them way out of proportion." Dr. Carlson suggests that by choosing your battles wisely, you'll be much more effective in winning those battles that are most important to you.

Those who constantly find themselves in battle mode usually end up losing the war because of depleted resources (health) or burned relationships. So the key is to determine what's most important to you, and to be willing to defer your agenda and consider others' opinions with as little bias as possible. Dr. Carlson says that this may involve reevaluating your priorities in life. Maybe that argument over who got the last cookie wasn't so important, at least not as opposed to whether your loved one stays away from a highly dangerous situation. Sometimes you'll just need to agree to disagree in order to live peaceably. Some people will not change their entrenched ideas, so you simply need to accept their differences because the alternative is a no-win situation. Some of those situations are none of your business, or you have no power to influence the decision: stay away from those battles. If you do enter in, make sure it's for the right reason. Are you upset that your employee turned in a late report, or that his doing so undermined your ability to get your report to your boss in time? Address the root cause, not the surface one.

Don't allow your ego to get in the way. Just because someone made a mistake doesn't mean they are out to get you. By letting someone get her way, you may actually be doing yourself a favor. If you go to battle, make sure you are standing on solid ground. If you're wrong, you could lose more than the battle. If it's not something that will matter in the long-term, let it go.

"Life is too short to spend it on warring. Fight only the most important ones, let the rest go." ~ C. JoyBell

SEPTEMBER 18

I will count my blessings

The next time you think your world has collapsed, consider the following story.

He was a husband and father of two young children, distinguished respiratory therapist at Oakland's Children's Hospital, outdoorsman, avid fisherman, strong, tall…now he was near death. Dave Lambert's body was shutting down. As blood began to clot, circulation in his limbs stopped. Heart failure appeared imminent. Unable to care for his rare condition, the hospital in Pleasanton, California transferred him to San Francisco General. Dave had contracted the rare form of Strep A—only about 2,000 cases a year are diagnosed worldwide—after treating an eight-year-old girl at Children's Hospital. Losing his spleen to Hodgkin's Disease years prior had apparently compromised his immune system's ability to fight the disease.

Now he lay helplessly in bed, gangrene ravaging all of his limbs. His hands, feet, arms, legs—even his nose—looked like they belonged on a shriveled mummy. "The doctors want to amputate all his limbs before the gangrene sets in below his elbows and knees," his wife, JoEllen, cried. "And I don't know what to tell them." If Dave lost his joints, he'd never walk again. Prosthetics would be useless. Despite heavy doses of painkillers, Dave screamed in pain, unable to make any sense of it all. Finally at the eleventh hour, JoEllen signed the permission papers. Dave survived and spent months recuperating in a hospital bed, unable to do anything for himself. A plastic surgeon rebuilt his nose, but the road to recovery would be long and unknown. When Dave was discharged from the hospital, he could do nothing by himself. Men from church carried him upstairs to go to bed; his wife and an assistant helped him go to the bathroom. He felt constantly overheated because his heart continued to pump blood at the same rate to limbs that no longer existed.

After Dave healed enough to accommodate some prosthetics fitted to his limbs, he began learning to live again. The journey proved hard, but Dave eventually skied the mountains of Lake Tahoe on his prosthetics, and he adapted to his new conditions by living a full life. Dave is an overcomer, because his vantage point from the deepest valley caused him to appreciate the journey to the top more than most.

Count your blessings.

"All the world is full of suffering. It is also full of overcoming." ~ Helen Keller

SEPTEMBER 19

I will take the road less traveled

In his landmark book, *The Road Less Traveled: A New Psychology of Love, Traditional Values and Spiritual Growth* (Touchstone, 1988), psychiatrist Morgan Scott Peck challenges the common assumption that life ought to be easy—that pain and challenges are to be avoided at all costs. He refutes the mindless notion that the path of least resistance is the correct path to a fulfilling life. Life is suffering, says Peck, so instead of denying it we should embrace difficulty in a disciplined way by delaying gratification, accepting responsibility, and dedicating ourselves to truth and balance—in order to achieve a healthy and meaningful life. Peck details how we must learn to deal with difficulties head-on and maturely. A frequent habit of avoiding these challenges and tensions—which is the general course of action taken by most—cripples people emotionally, psychologically, and spiritually.

A disciplined approach to life is key, suggests Peck, through a concept he calls "life-maps." During the course of our life, we are always engaged in the process of mapping our life and our environment through a very unexamined way. We never really take the time to ask ourselves about the way we're drawing our maps, why we're drawing them in a specific way. We go through life on autopilot, instinctively avoiding difficulty and suffering, seeking instead after comfort and pleasure. Peck challenges us to examine ourselves and to intentionally map out our lives based on reality, using a mentally healthful approach. Once we understand the misperceptions of our surroundings, and our false interpretations of love, we can discover true love.

"Love is not a feeling. Love is an action, an activity," Peck writes. "Genuine love implies commitment and the exercise of wisdom…love as the will to extend oneself for the purpose of nurturing one's own or another's spiritual growth…true love is an act of will that often transcends ephemeral feelings of love or cathexis, it is correct to say, 'Love is as love does.'"

Finally, Peck describes "grace" as the powerful force that originates from the unconscious and produces what he calls "the miracles of health," that are assisted by a force beyond our conscious will that nurtures spiritual growth. This road less traveled becomes the key to our ultimate success.

"It is only because of problems that we grow mentally and spiritually." ~ M. Scott Peck

SEPTEMBER 20

I will practice conceptual and solutions-based selling

In whatever position you may find yourself, selling is always an essential part of it. Conceptual and solutions-based selling are the most successful platforms. The misconception is that people buy a product, a service, or an idea. In reality, customers buy what they think the product or service will do for them. So as a sales person you must first understand what the customer wants to accomplish or gain, and then you need to connect your product or service to that concept. Once you've accomplished that, the customer's problem or need is satisfied. You have provided the solution.

It's a process that involves taking the time to learn about your customer. Ask questions, find out why they do what they do, what's working for them and what's not working. Focus on their results, their needs, and not on your own. This approach places you in the role of a consultant rather than just another sales person. You can distinguish yourself from your competition by positioning yourself as the "solutions person."

The steps of the sale begin with *gaining information*: ask open (who, what, why, when, where, and how) and closed (yes or no) questions. High gain questions that provoke thought are usually the best. Seek to understand the customer's situation, uncover their problems, determine how those problems affect their ability to be successful, and offer solutions for these problems using your product or service. Only after you've gained a clear understanding of what the customer wants to accomplish should you provide them with your product's features and benefits. Make sure to associate a unique benefit of your particular product to those needs identified through your questioning.

The final step is to gain commitment from your customer. Incremental commitment is fine, such as gaining an appointment for a follow-up meeting. However you should seek to gain higher degrees of commitment as the sales process moves forward until the customer fully buys into your product, service, or idea. A failure to commit means the customer doesn't believe your solution will satisfy their most critical needs, or they don't see the difference between what you have to offer versus their current provider. The key is to understand the customer's needs.

"Everyone lives by selling something." ~ Robert Louis Stevenson

SEPTEMBER 21

I will use the Oz Principle

In the *The Oz Principle: Getting Results Through Individual and Organizational Accountability* (Portfolio, 2004), authors Roger Connors, Tom Smith, and Craig Hickman discuss a philosophy that can be summarized in one word: ACCOUNTABILITY. Like Dorothy and her companions in the classic story *The Wizard of Oz*, the authors contend that we "really do possess the skills (we) need to do whatever (our) hearts desire" if we'll simply stop living below the imaginary "line" of *victimization* which strands us on a "yellow brick road" of blaming others for our problems.

The authors describe how to "live above the line" by assuming greater personal accountability through a four-step process: 1) *See It* - recognize and acknowledge the full reality of a situation; 2) *Own It* – accept full responsibility for one's current experiences and realities; 3) *Solve It* – change those realities by finding and implementing solutions to problems, while not dropping "below the line" again when obstacles present themselves; and 4) *Do It* – summon the commitment and courage to follow through with the identified solutions, especially when there appears a great risk in doing so.

Everyday challenges in peoples' lives can create detours along the road to accountability. Personal ownership must be chosen—it doesn't just naturally happen. Speaking of the various programs used by organizations to build accountability, the authors say: "…the essence of these programs boils down to getting people to rise above their circumstances and do whatever it takes to (ethically, of course) get the results they want," not only for themselves but also for everyone else involved in the enterprise. The discipline of staying "above the line" is hard, but well worth the effort. Rather than waiting for the wave of an imaginary wand, we need rather to tap into our own resources, the wherewithal within us and about us. As it turns out, as Pogo might have put it, "We have met the Wizard and he is us."

"Hearts will never be practical until they can be made unbreakable." ~ L. Frank Baum, The Wizard of Oz

SEPTEMBER 22

I will identify the threats and opportunities imposed upon me

No business stays the same, and with those changes come both significant opportunities and potentially damaging threats. Threats can include things like new regulations that prevent you from marketing in certain areas, or rising interest rates that increase your personal as well as business debt. Many of these influences are outside our control, but we can make the best of them through proper management.

One way is to use the SWOT Analysis that lists **S**trengths, **W**eaknesses, **O**pportunities, and **T**hreats to identify factors related to a product or business operation. Another is what Harvard professor Francis Aguilar created called a PEST Analysis that identifies the "big picture" factors that could force a major decision to either benefit from or minimize the forced change. Both are useful and are sourced through brainstorming sessions.

The first step of PEST is to determine the "**P**olitical Factors." These could be changes due to elections, new regulations, tax policies, corruption, legislative laws, and the timelines in which these will take effect. The second step involves brainstorming the "**E**conomic Factors," such as the growth or decline of the economy, job figures, variable exchange rates, the rising or declining levels of disposable income, credit availability, and global impacts. Third considerations are due to the "**S**ocio-Cultural Factors," like general shifts in public opinion, changing demographics, health related influences, educational shifts, customer values, social attitudes and cultural beliefs, and religious beliefs. The final part of PEST is to list out the "**T**echnological Factors." Are any disruptive technologies on the horizon? Are your competitors adopting new technologies? Are work patterns changing due to changing technologies? How are institutional or government research projects affecting future inventions, and how can we take advantage? Are there any technology networks that can help us?

After sourcing these key influences, brainstorm opportunities for each change. How can they open new markets or be used to develop new products? What threats could undermine our success and how could we respond? Finally, take action to plan accordingly.

"Difficulties mastered are opportunities won." ~ Winston Churchill

SEPTEMBER 23

I will develop my cultural intelligence

Most of us have heard of Emotional Intelligence (EI), but what is Cultural Intelligence? That's the question introduced by authors P. Christopher Earley and Soon Ang in their 2003 book *Cultural Intelligence: Individual Interactions Across Cultures* (Stanford Business Books). Whereas people with high EI are adept at understanding others' emotions, wants, and needs, people with high cultural intelligence are plugged into the values, beliefs, attitudes, and body language of people from different cultures. They use this understanding to empathize with others and to adjust their behaviors without stereotyping.

Culturally intelligent people who understand regional, international, and religious differences can use this insight to better communicate and negotiate with diverse people groups. According to Dr. David Livermore, an expert in cultural intelligence (CI), there are four components that form CI: 1) Drive – motivation to learn about a new culture or environment; 2) Knowledge – studying how culture shapes peoples' behaviors; 3) Strategy – factoring in cultural differences when planning and strategizing; and 4) Action – behaving in a culturally respectful way. The term "culture" can apply to any groups, such as different political persuasions, religious groups, age classes, and organizations or demographics with defined cultures.

Just as with Emotional Intelligence, those with Cultural Intelligence understand and act with the awareness that one plan or one approach does not fit all people and all situations. Besides knowing thyself, seek to know others and you'll both be happy.

"Tolerance, inter-cultural dialogue, and respect for diversity are more essential than ever in a world where peoples are becoming more and more closely interconnected."
~ Kofi Annan, former UN Secretary General

SEPTEMBER 24

I will overcome my prejudices

What's your favorite color? Is there any way to convince you to favor another color? Probably not—which means that you are prejudiced in favor of your color. The fact is, we all have prejudices. Some are harmless. When a prejudice causes someone to discriminate against another person, as in choosing not to do business with them, then that prejudice is harmful (to both the offender and the offended), and needs to be changed. Do you even know your prejudices? Did you know there's a test that can help you discover them?

The Implicit Association Test (IAT), developed by professors from Harvard, the University of Virginia, and the University of Washington, measures the two levels that all people operate within – the conscious and unconscious. In *Blink: The Power of Thinking without Thinking* (Little, Brown and Company, 2005), author Malcolm Gladwell describes the conscious level as "the decisions we make deliberately and things that we're aware of. I chose to wear these clothes. I choose the books I read." The unconscious level, however, tells you more about an individual's true feelings. Gladwell describes this as "the kind of stuff that comes out, tumbles out before we have a chance to think about it. Snap decisions. Our first impressions…how we think and how we feel (are) really important in things like prejudice and discrimination."

The aforementioned study showed that our environment and the society in which we live cause these unconscious feelings. Societal influences like the news can bombard viewers with pictures of ethnic drug dealers and bias a person against that race, even though consciously they do not think of themselves as prejudiced. We are a product of our world more than we'd like to think. Dr. Tony Greenwald, one of the psychologists who developed the test, says it's possible to change prejudice by showing positive images of the people against whom we're prejudiced. But the bad news is "that the change generally only lasts as long as the experiment (when the images are shown)."

The key is to immerse yourself in an environment that reinforces positive images in order to inculcate the goodness of those people into your unconscious mind. So we can change our prejudices by consistently exposing ourselves to positive representations of those against whom we hold a bias.

"Judgments prevent us from seeing the good that lies beyond appearances."
~ Wayne W. Dyer

SEPTEMBER 25

I will step up to the Kairos Moment

Renee's husband lay in the Emergency Room with life-threatening blood clots. She needed to be with him, and she needed to find a place for her two little children, just until the crisis cleared. Renee called her friends down the street to ask if they could babysit for a while. They said "no," using some inane reason, and that served as the beginning of the end of Renee's positive feelings toward them. Her husband recovered, but the friendship did not. "Kairos" moments are pivotal moments in time when we or others need help—usually during a crisis. They could be as traumatic as a sudden death in the family or as momentous as a wedding. If someone asks for your help during one of those kairos moments, or invites you to participate in them, you had best say "yes"—or else your moment of proof with them will turn into potentially lifelong disappointment.

The same applies to a boss or the CEO who calls in urgent need for you to take on a responsibility, perhaps because someone has just resigned. In that kairos moment you must not only respond with a "yes," but you must be willing to step up to the plate and do your very best to show yourself trustworthy and capable. When a kairos moment arises, people always remember who supports them. Those who make a concerted effort to help another during a time of great loss, who make the time and spend the energy to attend someone's wedding, or who show up for any other important occasion, are always fondly remembered. The feelings of gratitude on the part of the other person are lifelong. Remember how you felt when a kairos moment happened with you, and you asked someone to be there for you, and they said "no"? How did that make you feel? How long have you remembered that "offense?" Perhaps you felt slighted or snubbed.

When a crisis at work prompted Renee's boss to call her for help with a special project, she thought about the time she was in need. Because she said "yes," and then she did her best to go above and beyond the proverbial call of duty, she was rewarded with both a promotion and career-long favor with the boss. Kairos moments matter most in the scheme of life because they have the greatest impact. Be present for them.

"Act as if what you do makes a difference. It does." ~ William James

SEPTEMBER 26

I will live life deliberately

Time is a fleeting resource that can't afford to be wasted. If we don't choose to spend it deliberately, the circumstances around us will choose to spend it for us. To live deliberately means to live with intention. It means we pay attention to the opportunities, the environment, the people, and the needs around us. And we try to remain alert to the right choices. A deliberate life doesn't just hang out. It breathes quality of purpose and aim, based on the resources we either create or find in our midst. Free time is never really free—it's borrowed at a cost that must be repaid with either satisfaction or regret. And satisfaction comes with earning it; regret from simply letting time pass with no investment whatsoever.

If you decide to listen to the wind rustling through the trees, then make sure it's done deliberately, that it renews your strength and inspires you, rather than being a moment spent just "killing time." A deliberate life responds versus just reacting. Pick the right foods that will make you healthy and not just satisfy your sweet tooth or appetite. Decide when you will sleep, and exercise, and devote time to your most essential needs. Choose work that fits with your vision and dreams, instead of just getting by, because we are by nature purposeful and passionate people in need of more than a paycheck. And if the job is not what you love to do, then give it your all as a means to your end by loving what your job gives you.

Invest your resources—your time, your money, your energy—into what's most important to you by consciously asking yourself, "Has my first priority been paid?" After that's been taken care of, you can go onto the next and then the next. Seek people in need of your help. Don't wait for someone to fall over in front of you, crying "help me"—look out for the frowning face and turn it up with your smile. Offer to help someone. Choose the memories you wish to create and make them happen. Make life deliberate by giving it meaning. Don't hand the keys over to someone else by not driving it yourself.

"I went to the woods because I wanted to live deliberately, I wanted to live deep and suck out all the marrow of life, to put to rout all that was not life and not when I had come to die, discover that I had not lived." ~ Henry David Thoreau

SEPTEMBER 27

I will protect my reputation

You've spent years growing your reputation, but it can be ruined in just a few seconds and the damage to your future success could be incalculable. You need to be prepared to take steps immediately should you be the victim of rumors, electronic manipulation, or outright sabotage. When you discover that your reputation has been impugned, you need to jump into action without delay. Damaged reputations are like a crack in a damn that expands until the flood breaks through and creates irreparable harm.

To begin, try to hold your emotions in check—because representing yourself professionally is key to righting the wrong. Even if what others say is proven untrue, your behavior in seeking corrective action will create impressions in others for a long time. If the damage has happened from something you posted online in the distant past, contact the posting company to have it removed ASAP; and in the future, make sure to filter your postings with this thought in mind: what you post in the public domain can be viewed by thousands. You must be proactive in dealing with potential negatives.

Always have two Facebook profiles, one for friends, and a public one with maximum privacy settings for everyone else. Make sure to set a Google Alert for your name so that Google will send you email immediately anywhere your name is posted online. Be careful not to post emotional comments via email (that you wouldn't want the legal department to see). In fact, never write when you're angry, and never post your real name on blogs where people are discussing controversial issues.

If the damage has been done, actively promote your innocence to others. Silence makes others assume you're guilty. Recruit supporters to help defend you against any accusations. Seek those with authority or an irreproachable reputation for counsel and possible advocacy on your behalf. If you are guilty as charged, don't deny it. Fess-up to your failings and start making amends. If someone is bullying you or deliberately sabotaging your efforts, immediately address the issue. And if the bully doesn't stop, elevate the issue to someone in authority by showcasing your efforts in order to prove your merit. Stand up for yourself!

"A single lie destroys a whole reputation of integrity." ~ *Baltasar Gracian*

SEPTEMBER 28

I will control my responses

A lady went to a doctor and was diagnosed with a potentially fatal and contagious disease that is spread through saliva. She pulled out a notepad and began making a list. The doctor said, "Are you making out your last wishes?" She said, "Something like that. I'm making a list of people I'm going to bite." Getting even—that's human nature.

Arguably the most difficult thing in life to do is respond to someone who's hurt you with an act of goodness. In fact, the concept itself seems almost too esoteric. But the fact is that you can deny yourself revenge and those who witness your absolution will view you in a more positive light. Revenge almost always results in more damage than the original offense caused and often promotes further retaliation. When we're offended, the natural mindset is to consider the offender as the victimizer, and ourselves as the victim. The fact is that we can choose not to be the victim.

We begin changing this mindset by not responding in the heat of the moment. Count to ten, breath deeply, consider the good things in your life, and reason that they are 100 times more valuable than the outcome of revenge that will likely damage those good things. You need to let go of the offense, and if reasoning doesn't get you there, then try this visualization technique: dispose of any mementos—maybe imagine burning an email or mentally closeting the offender as irrelevant. Instead of negatively reacting to someone in his or her environment—like in the workplace—find a friend or spouse who will lend a sympathetic ear without letting yourself fall into a "pity party" or a constant verbal attack on the offender. Each time the offense resurrects itself in your mind, remind yourself that you've already relegated it to the trash heap of ignorant things people say or do. You might even be able to feel compassion for the damaged psyche that caused the offender to offload their troubles onto you, and consider whether the person against whom you seek revenge may be feeling as bad as you.

Anger only feeds on itself and eats away your joy, even your health. Exercise, prayer, or meditation can help relieve the stress from the offense. The need to get revenge only means that you're still a victim. But you're *not* a victim, so act like the overcomer that you are.

"It is often better not to see an insult than to avenge it." ~ Lucius Anneaus Seneca

SEPTEMBER 29

I will create change

Change happens, so embrace the opportunity to make it a positive experience. At any given point during the change process we can choose to live at the affect of change—be a change taker, or we can effect change in advance—be a change maker. Change makers proactively identify future problems and opportunities for improvement. They create a picture of what the organization will look like after the changes have happened, in order to present opportunities to those affected. Such vision helps motivate people. Then they initiate problem-solving discussions with key stakeholders using honest and open dialog.

Successful General Electric CEO Jack Welch once said that he valued change so much that he would risk throwing his company into confusion to make it happen. Change leaders use their discernment and insider knowledge to quickly form a core team comprised of people with the political influence, skills, and position authority to effect change by rallying the team behind a concise and motivating vision. Excellent collaboration and communication skills allow successful leaders to allay peoples' natural anxieties through confidence and good salesmanship.

Everyone going through change wants to know one thing: What's In It For Them (WIIFM). To advance change, the WIIFM must be identified and addressed through constant reinforcement. Significant change requires long-term goals, however short-term wins for the larger teams' WIIFM must be gained through recognition and encouragement for goal achievements. The WIIFM represents the opportunity that will occur as a result of the change.

Empowering individuals with the truth that leadership is a choice, not a title, fosters a spirit of continuous improvement. A positive culture reflects the unyielding optimism of its change makers to make it happen. You can be a change maker through a compelling vision and effective planning at any level by designing solutions that are in-the-flow, not above-the-flow. Keep it simple, keep it focused on the WIIFM, avoid over-predicting, trust people, listen to them, create a conversation, and be transparent.

"Individuals and organizations that are good react quickly to change. Individuals and organizations that are great create change."

~ Robert Kriegel, author of Sacred Cows Make The Best Burgers: Developing Change-Driving People and Organizations (Warner Books, 1997)

SEPTEMBER 30

I will do the right thing

Business icon Peter Drucker instilled a timeless paradigm shift years ago that argues that rather than *doing things right*, successful people must strive for effectiveness by *doing the right thing*. We all have twenty-four hours in a day, but what distinguishes successful people from their counterparts is what Drucker calls "their tender loving care of time."

The higher you climb within an organization, the more you will be at the affect of those you serve, which makes the issue of time more critical. Drucker suggests keeping a log and taking back control over your time. He details three common time grabbers that should be identified: 1) doing things that don't need to be done (eliminate those), 2) doing things that could be done better by others (delegate those), and 3) doing things that require others to do unnecessary things (again – eliminate and/or manage those). Leveraging strengths is key, even if it means hiring or using talent that poses some challenges, because *contribution is the only measurement of success that matters for the executive*. And contribution only comes with concentration, as explained by Drucker: "Effective executives do first things first and they do one thing at a time." This includes getting rid of futile initiatives or programs that either unnecessarily drain resources, or have never met expectations. Letting go of these drains is key to making progress.

Drucker explains that effective executives only solve problems once using widely applicable solutions that can be easily understood and used for a wide variety of problems, and they realize that doing nothing is an acceptable option. The final outcome of making a decision is taking action, which means making it a part of someone's responsibility. In his book, *The Effective Executive: The Definitive Guide to Getting the Right Things Done* (HarperBusiness, 2006), Drucker summarizes five key success factors: 1) allocating time based on the importance of returns – those activities that are "mission critical"; 2) tapping into peoples' strengths as well as your own strengths; 3) making contributions based on the unused potential in a job; 4) concentrating on the highest priorities one at a time; and 5) making decisions that are simple enough to apply across a broad range of areas, and that are executed by assigning responsibilities. By focusing on the majors, we can see clearly to do the right thing.

"Effectiveness is, after all, not a 'subject,' but a self-discipline." ~ Peter Drucker

OCTOBER

THINK DIFFERENT

OCTOBER 1

I will use reverse thinking

The classic way of solving a problem is to analyze it or its root cause. But there's another even more stimulating exercise for dissecting problems called *reverse thinking.* Instead of asking, "How can I solve this problem to achieve a desired outcome?," reverse thinking would formulate the question this way: "How could I create the problem?" Or "How can I arrive at the opposite effect of my desired outcome?"

This unconventional method tricks the mind by creating a different thought pathway that doesn't immediately stop at preconceived ideas—the "tried and true"—that may no longer *be* true. Once you've examined all the ways to solve the reverse problem, you can turn the solution around to meet the original challenge. Hopefully, you will have sourced some innovative solutions you hadn't thought about before.

Try this in a group setting that allows others to join in sourcing unique pathways. Here's an example: As manager of a flooring store, Avery is responsible for increasing revenue. The problem of maximizing the store's profitability versus accommodating the customers' desires can cause the overselling or overstocking of inventories that results in delayed projects or lost revenue. It's a problem that's been around for a long time, and Avery is skeptical that a better solution can be reached. However, he calls his team together and decides to use reverse thinking. He writes on the board, "How can we run out of inventory more quickly, and create larger inventories of poor selling flooring materials?" The team is startled by the question, but quickly begins suggesting ideas and Avery scribes them, without adding any commentary. One of the suggestions is to increase flooring prices for the high inventory materials, and to decrease pricing for the most popular items. The reverse solutions resulted in devising a sale that reduced overstocked items, which allowed for stocking of new and highly popular items, and a forty-three-percent increased profitability through a price increase on just two of the most popular items.

Reverse thinking is a good approach for creating innovative solutions to old problems, and it's a fun way to change paradigms.

"The mind ought sometimes to be diverted that it may return to better thinking."
~ Phaedrus

OCTOBER 2

I will define what success means to me

Success translates differently for each individual. Even those who define it in terms of status or wealth tend to alter their definition toward the end of life. What does success mean to you? Until you can answer that question in one or two simple sentences, the benchmark for assessing your progress will be a little like nailing pudding to a wall—runny and futile. Three questions can help us define success: 1) whose lives do I most want to impact?; 2) what contribution(s) do I most want to make in life?; and, 3) for what do I want to be known? Answering who and what is most important to our existence leads us to our signature purpose, "Why am I here?"

It's easy to let others define success for you, but don't allow your boss, your critics, your parents, your friends or any others to answer one of the most important questions in your life. It is imperative to proactively and assertively define your value and your target for success. This is one of the most important ways to create your future and enhance your career. Your self-defined success involves mapping out how you will create meaning in your life. That map should include the destination, as well as interludes along the journey. Success is largely measured by whether or not we find life meaningful, but it need not be summed up in just one final accomplishment.

Consistency of purpose can mean that success will represent a theme, a way of living, or a characteristic, such as being good to others. Many view success as a single victory, whereas it should represent a process toward fulfilling our meaning in life. That is why a person who has failed to achieve their goals can always turn their life toward a successful outcome. No one is a failure who gets back on track toward a life that's true to what is most worthwhile. Your success only requires that you do what is most important in giving you meaning today. You are never a failure as long as there is one more opportunity to succeed.

"Always bear in mind that your own resolution to success is more important than any other thing." ~ Abraham Lincoln

OCTOBER 3

I will choose my self-fulfilling prophecies

According to the law of self-fulfilling prophecies, people respond as others expect them to respond, as in "you get what you expect." A case in point involves bosses and teachers who tend to predict the performance of individuals under their supervision with uncanny accuracy because of this so-called law. Their expectations create a cycle of behavior that, when inculcated within their direct report or student, leads to the expected result regardless of the person's actual ability.

As people form expectations of us, they transmit their beliefs onto to us, either overtly or subtly by influencing our behavior through their actions, which naturally match their original expectation. Hence, their expectations become true. A supervisor inherits an employee who he perceives to be a laggard because of a prejudice based strictly on the employee's appearance. In truth, the employee's performance to date has been exceptional. However, the new supervisor assumes that the employee will not be reliable, so he gives the most important responsibilities to others in the workplace. Subsequently, information is withheld from this employee. From a lack of knowledge, the employee begins making mistakes, even missing a meeting because no one informed him of it. As a result of being out of the "loop," the employee's work appears negligent, thereby fulfilling the supervisor's expectation of him as a laggard. These kinds of self-fulfilling prophecies are motivation sappers. They undermine our self-confidence and negatively impact our ability to be successful. We can resist them by using an honest examination of our abilities and our situation.

If you find yourself in such a situation, think about the many times you did a great job, and recognize the obstacles that may be causing you not to perform at your highest level. If you can fix them, make it your aim to do so (as in asking for more information). Maintain your self-esteem by focusing on the facts and not taking everything to heart. Create realistic goals, and if your actions start to reflect the self-fulfilling prophecy, look for a way to make a change. Use self-affirmation by listing your strengths and abilities and by constantly reminding yourself that you are *terrific*! Always expect the best from yourself, and let that be your self-fulfilling prophecy.

"Whatever we expect with confidence becomes our own self-fulfilling prophecy."
~ *Brian Tracy*

OCTOBER 4

I will deal with my social anxiety

Have you ever gone into a meeting or other social setting feeling self-conscious? Do you ever feel like people are judging you? Social anxiety is the fear of being judged negatively by other people, and often leads to feelings of inadequacy, embarrassment, and nervousness. If you feel fine when you're alone but become anxious in social situations, you may be suffering from this anxiety. Studies have shown that social phobia is the third most prevalent psychological disorder in the United States. If your anxiety is debilitating to the point where you cannot socialize without your heart racing or muscles twitching, if you worry for days or weeks in advance or if you get sick, search for a specialist who uses cognitive-behavioral therapy to treat your phobia. Even though it's your mind tricking you into believing others are judging you, your self-consciousness is very real. You need to find the encouragement to get over it.

The first step in overcoming self-consciousness is to identify the negative thoughts that cause your fear of social situations. Let's say you are about to give a presentation and you say to yourself, "I'm going to do a terrible job. Everyone will hate it." The next step is to analyze and challenge your thoughts. Ask yourself, "Is my fear really legitimate? Will people actually interpret my nervousness as though I'm a failure? Do they really care?" Through this analytical process you can eventually replace your negative thoughts with a more realistic and positive perspective when assessing the causes of your anxiety. Start debunking false beliefs.

The truth is that no one can predict the future, mind reading is usually self-projection, we tend to blow things out of proportion, and people are generally not focusing on your negative ways. Learn to really see and listen to reality rather than dwelling on your own negative thoughts. You don't have to assume sole responsibility for conversations. Silence is OK. Others can share in making conversation. Focus on slow and steady breathing when you're in a social setting: four-in, two-hold, and six-out.

Don't just ignore the problem—gradually challenge yourself by introducing yourself to new people one at a time. Volunteer. Take a social skills or assertiveness training class to increase your confidence. Above all, don't give-up. A lot of people share in your fears and anxieties. You're not alone!

"Do not be afraid of tomorrow; for God is already there." ~ Author Unknown

OCTOBER 5

I will overcome the Peter Principle

In the late 1960s, Dr. Laurence Peter put forth an observation that people working in a hierarchal organization tend to be promoted up to their level of incompetence. Or as Dr. Peter simplified it, "The cream rises until it sours." Critics have charged that this theory, popularly known as the Peter Principle, completely ignores employees' potential to learn on the job and develop new competencies. It's true that some people who pursue greater responsibilities climb to a point beyond the reach of their skills or abilities, but usually people fail because of influences they could easily overcome.

If you find yourself in a position where you are under the looking glass, there are steps you can take to succeed. First, determine your short to medium goals (one-year and five-year) in order to be clear as to what you want. Try writing your ideal job description, and then try to fit as many of your ideals with the types of jobs that are available to you. Ask yourself what skills are missing in order to qualify for that ideal position. What can you do to develop these skills or experiences? Maybe you can do volunteer work, take courses, read books, or seek out a mentor. Don't look to immediately jump into a new position without equipping yourself for it, but if someone taps you for a position of leadership before you feel ready, be honest with yourself and your supervisor about your need to grow into it. Many who are chosen to lead others make the mistake of trying to lead their teams without currying favor with them. Leadership is earned, not bestowed. It's OK to ask questions of others, and to admit that you don't know all the answers. Listen to your new team. Get to know their strengths and weak areas. When you do make a mistake, own up to it.

Rarely does our life or career go exactly as planned, so remain flexible and equipped to handle new challenges by always building your proficiencies and keeping your options open to new possibilities. Know that in any new role you can't make everyone happy, but you can listen to others' opinions before making decisions that will impact your own success. You can take yourself to the next stage in your career by planning for it and continually preparing for new challenges. No one has to settle for a life of mediocrity.

"Competence, like truth, beauty and contact lenses,
is in the eye of the beholder." ~ Laurence J. Peter

OCTOBER 6

I will prepare for seminal (life changing) events

Skip's life changed dramatically six years ago when he was fired from his job. Now he looks back on his former life, slightly depressed and a little overweight, feeling sorry for the old Skip. Seminal events by their very definition influence later developments. Things like getting fired, turning a certain age, the diagnosis of a serious illness, or a lost relationship cause us to pause and reflect: "What am I going to do now?"

After Skip got fired, his contemplations led him to branch out on his own. After fifteen years in one field, he became a small business owner in a totally new industry. Today, Skip owns a bakery and coffee shop and loves it. When Skip turned forty, he faced another seminal event. He asked himself what the heck he was doing in life. That serious, moment-stopping question led Skip to an exciting new life.

What about you? What seminal events have shaped your life? Do you have any regrets? Are there any turning points that made things better? After all, it's your life and only you can live it. Seminal events force us to reflect, to reconsider the path we're on. Though sometimes beyond our control, they're to be welcomed rather than dreaded. What person doesn't wish to be more? Yet when the occasion to grow arrives by way of a shock or a dramatic turn of events, our human tendency is to go back to what's most comfortable. In our desire for a better future, we give way to yesterday's habits.

The key to fulfilling the desires you construct in your mind is to alter your response to seminal events. You know they're going to happen. They always do. They can turn the impossible (opportunities) into inevitable decision points that force us to think: "Why not?"

Consider planning these events in advance. That's right—plan the shock. What if you were diagnosed with a terminal illness today? How would you handle it? What if you were fired—then what? If you lost your closest loved one today, how would you reroute your life? The truth is, these events can quickly turn wishes into reality if we don't fall back into the rut of looking for another replacement. Sameness is truthfully never really the same. We can never fully go back. Awaken yourself to a new perceptual reality of what you can do if the foundation underneath you suddenly evaporates. These seminal events are finite. Don't waste them. Go forward and be more.

"Miss the moment (for opportunity) and you never get a chance again."
~ Aidan Chambers

OCTOBER 7

I will learn to speed read

If you're like most people, you read thousands of words each day from emails, reports, books, the newspaper, etc. What if you could spend less time reading and more time understanding important information? Learning to read more efficiently could be the most useful skill you can develop. Researchers discovered recently that your eyes visualize letters at the same time, typically two characters apart. Your brain then assimilates these images together to comprehend messages. The average person reads at a rate of 250 words per minute, which translates into reading a page in about one to two minutes. Speed-reading can help reduce this time to less than half, not to mention that your comprehension will increase through a better understanding of the primary message.

The first thing you must do is to clear your mind of any distractions, and you must not vocalize what you read. Multi-tasking actually slows you down, and sounding out what you read does the same. Reading two to ten blocks of words helps eliminate your verbalizing words and it also sparks greater conceptualization of ideas. The more words you block together, the faster you can read. The normal eye can span about one and-a-half to two inches at a time, which averages to about five words per page. When you read, try relaxing your eyes by using your peripheral vision to see entire sentences from beginning to end. This allows you to perceive the end of each sentence by skipping across the page until you condition yourself to automatically view the end of each line.

When you first learned to read, you were taught to look across and down, bringing to mind each word and sentence in order. When you read this way, you miss the core message by focusing on more information than is necessary. Overcome this by scanning pages, looking for general themes, headings, or highlighted points. Pay attention to key material instead of the superfluous stuff. This way you can reread any critical information that might get lost while skimming through the details, but be careful not to reread words unless you absolutely need to do so. You may find it useful to use a pointer to push your brain up to a faster pace. The more you practice these skills on a regular basis, the more efficient you'll become.

"I took the speed reading course and read War and Peace in 20 minutes—it's about Russia." ~ Woody Allen

OCTOBER 8

I will use a Pitch Idea for concepts

When you throw a pitch, sometimes it misses the target. That's bad, right? Not always. Throwing a pitch at someone can be successful even if it misses the mark because it offers a starting point for testing concepts and ideas. Not everything we envision can stand the test of scrutiny, so starting with a roughly drafted *pitch idea* can get the discussion going in lieu of gathering all of the necessary information, without having to draft a formal plan that needs to be airtight. This way you can instantly launch into a discussion of a new idea without finalizing the solution to a problem. You've heard people say, "Let me bounce an idea off you," which expresses a similar sentiment.

Creating an initial draft for a critical review allows you to gather feedback in advance of developing a final plan that is unassailable. Imagine your sales are declining and you need to devise a new sales strategy. Using your pitch idea, you could develop a sketch plan to change the sales targeting strategy. In this draft, determine those potential new customers that could utilize your product in greater numbers based on your initial assessments. Present your pitch idea to the key influencers and decision makers by making sure they understand you are only pitching a rough idea intended just for quick feedback in order to determine if the idea has any practicality.

Use this information gathering to confirm or amend your premise, and to develop a new pitch idea so that you can repeat this process until you are ready to create the final plan. Let others know you are working through the process of refining your idea in order to factor in their opinions and ideas as well. In essence, you are covering all the bases by benchmarking your idea with all of the people who will be involved in its potential success, and their involvement will also help you to establish greater buy-in from these persons.

Pitch ideas also keep the decision-making process moving forward, and help prevent wasted efforts that others will eventually deem unviable. An important caveat for using the pitch idea involves making sure that others understand your rationale. You don't want to be known as the person who creates unsound or crazy ideas. Make sure to clarify that these preliminary solutions are for testing in order to avoid mistakes.

"The difficulty lies not so much in developing new ideas as in escaping from old ones." ~ John Keynes

OCTOBER 9

I will use an Impact Analysis to change things

Have you ever witnessed a decision-making that could have been better thought out? Perhaps you've been at the affect of a change that made no sense in retrospect. Chances are the change agents didn't use a change Impact Analysis (IA), described by developers Bohner and Arnold as "identifying the potential consequences of a change, or estimating what needs to be modified to accomplish a change."

Factoring in the risks associated with change is key to an effective implementation. IA uses three types of techniques—traceability, dependency, and experiential—in order to uncover the risks of a change within an organization. In traceability IA, links between the systems effect of the change are measured—such as the impacts on different processes, people, and groups—as well as how the change will impact the organizational structure, values, and strategies. Dependency happens at a more detailed level such as designing models, blueprints, case mapping, static and dynamic algorithms, and simulations. A risk analysis will determine all of the variables that can negatively impact the overall desired outcome, and then a decision of "go" or "no go" will determine whether the next technique makes sense. The experiential technique actually pilots the change (beta sites) or tests its affect on the impacted institutions or individuals. This can also be preceded with market research or surveys in order confirm some assumptions going into the change process.

Having gone through this due diligence process, you'll need to next ask yourself whether it makes sense to go forward with the change given the negative consequences that surfaced through your risk analysis and pilot/survey results. If the answer is "move forward," you'll need to prepare the actions you will take to mitigate these consequences, including readying the people who will implement the change with justifications for the decision, and how they can advance solutions for any problems that might arise.

Most changes fail because they are created and implemented in a vacuum, with little feedback, inadequate preparation (due diligence), and disempowerment of the key stakeholders. Successful changes are thoroughly vetted through assessing their impact in the context of who and what will be involved.

"Chaos is inherent in all compounded things. Strive on with diligence." ~ Buddha

OCTOBER 10

I will bring out the best in others

What's the best you can do for someone else? How about helping to develop their talents, their job success, their education, or their overall health? Whether you do so as a parent or as a leader, helping others succeed makes you more successful. But because each person needs something different, the first step includes uncovering those needs. Discover their strengths and encourage their development toward an endeavor or a position that utilizes these strengths. Everyone shines in places where their talents and abilities can best be utilized. Find out what the person you're helping does best, and foster their growth toward a place suited to these qualities.

If someone is fitted where their abilities, talents, and passion draw them, they will be much more willing to work hard there to achieve high standards, and they will enjoy it more than something that demands lesser standards. People also tend to rise toward the level of comments made by those with influence over them. Treating someone like a star salesperson builds their esteem to become a superstar salesperson; praising someone's artistic abilities pushes them to live up to your praise; and encouraging a student's aptitude makes him or her want to excel. Ask the person you're helping what makes them want to be the best they can possibly be, and then foster that thriving environment by teaching them to succeed humbly, and to fail judiciously.

Finding out what a child or an employee wants to do, and then simply advising them to do it works wonders. Creating a little competitive challenge can help as well. They also need role models and challenges—someone and something to whom and to which they can aspire and a benchmark against which to assess their own development. Sometimes they need a push along with the encouragement, as long as it's done with a sincere attitude of caring for the other's best, as did John Wooden when he tended to correct his players more often than he praised, all with a caring heart and an enthusiastic spirit of continuous improvement. Energy feeds off of energy, and those who perceive that we're enthused about them almost always reflect that energy in their work and efforts. People generally sense whether you're on their side or not by the level of your encouragement and by your positive manners.

"Be with someone who brings out the best in you." ~ Author Unknown

OCTOBER 11

I will turn the other cheek

It runs completely contrary to human nature, and yet great leaders like Martin Luther King Jr. (MLK) and Abraham Lincoln practiced the concept of "turning the other cheek" as a means to accomplish hugely positive changes. The term was popularized by Jesus in his famous "Sermon on the Mount," in which he said not to resist evil, but rather "whoever smites you on your right cheek, turn to him the other also." Scholars say this teaching of returning "good for evil" represented the most revolutionary teaching during Jesus' life on earth.

Prior to this transformational paradigm, the general population practiced an "eye for eye" way of responding to wrongdoing (as stated in Exodus 21:23), which MLK said "leaves everybody blind." Several studies now confirm that those who can "turn the other cheek" are more successful. Ask someone why they seek revenge and they're likely to tell you their goal is catharsis, says Kevin Carlsmith, PhD, a social psychologist at Colgate University in Hamilton, N.Y. But according to a study he published in the May 2008 *Journal of Personality and Social Psychology*, exactly the opposite happens. In a series of experiments, he and colleagues Daniel Gilbert, PhD, at Harvard, and Timothy Wilson, PhD, at the University of Virginia, studied the reactions of students playing an investment game during which they felt cheated by others. Those who *turned the other cheek* were able to trivialize the event, Carlsmith said, making it easier to forget. But when we do get revenge, we think about it a lot. "Rather than providing closure, it does the opposite: It keeps the wound open and fresh," Carlsmith said.

Baseball great Jackie Robinson, who broke the racial barrier by being the first African-American Major League Baseball player, faced vitriolic and harassing comments as well as death threats from fans who resented his presence. Feeling justifiably angered by these kinds of taunts and threats, Robinson asked Brooklyn Dodgers executive Branch Rickey why he was chosen. "You want a player that doesn't have the guts to fight back?" Robinson asked, to which Rickey replied, "No, I want a player who's got the guts not to fight back." Instead of seeking revenge Robinson went on to become Rookie of the Year, MVP, and World Series Champion. He learned the true meaning of "turning the other cheek."

"The best revenge is to be unlike him who performed the injury." ~ Marcus Aurelius

OCTOBER 12

I will practice active listening

Great listeners tend to be great communicators because they connect with others and they understand how to respond appropriately. But few listen well. According to researchers, people generally remember less than half of what they hear, leading to misunderstandings and a lack of productivity in both the workplace and in personal relationships. You can improve your success using active listening, which involves an attentive or focused effort to understand the entire communication from the speaker, not just their words. Active listening also tells the other person they are being heard.

Have you ever felt when you were talking with someone that it was like talking into thin air? They just weren't plugged in? The key skill on the listener's part is to use *acknowledgement*, which can be as simple as maintaining eye contact, nodding, saying, "I hear what you're saying," or leaning forward with your body. Occasionally you should rephrase what the other person has just said, such as "So if I'm hearing you correctly, you're saying ______," "It sounds like you're saying," or just summarizing their conversation. *Reflecting* what the speaker says is a key listening skill that can be done through paraphrasing and asking questions to clarify important points.

It's also good to convey empathy for *how* what they just said is *affecting* you (the listener), such as saying, "I can understand how that must have made you feel." It's important to set aside your own agenda while listening, and don't mentally prepare a response without first making sure you've heard the entirety of what the other person has to say, both in words *and* in body language. Show that you're listening by using appropriate facial expressions, using an open posture, and encouraging the other speaker with words like "uh-huh" and "please continue."

Never interrupt the other person with questions or a response, and try to keep an open mind without judging their comments. Your general attitude should be respectful and sympathetic as you genuinely attempt to understand the speaker's perspective. You should be honest and straightforward, but always in a manner in which you would like to be treated. As you practice these skills, others are more likely to respond to you in kind.

"We have two ears and one tongue so that we would listen more and talk less." ~ *Diogenes*

OCTOBER 13

I will love more

When we get right down to it, how can we achieve success without love as our first priority? In our hurried lives, we often take for granted those who are closest to us. We often forget that to love anyone—in the purest (most innocent) form of the word—means we are acting out our most lofty purpose. Consummate love is unconditional. Tell that to the person who just went through a break-up, or the employee who feels unappreciated, or the friend who wasn't invited to an important event. They certainly don't feel unconditionally loved, and they're not about to return someone's offense with that kind of love.

The trouble with loving "more" is that our definition of love often carries with it qualifications such as, "If I'm treated a certain way, then I'll love (that other person)." The fact is no one can measure up to that level of expectancy all of the time. The key may be to just stop caring about what others do or say.

When Sheila stopped caring that her daughter Andrea said such terrible things, like "I hate you," she discovered that she could love her daughter limitlessly without attaching the need to correct Andrea's abusive language with her unconditional expressions of love. In an emotionally stable way, Sheila said, "You can hate me Andrea, but you will never stop me from loving you. Just the same, I will not tolerate your abusive language." For you, loving without judging might mean staying calm when your friend starts smoking again, or your spouse quits his job, or your co-worker snubs your luncheon invitation.

Real love can't always be at the affect of emotions, especially when tempers flare. That's because our brains mirror other's emotions. Anger triggers anger, anxiety elicits anxiety, despite how much we try to stop it. So when you deliberately return anger with calm, you begin disarming the other person, and when that loved one starts behaving more calmly, your unconditional love is more easily expressed.

Try shifting your attitude from simply responding to someone else to not caring about what he or she says or does. By practicing this form of desensitization, your ability to love more freely increases. You're no longer at the affect of other people, so that loving them acts as a soothing salve for open wounds.

"Pure love is a willingness to give without a thought of receiving anything in return." ~ Peace Pilgrim

OCTOBER 14

I will make my first 100 days successful

It's not a perfect measure, but the 100-day standard for gauging presidential effectiveness often holds true. The underlying reality is that presidents tend to be most effective when they first take office, when their impression seems fresh and new, and their aura of victory is most powerful. A similar but different dynamic occurs when anyone assumes a new position, whether that is starting a new job or being placed into a new position. We change jobs and positions so frequently during our career that learning how to make a positive initial impression is key to our future success for possibly years after these critical junctures. Just because you succeeded in the past doesn't mean you'll carry over this success for the next position. Your positive relationships may not carryover to the new place, or your skills may not be sufficient in your next step, so that the first 100 days becomes critical to setting the stage for how you will be perceived going forward.

Don't assume you will know exactly what to do. Ask people in your new environment for their advice, and especially inquire with key stakeholders as to their expectations of you. Create alliances and positive working relationships both within and outside of your team to help you in achieving your goals. Establish some early wins in order to create a foundation of credibility and to build momentum for future successes. As with new presidents who build their cabinets and try to make good on their campaign promises by practicing good politics, lasting success begins with creating positive first impressions as a person who can lead and be relied upon to make good choices, as well as to do what's best in the interest of the people within the organization.

The orientation process necessitates that you clearly understand the new requirements and expectations so that you can set your horizon for exceeding them. What's different between the president and you are that your campaign begins after you assume your new position, by building supporters for successfully meeting or exceeding the new requirements of the position. Your former successes are now history; it's time to make new ones. Don't be overly dismayed when you make mistakes, just surround yourself with advisors who can help you to grow.

"Out of your vulnerabilities will come your strength." ~ Sigmund Freud

OCTOBER 15

I will find a way to win

We've all heard the phrase: When one door closes, open a new one. Charlie Wedemeyer was a former football star at Michigan State University and a successful coach at Los Gatos High School, near San Jose, California. Then at age thirty, he was diagnosed with ALS, the incurable disease that attacks the nervous systems and destroys the ability of people to control their muscles. Given one to three years to live, Charlie continued coaching at Los Gatos. In 1984, six years after his diagnosis, he coached his Wildcats to the number four-rated football team in the country. However, after inspiring them to what seemed like a certain victory, a questionable penalty cost his team the league championship.

At ninety-five pounds and near death, Charlie took the loss as a sign that he needed to keep living in order to coach his team to victory. His nurse and his wife Lucy prayed for Charlie as he struggled to breath, and the three described God's presence as so strong that Charlie began to breathe again. When he opened his eyes, a flower whose buds had previously been closed was in full bloom. He took that as another sign from God to just trust in him and to carry on. After the toughest year of his life, Charlie continued coaching his 1985 Wildcats from his hospital bed.

Unlike his 1984 team, the '85 Wildcats were not expected to do well. But against all odds, they won the league championship and won throughout the playoffs before advancing to the state sectional championship. With seconds to go in the game, the Wildcats blocked a field goal attempt and won the game.

After achieving his dream as football coach, Charlie's body underwent extreme suffering and several times approached death. But again he felt called, this time to deliver the message of hope with his wife Lucy. Together, they began traveling the world. Lucy would interpret Charlie's language of blinks, eyebrow raises, and cheek twitches to communicate a message of hope and God's grace to thousands around the globe. "He was amazing, right 'til the end," said Lucy. Charlie died in 2010, thirty-two years after being diagnosed with ALS. He never accepted closed doors. He never allowed his challenges to overrule his purpose. We should all be inspired to do the same.

"Happiness often sneaks in through a door you didn't know you left open."
~ John Barrymore

OCTOBER 16

I will use positive affirmations to succeed

We usually get what we expect—what we really, truly believe. But few of us consider ourselves as invincible or that success is inevitable. Too many pre-programmed negative expectations cause us to avoid challenges for fear of failing, and then when the inevitable challenges come their way, we consciously or subconsciously expect to fail, and to no one's surprise, we do.

To change these patterns you need to make compelling statements that success is a fact, not just a possibility. Associate your affirmation with other occasions in which you've succeeded and discount your failures as merely "prep time" for your certain success. Be clear as to your goal, and then tell yourself that regardless of how many times you may need to reroute or alter your plans, you will succeed—somehow, someway. Leave no doubt that success is a foregone conclusion. Your positive affirmations should include statements like, "I deserve to be successful," "I am a success," "I can control my own success in life," "I always reach my goals," "I enjoy being successful," "I reject abuse from others," "I deeply believe in my abilities to succeed," "I deserve to be successful," "I am getting better each day," "I'm going to go after my challenge and succeed," "I will not allow temporary setbacks to keep me from succeeding," "I am strong and valuable," "People respect me," "The best is yet to come," "I forgive myself and others," "I am better because of my mistakes," "I accept myself without reservation," "I will seize this opportunity to prevail," and "I will find a solution to whatever problems come my way."

If your former programmed way of thinking resists believing in these affirmations, acknowledge them as part of your past and continue affirming your success with these positive declarations. Remember to be intentional and not merely emotional in saying them. Conviction will be instilled within your psyche when you repeat your affirmations regularly as a routine part of your day. Record them in a place where you can easily retrieve them, such as your wallet or your computer screen, to remind yourself of them during quiet times, breaks, lunchtime, and before sleep. Use them during goal setting and while visualizing your success. Start believing in yourself.

"You've got to win in your mind before you can win in your life." ~ John Addison

OCTOBER 17

I will be an ambivert

Which of these two personality types do you think would be the most successful in leadership, sales, and business in general: the extrovert or the introvert. Most would choose the extrovert—that outgoing person who is at ease in social settings, can strike-up a conversation at any moment, and gain their energy from being around people. Indeed, scholars such like Michael Mount of the University of Iowa, as well as several others, found that hiring managers tend to select extroverts for their positions, especially for leadership and sales positions. Certainly one would surmise that an extrovert would make a better sales person. Not true, according to a multi-analysis comprised of thirty-five research projects studying nearly 4,000 sales people, which found no correlation between sales performance and extroversion. Similar findings show that neither do extroverts make better leaders. Extroverts often fail to listen well, can talk over people, or they can appear too pushy or loud.

So are introverts more successful? No. A study by Adam Grant from Wharton's School of Management assessed extroverts and introverts and found that introverts earned average revenue of $120 per hour, whereas the extroverts faired slightly better by making $125 per hour.

Another group, however, earned a significantly higher revenue of $155 per hour, according to Grant's study. This group was called *ambiverts*—a term made-up by social scientists in the 1920s to explain people who are neither extremely introverted nor extroverted. On the scale of one to seven used by Grant to explain extroverts and introverts (with seven being the most extroverted, and one the most introverted), the ambiverts scored between three and five, and were described as being able to assert themselves, like the extroverts, without appearing too pushy. They were also not overly quiet, but maintained an appropriate tone with others.

The conclusion was that successful people should definitely keep themselves more in the middle, between the extremes of introversion and extroversion, and that hiring managers would do best to select candidates who could moderate their style. People generally do not appreciate those who come-off as too overwhelming (like extreme extroverts), or too reserved or quiet (like introverts). The key to success is to find balance.

"Love is essential, gregariousness is optional."
~ Susan Cain, Quiet: The Power of Introverts…

OCTOBER 18

I will use consensus decision-making

Gaining a consensus of agreement may not be the best approach when making a quick decision, but it's a good approach long-term. Group decision-making by its nature allows for a gathering of different ideas that forges an agreed upon decision that is acceptable by all. Thus it tends to lead toward higher levels of success, due to greater buy-in from members. Collective intelligence also tends to come-up with better results. Consensus decision-making forces groups to the highest level of interrelation, which is called collaboration, and leads to better solutions while promoting the growth of teamwork and trust.

Unlike voting, which is a means for choosing one alternative from several, consensus is the process of synthesizing many diverse elements into a cohesive strategy. Leaders who are confident enough to use consensus decision-making are careful not to allow one person's strongly held beliefs to overwhelm the whole group. They ensure that every member's input is valued in determining a solution that represents the best ideas from each person. Consensus does not require that everyone thinks that the decision made is absolutely the best one possible, however it does mean that during the process of arriving at a decision no one felt that his or her position had not received a fair hearing, or that they were not fully understood. The process takes more time, but it also exposes more people to develop their conflict resolution and interpersonal skills, which are two of the most foundational skills required for success.

Productive teams for consensus building should possess common values, good process management skills, and commitment to the common good. Discussion in the group should be initiated by placing a proposal for a solution on the table by the facilitator, allowing for changes. Differences should be clearly stated and acknowledged, and those who disagree should be required to propose their own suggestions and solutions in order to prevent the meeting from turning into a gripe session. Compromise with synergy and synthesis is key to integrating as many contributions as necessary. When consensus is arrived with no new changes requested, the facilitator should ask for any objections, and if none come forth, the decision is confirmed.

"A genuine leader is not a searcher for consensus, but a molder of consensus." ~ Martin Luther King Jr.

OCTOBER 19

I will place the past in the past

Letting go does not mean giving up, it means moving onto the next possibility. Releasing the past runs counter to our nature. Since childhood, we've desired to hold onto the trappings of what is familiar rather than moving onto the next adventure. Even when the past hurts, we feel that letting it go means quitting, and that our inability to right the wrong represents failure. In order to grow, we must come to accept that placing the past in the past means accepting what is done as settled. It means going to the next opportunity or the next relationship. Once the past is rightfully relegated to the present or future, only positive memories remain. After this is accomplished you will find that all of your experiences have finally come together into what should be and what must be. This includes the inevitable trials in life that help to increase our strength and wisdom.

Toward that end, you can look back and appreciate what has passed and ask yourself, "How did I survive all of that?" The human problem is not that we cannot learn new things, but that we must unlearn destructive things. Within the brain only a limited "storage bin" of cells can be used to contain information. We must use them wisely by choosing to resource only the constructive elements of our mind and by letting go of the destructive ones. Too often the false labels that abusers place upon us keep circling in our heads—like when they said, "You are not good enough" or "You are a failure." You need to sort out these false accusations from what people like about you, and what you like about yourself. Remove these past insults and memories from your present and future. Let go of the emotional clutter in your life by forgiving yourself and those who suffer from so much misery that they feel compelled to impose that pain on others.

We cannot change the physical past but we can change it mentally by rewriting the way we perceive the past and how we will deal with it going forward. The life that moves forward has been freed of the past.

"Let your past make you better, not bitter." ~ Author Unknown

"Don't let yesterday use too much of today." ~ Cherokee Proverb

OCTOBER 20

I will only control what is controllable

Far too much time is wasted trying to control what is outside our sphere of control. Don't allow everything you cannot control to have control over you. Countless people have sought after job security, only to be "downsized" by a top-level executive whom they never met and could not influence.

On any given day, we are presented with that which we can control, such as completing a task, and that which we cannot control, such as the economy, world events, or some decision maker with whom we have an unpredictable or nonexistent relationship. Generally other people cannot be controlled. They can only be influenced, since people make their own decisions. Tasks can be controlled only if they are measured against a predetermined objective. Any controllable must be directly related to our ability to achieve mastery over it. For example, the global affects of an economic downturn cannot be controlled, but our ability to manage our finances in order to maximize our financial security can be controlled. The decisions of a supervisor cannot be controlled, but the ability to meet her quantifiable and agreed upon expectations can be controlled.

Unclear expectations lead to uncontrollable situations, just as failing to define expectations in a relationship can lead to disappointment. The key is to build on what you can control and manage what you cannot. We control only that which we can assuredly achieve, which means that the only one you can control is you. Control yourself by controlling your thoughts and your actions, and you will live a satisfied life. *Think* on what is *good* and *do* what is *right*—this is the crux of controlling the controllable, and it must be practiced one intention at a time, because only you can control your thoughts and deeds. We have enormous control over our happiness and our small purposeful changes can have a big impact. It's up to you to make that happen.

"Don't spend your time on things you can't control. Instead spend your time thinking about what you can." ~ Benjamin Selekman, Harvard Business School

OCTOBER 21

I will find a mentor

All of us needed some type of mentoring during our lifetimes—like that knowledgeable and trusted counselor or teacher who volunteered their time to help you be successful. Before the information age dawned upon our modern world, mentors were close work colleagues, friends, or neighbors who naturally assumed a personal interest in your welfare. Today, with technologies bridging communications across the world, you can find your mentor anywhere there is a connection between a proven achiever in your field and you, even if you have to develop that connection from a point of no relationship—and even if you never meet! It's really not that difficult to find a mentor, because people *like* helping other people. Some companies or schools even have formal mentoring programs.

Your first step will be to determine what type of mentor you need. If it's a business/professional mentor, your primary mode of communication may be through email and phone calls. Never select a direct supervisor, and preferably choose someone outside of your division or circle of acquaintances. Establish upfront a convenient schedule or arrange times with your mentor before you begin. Prepare a list of questions or problems for your mentor, and solicit opinions from them, such as what worked and what did not work, paying particular attention to pitfalls they encountered and how they maneuvered around those events.

If you need a mentor in the academic/education field, you will probably need to schedule face-to-face session times with an expert in your subject matter. You can use video conferencing and chat rooms in lieu of personal meetings, but always make sure to address your specific problems/issues in a concise manner out of respect for your mentor's time. Athletic mentors almost always need to meet with you in person in order to conduct coaching sessions.

A mentor is a volunteer advisor, and not someone hired to do your work, so think about some value you can return as well—maybe a ride to the airport or some advice of your own. Once you get to know your mentor, ask her to assess your abilities and to introduce you to new perspectives. Show your appreciation to your mentor so she knows how useful she's been to you—maybe a small gift or a note to say "thank you."

"Mentoring is a brain to pick, an ear to listen,
and a push in the right direction." ~ John Crosby

OCTOBER 22

I will follow my calling

For years, Stacy would drag her slouched body to work, plop into her chair and begin completing her tasks with the enthusiasm of a sloth on sedatives. During a meeting in which her supervisor placed her on a performance improvement plan, Stacy was asked what she truly loved. "Artwork," she replied. "I'm not a painter, but I love artwork." "Then why don't you work in a gallery or something like that?" the supervisor asked. One year later Stacy found herself working in an art gallery in Carmel, California, and each day she arrived to work with a grin and perfect posture.

Three basic characteristics define our calling: passion, talent, and opportunity. Each gives voice to your vocation. Even the word "vocation" is rooted in the Latin word for "voice." Getting specific about what you want to do needs to combine the ideal of doing what you love with an honest assessment of your talents and abilities, followed by a search for jobs you can be passionate about. To help you find your "voice," determine five specific job titles that interest you. Then list other lifestyle factors that are most important to you, such as geography, travel, autonomy, weather, or proximity to family. Next, pick only one job title that best fits *all* of your lifestyle factors and make a deliberate commitment to pursue that position. If entrepreneurism is your goal, choose only one area of interest and invest your energies going down that road.

The key is to not become scattered during your search for the "perfect" calling. There may be no perfect calling. If not, seek a place where you can grow your passion by expanding responsibilities in your current position, or search for opportunities that may lead toward the ideal. Find the way to your passion and you will find your true voice in life.

"At the intersection of stuff you love to do, stuff you're good at, and stuff someone will pay you to do is your dream job." ~ Author Unknown

"Ignore the future, deal with the present. The question, 'What should I be when I grow up?' is wrong. Ask instead, 'What is next today?' We become adults one hour at a time, so what we do today matters." ~ Jessica Hagy

OCTOBER 23

I will get rid of excess baggage

Guilt, grudges, bad habits, worry, and stress can drag people down like heavy weights carried throughout their days. Anything that keeps you from doing your best drags you down. It doesn't take long before that extra weight becomes as normal as excess body fat, causing tiredness and disease. As with any malady, a treatment must be followed in order to keep the unhealthy influence from causing further damage. In the case of excess baggage, it must be dropped, and the sooner the better. The cure just may turn out to be forgiveness.

The Mayo Clinic reported that forgiving someone, even oneself, can lead to greater spiritual and psychological well-being, lower blood pressure, less anxiety, fewer symptoms of depression, and healthier relationships. Psychologists from Harvard, as well as many other notable institutions, say that holding onto the pain of a past event, such as an abuse or an unfair supervisor is best overcome through the practice of acceptance. We cannot change the past and may not be able to control a situation, but we can make a conscious and deliberate decision to relegate negative effects to history by accepting them as simple fact and releasing our resentment. Bad habits often result from anxiety caused by fears that typically begin with an inability to resolve hurt or insecure feelings.

Pledge today to release at least one excess baggage that holds you down. The key is to not delay—do it now. Your security lies in your inherent value, irrespective of anyone or anything. Say something like: "That's just the way it is. I forgive ________, and I'm moving on."

"We must be willing to get rid of the life we've planned, so as to have the life that is waiting for us. The old skin has to be shed before the new one can come." ~ Joseph Campbell

"Sometimes you've got to let everything go – purge yourself. If you are unhappy with anything…whatever is bringing you down, get rid of it. Because you'll find that when you're free, your creativity, your true self comes out." ~ Tina Turner

"Simplicity is making the journey of this life with just baggage enough."
~ Author Unknown

OCTOBER 24

I will grow upon my foundation

Build something upon your foundation that doesn't fit with its design, and your work may crumble. Fail to add to your foundation and you will be left with only a partial structure. Your foundation is comprised of what made you successful—your foundational advantages, your abilities, and what made your business a winner. It's what got you to where you are as a successful human being and as a professional, and as a leader. If we don't expand our foundations by expanding our abilities, if we don't add products, services, or even acquisitions to our business, we can lose ground to our competition and eventually regress. For you to continue succeeding you must grow—but carefully—and only toward something aligned with your foundation.

Don't immediately ask for positions you are not yet qualified to assume, but do build your skills in anticipation of one day applying for those positions. If you're responsible for building a business, make sure that any additions are correctly fitted to the company's foundation. For example, if the foundation of your business is making the best donuts in town, don't go creating a ski shop that's totally unrelated. It would be better to add coffee, or muffins instead—something aligned with your current customer base and similar to your current pricing structure, something that correlates with your brand identity. If your foundational talent is developing people, don't look for positions that will isolate you from others.

The key factor in your decision is the degree of synthesis with your existing talents or your existing business. Focus is often misunderstood in today's world, which prizes diversity. However, there's genuine value and potency in staying with what got you to the dance. Research shows that being perceived as the market leader, or as a leader in your field, dramatically improves your chances of succeeding in related ventures. Conversely, choosing something vastly different from your foundation compromises your chances for continued success. Businesses that stray from their foundation tend to lose customer loyalty, see additional costs due to unshared resources, and are required to invest more in order to compete in a new environment.

"Good order is the foundation of all things." ~ Edmund Burke

OCTOBER 25

I will understand the power of persuasion

Ever heard of a real estate or car salesperson say that someone else is interested in purchasing that house or car you're looking at, and if you don't buy it now you may lose it? How about a politician who frames a debate by explaining his position as "pro-life" or "pro-choice" because the word "pro" is more positive than the word "anti"? Social psychologist and author Robert Cialdini PhD explains in his book *Influence: The Psychology of Persuasion* (HarperBusiness, 2006) that all of us have certain "fixed-action patterns" that trigger automatic responses without us even realizing them. The example of the car sales person is what Cialdini calls the principle of *scarcity*—"buy it now or lose it." One well-understood principle of human behavior states that when we ask someone to do a favor for us, we'll be more successful if we provide a reason, using the word "because." Another example of a fixed-action pattern is that most people associate higher prices with better quality.

Cialdini also mentions the "contrast principle," which is how we compare two things presented one after another. If you are shown an attractive piece of jewelry followed by one that is less attractive than the first, the second will strike you as less attractive than it really is. This explains why many clothing sales persons are instructed to sell their most expensive items first.

Cialdini explains the "reciprocation principle," as when a person feels obligated to repay what another person has provided us, even if we don't want the added bonus. If a salesperson offers you a free refreshment, for example, you may feel more obligated to buy something from that person, whether you want it or not. Another principle is the rule of "commitment and consistency." You sign a petition and now you instinctively feel obligated to be consistent with your original stand, even if you feel less than enthused about it. In other words, the goal is to get it in writing.

Mirroring someone's movement or body language is known as "the chameleon effect" used in persuasion. Also social influence—what's called "herd behavior"—causes us to follow someone we like or someone we see as an authority. When we are unsure of ourselves, we are more likely to accept the actions of others as correct. Also, research tells us that people become fonder of people who eat with them—so take a client out for a meal.

"Who speaks to the instincts speaks to the deepest in mankind, and finds the readiest response." ~ Amos Bronson Alcott

OCTOBER 26

I will surround myself with people who force me to grow

Both the secure and highly successful agree: "surround yourself with people who don't always agree with you, and people who are smarter than you.'" Anything else is a recipe for mediocrity and potential failure. A crisis will be brewing in your organization and before you know it the entire business will be going down the drain, because people were either too afraid or too ignorant to say or do anything about it. Sometimes if you're in a position of authority you have to ask questions, no matter how trivial, in order to draw the information out of people. However, if you surround yourself with the right people they will feel comfortable bringing out the issues you need to know without being asked. Bottom line, the people surrounding you must be competent enough and inclined to share their knowledge and their opinions with you.

Choose for your team and your associates people with great natural ability and a "can-do" attitude. Watch out for that ambitious soul who is self-absorbed and whose only interest is to build his or her résumé at your expense. That person may laud you face-to-face and criticize you behind your back. Introduce your team or friends to your potential new member in order to glean their feedback as to your candidate's attitude as well as his or her aptitude. The more time spent together in advance of bringing him or her onboard the better.

Surround yourself with people whose talents and abilities fill your own talent gaps, and who are not afraid to challenge your decisions based on their knowledge and experience. You don't want anyone who will sabotage your efforts, so finding someone with good teamwork skills, and whose mission is aligned with yours is key. Your success will be dependent on developing your sense of security to the point where you feel comfortable in drawing into your circle of influence those who will bring the talent and audacity to do what's best.

"It's important to surround yourself with people smarter than yourself." ~ Ingersoll-Rand CEO Mike Lamach

OCTOBER 27

I will navigate across boundaries

As reported in the Harvard Business Review, seventy-one-percent of senior executives in major global companies ranked horizontal boundaries as their biggest challenge. According to the authors, what is commonly called "Silo busting" has become most essential for success in today's professional world. Collaboration across organizational boundaries is key, although only seven-percent of the senior executives surveyed considered that they do it effectively. Boundaries exist everywhere in life, and similar statistics apply for people in teams, across different countries, integrated businesses (mergers), and even within different communities.

Navigating across boundaries requires that we venture beyond our own confines and that we adapt to new environments by identifying common connections and mutual interests between different groups. Showing respect for people within the other group is the most foundational principle for navigating across boundaries. The second is a willingness to compromise and cooperate with each other. To do so, you need to discontinue your bias and expectations, place your agenda aside, and just listen to the other group members. Sharing is the key success factor in getting started, so you need to maintain an open mind while learning from others, valuing others' opinions and ideas. Poor communication will undermine an organization's ability to traverse across boundaries, so an open, honest, and consistent dialog between members must happen. Success requires that each person commit to owning the communication process. Moving forward together means progress; jockeying for position means regression—there's no standing still.

Disney-Pixar represents a good example of a merger where the two groups navigated through their own operating channels to emerge as a collaboration made in animated heaven. Conversely, the merger of Daimler/Chrysler ($37B) failed because of a corporate culture clash— many thought the high-end Daimler group swaggered in and attempted to tell the Chrysler group what to do. Had the two groups humbly asked more questions of each other in trying to balance the parts in relationship to the whole, they may have succeeded. Instead, they lost the main idea and could not focus on the big picture. Failure to navigate across boundaries cost them everything.

"As always in a musical collaboration: One has to like each other. As simple as that." ~ Klaus Schulze

OCTOBER 28

I will be an autodidact

Ernest Hemingway, actor Russell Crowe, Thomas Edison, Abraham Lincoln, and architect Frank Lloyd Wright were all autodidacts—self-taught persons who learned their genius on their own. They were ahead of their time. In this era the world of knowledge is turning over more or less completely every two to three years. The reason why you're doing something now may no longer exist. That's why you must be an autodidact in order to succeed.

Self-directed learners will be the most successful persons in the 21st century and beyond. Lifelong learning is now recognized by educators and employers as one of the most important competencies that people must possess. Self-taught individuals require less dependence on traditional educational venues, such as passive education activities, and greater participation in self-assessment, others' assessments, and the consistent acquisition of new skills and knowledge.

Traditional learning institutions establish goals through a teacher or school. Lifelong learning requires that the learner establish learning goals in relationship to life goals. Ongoing evaluation of learning in life is directed toward achieving these life goals.

In an article published in *Perspectives on Psychological Science: a Journal of the Association for Psychological Science*, researchers Todd Gureckis and Douglas Markant discovered that self-directed learning exposes people to information they wouldn't normally learn through traditional means. Hence, autodidacts tend to assimilate information better than conventional students.

An autodidact doesn't wait for someone to say, "you must learn this." Begin by establishing one to two learning tasks you want to complete for the day. Focus on one topic at a time. Filter out useless information by using the best resources aligned to your goal. Use what behavioral therapists call "loss aversion"—a consequence for failing—to keep you on goal. Surround yourself with similarly driven people. Make learning a lifestyle consistent with your life goals.

"Learning is not the product of teaching.
Learning is the product of the activity of learners." ~ John Holt

"You are only going to be as good as the people you surround yourself with, so be brave enough to let go of those who keep weighing you down." ~ www.livelifehappy.com

OCTOBER 29

I will read peoples' minds

No, you don't have to be a psychic to determine what's on peoples' minds. You just need to use some techniques and be observant in order to determine what someone is thinking. Once you do, you will be in a strong position to openly discuss things with that someone—and you might surprise a few people.

The first step is to profile the other person by studying their dress, body language, and how they respond to you. Your observations will help to construct a set of assumptions with which you can start projecting specifics about characteristics and background. Next you'll want to investigate some general insights about that person. If you ask questions positioned as statements, the other person will reveal things about themselves. If, for example, you notice his eyes begin drifting off, and he keeps checking his phone or watch, you could say, "you've got a lot on your mind, don't you?" Even if he says "no," you're still on the path to revealing what's on his mind, because the statement was simply a question. Most often, he will begin sharing more information about himself from these statement-questions.

So called "mind readers" use this same technique to entertain their audiences. They begin with asking a general question, like "someone here is going through a problem at work," and once someone raises their hand the "mind reader" already has a read on that person. General statements such as "you are facing a major decision" will generally elicit an affirmative, which establishes the initial credibility to uncover more information.

Since discovering a cluster of cells in the brain called "mirror neurons" that mirror or reflect another person's emotions, actions, and perceptions, scientists have actually proven that humans are natural mind readers. Considered to be the mirrors of the soul, eyes can help gauge the mind's thoughts. Enlarged pupils mean someone is interested or excited. So by mentioning something and observing the pupils, you can assess whether they are upset. Observing body language, facial expressions, and voice tones also give clues to people's state of mind. You just need to remain alert in order to pick up on these signals, and ask questions to confirm their truth.

"All things are ready, if our minds be so." ~ William Shakespeare, Henry V

OCTOBER 30

I will practice the seven C's of communication

So you want to be an effective communicator? Then follow the seven Cs when speaking or writing: 1) completeness, 2) correctness, 3) conciseness, 4) courtesy, 5) clarity, 6) consideration, and 7) concreteness. By using these Cs, you will communicate most effectively.

Completeness means providing the "what, where, who, how, and when" of what you express, including answering any questions that might arise from your message.

Correctness includes using the right form of expression, such as professional language in the workplace, as well as using the appropriate mode of communication (punctuation, visual aids, format).

Communicating *Concisely* ensures that your message is clearly understood by avoiding wordy expressions, staying on point, and not repeating yourself.

Courtesy respects the feelings, expectations, and customs of the audience, while also expressing appreciation. Instead of a store manager abruptly telling a customer that the "store is closed," she could say, "Thank you for shopping with us. I'm sorry to say that we are closing now, but we'll be open tomorrow." Maintaining

Clarity emphasizes the specific topic or goal, rather than saying too much at one time. Check your communication to see if you are using any unnecessary sentences or (filler) words such as "for instance," "sort of," and "basically." Showing

Consideration for the person reading or listening implies a level of understanding or empathy for them by displacing a "me-attitude" with a "we-attitude." Remaining sensitive to the audience's background, expectations, and views is key in order to avoid offending them.

Being *Concrete* means giving your audience a solid picture of what you are communicating by providing an appropriate level of detail with pinpoint focus. A bad example of using concreteness would be saying, "I am going to make you effective today." There's no imagery or detail in this sentence. A good example might be: "How much time do you spend duplicating your efforts? Today we're going to change that! By doing the job right the first time, you'll save time and enjoy your work much more." Note how the passion and details work.

"Genius is the ability to put into effect what is on your mind." ~ F. Scott Fitzgerald

OCTOBER 31

I will use an eternal focus

For years, Harvard instructor, practicing surgeon, and Duke University-trained neurologist Dr. Eben Alexander had dismissed near-death revelations of heaven and God as mere reactions of the brain's hard-wiring. Then in 2008 he contracted bacterial meningitis, a deadly infection that shut down his neocortex (the part of the brain that "makes us human") and sent him into a deep coma. He described his personal near-death-experience (NDE) as being ushered into a place both "pitch black" and "brimming with light" coming from an "orb" that interprets for an all-loving God. His best-selling book, *Proof of Heaven: A Neurosurgeon's Journey into the Afterlife* (Simon & Schuster, 2012), Alexander recounts those experiences. He wrote it knowing his story might jeopardize his professional reputation, particularly among skeptics like his former self. Dr. Alexander says that science cannot explain his experience, since he says his brain "wasn't working at all." "Our spirit is not dependent on the brain or body," he says. "It is eternal, and no one has one sentence worth of hard evidence that it isn't."

Whether you believe Dr. Alexander's NDE as real or not, the fact is our bodies are only temporary and very brief in the scope of all time. So from an everlasting perspective, are we made for eternity? If "yes," why do we almost never use our eternal focus? If we did, we would more easily dismiss the relatively miniscule hardships we face as fleeting moments. We would be asking ourselves questions like, "What do I really need while I am here to serve my purpose and prepare me for the next life?" We wouldn't just wait for some traumatic experience such as lying in a hospital bed with IV tubes hanging out of our body to think about what's next. We might better examine where our focus lies relative to our loved ones, time, money, our heart, or recreation to judge whether we are living for temporal satisfaction or improving our vision for a life beyond this one.

Living for eternity invites a whole new paradigm for how we live our lives in this world. You don't need to be religious to start thinking from an eternal focus. You just need to start preparing for the possibility that this life may not be all there is to your existence. Ask: Why am I here and where am I going—forever?

"All that is not eternal is eternally out of date." ~ *C.S. Lewis*

NOVEMBER

IT ALL COMES BACK TO YOU

NOVEMBER 1

I will practice the Law of Reciprocity

Are you making the Law of Reciprocity work for you? This law doesn't mean giving something of value for something received, or a tit-for-tat. In many ways it's related to the golden rule, "Do unto others as you want them to do unto you." But it goes even further. The Law of Reciprocity means helping others succeed, without any expectation of something in return. Paradoxically, this behavior results in greater returns than if we had asked for a reciprocated favor. Helping others deposits social capital into an expansive bank of people who may help you in the future, such that some person other than the one you directly helped may one day reciprocate your good deeds.

David Elliott works on behalf of an organization called *Halftime*, which helps professionals in the "second half" of their lives to get plugged into various philanthropic endeavors. He routinely meets with both acquaintances and strangers introduced to him through various network circles, and presents them with different opportunities to help them succeed in their "second halves." In the process, he also offers assistance to those struggling through mid-life crises and the like. Invariably, someone within David's extended network will reach out to him with opportunities that may be of interest to his organization or to him personally. David acts as the hub of the network and its central beneficiary as well, through the sheer satisfaction of helping others.

In his bestseller *The Tipping Point: How Little Things Can Make a Big Difference* (Back Bay Books, 2002), Malcolm Gladwell mentions a time-honored 1974 study called "Getting a Job," which interviews hundreds of professional and technical workers about their employment history. He discovered that fifty-six-percent found their job through a personal connection. It wasn't necessarily through their friends, but they were finding employment through acquaintances or friends-of-friends who had heard something positive about them.

The more social capital you invest in your network through helping others, the greater your return will be through the growth in your favorability reputation. The adage that "what goes around comes around" operates within your direct and indirect networks. In this living universe of exchanges, very few good works go unnoticed.

"Our attitude toward life determines life's attitude toward us." ~ John M. Mitchell

NOVEMBER 2

I will understand basic economics

Economics is basically the study of human behavior in the attempt to satisfy needs and wants. The foundation of economics is *scarcity*, as explained with the graph of Supply vs. Demand—the more demand there is for a product, the fewer the supplies of it, which elevates the price of the product. Economic decisions are based on the allocation of resources (for individuals time, money, or skill; for a country natural resources, labor force, and technology). The quantity (or supply) of a product produced is dependent on what people are willing to pay. If they are willing to pay more, the incentive to elevate supply increases. Demand is determined by price, such that the higher the price, the lower the quantity demanded, and the lower the price, the higher the quantity demanded.

The classic model says that as the price for a product rises, demand for that product will fall. However, if the manufacturer lowers the price of a product too much, demand will increase beyond what is available, resulting in a shortage. The desired state would be to establish a price point where the quantity supplied is in balance with the quantity demanded, which is called *equilibrium* (the quantity demanded equals the quantity supplied).

The two types of economics are *microeconomics* (the study of decisions by individuals and businesses in specific markets), which is determined by the above principles of supply, demand and price; and, *macroeconomics* (the study of the overall functioning of an economy such as economic growth, unemployment, recession, and inflation), which focuses on the national economy and the impact of interest rates, government deficits, etc. The size of the economy is determined by its Gross Domestic Product (GDP), which is the value of all the goods and services produced within our nation's borders in one year. The Federal Reserve controls the U.S. money supply and is the central banking system for the U.S. It replaces old currency with new currency and guarantees bank deposits. The Fed also affects the economy by moving interest rates, as well as selling and buying government securities. The Dow Jones Industrial Average is based upon the stock prices of thirty large blue chip U.S. corporations, and is used as a key economic indicator.

"In economics it is a far, far wiser thing to be right than to be consistent."
~ John Galbraith

NOVEMBER 3

I will value humanity

What do customers use to make their buying decisions? Two-thirds do not buy primarily based upon price. They buy on convenience, service, and word-of-mouth, according to TARP Worldwide Research. A study released by J.D. Powers shows that organizations that improve customer service increase shareholder value by fifty-two-percent. Customer experience no longer represents just a factor in determining operations; it has become a strategic driver for any business wishing to succeed. But it's not just treating the customer as king that drives success. It's a pervasive valuing of humans in general that causes the most sustainable levels of success.

Thriving businesses are built on treating both their internal and external customers *humanely*, according to Dr. Leonard Berry, author of *Discovering the Soul of Service: The Nine Drivers of Sustainable Business Success* (Free Press, 1999). Berry discusses fourteen outstanding companies from diverse industries that had a time-tested average age of thirty-one years of work, ranging from 120 employees to over 35,000. Trust-based relationships, value-driven leadership, and generosity were three of the nine drivers distinguished as being essential when establishing a humane organization. These values serve as the hallmark for all of the companies studied. What's also interesting is that only three of the fourteen companies had more than two CEOs in their history, thus allowing the leaders to develop the trust and principles of integrity and genuineness required to sustain success.

Restaurateur Drew Nieporent has been very successful in an industry where even the best leaders can fail. His restaurants span the world, having won every major restaurant award. He believes that building a values-based business is key to building an enduring business. "Restaurants are like children," he said. "They need your attention when they're young. You give them values and principles and hope they grow up strong." Successful CEO Mark Lortz started the company Therasense in the highly competitive diagnostic industry. Their success attracted the attention of healthcare giant Abbott Laboratories, which now owns the technology. He said, "You do something because it's the right thing to do, not just because you are making money from it." As these leaders prove, valuing humanity brings value to your business.

"A people that values its privileges above its principles soon loses both." ~ Dwight D. Eisenhower

NOVEMBER 4

I will build people's faith through story

If you really want someone to believe you, dispense with many of the facts and figures, and tell them a story—it's the key to building faith. Without a heart-grabbing story, what we offer can fall on deaf ears, according to authors Peter Guber, *Tell to Win: Connect, Persuade, and Triumph with the Hidden Power of Story* (Crown Business, 2011), and Annette Simmons, *The Story Factor: Secrets Of Influence From The Art Of Storytelling* (Basic Books, 2000), whose persuasive books preach the power of the story in business and life.

CEOs who just data dump through PowerPoint slides and spreadsheets can easily lose their audience. People in general are moved by emotion and develop faith in those who can inspire them. Several psychological studies have shown how our attitudes, hopes, yearnings, and values are strongly formed through story. Psychologists Melanie Green and Tim Brock explain that telling stories "radically alters the way information is processed." The more absorbed in a story someone becomes, the more that story changes them and their perceptions.

Perhaps the most convincing person in history, Jesus, used parables (stories) to drive home his points, and thousands of years later, most remember his stories as well or better than his words as the key drivers of their faith. Highly absorbed listeners of stories tend to believe them as truth, even if the storyteller is telling them something made-up. People who hear cold, hard facts tend to be more skeptical and want additional proof. When we hear a story it drops our mental guard. Master storytellers lull us into a rush of emotion in order to depress rational considerations, lose us in the imagination, and bring us to a surrendered belief in their truth.

This is the gospel of business today—to build a people's faith in what we offer through masterful storytelling. "Values are meaningless without stories to bring them to life and engage us on a personal level," says Annette Simmons, president of Group Process Consulting and a master storyteller. Fiction author Susanne Lakin (*Someone to Blame,* Zondervan, 2010) likens her work to telling people about her faith in a loving and forgiving God without being preachy. Many of her characters are based on real people whose storied lives tell more than mere strung out sentences could explain. Stories evoke emotions. You root for the protagonist and living within the story is the author herself—a messenger of love and forgiveness. We are far more likely to believe in a messenger who has captured our hearts through story.

"If history were taught in the form of stories, it would never be forgotten." ~ Rudyard Kipling

NOVEMBER 5

I will stick to my principles

Rory closed the door to seal off the last opening to the outside world, or rather the workplace outside his office. Now the four walls around him sounded silent, with only the faint hum of his desktop. He drilled into the photo of his wife and two giggly children, positioned perfectly on his desk so that he could see them from every angle—vestiges of the vibrant life that existed beyond his scant confines. In five minutes and twenty—make that eighteen—seconds, he would meet with his boss to explain why he had defied company policy by holding a Bible study on company property. It was not the first such meeting. He'd already met with Human Resources, and faced a series of meetings to determine how culpable he was in the matter. *It was just a stupid little Bible study*, he thought. *Why the big fuss*? Yeah, he'd arranged it. Talked to a few co-workers asking them if they'd like to participate. But it wasn't proselytizing, like they claimed. Not in a gazillion years would he have imagined losing his job over such an inane thing. Heck, he wasn't even the proselytizing type. Each person was entitled to their own faith was his belief. But that didn't matter now.

He walked into his boss's office. "Hello, Rory," she said, with the tone of an executioner. "I think you know why we're meeting. You defied company policy, and because of your actions, you severely offended an employee on campus." *Offended my foot*, he thought, *the person even said he might like to attend. Called himself a Christian, for goodness sake.* That same humming noise that reverberated from each work desk now sounded like the dirge of a funeral bell tolling. *Just get it over with*, his shaking knees spoke. He'd been a model employee up until now. Good reviews, liked by his coworkers. Just because *someone else* suggested he lead-up a luncheon Bible study with no knowledge of how it violated company policy—this was fair? This was justice?

"All I want now is an apology that what you did was wrong," his boss said as she drew in a deep breath. But he wasn't wrong. He'd done nothing intentionally wrong. "I can't do that Sarah," he answered. "If I admitted wrongdoing, I believe that would justify an unfair practice. I'll take the punishment," Rory sighed. So that was it. He'd taken a stand. His wife and kids would be proud.

"While values drive behaviors, principles govern consequences." ~ Stephen Covey

NOVEMBER 6

I will not be a workaholic

Hard work is an important ingredient of success, but when someone values work over everything else, even when it negatively affects health and family, they've crossed over the line to workaholism. If you've gone well beyond what's necessary and have no other interests or activities, you may be the victim of a negative addiction. In Japan, workaholism is called "karoshi"—death by overwork—and it's estimated to cause 1,000 deaths per year. Workaholics have experienced a condition known as "leisure illness," when workers actually get physically sick on vacations and weekends as they stop working and make a futile effort to relax.

With massive layoffs in the United States, the remaining employees are often forced to assume more responsibilities to cover for those laid-off. The number of hours people work is increasing, as verified by the U.S. Census and CPS data, which shows that workers averaging more than forty-eight hours per week is higher today than it was twenty-five years ago. Surveys now reveal that the average workweek is nearing fifty-six hours.

"The way we're working isn't working," says Tony Schwartz, founder and CEO of *The Energy Project*, who uses studies and statistics that show long days are not productive days. One case study Schwartz cites is about young accountants expected to work fourteen-hour days during tax time. He taught these accountants to be more efficient by reducing distractions and focusing on tasks without interruption. They reduced their work time and actually got more done.

Workaholics actually tend to be less effective than other workers because they have trouble entrusting their co-workers, which makes them poor team players. Or they become disorganized compared to others because they take on too much work. If you're a workaholic (not just a hard worker), try resetting your expectations of what you can do in a day. Pace yourself with the appropriate mix of "normal times," rest, and those occasional times when you need to really push to get something done. Gradually cut down the numbers of hours you work each week. Prioritize your time for recreation, sharing at least one activity with family and friends. Exercise each day, even if it's only stretching. Delegate or share work. Refuse to feel guilty when you're not working. Enjoy the increased productivity.

"It's all about quality of life and finding a happy balance between work, family and friends." ~ Phillip Green

NOVEMBER 7

I will plan a great dinner out

Meals with important clients, business associates, or even that special person in your life can make a lasting impression, so make sure you leave a positive one. The first rule is to select a restaurant you know. Risking a new restaurant without any knowledge of the menu or quality of food could prove embarrassing. If you're meeting people at the restaurant, make sure the location is easy to get to. Picking a high-priced restaurant may seem like an impressive choice, however the price of the meal says something about the price you are charging your customer, so it's best to select a midrange-priced restaurant. Ask your guest(s) if they prefer any types of foods, and if you're not sure, choose a restaurant with several food style choices. If possible, review the menu online in advance of your dinner to plan your choices in advance – especially the wine selection. Unless you are traveling with your guest(s), get to the restaurant about fifteen minutes early in order to prepare for the meal.

At business dinners, wines usually accompany the meal, and can be the trickiest part of the dinner. Chat with the sommelier without the pressure of your guests watching so you can discuss price options; this way when you order at the table you can zero in on the best choice. Feel free to enlist wines from beyond California and Europe—safe bets are a red malbec from Argentina, a sauvignon blanc from New Zealand, or a Kingston Tobiano Pinot Noir from Chile. Try to select a unique wine with the sommelier because an unfamiliar wine is more likely to impress your associates. Ordering a lighter white, like a pinot grigio or sauvignon blanc for the table as an aperitif can set a welcoming tone. After preselecting your wine choices, you may ask your guests if they prefer red or white, then select from the sommelier's or manager's recommendations. If you didn't preselect, it's fine to pick one or two brand name wines (note: California cabs and chardonnays are safer choices than more arcane European options).

Prearrange payment with your server. When dining, allow your guest(s) to order first, and then select a meal closest to the price of their dish so that they will not feel embarrassed ordering the salad while you ordered the filet mignon, or vice versa. Then enjoy! You're going to have a great dinner out.

"Get to know the chef and you will start to enjoy dining out even more." ~ John Walters

NOVEMBER 8

I will figure out what I don't want

Almost as important as figuring out your life's mission is to identify obstacles—those things likely to prevent you from fulfilling your mission. In other words, figure out what it is that sucks the life out of you, what would you like to change, what habits and attitudes are not aligned with your life's mission, and what activities are not in agreement with your goals and objectives. *Anything* that doesn't fit with your mission and purpose in life is probably keeping you from living a fulfilling life. Make a list of these unwanted things and really think through the cost of keeping them.

Next to these things, list out those things that are aligned with your mission. Keep this list in a place where you can view it frequently in order to maintain your focus on the goals you've established. Start getting rid of the things you do not want, and maintain or start obtaining the things you do want. This simple process will cause you to advance your mission so quickly that you may be wowed at the progress you've made.

Perhaps the hardest part in this process is getting rid of damaging relationships, like people who forecast doom and gloom based strictly on their own experiences, or self-centered persons who consider the world to rotate on their own axis. Needy people almost always fail to see the needs of others. You don't need these people, nor those on the other end of the spectrum who easily heap unconditional praises on you—while failing to tell you what or how you could be doing things better. We all need honest and helpful friends who do not gossip. Gossipers may tell you the inside scoop about others, but they're also telling others the inside scoop about you. We also don't need backstabbers whose only protected back is their own, or naysayers who always seem to come-up with a reason why your ideas won't work, even when others affirm them. Conversely, your "want list" of relationships should include people with meaningful goals, a positive mission in life, and a foundation of integrity.

Surround yourself with the resources and influences that will get you to closer to your mission, and get rid of the stuff, the relationships, and the activities that are holding you back. It will be hard to give-up some of these things, but the benefits will far outweigh the pain in doing so.

"You want a good life, get rid of bad people…
It's amazing how quickly it changes." ~ Marlon Wayans

NOVEMBER 9

I will just do it

Why do you suppose the famous "Just Do It" Nike tagline resonated with more people than perhaps ninety-nine-percent of all taglines? Perhaps because there is such a widely understood gap between what people know to do, and their actually, actively doing it. It's also why companies who pour thousands into training their people all too often discover that these people fail to practice what they've been taught.

One of the best organizations for inculcating training into their members with over ninety-five-percent compliance in applying their new skills is the U.S. military. The military uses simulations and live ammunition exercises to prepare soldiers for combat. Surgical residents, airline pilots, and professional athletes follow the same strategy. They use mental skills, like maintaining a high level of self-motivation, setting high-realistic goals, using positive self-talk, using positive mental imagery, managing emotions, and maintaining concentration, which are applied through training by first assessing their proficiencies in these areas, then teaching the skills that need improvement, and finally reassessing the person's proficiency in each of the skills in order to evaluate progress.

Those who *Just Do It* are effectively trained through experiential training: *See One, Do One, Teach One*. The final steps of performing the skills and being able to teach them proves that knowledge has been acquired and transferred. In *The Knowing-Doing Gap: How Smart Companies Turn Knowledge into Action* (Harvard Business School Press, 2000), authors Jeffrey Pfeffer and Robert I. Sutton remind us that knowing is not the problem, as evidenced by $60 billion in corporate training each year. They say, "There are fewer and smaller differences in *what firms know* than in their *ability to act* on that knowledge." Leading the list of reasons this is not happening, the authors say, is pointless communication. Just talking about innovative strategy and improvements or holding mission-statement retreats resembles action in effort alone. The authors suggest that the "Knowing-Doing Gap" originates from fear. Creating a culture that encourages action—even when it fails—helps to drive out that fear. Surgeons have done this through openly sharing mistakes with their colleagues. Businesses should follow this example, by sharing their failures and learning, and rewarding second tries. Just do it.

"The difference between who you are and who you want to be is what you do."
~ Bill Phillips, fitness and transformation leader

NOVEMBER 10

I will help others become more of what they already are

In the rule-changing book, *First, Break All the Rules: What the World's Greatest Managers Do Differently* (Simon & Schuster, 1999), former Gallup Inc. employees Marcus Buckingham and Curt Coffman published the results of a vast survey, using data collected over twenty-five years, to reveal what good management looks like. They asked the question: "Do managers matter?" The Gallup results proved managers have a huge impact on the success of an organization. According to survey results, great managers delivered larger sales, better profitability, and lower turnover than poor managers. With over one million workplace interviews, Gallup was able to determine what qualities constitute a good manager. Consistently, the researchers heard the same message: "(Great managers) help each person become *more and more* of who he (or she) already is."

The 80,000 highly rated managers interviewed identified that the success of their employees resulted through a focus on their natural strengths as opposed to correcting their weaknesses. This research represented a dramatic shift from the conventional wisdom of making an employee fit into a position to one of discovering the *right position for the employee*—the key being to hire the right talent for the job, instead of trying to reform the new hire's talents. As an example, the authors studied the seven men chosen to champion NASA's unsuccessful Mercury space program. All the candidates chosen possessed the necessary experience as military test pilots. However, despite two years of uniform training, each astronaut performed differently. In the new environment, some performed flawlessly, while others committed mission critical errors because the hiring directors didn't factor in the individual talents of each astronaut. For example, during liftoff one astronaut's pulse reached 150, whereas Neil Armstrong's pulse never exceeded eighty—which indicated how each astronaut's natural abilities would adjust to the mission.

Subsequent to the book's impact, hiring managers began using behavior-based questions during interviews such as, "Explain to me an experience where you...?" These types of questions helped distinguish the ready responses that could identify a consistent application of a desired talent. Uncovering what the candidate experienced as "satisfying" helped determine where he or she would feel most secure. Those who enjoyed resolving problems specific to the job faired best, such as police officers who relished fighting injustice and thrived during tense conflict. Helping others become more of who they already are satisfies your life purpose as well.

"He has a right to criticize, who has a heart to help." ~ Abraham Lincoln

NOVEMBER 11

I will practice ergonomics

Most on-the-job injuries result from repetitive movements, poor posture, heavy lifting, bending over, and falling. Sitting in the same position for a long time and making repetitive movements can strain your muscles, nerves, joints, and spine, which can lead to tendinopathy and bursitis, and over time they can cause long-term health problems. Workplace ergonomics can help you be more comfortable at work and can lower stress and injury.

General ergonomic strategies begin with getting up and walking around every twenty to forty minutes, and taking frequent one to two minute short breaks that aren't breaks from work, rather they are breaks from using frequently strained muscles and joints, such as routinely resting and stretching your fingers when typing. Keep your feet flat on the floor and position your computer monitor so that your eyes are level with the top of the screen. The center should be fifteen degrees below your line of sight and approximately an arm's length from your body. Try to place your work in front of you and sit tall while you work. Change your position often. When typing, your wrists should be in a straight, neutral position in line with your forearms (not bent upward). The telephone should be able to be used with your head upright and your shoulders relaxed. You should have a chair with lumbar support. If that's not possible, try using a small pillow to relieve pressure on your lower back. Instead of twisting to face your work, turn with your entire body.

Alan Hedge, PhD, professor of ergonomics at Cornell University, recommends finding a chair that swivels and rolls and advises using the one-inch seat rule: when sitting back, there should be at least a one-inch gap between the edge of the seat and the backs of your knees, and the seat of your chair should be at least one-inch wider than your hips and thighs. The back of your chair should be wide enough for your back, but not so wide that it restricts your arm movements. Hedge also suggests chairs with headrests for those who need to reduce neck and shoulder strain. If your job must be performed standing, you should be provided with a chair or stool so you can sit down at frequent intervals. You should also give your eyes a break by looking away from the computer monitor and regularly focusing on an object in the distance. Avoid the "inverted v-curve" (ninety degrees) when bending, because it creates greater strain on your back. Excessive force on your joints can create potential for fatigue and injury.

"Prepare and prevent, don't repair and repent." ~ Author Unknown

NOVEMBER 12

I will cover all the bases

Managing all your key influencers and decision makers is key to the success of any project or sale. Key influencers are those who impact your ability to achieve your goals and objectives without necessarily having the position authority to make final decisions. Decision makers are in a position of power to make those decisions. Both influencers and decision makers are the key stakeholders in your success. Fail to engage and gain support from any one of these stakeholders and your efforts could fail as well. Keeping track of who they are and the status of their position is vitally important. The final stage of your success is to convince these stakeholders of your goals in order to gain their support for them.

Maintain a spreadsheet or file worksheet with the following column headlines in order to track progress: 1) Project/Account Name; 2) Stakeholder Name & Position (I = Influencer or D = Decision Maker); 3) Degree of Influence (H = High, M = Medium, L = Low); 4) Current Status (C = Champion/Supporter, N = Neutral, S = Skeptic); 5) Key Interests & Needs; 6) Actions (for you to take in order to move them to a strong supporter status). List your stakeholders in order of importance in achieving your goals. Make sure that all of your decision makers are prioritized first, and that your communication with them meets with their expectations (in terms of frequency and form of communication) as well as your needs.

Under "Key Interests & Needs," list what benefits the stakeholder wants in order to support your project or sale. Under the "Actions" column, note what you need to do to move the stakeholder to a "Champion" status—someone who will enthusiastically support your project or offering; for a "Skeptic," note what actions will be necessary to at least neutralize their resistance. Include measureable actions with dates for completion. When potential challenges arise, check-in with the expectations of your stakeholders as far in advance as possible of a problem's manifestation in order to protect your status with them.

By keeping track of your key influencers and decision makers and the actions you must take, you can more easily plan your strategy and prioritize your actions. And by covering all the bases you will avoid surprises and boost support.

"Thoroughness characterizes all successful men. Genius is the art of taking infinite pains…" ~ Elbert Hubbard

NOVEMBER 13

I will succeed through my mid-life challenge

It may happen when you're thirty or when you're sixty, but eventually you will probably start thinking that something's missing in your career and life. Often, that period of life seems to trigger all kinds of things—like empty nest syndrome, menopause, affairs, sudden buys of sports convertibles—to name only a few. Here's the dichotomy: we are living longer and yet, according to surveys, we are experiencing our midlife crises at younger and younger ages. Your personal success in getting through this period requires a little soul searching and a little crisis management—a few don'ts and dos.

Don't worry excessively about work—the proverbial grass is always greener on the other side, and what may seem a better job somewhere else may simply be wishful thinking or a rose-colored perspective. Don't abandon your partner—he or she may not look as appealing as they did in youth, but you're not fresh from the factory either. Check your imagination. Those young people probably aren't adoring your body or face anymore—you broke up with that sweetheart you never hooked-up with for a reason. So keep your partner and seek some marital counseling if necessary. Don't buy expensive midlife toys in order to fulfill youthful fantasies. Those people staring at old dudes on racing bikes aren't really admiring them.

Do be thankful for what you have. Count your blessings. If you've genuinely lost enthusiasm for your work take some time to align your interests with your abilities, and make a long-term plan to guide you toward a more fulfilling vocational life. You can't depend on your current workplace to provide nourishment for your soul (that's not its business), so spend more time with friends to discuss your ideas, and how you can reenergize yourself, and then take personal responsibility for making some life changes.

Determine what's most important to you and develop a work pathway, starting with short-term objectives and leading to long-term goals to get there. Dr. Colette Cozean, inventor of the arthroscope and successful CEO many times over, did this when she started a missions group that travels to Africa twice a year to aid the poor. She now mentors other CEOs and brings leaders together to engage them in philanthropic endeavors. She turned her midlife from crisis to purpose, as can you.

"Midlife crisis…that moment when you realize your children and your clothes are the same age." ~ Author Unknown

NOVEMBER 14

I will do fun team-building exercises

Want to have some fun and make your team or circle of friends more cohesive at the same time? Then try these team-building exercises—they really work!

The **"Bonding Belt"**: the goal is to get from point A to point B as a team while "stuck" together (with film, rope or tape), as quickly as possible. To begin, give the team members five minutes to discuss their strategies. At the end of this time they should be banded and ready to go. Make sure the start and finish lines are clearly labeled. Then let your teams go, and keep track of their end times. Once they finish, allow the teams time to re-strategize their next attempt in order to beat their previous score. This exercise forces teams to strategize effectively by forcing them to consider different alternatives.

Here's another game: **"Back-to-Back Drawing"**: divide the group into pairs, and have each pair sit on the floor back to back. Give one person in each pair a drawing of a shape, and give the other person a pencil and pad of paper. Ask the people holding the drawing to give verbal instructions to their partners about how to draw the shape—without telling the partners what the shape is. After they've finished, ask each pair to compare their original shape with the actual drawing, and ask them to consider how well they communicated with each other in sending and receiving communications. This exercises challenges the teams to think of how they can communicate more effectively.

Here's the final game: **"Personal Best"**: Ask the participants to think back over their careers and choose a moment when everything great about themselves came out best and they were performing at their personal best. Maybe it was a completing an important project; maybe it was a day when they did something special for a person in need. Perhaps it was when they mentored someone who became successful. Tell them in advance that you want them to share that experience with the group and give them ten minutes to prepare specific details. Let each participant share, and allow for comments, laughter, and just good conversation—about forty minutes to an hour. Debrief the exercise and ask for common themes then ask: "How can you create a workplace in which these themes occur more often?" Yes, even work can be fun when done by a cohesive team.

"The ratio of 'we's to 'I's' is the best indicator of the development of a team."
~ Lewis B. Ergen

NOVEMBER 15

I will strive for the group's performance

Together we rise, divided we fall. Isn't that the way it seems to go? How do we know when we've "arrived?" Perhaps we can agree that the ultimate goal is performance. When all the rowers in a boat are in sync, maximum potential is achieved. But no team begins that way. New teams go through stages of developing, just like any new relationships. They are the same five stages: Forming, Norming, Storming, and Performing. Bruce Tuckman, who demonstrated that all these phases are necessary and inevitable in order for teams to grow, to resolve problems, to discover solutions, and to deliver results, first proposed these stages in 1965. About ten years later, Tuckman added a fifth stage to the model: Adjourning.

In the Forming stage individual behavior is driven by a yearning to be accepted by the other group members. The "Forming" stage provides comfort to the members, however the avoidance of conflict and a fear of upsetting each other gets in the way of achieving results. In the "Norming" stage, group members begin to establish goals and expectations. During the process, conflicts typically arise—which brings us to the "Storming" stage. This is when members generally air their dissatisfaction and begin to work through conflicts that erupt through challenging member roles within the group.

When conflict resolution skills are effectively practiced within the group, and a coalescing of differing opinions develops from a shared desire for the team's success, the "Performing" stage results, and this is what ultimately defines a well functioning team. This stage is characterized by a condition of interdependence and adaptability forged by mutual trust in each other. Roles may change during the "Performing" stage, however the group's cohesiveness, loyalty, and morale all remain high.

The last stage, "Adjourning" (or what some call the "Mourning" stage), occurs as team members place closure on projects and tasks, and prepare for a new group experience. This is really the end of the group, and is a time for reflection as to what worked well and what could have been improved. Tuckman's model has become a standard explanation for group development and team dynamics, and helps teams keep tabs on their progress. How is your group doing?

"Teams share the burden and divide the grief." ~ Doug Smith

NOVEMBER 16

I will believe in the Cassandra Truth

You try your hardest to tell someone that the company is headed in the wrong direction and that your solution will save the day, or that your friend's newest relationship will only end-up hurting him or her, or that an associate's demise is coming if he or she keeps treating people like they're stepping stones on the way to a loftier position. Sadly, these people look at you like you are loony and send you away. What's a lone messenger of truth to do? That's the dilemma of someone who practices the *Cassandra Truth*, based on a mythical Greek prophetess whom Apollo placed a curse upon, ensuring that nobody would believe her warnings. In other words, the Cassandra Truth represents *a truth that ought to be believed but isn't.*

Perhaps you've been guilty of not believing in the truth. If so, you're probably making statements like, "It's too good to be true"; "If I can't see it, touch it, or understand it, it isn't real"; "(So and so) burned me once, so I'm never going to trust them again"; "That used to be true, but things have changed"; "I used to believe, but then I grew-up (or got educated)"; "They're all hypocrites, so why should I believe them?"; "(He or she) will never change"; "I'm never going to be successful at this." These excuses can rob us of our opportunity for success, quench our desire to live beyond the limits of ourselves, and steal away our joy. They prejudicially dismiss something that may in fact be true.

The truth in stretching and growing ourselves can be a painful process, and many would rather just leave well enough alone. The fact remains, however, that any truth yet undiscovered still remains a truth. Whether we agree or not, the laws of nature as well as the inevitability of change will impose themselves upon us whether we like it or not, so it's best that we deal with them and not instantly shun what others tell us, or what seem implausible, without giving them a fair hearing.

When someone gives you advice, even if it's someone who doesn't have your best interests at heart, attempt to validate what you hear with those who are committed to your success. Ask your mentor, your accountability partner, or your friends: "Does this seem correct?" Then do some research to further validate a Cassandra Truth, because if you miss it due to your own bias—who knows what you might be losing?

"Pretending to be someone you're not is a waste of the person you are." ~ Kurt Cobain

NOVEMBER 17

I will raise average performance

Think criticism is more effective than praise? Wrong! This is one of those accepted practices that research has debunked. The belief that criticism is likely followed by improvement may be correct. However, according to a revealing article by Linda Hill and Kent Lineback there's another factor going on, called "regression to the mean," that explains the long-term effect. Hill and Lineback's research reveals that we all exhibit an average performance level over time, but actual performance varies from task to task. By tracking performances over time, great performances are usually followed by only moderate performances more closely related to the average of a person. The same pattern works in reverse when a better performance follows a poor one. This is all part of the variability of human performance. Therefore, when the boss criticizes you for performing less than your own average, you will tend to perform better thereafter *simply because* your natural pattern is to return to your own average. This would have occurred even if your boss hadn't criticized you.

The studies showed the same results in response to praise, where the next performance tended to be worse just because your propensity is to return to your average. Because bosses either consciously or intuitively notice improved performances following criticism of poor performance, they're inclined to criticize more frequently.

Instead of focusing on improving task performance, we should be focusing on *increasing average performance.* This happens by focusing on what people do well. The evidence is overwhelming that positive reinforcement—building on strengths and encouraging constant improvement—produces increased average performance far more than just finding fault with others. A corroborating study by academics Heaphy and Losada, and published in the Harvard Business Review, showed that low-performing teams received almost three negative comments for every positive one. Conversely, focusing on people's strengths increased their performance by sixty-two-percent. The study found the best ratio of positive to negative comments to improve performance was six to one. This ratio was also shown to help marriages. Thinking and speaking positive really can help raise anyone's average.

"You can't let praise or criticism get to you. It's a weakness to get caught up in either one." ~ John Wooden

NOVEMBER 18

I will remain faithful to my roots and my personal values

Sam Walton, founder of Wal-Mart and the greatest merchant of the twentieth century, started with a small town store in Newport, Arkansas back in 1945. By the first part of the twenty-first century, his retail giant chain had grown to the number one Fortune 500 company. How did he go from rags to the top pinnacle of success? He always remained faithful to his roots, and to his personal values. Despite being named Fortune's richest man in America in the mid-nineteen-eighties, he still drove the same old pickup truck "with cages in the back for [his] bird dogs," and got his hair cut at the same barbershop near the town square.

While sticking to his roots, Walton also stuck to his fiercely competitive nature. He played quarterback for his undefeated football team, he was first in the history of Missouri to be awarded Eagle Scout status, and he played on his undefeated basketball team despite being a scant five-feet-nine-inches tall. After serving in the Navy during World War II, Walton moved to a small town in Arkansas, out of respect for his wife Helen's wish to live in a town no larger than 10,000 people. Walton was committed to his marriage and loyal to those for whom he was responsible. He bought a little five-and-dime in Newport, and over the next fifteen years expanded his company to sixteen stores, always focusing on smaller markets, staying true to his small town roots, while the other big discounters like Kmart, Woolco, and Target cannibalized each other, fighting over big markets.

It was the culture Walton created that distinguished him most, and it's simply valuing other people. In the beginning, Walton's store managers actually invested money in the stores they managed, giving them "skin in the game." Walton constantly improved his stores by stopping at other retailers to study their tactics. His energy and commitment to people and improvement destined his success. It kept his employees with him during the early days, when money was tight. His small-town values stuck with him as he grew organically from several small-town, niche markets to an ever-expanding influence. Walton characterized his attitude when he expressed his disgust at "overpaid CEOs who're really looting from the top and aren't watching out for anyone but themselves" – that "really upsets me," he said. He never lost touch with his roots. That philosophy worked for him. It will work for you too.

"High expectations are the key to everything." ~ Sam Walton

NOVEMBER 19

I will give back to charity

His net worth at this writing is $66.2 billion. So does that make Bill Gates a successful person? Does being creator of the world's largest software maker, Microsoft, better describe Mr. Gates as a success? No. What really caps off this extraordinary achiever's success is his decision to donate billions to charity, thereby literally giving away his position as the world's richest man. Additionally, he started a campaign with fellow billionaire Warren Buffet to gain pledges from more than thirty U.S. billionaires to give at least fifty-percent of their wealth to charity. Now that's success!

Not only can giving enhance people's success in the eyes of those who benefit from their generosity, it can actually increase the giver's wealth. Sound like a paradox? At a Family Philanthropy Conference in San Diego, Arthur C. Brooks, President of the American Enterprise Institute and author of *Who Really Cares: The Surprising Truth about Compassionate Conservatism* (Basic Books, 2006), shared extensive research showing that giving leads to happiness *and* to more wealth. A $2 billion, or one percent, increase in charitable giving leads to a $39 billion increase in the gross domestic product, a standard measure of a nation's wealth. "Because of what you do, we are a richer, happier, healthier nation..." Brooks told his audience.

At the micro level, a family that gives $100 or more earns, on average, more money the subsequent year. Studies show that giving releases endorphins that make you happier. What's more, those who give their resources and time to others are generally perceived as leaders, and leaders attract success. Besides all that, it's just the right thing to do.

Think of this: if each of us contributed just ten percent of our wealth to charity, we could end world hunger, heal all of the children with treatable diseases in third world countries, provide education and better opportunities to everyone who could not otherwise afford them, and provide disability assistance to those who have none. According to The National Philanthropic Trust, sixty-five-percent of households give to charity, and by the year 2055, some $41 trillion will change hands as Americans pass on their accumulated assets to the next generation. Let's all commit to giving more of our wealth and time to those in need. It's the proverbial win-win—and it feels so good!

"Sometimes a small thing you do can mean everything in another person's life." ~ Author Unknown

November 20

I will gain control of my life

Stress seems to be a fact of life. The financial burdens keep piling up, you can never do enough at work, and your responsibilities are always front and center. The good news is, you can control much of what causes you stress. Indeed, just realizing that you're in control of your life is the foundation of stress management.

The first step is to identify what's causing stress in your life. Writing in a journal or talking to friends can help you sort out causes and feelings. Then decide what causes are within your control, and what can be avoided. Sometimes how you cope with stress actually leads to *more* stress—like overeating or under eating, drinking too much, withdrawing from friends and family, being short tempered, or procrastinating. Replace any of these bad habits with better coping mechanisms by changing your situation or your attitude toward stress causers.

There are four basic responses to these causes that can relieve stress: avoid them, change your response to them, adapt your life around them, or simply accept them. To avoid the causes of stress, consider reducing or eliminating associations with people who cause you stress, avoid situations that induce stress—like heavy traffic by changing your schedule—and reduce your to-do list by saying "no" to more than you can handle. If avoiding the cause of stress is not possible, try altering your response to it. Be willing to negotiate a healthful alternative, be assertive with those who are not considerate of your needs, be honest and open with your feelings of discomfort, and manage your time more effectively. You can also regain control by adapting to a stressor that can't be avoided or altered. Exercising, getting enough sleep, and eating properly are three areas you can change to reduce stress. Try reframing the cause of your stress with a more positive perspective, such as looking at that traffic jam as a time to think through things and listen to some good music. Think long-term: is this really something that will be important in a month or year?

Finally, if what causes you stress is something you need to live with, such as an illness or a job loss, do your best to accept it and look for the silver lining. Share your feelings with others, learn to move on, and find time for relaxation.

"We don't see things as they are, we see them as we are." ~ Anais Nin

NOVEMBER 21

I will synthesize information

Dr. Howard Gardner, in his Harvard Business Review article "The Synthesizing Leader" (*The HBR List: Breakthrough Ideas for 2006*), explained that the single most important trait of future leaders in world development is the ability to synthesize information. Synthesizing which information to utilize includes, in addition to other things, developing standards for selection, such as discerning credibility and relevance. It also includes the ability to answer the questions: "Does this information form a coherent story?" and "Do these trends make sense?" With a plethora of data coming from multiple and global sources, selecting which chunks of information are worthy of one's limited attention is a key competency for success, and ultimately, for being a strong leader.

A leader synthesizes information, while a manager analyzes. A leader requests that his or her managers provide status reports and other critical statistics, and then the leader considers all of the data and tries to synthesize it into a basic statement followed by a direction for the entire set of problems. Essentially, synthesis entails dealing with abstract concepts to create a vision or broad strategic plan, whereas analysis deals with details to provide a tactical response. Leadership assesses the long-term impact of the information and circumstances, whereas management considers short-term goals. Leadership defines the next big thing to bring the organization to the next level of success, whereas management is concerned with effectively executing the plan by controlling processes and tracking progress. Leaders use information to see the broader view. They take various facts and observations and connect the dots to create a clear picture of what is likely to occur in advance of it happening. In other words, they put their organization on the offense.

Leaders understand how to clear through data by looking for the ten to twenty percent of information that will return eighty to ninety percent of the value. They think in terms of a sequence of importance and consequence, laser focus on goals, factor in constraints, formulate alternative courses, and develop back-up plans should decisions go wrong. Leadership in the twenty-first century will require a new paradigm that can form information into breakthroughs.

"Leadership is a choice, not a position." ~ Stephen Covey

NOVEMBER 22

I will deal with interview rejections

We all have experienced them: that hurtful email/letter/phone call that says you didn't get the job. It's hard, especially if you've faced several rejections during your job search. You may have felt the interview went positively, and then the surprise and frustration settles in after the rejection arrives. It's important to understand that the way you handle these rejections is just as important as your experience and skills when seeking out a new position. Allowing rejection to jiggle your self-confidence can make you doubt your abilities, which can negatively affect future interviews and tempt you to give-up. It sounds cliché, but you really can't take it personally. There are many factors that could have gotten in the way.

Most rejections reflect more on the other person, the rejecter, and how they're bias perceives their needs, than they do on you. That you weren't the perfect match doesn't mean that you're not an outstanding professional with excellent attributes and talents. In fact, not getting the job may have saved you from a grueling future with someone who would not have been a good fit for you. Rejection can strangely place our minds in a tailspin where our collective unconscious takes over and starts replaying our failures. Don't let that happen! Refuse to let past failures resurrect themselves in your head. Stay present and future focused. Counter the tendency to focus on your weaknesses by focusing on what you're really good at. What are you passionate about? Don't blame yourself for not being perfect.

Keep in mind that rejection is not feedback, and it's perfectly acceptable to politely ask the employer for more detailed feedback about your interview to help you improve the next time around. But know that interview feedback is often very general. So seeking out mentors and peers for advice may provide you with more valuable insight. It's important to keep learning and developing, especially if you're not currently employed, to keep your skills sharp, whether through volunteering with a company of interest or gaining additional education/training. Accept that rejections are a part of the job search. Buffer yourself emotionally to handle the disappointment that comes with rejection. You're not alone—rejection happens to countless people. Keep it in perspective; other's decisions don't necessarily reflect on you.

"A rejection is nothing more than a necessary step in the pursuit of success." ~ Bo Bennett

NOVEMBER 23

I will self-regulate

Feeling out of control angry after someone offends you? Are emotions ruling you instead of you ruling them? Is life out of balance? Maybe you, like most of us, need to improve your self-regulation skills. Self-regulation is the ability to act in your long-term best interest, consistent with your strongest values. When we betray our strongest values, we feel guilty and unsatisfied. Emotionally, self-regulation is the ability to calm yourself when you're upset and uplift yourself when you're down.

Our brain is continually sensing and reacting to the needs of the body. Internal "thermostats" regulate our internal (bodily) and external (environmental) systems, such that when they sense imbalance (stress), they activate the brain's alarm systems to retrieve what the body needs. Much of this regulation occurs beyond our awareness, but as we grow, we can start to manage our own regulation. When the internal system needs water or the external system is threatened, our "thermostat" tells us, so that we can find water and prepare to respond to threats. Emotions actually send chemical signals to the brain, muscles, and organs of the body that prepare us to take action based on self-regulation.

Key to the process of self-regulating stress, hunger, thirst, and emotions is to read your body's signals. Many of the sensations we feel when we are "out of regulation" are because we lack awareness of ourselves or we cannot control our internal and external systems. Self-regulation happens when we focus on our values rather than our feelings. Saying "I feel bad" focuses on what is wrong, and if you blame someone else you become angry and want to get even. A focus on values says, "I'm better than this," which translates into the values that make you unique and resilient.

Self-regulation expert and psychologist Barry Zimmerman, PhD, suggests these means for self-regulation: goal setting, seeking out advice (such as being mentored), focusing on your values and standards, self-motivation, and adapting. In other words, consistently monitor your behavior, thoughts, and strategies, and change some aspects of your current functioning to make them consistent with your highest values. When you begin to live up to your values, your circumstances take a back seat—and you are self-regulating.

"Never violate the sacredness of your individual self-respect." ~ Theodore Parker

NOVEMBER 24

I will own it

You just bought a new car. You didn't lease it—you own it. And because of that pride of ownership you wash it routinely and keep the interior immaculate to keep it looking new. Shortly after making this purchase, you go on a vacation and rent a car. It doesn't matter that you leave your trash in this car or drive it less carefully, because it's a rental, right? Who takes care of a rental with the same attention as something they own? Well, the same principle applies to our decisions, and the decisions made by others that we are charged to implement.

Say your boss tells you the company needs to realign its resources by cutting back on expenses. Would you go to your direct reports and say something like, "My boss told me we have to cutback. I know—I don't like it either—but we have to do what the boss says"? Or would you say to your employee, "In order to meet our numbers, we all need to pitch-in. So I'm asking each of us, including you and me, to cutback on expenses." The first statement wasn't "owning it," it was passing responsibility onto the boss. In the second statement, the person who gave the marching orders was never even mentioned. You owned the decision and considered it as if you had come-up with the idea. That's the difference between owning a decision and just "renting" it from someone else.

Successful people own their decisions, whether they made them or someone else to whom they are responsible made them. If something has to be done, each of us needs to own the responsibility and not just pass on it or make excuses. Accept your leader's decisions as if they are your own—as if you made them—with the faith that it will lead to something good. You also need to feel good about your choices in order to allow you to confidently make decisions in the future.

Having faith in yourself and others to own your decisions empowers you, gives you more joy, builds your credibility, and makes you the master of your domain. Author and pastor Chuck Swindoll once said, "I'm convinced that life is 10% what happens to me and 90% how I react to it." Said another way, "Life is what I make happen from what happens to me." Owning your decisions make them yours, and because you own them, you take care of them, and that leads to a happy state of mind.

"Life is what happens to you while you're busy making other plans." ~ John Lennon, from Beautiful Boy

NOVEMBER 25

I will work smarter

Perhaps you've heard of the Pareto principle (also known as the eighty-twenty rule and the principle of factor sparsity), which states that, for many events, roughly eighty-percent of the effects come from twenty-percent of the causes. Using this as a principle, which many businesses do, we should all ruthlessly get rid of the eighty-percent (of our day) time wasters in order to devote our efforts to the twenty-percent of activities that will return eighty-percent of our profit. So how do we do that?

In his best seller, *The 4-Hour Workweek: Escape 9-5, Live Anywhere, and Join the New Rich* (Crown Publishing Group, 2007) Tim Ferriss writes about what he calls a *lifestyle design.* It involves not burning out, deferring the joys of life, and redefining the rules of the game to live the good life now. The key is to outsource as much as possible of the eighty-percent that impedes our success. Tradition tells us that elimination is about time management, but Ferriss suggests we simply forget about time management and focus instead on getting the really important and results-producing tasks done. There's a difference, he says, between efficiency and effectiveness. Choose to be effective. The key is to avoid building a business or operation that requires your constant presence, because that just sucks up all your time. Give the people who work for or with you specific instructions and empower them to do the job (limit things that require your approval), and for tasks that can't be delegated use outsource vendors to do most if not all of the non-essential eighty-percent.

Make yourself mobile, unrestricted by office space or location, so you can conduct business anywhere at anytime. This allows you to leverage your time and efforts across the globe. Through outsourcing, you've eliminated the need to make numerous time-consuming decisions by building a self-sustaining system. Also eliminate the twenty-percent that is causing eighty-percent of the problems, like emails, high-maintenance people and clients, etc. Apply *Parkinson's Law*, which states to not allow tasks to absorb more importance than they merit by swelling to fill all available time. You can actually limit tasks to the most important ones by shortening your work time! Eliminate as many of the unessential inputs as you can so that you can major in the majors. Batch weekly chores and keep to a schedule. Ferris finally suggests eliminating things before delegating them and if you can't measure it, it doesn't count toward anything. Now that's working smarter.

"Those who wish to sing, always find a song." ~ Swedish Proverb

NOVEMBER 26

I will overcome temptation

Without any question—without a single doubt—the biggest problem that decent people have is temptation. Succumbing to temptation has torpedoed more careers and relationships than ships sunk by the entire submarine fleet of every country throughout history.

There's a story about a dog whose master laid out dinner for his family, but the dog would find a way to sneak over to the meat and eat it. So the master began slapping a piece of newspaper to startle the dog every time it went after the meat. Eventually the dog learned not to even look at the meat, somehow realizing the temptation to disobey would be too great. Instead, the dog looked steadfastly into his master's face and never took his eyes off him.

That's how temptation works. As long as we stare at it, as long as we even think about that forbidden pleasure, we remain susceptible. But like the dog, if we religiously look at our loved one, if we consider how that person or others we care about could be hurt if we blindly turn away from them and go after the temptation, then our attention is forced onto the people and things most important to us. Those temptations that would otherwise torpedo us lose their power.

It's not enough to trust in our guiding values to steer us away from the unhealthful allures of this world—although values are essential. We must consistently train our gaze onto the reasons for our true joy, those that edify us and bring out our best nature. The mental hard work of considering the consequences could keep you from that tempting chocolate, because your health is one of the most important things in your life. Try visualizing yourself walking away from an unhealthy relationship and toward your loved one, eyes fixed on the one you would never wish to disappoint. Turn your mental gaze on the your family, your health, your career, your friends, your home—all the things for which you can be grateful—to ground you from temptation. And if all else fails, just run from it. Go exercise, take up a new hobby, go out for an activity, or even move. Then celebrate the fact that you cherished your best. Be an overcomer.

"Discipline is remembering what you want." ~ David Campbell

NOVEMBER 27

I will speak without the corporate jargon

Ever spoken with someone outside the workplace and their eyes started to glaze over, or worse yet, roll back in their head? Perhaps you've been speaking the annoying corporate jargon that keeps people from just telling it like it is—and prevents others from hearing you at all. It's become an epidemic problem with professionals, and it's time to stop sounding like an office parrot. Corporate jargon includes slang like "robust," "best practices," "core competency," "throw under the bus," "thought-leader," "face time," "circle back," "boilerplate," "action item," "change management," "drinking the Kool-Aid," "game plan," "on your plate," "hardball," and "bang for the buck," to name a few. These kinds of terms obscure your message by adding layers of wordiness. They come off sounding evasive, or just plain bothersome.

If you find yourself speaking corporate jargon, stop, and talk straight. Start by bringing your genuine self to work. Don't try to sound like a programmed talking point. Instead, use some self-deprecating humor such as, "I'm in shape. Round is a shape, right?" People will be eager to listen to someone who is funny at their own expense. For years professionals have been programmed to sell their ideas, which has inculcated a sales mindset even when speaking in the break room and during off hours. If you want to connect with someone on a human level, stop selling and start sharing your heart. If you have to communicate hard news, like a cutback or disciplinary action, don't hide behind legalese or "HR gobbledygook," as in using terms like "redeployment" and "workforce optimization." You can be honest and protective of company policy at the same time, but sounding like an infomercial or a company recording just doesn't help anyone.

Use clear but compassionate language. Whether you're speaking to the boss or to an acquaintance, speaking succinctly and with energy usually works well. Don't tell others, share with them. Acknowledge their comments and listen to what they say without thinking about your next clever thing. People won't want to listen to you if they feel like they're not being understood. The highest level of human communication comes with language that is original to you. So speak the same to anyone you meet. And by all means stop with the corporate slang—we're better than that.

"Bull has become the language of business." ~ Why Business People Speak Like Idiots: A Bullfighter's Guides (Fugere and Hardaway, Free Press, 2005)

NOVEMBER 28

I will develop common sense

Rational people can do irrational things, like gambling all their money on the stock market. Everyone lacks common sense from time to time, or "practical intelligence" as some have called it. It's one of the most essential keys to success, but it isn't so common these days. Practicing good judgment in the moment, and reacting with good reasoning when life throws us a curve ball can be a learned skill. Much of common sense comes from experience, which is why people who've been there and done that are treasure troves from which to learn about common sense. These people are your elders, your mentors, those who are experienced in work and life. So the first key in developing common sense is to glean from those wiser than yourself in situations where you have little experience.

Most of us think from a limited perspective that prevents us from seeing alternative approaches that may be better than our preconceived notions. So therefore our reactive or "fallback" behavior is to do what seems normal. But normal isn't necessarily right. Sometimes we need to take a time-out, and seek advice or process a response in exception to our immediate assumptions. We depress common sense when we automatically apply our conditioned or biased thinking without adapting to the current circumstances. This also happens when emotions take over, or when prejudice or social fads override our ability to synthesize the common experiences of those who consistently make good choices, while also mentally processing different responses and their consequences.

Many of us are suffering from obsessive "get it done," which means we are prioritizing getting something done over thinking through the consequences. So take time out each day to deliberate on what to do. Thinking through "what ifs" prepares you to make better quick decisions when the situation demands it. What we call "basic common sense" relates to fundamental knowledge such as taking care of your health, respecting other's rights, understanding your limits, keeping safe, and knowing accepted facts. Advanced common sense comes from valuing different ideas, thinking proactively, and being curious. Take time for introspection and for gaining experience. But in a rush, trust your hunches.

"Common sense is genius dressed in its working clothes." ~ Ralph Waldo Emerson

NOVEMBER 29

I will self-manage

Two gentlemen walk into a hardware store at the same time, one an athletic type with a ready-made smile, the other a tall pudgy man with a fixed frown. A salesman approaches the two men to ask them what they need. The cheerful guy asks for twenty size 6 x ¾" screws to finish some cabinets he's promised to the customer by next Friday. He plans on completing the project early since he's been "religiously" sticking to his schedule. The tall dour guy says he's been working on a home project "off and on for months now," and he bought the wrong materials and now needs to find the correct ones. Which one is more self-managed? Correct! The cheerful athletic customer has stuck to his plan (meaning he's demonstrated *strong organizational skills*), he appears to like finishing projects ahead of schedule (meaning he's developed *effective productivity habits*), and he knows exactly what he needs to get the job done (demonstrating a *strong sense of self-discipline*).

Success depends on taking effective action, and the key to effective action is our ability to focus attention on where it's most required. One of the greatest impediments to good self-management is procrastination—a common problem for most of us. One technique for not putting something off is to do the difficult thing first. Try making a commitment to doing one "difficult thing" a day up front, and this will have a dramatic effect on your ability to accomplish the rest of your responsibilities.

The cheerful guy who self-managed his project made plans for his entire week beginning the first day of the week, and he kept the list with him while working, which also kept him from time-killing distractions. On his list he noted how many minutes he would commit to each task, and rarely strayed from it. Another technique the cheerful guy used was visualizing the completed task, especially completing the unpleasant tasks, and conversely he envisioned the consequences of not completing the tasks on time (an unhappy customer), associated with the cost of not doing the task on time (lost revenue or hiring extra help). Being self-managed involves tackling the tough issues by living your values and honoring your word. There are good reasons why one man wore a smile, and the other a frown.

"Always do right. That will gratify some of the people and astonish the rest."
~ Mark Twain

NOVEMBER 30

I will empower people and teams

According to studies of companies whose employees love where they work, the less hierarchy at a company, the greater the likelihood that most people will feel empowered and motivated. One such company is Whole Foods Market, Inc., whose CEO John Mackey said, "We've made adjustments to keep the external and internal equity perspectives in balance." Mackey's company caps the maximum allowable ratio of the highest cash compensation to average employee compensation to address internal equity, and they've never lost a top executive to a competitor.

Some companies in other countries, like Japan, maintain a system where the highest-paid employee makes just six to eight times what the lowest-paid earns—an astounding departure from the 380-1-spread between the CEO and average worker pay among the S&P 500 (according to the 2011 research conducted by Executive PayWatch).

Asking royalty to relinquish their crowns in the name of fairness creates an empowering environment, by eliminating much of the divide between executive management and the people who work "under" them. Empowerment is about giving up not only some control, but status as well, in order to improve others' sense of confidence, comradery, and self-awareness.

Part of empowerment means getting employees to want to be a member of the team and to succeed. Setting the tone of "we're all in this together" is key. Besides leveling the playing field, frequent and open communication is another way in which to empower others. Current information and company updates should be provided in order to give employees a sense of importance and inclusiveness.

Employees who feel plugged into the company's decisions are more apt to be inspired and to want to promote the success of the company. A strong recognition system for ideas and contributions also motivates people to want to do more. This involves more than just sending an email. Taking the time to talk in person shows you care. Another key ingredient for empowering and motivating others is to involve them in the planning and decision making process. Also, the more brains you have thinking about an issue, the better your chances that all options have been explored and to create an optimal result for the company.

"The most common way people give up their power is by thinking they don't have any." ~ Alice Walker

DECEMBER

BE A GIFT

DECEMBER 1

I will heed the red flags of affection

Amy lived a life of strong values like honesty, faith, and generosity. She liked strong men—especially successful ones. One day she met a man at the store in which she worked who appeared confident, well groomed, and handsome. For their first date, he took her to an expensive restaurant in Chicago and picked her up in a red Ferrari sports car. They fell in love, and ten months later Amy gave birth to the couple's son. After almost two years of marriage, Amy began noticing some bazaar behaviors. Her husband would stay out all night, friends of his that she met were brash, rough, and used vulgar language. One day a friend of Amy's pounded at the door. "You've got to get out of here now!" her friend said. "Your husband is a crime boss and a sex slave trader, and he's planning to take your son!" Terrified, Amy ran for her life and never returned. She found out later that her friend was right. What happened? How do people end up in unhealthy relationships, despite warning signs that this partner was bad news? Not everyone ends up in the kind of trouble Amy encountered, but even slightly damaging relationships can blind us to reality.

Love *is* truly blind, as researchers at the University College London discovered using MRI machines. "Feelings of love lead to a suppression of activity in the areas of the brain controlling critical thought," they learned. "It seems that once we get close to a person, the brain decides the need to assess their character and personality is reduced." Not only that, but chemicals that make us feel good and hormones such as oxytocin and dopamine cloud our judgment even more so. We can become essentially "high" on love, making us ignore the red flags right before our eyes. In some cases like Amy's, a person can pass off negative alerts by using excuses like "he'll get better," or thinking she can improve him.

Marriage expert Dr. John Van Epp, author of *How to Avoid Falling in Love With a Jerk* (McGraw-Hill, 2008), says, "The good doesn't always last, and the bad usually gets worse." It's important that we heed the red flags, like when a person's strongest values contradict ours, even a little. Take note of their friends. Are they people you respect? Observe how they treat others, like waiters and others in the service industry. Is she courteous? Is he violent? Do you argue a lot? Does she make you feel guilty when you want to spend time apart? Does he never take responsibility for bad behavior? All of these red flags signal "stop"—and re-consider whether further involvement is worth it.

"Love is blind and lovers cannot see the pretty follies that themselves commit."
~ William Shakespeare, THE MERCHANT OF VENICE

DECEMBER 2

I will maximize my weekends

As responsibilities expand our workweek and shrink our free time, it's important to make the most of our weekends. A study published in the *Journal of Organizational Behavior* found that some weekend endeavors can help recover from the stress of the workweek, while others don't. Charlotte Fritz, Ph.D., from Portland State University, proposed, along with her co-authors, that weekend activities should decrease negative emotions (stress, fatigue and anger) and increase positive ones (happiness, confidence and peace of mind). They arrived at four factors to improve the positives and decrease negative feelings: 1) take more time to relax (by choosing "activities that you don't have to force yourself to do or that require very little effort to initiate"); 2) challenge yourself (take-up a new hobby, a new sport, or learn a new skill that can build your competency and create more energy); 3) detach from work (try not to even think about work during the weekend so you can do other things); and 4) don't store-up all your errands for the weekend (try fitting in some of your most undesirable chores during the week so that you can relax more on the weekend).

Time management expert Laura Vanderkam, in her e-Book, *What The Most Successful People Do On The Weekend: A Short Guide to Making the Most of Your Days Off* (Portfolio, 2012), suggests that instead of just plopping down on the sofa to watch T.V. or doing something by default, you choose to decide how your time is spent. Vanderkam writes that "even loafing time must be consciously chosen, because time will be filled with something whether it's consciously chosen or not." Some of us are good at planning for the week's schedule, but experts say that you must plan for the weekend as well, and remain disciplined in following through with your weekend commitments.

Harvard psychologist Daniel Gilbert claims in his book, *Stumbling on Happiness* (Knopf, 2006), "The greatest achievement of the human brain is its ability to imagine objects and episodes that do not exist in the realm of the real." Gilbert writes about anticipation, which translates into happiness, and the joy that results from planning your activities for the weekend. Maybe you've been dreaming about going someplace new, or doing something different, or revisiting a favorite location. Planning in advance allows you to do what you've always wanted to do—on the weekend.

"I'm learning the power of going away for the weekend and keeping myself company." ~ *Zoe Saldana*

DECEMBER 3

I will practice the law of forgiveness

A master in stained glass, Courtney bid on a project to replace the windows of an old chapel located within the huge fields of cemetery space in Colma, near San Francisco. The job was worth several thousands, and Courtney labored for weeks over the new designs. The cemetery director took Courtney's designs, studied them for a few days, and then called her to politely decline her services. Years later, Courtney decided to revisit the old chapel, and was flabbergasted to see that the windows were exactly formed according to her designs. Apparently the director gave her plans to someone else who probably charged less money. After a period of hurt and anger, Courtney practiced forgiveness and eventually got back her peace of mind.

Confucious said, "Before you embark on a journey of revenge, dig two graves." The law of forgiveness tells us to forgive (not justify) anyone who has caused you pain or suffering. In return, we will escape the consequences of anger and hidden hostilities that come with thoughts of revenge. Sometimes the offender is actually awakened to his or her misdeed through our choice to forgive. Most people who harm us are acting out of insecurity, ignorance, abuse, or extreme unhappiness. These negative people then filter their thoughts and actions through their negative lenses and are either blind to the hurt they impose on others, or they choose to ignore their responsibility for committing something wrong. They become self-centered with a warped sense of judgment.

Once you've realized that the person who offended you is damaged and will ultimately live with the consequences of their toxic behavior, you can begin to forgive them. This in turn releases you from the toxic burden of avenging yourself, and frees you to become stronger, more tolerant, compassionate, and better. In Courtney's case, she learned to not always trust others with her designs by retrieving them after their review, and by requiring a signed disclosure agreement. She forgave the director for being such an insecure, greedy, and selfish person that he needed to stoop so low as to steal from her. In return she grew wiser and stronger. Forgiveness is an attitude shifting approach for relieving the stress of pent-up hostility, and it empowers you as a superior.

"The weak can never forgive. Forgiveness is the attribute of the strong."
~ Mahatma Gandhi

DECEMBER 4

I will create memorable experiences

Walt Disney World doesn't just sell entertainment. Starbucks doesn't just sell coffee. The Hard Rock Café doesn't just sell food and drinks. These iconic businesses sell experience. Joseph Pine and James Gilmore first introduced the concept of *The Experience Economy: Work Is Theater & Every Business a Stage* (Havard Business School Press, 1999). They use the changing nature of birthday parties to illustrate an evolution of economic value from commodities to goods and services, and currently to experiences.

Before the introduction of places like Chuck E. Cheese's, birthdays typically centered on Mom baking a birthday cake and having her child's friends over for a party. Now parents bring their children to places like Chuck E.'s for pizza, games, and a show. It's an experience. The cost of the cake might be just a few dollars, but the cost of an experience could be many times that, and parents are willing to pay more for a fun and memorable experience that can last a lifetime. Companies demand premium pricing by creating experiences distinguished from that of their competitors. Pine and Gilmore's extensive research bears this out, showing that companies who do a good job producing experiences grow faster than goods or services based companies.

The extent of success in developing a good experience is measured as a matrix of guest participation and the connection the guest has with the event. The four "experience realms" explained in *The Experience Economy* are: 1) *entertainment*, where the audience watches passively; 2) *education*, with a higher level of participation, like a hands-on experience at a discovery museum; 3) *escapism*, like visiting a casino, or an Internet chat room where the participant is fully connected and involved; and, 4) *esthetics*, with high immersion yet low physical involvement, like a visit to an art show or an outdoor mall.

The key to creating a great experience is to incorporate all four realms by staging a "rich, compelling experience." Disney does a great job of this through a well-established corporate culture of creating memorable experiences for their "guests." Amazon creates an online experience by using personalized recommendations, and encouraging customer participation in the form of reviews and wish lists. Creating a positive customer experience today means more than a smile and good service—it means creating lasting impressions.

"You cannot create experience. You must undergo it." ~ *Albert Camus*

DECEMBER 5

I will act with moral intelligence

Moral Intelligence is a term for the mental capacity to determine how to apply universally accepted moral principles to our personal values, goals, and actions. The key is to act on these moral principles, such as living with integrity, correctness, responsibility, empathy, forgiveness, compassion and forgiveness. Simply knowing right from wrong isn't enough; the morally competent person must actually do what's right. Vital for both personal and organizational success is a consistent and intentional commitment to our moral principles, and it begins with being self-aware. Are these principles at the forefront of your thinking? Can you discern those occasions when you are morally intelligent (know right from wrong) but are morally incompetent (not practicing right from wrong), so that you can realign your actions with your moral principles? This is what we call our moral compass—maintaining a directional focus on our core principles.

As human beings, we naturally cannot function at a satisfying level unless we are faithful to our moral compass. We also thrive in environments that nurture these moral principles, and conversely we go into survival mode when these principles are not in action, in order to protect ourselves. True leaders nurture moral intelligence wherever they go, such as listening to team members instead of telling them, showing genuine concern for an employee's well being, and when appropriate placing the agenda of someone else above your own. Practicing moral intelligence is a trained skill that is instilled as a consistent mode of behavior through repetition, by overriding the brain's tendency to react impulsively and selfishly with a concerted effort, and self-awareness to follow one's core moral principles. Just giving lip service to doing the morally right thing doesn't accomplish anything unless others at your affect respond with greater motivation, enthusiasm, comfort, and empowerment.

Said another way, moral leadership occurs when others start behaving in a more morally principled way because of your example. So make fewer excuses, take responsibility for your actions, keep commitments, be honest, show tolerance, avoid those little white lies, uphold integrity and communicate respect to others. Our world needs your example.

"Happiness and moral duty are inseparably connected." ~ George Washington

DECEMBER 6

I will build on my strengths and develop my weak areas

Healthy organizations commonly require that their members create a development plan for their personal and professional growth. Some use a form of 360 Feedback, where coworkers provide their assessment of an employee's strengths and areas for improvement, and next the supervisor and/or employee determines a plan for development in order to improve skills in those identified areas. This practice proves healthful for any individual, whether in the workplace or at home.

Try these two different exercises: first ask your supervisor, direct reports, and at least two other coworkers to provide you with one to three strengths and one to three areas for improvement; then do the same for your significant other and at least three friends. Choose the one or two most consistent comments/themes for your strengths and weaknesses. Create a plan for developing one to two skills for your two weakest areas, and determine one to two ways in which you can build on your strengths for both your professional and your personal lives.

The average person can fully develop no more than three skills in a year; so don't overload yourself with a laundry list of plans. Make the skills simple enough and clear enough to remain top of mind, such as improving public speaking or conflict resolution skills, and then select the seminars, books, coach, mentor, or other resources that will help you achieve your plan. Go through the same exercise of asking for feedback toward the end of the year to assess whether you are practicing your newfound skills. A healthy person is someone committed to self-improvement. Let others help you make it happen.

"There is nothing noble in being superior to your fellow man; true nobility is being superior to your former self." – Ernest Hemingway

"There is only one corner of the universe you can be certain of improving and that's your own self." – Aldous Huxley

"If you do not change, you can become extinct!"
~ Spencer Johnson, author of Who Moved My Cheese

DECEMBER 7

I will build others up

Encouragement keeps us going in times of change and trouble. An experiment was once conducted to measure the human capacity to endure pain, by assessing how long a barefooted person could stand in a bucket of ice cold water. The researchers found that when there was someone else present who offered words of encouragement, the person standing in the icy water tolerated pain twice as long as when no one is present. Affective Psychology expert Richard Davidson, PhD., relates this phenomenon to the emotional style that defines our outlook. He says by finding and making opportunities to compliment others, you can actually train your brain to see the good in people, as well as the good in yourself and life in general.

In Kathryn Stockett's wonderful bestseller, *The Help* (Amy Einhorn Books/Putnam, 2009), she demonstrates this concept of positive reinforcement. Her character Aibileen Clark encourages a little girl, Mae Mobley, by consistently telling the girl: "You is kind. You is smart. You is important." In so doing Aibileen helps transform the mindset of racial prejudice in the white dominated society with the affirmations she tells to the little girl, whom readers hope grows up to overcome the negative expectations instilled by her bigoted parents. Encouragement has a powerful reciprocal effect that both builds up the receiver and builds up the giver. Nothing is deducted from us for offering a compliment.

All too often a fixation on our own agenda, or insecurity, or a lack of well being in our own life prevents us from giving a sincere compliment to another. But encouraging others can come in multiple and painless forms, like expressing your genuine interest in someone, acknowledging what's important to them, offering support and help in times of need, or giving someone words of praise. Even asking for advice shows you value and respect others' opinions and value them as a person. Wouldn't our workplace and our world be a better place if the standard practice among people would be to encourage one another? Think of how many lives would be transformed simply by seeking the positives in each other, and then actively expressing them. Perhaps the biggest transformation will happen to you.

"In the end, everything will be okay. If it's not okay, it's not yet the end."
~ Fernando Sabino

DECEMBER 8

I will make my home and workspace positive

Most of your time is spent at both your home and your workspace; in fact, more and more people are including their primary workspace in their home. So doesn't it make sense to make both spaces inviting, optimistic, and positive? Several researchers agree that designing and filling your home and workspace with uplifting reminders, like pictures of your favorite getaway or your family gives you a more positive outlook on life. Occasionally changing those pictures and the scenery around you also helps keep your perspective fresh and free from rote thinking.

In your workspace, create an energizing flow with everything you need to get to and see within a 180-degree rotation and within reach. Think of what inspires you, or takes your breath away. Those are the things with which you should surround yourself. Perhaps it's a valued collection, or a particular landscape. Whatever it is, place it directly in front of you. In your home, put it in a place where you will see it often, such as the family room or kitchen.

The color of your home and workspace will have a dramatic impact on your perspective. Although each person can have a different interpretation, color theorists in general believe certain colors evoke specific emotions: yellow elicits happiness; green presents a restful state to the eye; red increases the energy level within a space; blue (like the ocean) calms and soothes; and orange revitalizes the senses and is the color of adventure and social communication.

Plan for storage by anticipating the expansion of stuff in your workplace and home. If you currently need a three-shelve storage container, plan for six shelves. One of the most uninspiring places in which to live and work is cluttered with stuff that should have been tucked away in files, closets, or storage bins. Having stuff scattered about only adds to a sense of stress and being overwhelmed. So remember to plan for future growth, including expanding families and all of those books you intend to read.

Finally, choose dimmer lighting since, according to the British Medical Journal, this type of lighting decreases blinking and lessens drying of the eyes. Make sure you have plenty of ambient lighting. Good spatial layout, alternating pictures and photos, mood colors, pleasant smells, greenery (if you're not allergic), adequate storage, and pleasant lighting all add up to a positive and optimistic home and work environment.

"Talent hits a target no one else can hit; Genius hits a target no one else can see."
~ Arthur Schopenhauer

DECEMBER 9

I will trust my gut feeling

Some follow their instincts first when making decisions, while others insist on using their intellect for the final determination. Several studies have shown that instinct as much as intellect leads to the right decision. Professor Marius Usher of Tel Aviv University's School of Psychological Sciences and his fellow researchers found that participants who were forced to choose between two options based on instinct alone made the right choice up to ninety-percent of the time. Usher and others point to a person's ability to average value based on a repository of stored information in the brain.

As we accumulate knowledge, the brain begins to recognize patterns, and then it unconsciously organizes these patterns into groups of information—a mechanism the late social scientist Dr. Herbert Simon called "chunking." Our long-term memory stores these clusters of patterns into a larger composition that can be recognized as an impulse of intuition. Of course that commonly called "gut feeling" is not flawless, but it can be an important part of the decision-making process. It's actually a form of unconscious reasoning that comes from our brain's stored information.

Athletes in particular excel by trusting their instincts after extensive study and practice. During game time, overthinking can impede their ability to react quickly, so they allow intuition to direct their activities. In the professional environment when time is limited, "gut decisions" can often lead to greater progress, especially if corroborated with others and the facts. Steve Jobs said about trusting his gut, "it never let me down, and it has made all the difference in my life." That small voice that nudges you when you're conflicted between two choices is real. Trust your gut.

"Trust your hunches. They're usually based on facts filed away just below the conscious level." ~ Joyce Brothers

"I believe in intuition and inspiration…at times I feel certain I am right while not knowing the reasons." ~ Albert Einstein

DECEMBER 10

I will develop my competitive intelligence

If you work with a business or are in an environment with others competing for a similar position or the same capital pool as you, you need to develop your Competitive Intelligence (CI). CI is the ethical gaining and analysis of competitor and marketing information from available sources in order to make strategic decisions. Peter Drucker said it well: "The purpose of information is not knowledge. It is being able to take the right action." CI provides early warnings about changing market trends as well as transformative steps being used by the competition in order to significantly influence customers and untapped markets. CI differs from Business Intelligence (BI) in that BI is focused on gathering and analyzing customer data and analyses of business influences through statistical and quantitative reviews; though, both CI and BI are often are used to make informed decisions.

The first step of the CI process is to engage the key stakeholders (marketing, sales, research and development) to understand what you already know, what you will do with the CI, who needs to receive the CI, what is the cost to gain it and the cost of not gaining it. Next, target the resources you will need to achieve your goal, probably using an automated intelligence tool using keywords and other specifications. Establish your validation criteria to qualify only information of strategic benefit and to discard extrinsic information that is not relevant to the strategic intent. Once you've qualified the intelligence, perform an extensive analysis to determine the key drivers behind the competitor's actions and the market influences that caused them, such as economic shifts or migrating customer wants—think of framing intelligence in terms of what results you can place into action. Then decide who needs to know your findings and recommendations and ensure that you gain feedback from each of the key stakeholders as to how they respond to your intelligence.

The final step is to make a decision, based on the influence of your CI, that will positively impact your position and that of your company. The ensuing strategic decision will determine the broad direction in which you and the organization will embark, based on the trust the decision makers have in the value of your CI.

"If you don't have a competitive advantage,
don't compete!" ~ Jack Welsh, CEO General Electric

DECEMBER 11

I will know the competencies of success

What makes someone competent? There are many competencies that generally lead to success, and it's important to understand them in order to develop them in others and yourself. These competencies came from a content analysis of many sources, and were published in *FYI: For Your Improvement, A Guide for Development and Coaching* (Lominger Ltd Inc., 4th edition, 2004). In alphabetical order, a person who is competent as a professional demonstrates proficiency in the following abilities: action-oriented, able to deal with ambiguity, approachable, able to deal well with her boss, strong business acumen, mature career ambition, cares about direct reports, comfortable around higher management, good command skills, compassionate, composed, good conflict management skills, skilled in confronting people, creative, customer-focused, timely with decision making, makes quality decisions, delegates appropriately, develops direct reports and others, knows how to direct others, manages diversity, strong ethics and values, fair to direct reports, applicable functional/technical skills, knows how to hire and staff, good sense of humor, an ability to inform others as needed, innovation management skills, integrity and trust, intellectual horsepower, interpersonal savvy, able to learn on the fly, good listening skills, shows managerial courage, manages and measures work, motivates others, negotiation skills, agile within the organization, organized, deals with paradox, patient, good peer relationships, perseveres, open (admits mistakes, shares about himself), continuously learns, keeps perspective, plans well, has political savvy, good presentation skills, sets priorities, problem solving skills, process management skills, drives for results, self-develops, good self-knowledge, can size-up people, can stand alone, shows strategic agility, manages through systems, builds effective teams, learns technical needs, good time management skills, knows total work systems (Six Sigma), understands others, manages vision and purpose, good work/life balance, written communication skills, produces quality work, delivers timely output, uses resources effectively, adds value to the customer, can operate independently, good teamwork, productive work habits, develops skills, and walks the talk.

For more advice on how to develop each of these areas, read *FYI* by Michael Lombardo and Robert Eichinger; it's an excellent reference book—useful for writing reviews as well as identifying your own areas for development.

"If a leader demonstrates competency, genuine concern for others, and admirable character, people will follow." ~ T. Richard Chase

DECEMBER 12

I will perform well before the big dogs

It may happen during a presentation watching someone in the audience tapping his feet. Then someone whispers to another person, or starts texting in the midst of your speaking. It may happen when you're at a social event, talking with upper management or some other important person, and you think they're judging your every word by looking you up and down. You worry that you're being ineffective, or that they're disappointed, or that your hair is messed-up. Sound familiar? You suffer from performance anxiety—and you're not alone.

First, maintain your cool by keeping your mind from drifting. When reading into others' peculiarities or if their status distracts you, you become unable to concentrate, you become nervous and the result puts you off your game so your memory lapses and you make errors. Consider what's the worst that can happen, and then prepare for these possibilities in advance of going before the big dogs. Remind yourself that, if you're presenting, you have practiced to the best of your ability. In a social situation, you are who you are, and you need to envision that "big dog" as your peer, not the one who controls your future. Visit the place in which you will be speaking in advance to gain some comfort in the actual setting. When you are front and center, make sure not to judge yourself. Doing so removes you from being present-minded and disrupts your natural thought process. Reserve any judgments for after the event; just keep motivating yourself without the rhetorical dialog that can play in your head. Believe you are doing exactly what you need to do in the moment. Don't over interpret reactions or second-guess yourself. Most of the time such thoughts are absolutely false and a waste of energy. Staying in the moment is key, without projecting yourself into either the past or the future.

Single out the one aspect of your presentation or personhood that is most important before you're actually before the audience or "big dog," such as standing tall or speaking clearly, and you'll be more confident going forward. Finally, slow down, compose yourself, trust yourself, and be yourself.

"The greatest weakness of all is the great fear of appearing weak."
~ Jacques Benigne Bousset

DECEMBER 13

I will feel comfortable in my own skin

You know them when you meet them. They exude confidence and are not afraid to share their authenticity with the world through an extraordinary self-awareness and self-appreciation that is neither cocky nor contrived. To be one of those exceptional persons who feel comfortable in her skin, the first step is to admit your whole person, frailties and strengths, and to love every part of you. It's not a cliché kind of self-love, but rather a justified understanding that you deserve a special place in the world and that your merit is not based on earning, but on simply being who you are. Stop trying to make excuses for your flaws and embrace mistakes as an opportunity to learn. Forgive everyone who has offended you or caused you harm and take ownership of your emotions. Don't just tolerate the negative stuff, either discard it or appreciate its benefit in making you better.

Identify those reoccurring nuisances that crop up in your life over and over—a type of unhealthy relationship that feeds your insecurities, jobs that suck the joy out of you, habits that provide seconds of false comfort and years of suffering—and steel your resolve to learn from them so you can move on and break the cycle of repetitive failings. No one feels completely at ease in every situation. Each of us harbors the same fears, the same yearnings to be free, the same self-doubts that can only be assuaged through a belief in a grander purpose, a transcendent God that will make it all right.

Feel free to dream beyond your ability to believe. Live wholeheartedly without fear of being hurt or of failing—because you are the most wondrous creation on the face of this earth!

"Being comfortable in your own skin and content with your own company is a magical gift to yourself and everyone in your life." – Patricia Alexander, Book of Comforts: Simple, Powerful Ways to Comfort Your Spirit, Body & Soul (Blue Ephiphany, 2006)

"Self-awareness gives you the capacity to learn from your mistakes as well as your successes. It enables you to keep growing." ~ Larry Bossidy and Ram Charan, EXECUTION: THE DISCIPLINE OF GETTING Things DONE (Crown Business, 2002)

"Know Thyself." ~ Socrates

DECEMBER 14

I will wait for the parade to pass before judging how it will end

Waiting is so hard. Waiting in line. Waiting for an answer. It can cause impatience— some just throw up their hands and give up. But you must wait for the ending. You never know from where you stand whether the ending will be a good one or not.

Never in a hundred years would Josh Opperman think that returning to his New York apartment to find his fiancée gone and only an engagement ring left behind would turn into a fortune. When he tried to return the ring, the jeweler offered Josh just thirty-five-percent of the purchase price. So seeing an opportunity, he founded the website *I Do...Now I Don't*, which buys engagement rings from ended relationships and resells them to wooers searching for a good deal. He now sells hundreds of rings.

Imagine if a mother giving birth just decided to stop pushing because the suffering was just too great? If Soichiro Honda decided to stop pushing and waiting for some success after his piston plant was destroyed in an earthquake and after he failed in infiltrating the Japanese minicar market, he would not have ultimately succeeded creating the automobile giant Honda, despite the opposition of the Japanese government.

Waiting can be good. The international dating service *It's Just Lunch* advocates that clients not look at photos, because photos lead to hasty reactions. Instead, they advise clients to go to lunch and wait until the end of the lunch to decide whether to go out on a second date. Frank Partnoy, author of *Wait: The Art and Science of Delay* (Public Affairs, 2012), explains that delayed apologies gives the wronged party a chance to process their feelings, making your apology more meaningful. Partnoy advises us to, "Just take a breath. Take more pauses. Stare off into the distance. Ask yourself the first question of this two step process: What is the maximum amount of time I have available to respond?" This approach can free up time (like delaying a response) to spend it on something else of greater importance. The key is don't make snap decisions without knowing all the facts and without processing. Sometimes, as when Ralphie in the movie *A Christmas Story* (1983), became sad upon not seeing his BB gun under the Christmas tree, we just need to wait—because it's hidden somewhere else.

"Success is 99 percent failure." ~ Soichiro Honda

DECEMBER 15

I will survive the test of character

Arthur Miller's play, *Death of a Salesman*, represents an emotional portrayal of father and washed-up salesman Willy Loman, who wishes to live out his aspirations through his son Biff. Although Happy, Willy's other son, would like to follow in his father's footsteps, Willy's desire is for Biff, a former high school star athlete whose adult life has been a constant string of setbacks.

The play begins with Biff and Happy making a business proposition in an effort to pacify their father. Willy wants so much to make-up for Biff's lost potential, but instead he gets angry with his boss for refusing to give Biff a job and Willy gets fired. Meanwhile, Biff fails to get a job in town, and then impulsively steals a fountain pen. No one knows what sent Biff adrift until it is discovered that years earlier, when Biff went to see his father in Boston, he'd caught him in an affair. Finally, Willy and Biff argue. Biff forgives his father, leading Willy to hope Biff will now pursue a career as a salesman. In the end, Willy kills himself by intentionally crashing his car so that Biff can use the life insurance money to start his business. At Willy's funeral, Biff reaffirms that he does not want to become a salesman. Happy follows in his father's footsteps.

This poignant story of misplaced aspirations, dishonesty, and failed character illustrates a moral for today and probably all-time. One need only think back to the lies and deception that befell Enron because of Ken Lay and Jeff Skilling's shell games back in 2001 to be reminded that honesty and character—and striving for the genuine interests of others—matter most. Willy Loman is like many who fail to realize that dreams must be real, while the Biffs of this world must follow their true calling, and the Happys of today should be encouraged. We all need to know that ordinary isn't bad.

Lessons are always framed from the point of view of character. The classic definition of character is: *the mental and moral qualities distinctive to an individual.* However, Polonius said it best in Shakespeare's *The Tragedy of Hamlet, Prince of Denmark*, when he declared, "To thine own self be true, and it must follow, as the night the day, thou canst not then be false to any man." This is true character.

"Character is much easier kept than recovered." ~ *Thomas Paine*

DECEMBER 16

I will manage "The King"

People in positions of power over us will determine our standing, whether we like it or not. Ignoring them, or not treating them correctly, can be deadly. They are CEOs, executives, high-ranking officials, bosses, and any other persons of influence within an organization who rule their domain as if it were their own kingdoms. These "kings" typically surround themselves with those who will serve and defend them. They are power brokers who instinctively command others by keeping them in places of uncertainty while securing their own stable foundation. These kings exude a strong exterior, but inside they are acutely sensitive to how people treat them, and how they are perceived.

If you are at the affect of a king, even if you are one of these kings, you should know how to deal with kings in order to ensure your own success. If you don't, chances are the king will perceive you as either a threat or a disposable resource that can be discarded at their discretion. Some argue that these powerful and often disruptive personalities don't belong in a team setting, but they are the ones who typically get things done, and that's why you see these bold, confident, and often charismatic kings in high-level positions.

To become a trusted ally of the king you will need to position yourself as a part of his protected realm, so the king will feel you are a trusted member to be shielded and cared for. If the king sees you as being outside of his realm, he may perceive you as a potential enemy or as someone not worthy of his attention. That's why you need to make sure that the king sees you as a part of *his* team, actively engaged in his vision, and that the king understands what value you bring to his plans. You need to be front and center in order to be recognized for new positions, projects, or promotions. If you hide from the king, or try to work under the radar, you may be deprived of the king's bounty, which means your resources may dry-up, or your political capital will be shrunk, along with a declining career. These are cold and hard realities, but good kings truly care for their team. Bad kings abuse their power, spend more of their energies in preserving their power rather than on driving their goals, and bully others instead of motivating them. Get close to the good kings.

"Never allow a person to tell you no who doesn't have the power to say yes." ~ Eleanor Roosevelt

DECEMBER 17

I will build my personal identity

A personal identity, or brand, refers to the way other people perceive you. Are you trustworthy? Are you an expert? Are you intelligent? It's the first notion of you that pops into someone's head after hearing your name. In order to build your personal identity so that others perceive you the way you want to be noticed, you first need to define what makes you special.

Don't try to be like the other person. Establish goals for what you desire your public image to be. If you want to be seen as the expert in home design, you will need to become the authority in high-end design with the experience and talent that showcases your authority on the subject. Think about the key messages with which you want others to associate you. Do you want to be about finding the latest and greatest, or do you want to be the upscale aficionado? Once you've identified your specialty, you need to hone in on developing specific expertise in that area. Your style must also match your identity. Are you the empathetic listener who identifies with her clients, or are you the suave professional who can work with the best of them? Now add a tag line to your identity, such as, "The trend designer—imaginative aficionado to help you discover and manifest your dream home."

Keep in mind that YOU are your identity, so be consistent in representing who you are. Every day you must bring forth the standard of expectation you have established for yourself and the people around you. When you see yourself through the lens of your personal identity, you will become more mindful of who you need to be with others. This isn't pretending or acting—remember that your personal identity is who you are—you just want others to see YOU. Try to gain as much exposure as you can without seeming like a publicity hog, so that when someone thinks of a project or subject that fits your identity, they think of you.

Be sure to continually refresh your identity with new ideas and concepts in order for others to view you as a leader. This requires continuous learning about what's new in your field, and developing the skills necessary for performing at a high level. Use your tag line to network with your connections, and by corresponding with those in social media who are aligned with your identity. Getting people talking is key.

"The value of identity of course is that so often with it comes purpose."
~ Richard R. Grant

DECEMBER 18

I will build or rebuild trust

Building (or rebuilding) trust can take months—sometimes years—to make happen; sadly, it can be lost overnight. Trust is built on reliability and doing what's right—a huge factor in determining your success. In any relationship, being considered trustworthy builds respect and commitment, as well as a supportive and stress free environment. We build trust one-step at a time, by proving our dependability and honesty along the way, until eventually our level of trust reaches the point where we can completely let down our guard with another person. Some people are more trusting than others. Others need to observe what you do. Do you keep your word? Are you on time for meetings? Do you follow through on commitments? Do you own up to your mistakes?

If you're in a new relationship, or in a situation where you need to rebuild trust, there are certain steps that will get you there more quickly. The first is obvious: Be honest. Do what you say and say what you mean. There's no such thing as a "little white lie"—they are all just lies. Don't cheat on expense reports; don't say things you don't mean. Second, be transparent while using good judgment. Have you ever experienced a conversation where someone shared something with you by saying, "just between us"? These kinds of secret conversations damage trust, as do unnecessarily harsh and unsolicited criticisms, even if they are followed with an apology. Consider that the damage has already been done. Instead, share things about yourself, including the parts you may not like.

To be trusted you need to be candid enough to appear vulnerable and authentic to the other person. By revealing your defects, you are laying the groundwork for the other person to be more trusting, since you've gone first. You're saying in essence, "I'm sharing some sensitive things about me, because I trust you enough to accept me as I am." Almost always the other person will return the favor, thus taking the relationship to a deeper level of trust. Keeping a mutually advantageous attitude toward one another is key. This means being willing to share your knowledge, your concerns, even your privileged information without any hidden agendas. Giving without expecting anything in return always builds trust.

"A man who trusts nobody is apt to be the kind of man nobody trusts."
~ Harold MacMillan

DECEMBER 19

I will write my obituary while living

One crisp morning, a man of great wealth opened his newspaper. As was his daily curiosity, the man reviewed the obituary column to read about the poor souls who had recently departed. One obituary immediately struck him with blood curdling horror: it was his own. After nearly fainting, the man called the editor to ask why the paper had reported him as dead. "We are so sorry sir, we reported the death of the wrong person by mistake…." On and on the editor profusely apologized for upsetting the accomplished, fashionable gentleman. After calming his nerves, the man sat down and began contemplating his life. He again picked up the newspaper and decided to fully read the article.

The obituary read, "Dynamite King Dies." Another startling commentary read: "He was the merchant of death." The man threw the newspaper down. "Is this how I will be remembered?" he gasped. The question stormed in his head until a resounding "NO!" blurted from his mouth. "I will not accept what I have done as my final legacy," he said. From that moment forward, the man dedicated his life's work toward peace. The man's name was Alfred Nobel. He was the inventor of dynamite, but his legacy is known today as the Nobel Peace Prize. It is the award he funded.

What would you like your legacy to be? Do you need to redefine your values, or will you be remembered for your generosity and loving-kindness based on your contributions today? The legacy you leave is based on your final chapter—on how your story ends, as well as how you got there. Your legacy comes from the storyline that expresses the difference your life made. Consider where you've been, where you are now, and where you are headed. A positive legacy explains our journey from success to significance. By living our lives with intention, we determine our desired legacy. We make our own world a better place than it was before we influenced it. Choosing a life of lasting significance over temporary success takes determination and purposefulness.

"The greatest use of life is to spend it for something that will outlast It." ~ William James

DECEMBER 20

I will use the right kind of power and influence

Do you have power? What type of power produces the greatest results? Those with position power who can fire you or give you a raise with little other influence do not motivate others to perform at their highest level. Motivation is best derived from those who gain their power through admiration, or because they are experts. They don't necessarily have formal leadership roles, but they positively drive others' behaviors because of their personal attributes and skills.

A notable study of power conducted by social psychologists John French and Bertram Raven in 1959 and updated in 2008 divided the types of power into five different forms. They determined that social influence is defined as "change in the belief, attitude, or behavior of a person (the target of influence), which results from the action of another person (an influencing agent)," and social power as the potential for such influence. They identified five bases of power: 1) **Legitimate** – derived from the belief that a person has the right to make demands, and expect compliance and obedience form others; 2) **Reward** – derived from one person's ability to compensate another for compliance; 3) **Referent** – derived from a person's perceived attractiveness, worthiness, and right to respect from others; 4) **Expert** – derived from a person's superior knowledge and skills; 5) **Coercive** – derived from the belief that a person can punish others for noncompliance.

It has been shown that when employees in an organization associate a leader or person of influence with Expert or Referent power, they are more engaged, more devoted to the organization, and are more willing to go the extra mile to reach the organizational goals. Those with Legitimate Power can lose the respect of others by losing their position or followers, and those with Reward Power generally don't have complete control over salary increases or promotions. Those with Coercive Power who use threats can cause demoralization and a very harsh environment.

What is your source of power? Are you using your expertise and interpersonal skills to influence others, or are you simply throwing your weight around? Are you taking time to listen, convince, and earn the respect of your followers? Using Expert and Referent Power leads to success.

"A leader is one who knows the way, goes the way, and shows the way."
~ John C. Maxwell

DECEMBER 21

I will use the right keys to start a business

So you want to start a business. Find a partner who can be your soul mate in stoking your vision. The key is to focus on making something significant—not money. Significance starts when you're passionate about something, but it comes to fruition when your product or service makes others more productive or makes their lives more enjoyable. Usually this means that you are offering a solution to a problem, or that you're preserving something of value to others.

To make sure you've got the sizzle to bake your idea into reality, you'll need a mission statement—but not with those boring words like "delivering superior service or products." Give it life by making it concise and inspiring in fifteen words or less, like Nike: "To bring inspiration and innovation to every athlete in the world." Think outrageously. Amazon didn't build its retail book business by carrying more than the average number of two hundred thousand plus titles, it committed to carrying two and-a-half million. You will need to break your old thought patterns to adopt new ones for creating a customer base that is fiercely loyal, versus trying to be all things to all people. Harley-Davidson's CEO, Richard Teerlink, for example, gave his biker customers "adventurous pioneer spirit, the wild west…"

Make sure not to get bogged down with lengthy business plans and analyses. Make products that are intuitive. Get the product or service out there as quickly as possible, even if you have to use a pilot or prototype. Ideally, you've got a product or service that is exclusive or at least different, and that offers high value to customers. By value you need enough people who want to buy your product, but if you're in a large market space, without much differentness, you can only compete on price. You need something people really want, and perceive as unique. Whereas niche positioning is important, you also should to get your message out to a broad audience of people who are early adopters of new things. Think wide and shallow at first—not narrow and deep. If you need to raise capital or make presentations, narrow your slides to no more than fifteen, limit your pitch to thirty minutes, and use thirty-point font to present only the most salient points. When you hire people, look for people passionate about your business. Try hiring people whose skills fill your skill and knowledge gaps. Involve your most enthusiastic customers and employees in as many activities as you can. They are your best promoters.

"The way to get started is to quit talking and begin doing." ~ Walt Disney

DECEMBER 22

I will unmask the most common myths about success

Critical to understanding the keys to success is exposing the myths of success. The first myth is that you need to be a "workaholic" to succeed, even though working hard is a common characteristic among nearly all successful people. The key is to work more wisely, by delegating and carefully selecting what needs to be accomplished, and to make the most of your time when you are not working.

The second myth is that you need advanced degrees from well-known universities. With so many charging exorbitant fees, leaving mountains of debt for students (or parents) to climb, advanced degrees may not make the most sense. While having these degrees help you stand out, how you present yourself, and demonstrating that you can deliver results often has a greater impact on your success.

Another myth is that overnight success is possible. Most people persevere for a long time, and they experience several setbacks before finally achieving success. You can keep your sky-high dream alive while keeping your feet planted on the foundation of what you have right now in order to better cope with periodic failures along the way.

That luck is a huge factor in success serves as another myth. Sure, some people get better breaks than others, but the fact is, if you want something you have to earn it. Or maybe you just need to elevate your goals a little bit.

One myth that can sound disturbing—but really isn't—is that employers always want you to be yourself. While employers do value your unique skill sets and experience, they also expect you to follow company rules and guidelines. The key is for you to assimilate with those expectations and with the culture, without losing your genuineness.

The idea that if you work hard and are doing a good job you'll invariably succeed is another myth. Some great contributors can go unnoticed if they don't make their contributions visible and others don't value what they've done. So instead of toiling away, start asking those in positions of influence for their feedback of your efforts, and if they don't know about your work, tell them about the great things you are doing and check-in periodically to make sure you're on the right track. Success doesn't just happen. It's an intentional goal and well worth the effort.

"Myths are a waste of time. They prevent progression." ~ Barbara Streisand

DECEMBER 23

I will delegate

Ever heard of "Superprofessional"? NO, you haven't. That's because there is no professional superhero—no one can do it all! Sorry to break the news to you, but it's not you, either. You're not made of steel and your superhuman powers are, well, *not* superhuman. So take off the cape and start showing trust in the talent around you. No one succeeds alone. If you're feeling overwhelmed, call Captain Delegation to the rescue! If you allow delegation to be your partner, you won't let others down by not being able to do enough—you'll be successful. Of course you can't delegate everything, but if someone else has the necessary expertise and knowledge to do the task, pass the baton.

Many times delegating a task allows the other person to develop their skills. This works especially well for reoccurring tasks that are similar, and for non-critical tasks (other than hiring your team). The ideal delegation candidate would already have the skills and knowledge to do the job, but if not, you'll need to ask yourself if you have time and resources to train him or her. Check the person's attitude and long-term goals and interests to determine if there's a fit, as well as whether they can shift their existing workload to accommodate yours. Clarify the desired outcome with your delegate; identify the specific responsibilities and boundaries, including the channels of authority and accountability. Tell them who needs to know about their work and who should be asked for permission. Inform your delegate as to whether he or she can act independently, and if not, how often and to whom does he need to report actions or results. Remember that you're ultimately accountable, so the delegate's abilities should match the level of the job, and they should be related to their current level of performance. Be sure to maintain consistent communications with your delegate, especially at the onset of the task, and by all means give credit where credit is due.

The best delegators focus on the results, not the detailed process. By leaving the delegate to navigate his or her own solutions, you may learn something new as well. Don't allow the delegate to shift the task back to you by answering all of their questions. Allow them to develop their resolution skills, but let your delegate know that you must be made aware of problems. Stay informed while trusting your team.

"No person will make a great business who wants to do it all himself or get all the credit." ~ *Andrew Carnegie*

DECEMBER 24

I will follow my North Star

Life coach Martha Beck loves turtles—their hard shell protects them from the dangers in life; a soft and sensitive underside; slow but steady wins the race; and occasionally the turtle sticks out its head so that it can move forward. Getting ahead, the turtle way, is how Beck explains it in *Finding Your Own North Star: Claiming the Life You Were Meant to Live* (Three Rivers Press, 2002). It's that bright light fixed over the place where we can find our saving grace, even in the darkest of times. The knocks and changing directions of life can strand us, keeping us from our loftiest dreams, or any degree of happiness when we're mired in the muck of circumstances. Beck explains human nature as a division of two selves—that part of us that has learned to live in harmony with others, giving-in when needed, and that other part that too often hides behind a mask to cover our more vulnerable and truest core self.

Finding balance between the two halves is key to finding success in life, she contends. We cannot have one without the other in order to follow our path toward the North Star. Too much core self and we become irresponsible members of society. Too much social self, and we lose touch with our heart, falling into superficiality, losing sight of our dreams and wearing our mask so much that we forget our true face. Eventually unhappiness signals our first clue, followed by an internalization of our sadness that can manifest into chronic fatigue, irritability, even illness. People who behave badly are not so much evil, Beck says, as they are in pain as a result of detachment from their core self. Beck embraces change as a fact of life that keeps us young and vital, just as flexing a muscle keeps it strong. Like the turtle, we need to stretch out our neck from the protective covering of our shell to experience the bounty of life. It's the trials, the testing in life that make us "heroic," and equips us with the abilities to move forward. Beck's advice is to keep oneself positive, surround oneself with encouragers and positive influences.

"Change hurts," she warns… "To complete it, you'll have to kill off the old You," and allow the birth of a different You. You must maintain your North Star focus throughout life's trials in order to reach your saving grace—your dreams. After all, turtles are destined to cross the finish line. Slow and steady wins the race.

"Trials teach us what we are; they dig up the soil,
and let us see what we are made of." ~ Charles Spurgeon

DECEMBER 25

I will give my greatest gift

The Christmas season brings with it a spirit of both giving and receiving. Children eagerly anticipate opening wrapped packages delivered, many presume, by Santa Claus himself. Exchanging gifts is a tradition long practiced for many special occasions as expressions of love and caring toward others. Besides the material things, the entertainment, or financial assistance we might give to friends and family, what is the greatest gift you can give? When that question was posed to well over a hundred people, a surprisingly consistent number of them (over ninety-percent) said basically the same thing: their "love," their "heart," "themselves." Even when pressed to consider vast luxuries as gifts, most would give up just about anything to preserve the genuine warmth and support of loved ones. That's the power of love—the greatest gift of all. We cannot wrap it, we cannot buy it—and yet it comes at quite a price.

True love and caring are forged through the costs of sacrifice, disappointment, forgiveness, and pain. However, the gains in return for these hardships are comfort, hope, trust, and joy. These are the hallmarks of love, and they can only be given freely, with a no-return policy. True love operates as a function of the heart, and even though we may separate from one another for various reasons, true love never dies. It lives as vibrantly as the blood pulsating through our veins, bleeding sometimes through our failings and the failings of others; however, the gift of true love once given lives on.

True love, what some call agape or pure, unconditional love, is the lifeblood of our success. Without it, any achievements wither into nothing. With it, our achievements can bless others as well as ourselves. That's the beauty of love—it translates into a life well lived. Regardless of your religion or non-religion, use this day to share your greatest gift with others, and never stop giving it. Look for people with whom to share this gift for a lifetime—those who are lonely, those who need a friend, those who share your values, those who share a kindred spirit with you. Liberally give the gift that brings lasting fulfillment. By doing so you will surpass any other gift that may come your way during your journey of success, for it guarantees an enriched life and the ultimate success.

"The course of true love never did run smooth." ~ William Shakespeare

DECEMBER 26

I will stay relevant

With a changing workplace, a changing global economy, changing communication channels and an ever-expanding base of knowledge, it's become increasingly difficult to stay relevant in business and in the workplace. To do so you have to think outside the box, know something others don't know, develop your skills and cultural intelligence, stay flexible and listen to diverse ideas, and practice new ways of communicating. Out of the box thinking challenges assumptions, but it also reframes ideas to consider them in a new way. It uses lateral thinking to look at problems from many angles instead of tackling them head-on. Regardless of where you work, you will gain recognition if there is something you know or can do that others have not thought of or are not capable of doing.

The commoditization of talent within organizations offers those with specialized knowledge a way of differentiating themselves and gaining notice. For example, one fifty-plus-year-old person in his office had become phenomenal at creating stunning presentation programs, so guess what? Executives started asking him to design their presentation slides. In today's environment, contributors need to develop a diverse set of skills. Learning new skills both inside and outside the workplace through continuous education and skill building exposes you to the various industry changes, and raises your intellectual value to your organization. Developing your cultural literacy is also important if you're in an international business environment. Network with those of other cultures and international businesspersons to learn all you can. Try learning a new language. You don't need to be fluent—just try to be conversant.

Staying relevant is all about adapting to changing dynamics and learning about diverse cultures and approaches. Push yourself outside of your comfort zone. Stay informed. The online world has revolutionized meetings, presentations, data visualization, and the breadth of socializing and connecting with others. Keep up with the latest and greatest. Besides staying current, relevancy requires that we listen and learn (as well as unlearn dated habits) and stay open to new ideas.

"The illiterate of the 21st century will not be those who cannot read and write, but those who cannot learn, unlearn, and relearn." ~ Alvin Toffler

DECEMBER 27

I will give out valuable performance reviews

Ed, a successful senior executive who worked for a global banking firm, came over to his peer's office after his year-end performance review and said through his flushed face, "I'm quitting! They don't care about any of the work I've done! I'm doing more work, no thanks, and all they want is *more* work out of me!" Ed, in fact, quit five days later, without another job lined up.

Performance reviews can make or break a person's success, and there are common mistakes supervisors make to demotivate and even anger their direct reports. One of the reasons for this is that supervisors are not specific enough. They're often pushed by HR to get their reviews done on schedule, so they rush through the process, saying something like, "Oh by the way, Angie, can I have just fifteen minutes of your time to complete your performance review?" A year's worth of work for a quickie review with general comments such as, "You're doing a (____) job" doesn't improve performance.

The key is telling the direct report *specifically* how they met (or did not meet) their goals, and how they can build on their successes and improve in the future. No one should be blindsided by a review, because the discussion about performance should be ongoing by periodically checking in with the report about progress versus goals. It should also include plenty of appreciation for good work, and it should be straightforward but kind in communicating areas for improvement. Just be truthful.

One of the biggest disservices to people is not helping them improve. This unfortunately happens in classic avoidance style, with some negligent supervisors keeping people's "head in a cloud," wondering why they're not being more successful. The problem with annual or semi-annual reviews is that the feedback can be skewed toward recent events as a basis for assessing the entire year's performance. This is unfair to the employee. A comprehensive review reveals what's working and what's not working over an extended time period, and it's slanted in favor of the positives. It should also include a discussion around career goals and a development pathway to get there, if the person's ambitions are realistic. If you're on the receiving end, you should ask this of your boss. Also, give your boss a self-assessment beforehand.

"Feedback is the breakfast of champions." ~ Ken Blanchard

DECEMBER 28

I will manage information effectively

Have you ever been on the phone with someone who needed some information you'd filed and you just couldn't find it on the spot? The ability to organize information directly impacts your success. Start by making the commitment to not spend more than thirty minutes a day between email and administrative overhead. To prepare for this commitment, savagely delete old and unnecessary files. Decide if each file is relevant to something important, and if not, get rid of it. When you receive information from someone, it's tempting to "place it somewhere" in a pile. Use the five-minute rule: if taking immediate action on the file will use five minutes or less, take care of it as soon as you encounter it, as suggested by David Allen in his book, *Getting Things Done: The Art of Stress-Free* Productivity (Viking Adult, 2001).

Allen says you can avoid accumulating a long to-do list by immediately taking care of a task you encounter, as long as it will take no more than minutes. If you need to file it, store the information in paper or computer files by category, and in a consistent method, such as dividing folders by project and by customer—you can even give them a unique appearance or color for each category. If you prefer to keep current work on your desk until it's completed, make sure to periodically (every week to two weeks) move this work into your completed files.

Make sure not to overload files by creating subfolders for subjects like expenses and presentations. If you wish to archive paper documents, make digital copies using a scanner. Organize your documents by noting a date on it so that you can easily source specific information. Allen suggests using a "tickler file" as a reminder system intended to act as an adjunct to your regular calendaring and scheduling system.

Use the forty-three-folders system, with thirty-one numbered "day" folders and twelve labeled with the months of the year. Using this system, anything you need to be reminded of on some future date goes into your tickler file. Each morning, that day's folder is retrieved and the contents placed into your inbox, and whatever you placed there days, weeks, or months earlier is readily available when you need it. If you don't complete some work items by the end of the day, transfer them to the folder for the next convenient day. Finally, don't try to do everything. Focus only on a few key tasks.

"Information storage has to take place at the unconscious level." ~ Paul G. Thomas

DECEMBER 29

I will develop a Cumulative Advantage

You've heard the saying: "the rich get richer and the poor get poorer." Some sociologists (like Robert Merton who coined it as the "Matthew Effect") say it's true, according to the principle of Cumulative Advantage. Society demonstrates this principle. Students who get A's receive more attention and therefore better teaching. The most athletic youngsters receive the most coaching. Type A directors are given more challenging development opportunities in the workplace.

A study at Iowa State University by psychologists Guyll Madon and Willard Spoth studied the synergistic accumulative effect of parents' beliefs on children's drinking behavior, and discovered that negative self-fulfilling prophecies instilled within children can actually increase their chances of developing alcoholism. So are we predestined toward success or failure? Not necessarily so, according to Daniel Rigney, author of *The Matthew Effect: How Advantage Begets Further Advantage* (Columbia University Press, 2010). He says that the process "feeds back upon itself." For example, when children read more often, making them better readers, it creates a "self-perpetuating cycle." In other words, you *can* alter the Cumulative Advantage (such as being born with certain physical or resource/wealth advantages) by committing to vital habits, such as those we've outlined in *Daily Keys to Success.*

Rigney says that "success tends to breed further success," but we can change that cumulative effect by changing our habits. Consider Dr. Ben Carson, who escaped poverty to become a famed neurosurgeon, or Abraham Lincoln who was primarily self-taught, or Daniel "Rudy" Ruettiger who, despite his small size, fulfilled his aspiration to play football at Notre Dame (as depicted in the popular 2005 film, *Rudy*). Rudy's story also goes to show that despite our natural abilities in comparison to others, we can still initiate a pattern of success that can lead to alternate paths of success—Rudy later became a motivational speaker. The key, as with Abraham Lincoln, is to use failure as a motivator, not allowing it to derail us from our pathway to success. The advantage of incumbency in presidential elections demonstrates that when success is eventually achieved, it tends to lead to further success, and is incrementally developed.

"We are not retreating—we are advancing in another direction." ~ Douglas MacArthur

DECEMBER 30

I will use "The Balanced Scorecard"

One of the major reasons most strategic plans fail is that they are either inflexible (done only once a year) or they are too unwieldy to remain top of mind. Increasingly, organizations are using the balanced scorecard (BSC) as a performance management tool that makes strategy a continual process—not just a fixed endpoint. BSC measures four key areas of progress: **Learning & Growth** (personal development, employee satisfaction, information systems, etc.), **Internal Business Processes** (quality control, regulatory affairs, cycle time, etc.), **Customers** (market share, satisfaction, etc.) and **Financial** (revenue, profit, etc.).

The exceptional BSC concept put forth by Drs. Robert Kaplan and David Norton is that if you are measuring only financial results, you are only assessing past performance, or "driving by looking in the rear-view mirror." Financial results are *lagging* indicators of progress. Conversely, Learning & Growth, Internal Business Processes, and Customer Relations are *leading* indicators—they happen *before* the organization prospers or fails. The key is developing an "instrument panel" of measurements that are consistently updated to give you a real time (current) read on how you are doing. This objective system is ideally shared with all of the key stakeholders within the organization.

Even if some sensitive financial information cannot be shared, you can share select key information such as sales and revenues for the month and employee and/or customer summary feedback for the week or month. This cross-functional sharing of strategic metrics expresses the links between human and physical indicators to achieve an organization's strategic priorities. Thus, the scorecard enables companies to modify strategies to reflect real-time learning by: 1) translating the vision into operational goals; 2) communicating the vision and linking it to individual performance; 3) determining the business plan and metrics; and 4) providing feedback and learning so that the strategy can be adjusted accordingly. BSC is a looping mechanism that empowers the organization to make collaborative decisions that factor in the changing dynamics influencing the market and organization, and keeps the attention on strategic issues.

"However beautiful the strategy, you should occasionally look at the results." ~ Winston Churchill

DECEMBER 31

I will continuously learn

There are a lot of reasons for success, but none bigger than continuous learning. Whether you're an individual or you represent an organization, staying plugged into the "mind of information" around you is key. As an individual, begin to gather information by subscribing to magazines and trade journals, read books, attend seminars facilitated by experts in your chosen field (ask them questions and for their advice), blog with these experts, send for and study literature on companies, talk to employees and other business people about the industry leaders, and the up and coming companies in your area of interest.

If you're a leader within an organization, your strategic imperative is to interconnect the various functions into a true system, where each function operates as a whole. Probably the biggest complaint within organizations is that leaders don't tell people what's going on, and how they are connected. People do not know nearly as much as their leaders think they do. The concept of *systems thinking* (for continuous learning organizations) was defined by Peter Senge in his best seller, *The Fifth Discipline: The Art & Practice of The Learning Organization* (Currency, 1990), as when an organization works as a united system and consistently learns from its experiences and shares this learning throughout the organization. When people operate in a vacuum, mistakes happen. The job of sharing knowledge, or Knowledge Management, keeps the same problems from occurring over and over by keeping everyone united, on the same page, and driven by the same point of view. Possible solutions include a centralized shared database and even over-communication about critical processes or projects.

Continuous learning as a person and as an organization adds wealth. Even if you lose all of your money and your property, you cannot lose your most important asset—knowledge. As contemporary economist and entrepreneur Paul Zane Pfizer said, "prosperity belongs to those who learn new things fastest." Your journey of success began with learning about your new world through observing your surroundings, and those in your midst. If you're a continuous learner, the journey will never end. Someday—perhaps today—people will study you and learn from your success. Make sure to tell them that you earned it—for the ones that mattered most.

"Best is good. Better is best." ~ Lisa Grunwald

ACKNOWLEDGMENTS

I am who I am first and foremost because of God, second because of my loved ones, and third because of those who challenged me—both the ones who desired my success, as well as those who didn't much care for me. Today, I am grateful for everyone who helped form "Randy Kay Inc." Sometimes I'll look back and think that so or so was the proverbial "thorn in my side." But in reality, that challenging person made me stronger. Of course, it's the ones who supported me the most who I appreciate the most.

I was an agnostic for much of my life before I met God through Jesus Christ, and after personally experiencing the Big Guy, I became a softer person. Not a perfect or necessarily even a better person—just more caring. So kudos to my Maker for continuing to show me mercy and grace while I screwed up and made a mess of things, and for giving me time on this earth to find my way and help others.

I don't strive to be famous or unbelievably wealthy. Rather, my goal is to be known as someone who remained faithful in living out his uniquely created personhood, and who blessed others. If anyone can say that about me, then it is because of those who afforded me the opportunity to be involved in their lives. My parents, Robert and Norma Kay, instilled within me a sense of integrity and purpose. They gave me unconditional love, served as spectacular role models, and for that I am eternally grateful.

Then I met my wife—my lovely and intelligent wife Renee—who first loved me because of who she saw on the surface, and who then grew to love me, warts and all. She is the crowning jewel of my success, and the inspiration for *Daily Keys to Success*, because it was she who first suggested it. Renee, you are the reason I do what I do.

Of course, my children, Ryan and Annie, are the fruits of my success. When I look upon the rock of integrity, my son Ryan Kay, I see the person I always hoped he would be. And, when I look upon my beautiful Annie, full of wisdom and strength, I see the wonderful daughter for whom I prayed.

Finally, but certainly not last, are the friends, coworkers, customers, key acquaintances, and influencers who in absentia gave me the content for *Daily Keys to Success*. My experiences with you, filtered through my own understanding, produced whatever insights others gain in reading their *Keys to Success*. Some of you know who you are—we spent time together, labored together, and experienced the joys and sadness of life together. Thank you for sharing your life with me. Even if we never met or barely knew each other, such as the speakers, teachers and authors who inspired me, I consider you my mentors and guides. For my friends, I cannot thank you enough. You gave me your time and pieces of your life, just because you considered me valuable enough to invest those precious resources expecting little in return.

For you, my readers—thank you for sharing this journey with me. In fact, it's to you I am most appreciative for this book, because it's you who give *Daily Keys to Success* a reason for being.

~ Randy Kay
May 16, 2013

CREDITS

Alessandra, Tony, PhD and Michael O'Connor, PhD. *People Smart in Business*. Alessandra & Associates, Inc., 2009.

Beck, Martha. *Finding Your Own North Star: Claiming the Life You Were Meant to Live*. Three Rivers Press, 2002.

Branden, Nathaniel. *The Psychology of Self-Esteem*. New York: Jossey-Bass, 2001.

Bronson, Po and Ashley Merryman, *NurtureShock*. New York: Hatchett Book Group, 2009.

Carnegie, Dale. *How to Win Friends and Influence People*. Pocket Books, Paperback Special Annieversary Edition, 1998.

Cialdini, Robert, PhD. *Influence: The Psychology of Persuasion*. Collins Business Essentials, 2007

Carter, Sherrie Bourg. "8 Easy Organizational Tips to Increase Your Productivity at Work." Psychology Today, September 18, 2011.

Collins, Jim. *Good to Great*. New York: HarperCollins, 2001.

Csikszentmihalyi, Mihaly. *Flow: The Psychology of Optimal Experience*. Harper Perennial, 1991.

Dixon, Matthew and Brent Adamson. *The Challenger Sale: Taking Control of the Customer Conversation*. Portfolio Hardcover, 2011.

ExecuRead. "Speed Reading Facts." http://www.execuread.com/facts/facts.

Ferriss, Timothy. *The 4-Hour Workweek: Escape 9-5, Live Anywhere, and Join the New Rich*. Harmony, 2009.

Freeman, John. *The Tyranny of E-Mail*. New York: Scribner, 2009.

Gladwell, Malcolm. *The Tipping Point: How Little Things Can Make a Big Difference*. Bay Back Books, 2002.

Goleman, Daniel. *Emotional Intelligence: Why It Can Matter More Than IQ*. Bantam, 2006.

Hawkins, Jeff. "Voices of Innovation." Bloomberg Businessweek. http://www.businessweek.com/magazine/content/04_41/b3903463.html.

Hersey, Paul, PhD. The Situational Leader. Center for Leadership Studies, 1997.

Kahneman, Daniel. *Thinking Fast and Slow*. Farrar, Straus and Giroux, 2011.

Kantrowitz, Barbara, and Karen Springen. "What Dreams Are Made Of." Newsweek, August 9, 2004.

Kawasaki, Guy. *The Art of the Start*. Portfolio, 2004.

Kelly, Tom. *The Art of Innovation*. New York: Doubleday, 2001.

MacKay, Harvey. *Swim with the Sharks without Being Eaten Alive*. Collins Business, 2005.

Maxwell, John. *Failing Forward*. Thomas Nelson; Reprint Edition, 2007.

MindTools. "Get Started With Mind Tools."

http://www.mindtools.com/pages/article/get-started.htm#.

Nightingale, Earl. *Think and Grow Rich*. Brilliance Audio, 2011.

Peck, M. Scott. *The Road Less Traveled: A New Psychology of Love, Traditional Values, and Spiritual Growth*. Touchstone, 2003.

Robbins, Anthony. *Awaken the Giant Within*. New York: Free Press, 1991.

Simmons, Annette. *The Story Factor: Inspiration, Influence, and Persuasion Through the Art of Storytelling*. Basic Books, 2006.

Thomas, Kenneth and Ralph Kilmann. *Thomas-Kilmann Conflict Mode Instrument*. CPP, Inc., 2002.

Walton, Sam. *Made in America – My Story*. Bantam Gooks, 1993.

Watkins, Michael. *The First 90 Days: Critical Success Strategies for New Leaders at All Levels*. Harvard Business School Press, 2003.

Ziglar, Zig. *Secrets of Closing the Sale*. Felming H. Revell, 2006.

Zook, Chris. *Beyond the Core: Expand Your Market Without Abandoning Your Roots*. Harvard Business School Press, 2004.

ABOUT THE AUTHOR

RANDY KAY IS A BUSINESS leader, entrepreneur, trainer, and coach who, as an executive and advisor to start-ups and several Fortune 500 companies, has contributed to the success of thousands of top performers. His numerous promotions and attainment of the highest accolades within each of the organizations in which Kay has participated speak to his career success, while his leadership in charitable organizations and strong family life give voice to Kay's personal success. As Chief Executive Officer of the strategic and human resources company, TenorCorp, Kay counsels and supports market-leading organizations all over the world. He has lectured at several companies and teaching institutions such as his alma mater, Northwestern University, as well as at several religious institutions following his ordination as a minister. Kay's writings and teaching are changing the way professionals and contributors of all kinds define and work toward success.

Find out more at www.randywkay.com.

THANKS FOR READING

DAILY KEYS TO SUCCESS

I HOPE YOU'VE GAINED SOME transforming insights for your life and career through these keys. Please don't just put this book on the shelf to collect dust—it's not like a fine red wine that gets better through aging. Pick it up once in awhile and look for some key you can use to open the door to a fresh advance in your life. Many of the keys are timeless and yet, even as technologies and musical tastes change, no one in the history of the world has yet to experience *your* success. That's because no one exactly like you has ever before graced this earth—or ever will again.

Although I probably don't know you, I feel we've shared something very important together through these pages. Let's continue the journey. Please visit www.randywkay.com and share with me where you are on your road of success. And remember this, my friend—even if you find yourself in the valley, the peak of your success always lies in front if you, if only you keep growing and giving.

~ *Randy Kay*

INDEX

Made in United States
Troutdale, OR
12/28/2023

16504524R00236